organizational

D0245581

organizational
behaviour
Integrated Readings

David Buchanan and Andrzej Huczynski

Prentice Hall
London ■ New York ■ Toronto ■ Sydney ■ Tokyo ■ Singapore ■
Madrid ■ Mexico City ■ Munich ■ Paris

First published 1997 by
Prentice Hall Europe
Campus 400, Maylands Avenue
Hemel Hempstead
Hertfordshire, HP2 7EZ
A division of
Simon & Schuster International Group

Typeset in 10.5/11.5pt
by Mathematical Composition Setters Ltd, Salisbury Wiltshire

Printed and bound in Great Britain
by Bath Press

Library of Congress Cataloging-in-Publication Data

Available from the publisher

British Library Cataloguing in Publication Data

A catalogue record for this book is available from
the British Library

ISBN 0-13-234345-2

1 2 3 4 5 01 00 99 98 97

Contents

Aims and guide

The aim of this text is to provide an innovative set of twenty-three readings in organizational behaviour, to complement the third edition of our book *Organizational Behaviour: An Introductory Text* (1997). That text has two introductory Chapters, and five Parts, and there is one reading here to accompany each chapter in the core text. This collection of readings forms a key part of a total learning package which includes:

- a comprehensively revised and updated third edition of the core text
- a student workbook
- an instructor's manual
- this book of readings linked to the text of the third edition.

In the pressured, semestered, modularized world of higher education, how can we ensure that students are adequately exposed to a broad and complex subject area like organizational behaviour? A single text typically offers a limited perspective. It has become difficult to give students access to the rich journal literatures related to this subject. Libraries are not resourced to deal with large student groups looking for a limited number of specialist articles. Copyright laws restrict the wholesale copying of journal articles for students, even for educational purposes. Department budgets reinforce this restriction anyway. One solution to these difficulties lies with a collection of readings such as this. This collection has two main advantages over other readings texts. First, the readings are linked directly to the core textbook. Second, each reading is prefaced with a brief set of learning objectives and learning activities. Students are thus in no doubt about the purpose of the reading, what they might take from it, and how this relates to the main text.

This structure does not prevent instructors from using this collection of readings in other ways and for other purposes. Many of these readings relate to a number of different topics and the link to a single textbook chapter is in some instances determined by emphasis. These articles can be built into the reading guide for a course of study in different ways, and not necessarily in the sequence presented here. Additionally, these readings can be most effective if they are linked to the instructor's assessment strategy. Some of these readings can be used as the basis for coursework, for a module assignment. The links to the main text make it possible to structure examination questions that require a knowledge of both textbook chapter and one or more relevant readings. Many of the learning activities are designed to give the student notes and ideas that can be used in assignments and for examination answers.

The readings have been selected, in terms of content and learning activities, with a number of criteria in mind. First, they are chosen to provide a richer, deeper understanding of the key contributions, themes, issues and controversies covered in the main text. Second, they have been chosen as effective vehicles for self-study and independent learning. Third, we have tried to collect materials difficult for the student or instructor to get from libraries. This book has been designed as a personal study guide which complements the core text and the student workbook. It is not designed for lecture theatre or tutorial room use.

This book incorporates a number of unique features.

1 learning objectives

Each reading is prefaced with a set of learning objectives. These are designed to assist independent self study. These are not designed to discourage students and instructors from using these readings in other ways, depending on the aims of their particular courses. However, books of readings typically incorporate only an introduction to their collection, and occasionally include a brief summary of each section into which material has been organized. The reader is typically given little or no guidance with respect to why particular readings have been chosen, or what the reader should expect to take from each reading. We regard that approach as inappropriate.

2 learning activities

Each reading is accompanied by suggested learning activities, linked to the core text, and designed to challenge and extend the reader's knowledge. Most books of readings leave instructors and students to devise their own learning methods – typically, this involves reading the chapter and writing an essay. This text is distinctive in going beyond that limited approach, in providing specific guidance on self-study. Suggested learning activities address theoretical and conceptual issues, practical organizational implications, and key debates and controversies. These suggestions, however, do not prevent instructors and students using the materials in other ways appropriate to their organizational behaviour course and its assessment strategy.

3 keyed to the core text

The learning objectives indicate the chapters and materials in the core text relevant to each reading. In this way, we hope to take readers significantly beyond the core text's introductory materials. This will be achieved by offering other perspectives, by generating controversy and criticism, and by filling gaps where appropriate in the introductory material.

4 blended contributions

The readings include a mixture of materials from a wide range of historical and contemporary sources. They are drawn from widely differing sources and contexts, originally written for different purposes, and we hope that the individual items will find a new voice and freshness in being brought together in this particular collection. No attempt has been made to offer readings balanced in length and style; some are the length of conventional book chapters or journal articles, and some are relatively short. Most books of readings rely exclusively either on journal reprints or commissioned chapters (sometimes from conference papers). We hope that this collection has a much livelier and less conventional 'feel'.

5 depth and integration

Some readings have been chosen to take readers into greater depth in specific areas. Others have been chosen because they provide insights into the ways in which the issues covered in separate chapters in the core text are interrelated. It is inevitable in a more or less conventional introductory text that topics are covered in a basic and sequential manner that disguises the complexities of many issues, and that implies relatively watertight compartments of knowledge. This text seeks to illustrate both the complexity and overlap in the field of organizational behaviour, thus complementing the core text in a valuable and challenging way.

Acknowledgements

We should like to acknowledge the contributions of those who helped to devise some of the learning activities associated with the readings. These include Louise McLaughlin (Reading 7); Claire Maitland (Reading 8); Michael Boyle and Lindsay Johnston (Reading 9); Christiane Zehetner (Reading 11); Catherine Hallett (Reading 14); and Erwin de Groot and Robert Frew (Reading 15).

the ORBIT series

We hope that you enjoy using this book, and that it lives up to your expectations. However, we would welcome your suggestions on how it could be improved. We would like to invite you to send us criticisms, sugestions, ideas and general comments about this book, or indeed about any of the four books in the ORBIT series: core text, readings, student workbook, instructor's manual. We would like to learn about features which you liked, as well as about features which you think could be changed, dropped or improved. Your advice will be used to improve these books, and all sugestions will be fully acknowledged. The simplest way to do this is through email, and here are our addresses. We look forward to hearing from you.

David Buchanan d.buchanan@dm.ac.uk
For chaps 1–6, 16, 17, 19, 20 and 23

Andrzej Huczynski a.a.huczynski@mgt.gla.ac.uk
For chaps 7–15, 18, 21 and 22

introduction to organizational behaviour

a century of organizational behaviour (1973)

'The short and glorious history of organizational theory', by Charles Perrow, *Organizational Dynamics*, Summer 1973, pp. 32–44.

Organizational behaviour has its roots in American social scientific theory and organizational practice. This article, written by the organization theorist Charles Perrow, traces the development of the subject this century, and offers an assessment of progress, up to the mid-1970s. Perrow thus offers an interesting, if biased, historical perspective, and also provides a benchmark against which developments since this article was written can be assessed.

learning objectives

Once you have read and understood this article, you should be able to:

1 Explain the development of the field during the twentieth century in terms of the main contributors, theoretical perspectives and practical implications – and in terms of the increasing sophistication of our understanding of organizational behaviour.
2 Realistically assess progress in this field, with respect to the development of theory, and with respect to the development of ideas and techniques that have practical value.
3 Locate contributions to the field of organizational behaviour since this article was written, with respect to how they depart from and/or build on previous contributions.

learning pre-requisites

The material covered in the article touches almost every main theme covered in the core text. However, the article is particularly relevant to Chapter 1, Introduction, where the term *organizational behaviour* is defined. A subject area can be defined also in terms of the topics, issues and controversies that its adherents find engaging. Perrow thus presents an alternative definition of the field in this wide historical coverage. Chapter 1 also identifies *the organizational dilemma* facing attempts simultaneously to fulfil individual and corporate needs and aspirations. Perrow frames this dilemma in terms of the protracted and inconclusive struggle between what he calls 'the forces of light and the forces of darkness'.

learning activities

1 Using the table on the next page, or your own version of this, construct a *timeline* which identifies, decade by decade:
  ▶ the main figures contributing to organizational thought and practice – the 'big names'
  ▶ the theoretical stances or perspectives adopted by those figures
  ▶ the prescriptions or practical organizational guidance which they advocated

▶ aspects of the wider social, economic and political context that may have shaped the ideas and interests of those working in the field of organizational behaviour.

2 As your course unfolds, and as your knowledge of the subject develops, bring your timeline up to date by filling in contributions during the 1970s, 1980s and 1990s.

	Big names	*Theoretical perspectives*	*Prescriptions*	*The whole context*
↑ 1900s				
↑ 1910s				
↑ 1920s				
↑ 1930s				
↑ 1940s				
↑ 1950s				
↑ 1960s				
↑ 1970s				
↑ 1980s				
↑ 1990s				

READING
1

The short and glorious history of organizational theory*
Charles Perrow

From the beginning, the forces of light and the forces of darkness have polarized the field of organizational analysis, and the struggle has been protracted and inconclusive. The forces of darkness have been represented by the mechanical school of organizational theory – those who treat the organization as a machine. This school characterizes organizations in terms of such things as: centralized authority, clear lines of authority, specialization and expertise, marked division of labor, rules and regulations, and clear separation of staff and line.

The forces of light, which by mid-20th century came to be characterized as the human relations school, emphasize people rather than machines, accommodations rather than machine-like precision, and draw their inspiration from biological systems rather than engineering systems. They have emphasized such things as: delegation of authority, employee autonomy, trust and openness, concerns with the 'whole person', and interpersonal dynamics.

The rise and fall of scientific management

The forces of darkness formulated their position first, starting in the early part of this century. They have been characterized as the scientific management or classical management school. This school started by parading simple-minded injunctions to plan ahead, keep records, write down policies, specialize, be decisive, and keep your span of control to about six people. These injunctions were needed as firms grew in size and complexity, since there were few models around beyond the railroads, the military, and the Catholic Church to guide organizations. And their injunctions worked. Executives began to delegate, reduce their span of control, keep records, and specialize. Planning ahead still is difficult it seems, and the modern equivalent is Management by Objectives.

But many things intruded to make these simple-minded injunctions less relevant:

1 Labor became a more critical factor in the firm. As the technology increased in sophistication it took longer to train people, and more varied and specialized skills were needed. Thus, labor turnover cost more and recruitment became more selective. As a consequence, labor's power increased. Unions and strikes appeared. Management adjusted by beginning to speak of a cooperative system of capital, management, and labor. The machine model began to lose its relevancy.

2 The increasing complexity of markets, variability of products, increasing number of branch plants, and changes in technology all required more adaptive organization. The scientific management school was ill-equipped to deal with rapid change. It had presumed that once the proper structure was achieved the firm could run forever without much tampering. By the late 1930s, people began writing about adaptation and change in industry from an organizational point of view and had to abandon some of the principles of scientific management.

3 Political, social, and cultural changes meant new expectations regarding the proper way to treat people. The dark, satanic mills needed at the least a whitewashing. Child labor and the brutality of supervision in many enterprises became no longer permissible. Even managers could not be expected to accept the authoritarian patterns of leadership that prevailed in the small firm run by the founding father.

* Reprinted by permission of the publisher from *Organizational Dynamics*, Summer 1973. Copyright 1973 by AMACOM, a division of American Management Association, New York. All rights reserved..

4 As mergers and growth proceeded apace and the firm could no longer be viewed as the shadow of one man (the founding entrepreneur), a search for methods of selecting good leadership became a preoccupation. A good, clear, mechanical structure would no longer suffice. Instead, firms had to search for the qualities of leadership that could fill the large footsteps of the entrepreneur. They tacitly had to admit that something other than either 'sound principles' or 'dynamic leadership' was needed. The search for leadership traits implied that leaders were made, not just born, that the matter was complex, and that several skills were involved.

Enter human relations

From the beginning, individual voices were raised against the implications of the scientific management school. *Bureaucracy* had always been a dirty word, and the job design efforts of Frederick Taylor were even the subject of a congressional investigation. But no effective counterforce developed until 1938, when a business executive with academic talents named Chester Bernard proposed the first new theory of organizations: Organizations are cooperative systems, not the products of mechanical engineering. He stressed natural groups within the organization, upward communication, authority from below rather than from above, and leaders who functioned as a cohesive force. With the spectre of labor unrest and the Great Depression upon him, Bernard's emphasis on the cooperative nature of organizations was well-timed. The year following the publication of his *Functions of the Executive* (1938) saw the publication of F. J. Roethlisberger and William Dickson's *Management and the Worker*, reporting on the first large-scale empirical investigation of productivity and social relations. The research, most of it conducted in the Hawthorne plant of the Western Electric Company during a period in which the work force was reduced, highlighted the role of informal groups, work restriction norms, the value of decent, humane leadership, and the role of psychological manipulation of employees through the counseling system. World War II intervened, but after the war the human relations movement, building on the insights of Bernard and the Hawthorne studies, came into its own.

The first step was a search for the traits of good leadership. It went on furiously at university centers but at first failed to produce more than a list of Boy Scout maxims: A good leader was kind, courteous, loyal, courageous, and so on. We suspected as much. However, the studies did turn up a distinction between 'consideration,' or employee-centered aspects of leadership, and job-centered, technical aspects labeled 'initiating structure.' Both were important, but the former received most of the attention and the latter went undeveloped. The former led directly to an examination of group processes, an investigation that has culminated in T-group programs and is moving forward still with encounter groups. Meanwhile, in England, the Tavistock Institute sensed the importance of the influence of the kind of task a group had to perform on the social relations within the group. The first important study, conducted among coal miners, showed that job simplification and specialization did not work under conditions of uncertainty and nonroutine tasks.

As this work flourished and spread, more adventurous theorists began to extend it beyond work groups to organizations as a whole. We now knew that there were a number of things that were bad for the morale and loyalty of groups – routine tasks, submission to authority, specialization of tasks, segregation of task sequence, ignorance of the goals of the firm, centralized decision making, and so on. If these were bad for groups, they were likely to be bad for groups of groups – i.e., for organizations. So people like Warren Bennis began talking about innovative, rapidly changing organizations that were made up of temporary leadership and role assignments, and democratic access to the goals of the firm. If rapidly changing technologies and unstable, turbulent environments were to characterize industry, then the structure of firms should be temporary and decentralized. The forces of light, of freedom, autonomy, change, humanity, creativity, and democracy were winning. Scientific management survived only in outdated text books. If the evangelizing of some of the human relations school theorists were excessive, and, if Likert's System 4, or MacGregor's Theory Y, or Blake's 9 × 9 evaded us, at least there was a rationale for the confusion, disorganization, scrambling, and stress: Systems should be temporary.

Bureaucracy's comeback

Meanwhile, in another part of the management forest, the mechanistic school was gathering its forces and preparing to outflank the forces of light. First came the numbers men – the linear programmers, the budget experts, and the financial analysts – with their PERT systems and cost-benefit analyses. From another world, unburdened by most of the scientific management ideology and untouched by the human relations school, they began to parcel things out and give some meaning to those truisms, 'plan ahead' and 'keep records.' Armed with emerging systems concepts, they carried the 'mechanistic' analogy to its fullest – and it was very productive. Their work still goes on, largely untroubled by organizational theory; the theory, it seems clear, will have to adjust to them, rather than the other way around.

   Then the words of Max Weber, first translated from the German in the 1940s – he wrote around 1910, incredibly – began to find their way into social science thought. At first, with his celebration of the efficiency of bureaucracy, he was received with only reluctant respect, and even with hostility. All writers were against bureaucracy. But it turned out, surprisingly, that managers were not. When asked, they acknowledge that they preferred clear lines of communication, clear specifications of authority and responsibility, and clear knowledge of whom they were responsible to. They were as wont to say 'there ought to be a rule about this,' as to say 'there are too many rules around here,' as wont to say 'next week we've got to get organized,' as to say 'there is too much red tape.' Gradually, studies began to show that bureaucratic organizations could change faster than nonbureaucratic ones, and that morale could be higher where there was clear evidence of bureaucracy.

   What was this thing, then? Weber had showed us, for example, that bureaucracy was the most effective way of ridding organizations of favoritism, arbitrary authority, discrimination, payola, and kickbacks, and, yes, even incompetence. His model stressed expertise, and the favorite or the boss's nephew or the guy who burned up resources to make his performance look good was *not* the one with expertise. Rules could be changed: they could be dropped in exceptional circumstances; job security promoted more innovation. The sins of bureaucracy began to look like the sins of failing to follow its principles.

Enter power, conflict, and decisions

But another discipline began to intrude upon the confident work and increasingly elaborate models of the human relations theorists (largely social psychologists) and the uneasy toying with bureaucracy of the 'structionalists' (largely sociologists). Both tended to study economic organizations. A few, like Philip Selznick, were noting conflict and differences in goals (perhaps because he was studying a public agency, the Tennessee Valley Authority), but most ignored conflict or treated it as a pathological manifestation of breakdowns in communication or the ego trips of unreconstructed managers.

But in the world of political parties, pressure groups, and legislative bodies, conflict was not only rampant, but to be expected – it was even functional. This was the domain of the political scientists. They kept talking about power, making it a legitimate concern for analysis. There was an open acknowledgment of 'manipulation.' These were political scientists who were 'behaviorally' inclined – studying and recording behavior rather than constitutions and formal systems of government – and they came to a much more complex view of organized activity. It spilled over into the area of economic organizations, with the help of some economists like R. A. Gordon and some sociologists who were studying conflicting goals of treatment and custody in prisons and mental hospitals.

The presence of legitimately conflicting goals and techniques of preserving and using power did not, of course, sit well with a cooperative systems view of organizations. But it also puzzled the bureaucratic school (and what was left of the old scientific management school), for the impressive Weberian principles were designed to settle questions of power through organizational design and to keep conflict out through reliance on rational-legal authority and systems of careers, expertise, and hierarchy. But power was being overtly contested and exercised in covert ways, and conflict was bursting out all over, and even being creative.

Gradually, in the second half of the 1950s and in the next decade, the political-science view infiltrated both schools. Conflict could be healthy, even in a cooperative system, said the human relationists; it was the mode of resolution that counted, rather than prevention. Power became reconceptualized as 'influence,' and the distribution was less important, said Arnold Tannenbaum, than the total amount. For the bureaucratic school – never a clearly defined group of people, and largely without any clear ideology – it was easier to just absorb the new data and theories as something else to be thrown into the pot. That is to say, they floundered, writing books that went from topic to topic, without a clear view of organizations, or better yet, producing 'readers' and leaving students to sort it all out.

Buried in the political-science viewpoint was a sleeper that only gradually began to undermine the dominant views. This was the idea, largely found in the work of Herbert Simon and James March, that because man was so limited – in intelligence, reasoning powers, information at his disposal, time available, and means of ordering his preferences clearly – he generally seized on the first acceptable alternative when deciding, rather than looking for the best; that he rarely changed things unless they really got bad, and even then he continued to try what had worked before; that he limited his search for solutions to well worn paths and traditional sources of information and established ideas; that he was wont to remain preoccupied with routine, thus preventing innovation. They called these characteristics 'cognitive limits on rationality' and spoke of 'satisficing' rather than maximizing or optimizing. It is now called the 'decision-making' school and is concerned with the basic question of how people make decisions.

This view had some rather unusual implications. It suggested that if managers were so limited, then they could be easily controlled. What was necessary was not to give direct orders (on the assumption that subordinates were idiots without expertise) or to leave them to their own devices (on the assumption that they were supermen who would somehow know what was best for the organization, how to coordinate with all the other supermen, how to anticipate market changes, and so on). It was necessary to control only the *premises* of their decisions. Left to themselves, with those premises set, they could be predicted to rely on precedent, keep things stable and smooth, and respond to signals that reinforce the behavior desired of them.

To control the premises of decision making, March and Simon outline a variety of devices, all of which are familiar to you, but some of which you may not have seen before in quite this light. For example, organizations develop vocabularies, and this means that certain kinds of information are highlighted, and others are screened out – just as Eskimos (and skiers) distinguish many varieties of snow, while Londoners see only one. This is a form of attention-directing. Another is the reward system. Change the bonus for salesmen and you can shift them from volume selling to steady-account selling, or to selling quality products or new products. If you want to channel good people into a different function (because, for example, sales should no longer be the critical functions as the market changes, but engineering applications should), you may have to promote mediocre people in the unrewarded function in order to signal to the good people in the rewarded one that the game has changed. You cannot expect most people to make such decisions on their own because of the cognitive limits on their rationality, nor will you succeed by giving direct orders, because you yourself probably do not know whom to order where. You presume that once the signals are clear and the new sets of alternatives are manifest they have enough ability to make the decision but you have had to change the premises for their decisions about their career lines.

It would take too long to go through the dozen or so devices, covering a range of decision areas (March and Simon are not that clear or systematic about them, themselves, so I have summarized them in my own book), but I think the message is clear.

It was becoming clear to the human relations school, and to the bureaucratic school. The human relationists had begun to speak of changing stimuli rather than changing personality. They had begun to see that the rewards that can change behavior can well be prestige, money, comfort, and the like, rather than trust, openness, self-insight, and so on. The alternative to supportive relations need not be punishment, since behavior can best be changed by rewarding approved behavior rather than by punishing disapproved behavior. They were finding that although leadership may be centralized, it can function best through indirect and unobtrusive means such as changing the premises on which decisions are made, thus giving the impression that the subordinate is actually making a decision when he has only been switched to a different set of alternatives. The implications of this work were also beginning to filter into the human relations school, through an emphasis on behavioral psychology (the modern version of the much maligned stimulus-response school) that was supplanting personality theory (Freudian in its roots and drawing heavily, in the human relations school, on Maslow).

For the bureaucratic school, this new line of thought reduced the heavy weight placed upon the bony structure of bureaucracy by highlighting the muscle and flesh that make these bones move. A single chain of command, precise division of labor, and clear lines of communication are simply not enough in themselves. Control can be achieved by using alternative communication channels, depending on the situation; by increasing or decreasing the static or 'noise' in the system; by creating organizational myths and organizational vocabularies that allow only selective bits of information to enter the system; and through monitoring performance through indirect means rather than direct surveillance. Weber was all right for a starter, but organizations had changed vastly, and the leaders needed many more means of control and more subtle means of manipulation than they did at the turn of the century.

The technological qualification

By now the forces of darkness and forces of light had moved respectively from midnight and noon to about 4 A.M. and 8 P.M. But any convergence or resolution would have to be on yet new terms, for soon after the political-science tradition had begun to infiltrate the established schools, another blow struck both of the major positions. Working quite independently of the Tavistock Group, with its emphasis on sociotechnical systems, and before the work of Burns and Stalker on mechanistic and organic firms, Joan Woodward was trying to see whether the classical scientific principles of organization made any sense in her survey of a hundred firms in South Essex. She tripped and stumbled over a piece of gold in the process. She picked up the gold, labeled it 'technology,' and made sense out of her otherwise hopeless data. Job-shop firms, mass-production firms, and continuous-process firms all had quite different structures because the type of tasks, or the 'technology,' was different. Somewhat later, researchers in America were coming to very similar conclusions based on studies of hospitals, juvenile correctional institutions, and industrial firms. Bureaucracy appeared to be the best form of organization for routine operations; temporary work groups, decentralization, and emphasis on interpersonal processes appeared to work best for nonroutine operations. A raft of studies appeared and are still appearing, all trying to show how the nature of the task affects the structure of the organization.

This severely complicated things for the human relations school, since it suggested that openness and trust, while good things in themselves, did not have much impact, or perhaps were not even possible in some kinds of work situations. The prescriptions that were being handed out would have to be drastically qualified. What might work for nonroutine, high-status, interesting, and challenging jobs performed by highly educated people might not be relevant or even beneficial for the vast majority of jobs and people.

It also forced the upholders of the revised bureaucratic theory to qualify their recommendations, since research and development units should obviously be run differently from mass-production units, and the difference between both of these and highly programmed and highly sophisticated continuous-process firms was obscure in terms of bureaucratic theory. But the bureaucratic school perhaps came out on top, because the forces of evil – authority, structure, division of labor, and the like – no longer looked evil, even if they were not applicable to a minority of industrial units.

The emphasis on technology raised other questions, however. A can company might be quite routine, and a plastics division nonroutine, but there were both routine and nonroutine units within each. How should they be integrated if the prescription were followed that, say, production should be bureaucratized and R&D not? James Thompson began spelling out different forms of interdependence among units in organizations, and Paul Lawrence and Jay Lorsch looked closely at the nature of integrating mechanisms. Lawrence and Lorsch found that firms performed best when the differences between units were *maximized* (in contrast to both the human relations and the bureaucratic school), as long as the integrating mechanisms stood half-way between the two – being neither strongly bureaucratic nor nonroutine. They also noted that attempts at participative management in routine situations were counterproductive, that the environments of some kinds of organizations were far from turbulent and customers did not want innovations and changes, that cost reduction, price and efficiency were trivial considerations in some firms, and so on. The technical insight was demolishing our comfortable truths right and left. They were also being questioned from another quarter.

Enter goals, environments, and systems

The final seam was being mined by the sociologists while all this went on. This was the concern with organizational goals and the environment. Borrowing from the political scientists to some extent, but pushing ahead on their own, this 'institutional school' came to see that goals were not fixed: conflicting goals could be pursued simultaneously, if there were enough slack resources, or sequentially (growth for the next four years, then cost-cutting and profit-taking for the next four); that goals were up for grabs in organizations, and units fought over them. Goals were, of course, not what they seemed to be, the important ones were quite unofficial; history played a big role; and assuming profit as the preeminent goal, explained almost nothing about a firm's behavior.

They also did case studies that linked the organization to the web of influence of the environment; that showed now unique organizations were in many respects (so that, once again, there was no one best way to do things for all organizations); how organizations were embedded in their own history, making change difficult. Most striking of all, perhaps, the case studies revealed that the stated goals usually were not the real ones; the official leaders usually were not the real ones; the official leaders usually were not the powerful ones; claims of effectiveness and efficiency were deceptive or even untrue; the public interest was not being served; political influences were pervasive; favoritism, discrimination, and sheer corruption were commonplace. The accumulation of these studies presented quite a pill for either the forces of light or darkness to swallow, since it was hard to see how training sessions or interpersonal skills were relevant to these problems, and it was also clear that the vaunted efficiency of bureaucracy was hardly in evidence. What could they make of this wad of case studies?

We are still sorting it out. In one sense, the Weberian model is upheld because organizations are not, *by nature*, cooperative systems; top managers must exercise a great deal of effort to control them. But if organizations are tools in the hands of leaders, they may be very recalcitrant ones. Like the broom in the story of the sorcerer's apprentice, they occasionally get out of hand. If conflicting goals, bargaining, and unofficial leadership exist, where is the structure of Weberian bones and Simonian muscle? To what extent are organizations tools, and to what extent are they products of the varied interests and group strivings of their members? Does it vary by organization, in terms of some typological alchemy we have not discovered? We don't know. But at any rate, the bureaucratic model suffers again; it simply has not reckoned on the role of the environment. There are enormous sources of variations that the neat, though by now quite complex, neo-Weberian model could not account for.

The human relations model has also been badly shaken by the findings of the institutional school, for it was wont to assume that goals were given and unproblematical and that anything that promoted harmony and efficiency for an organization also was good for society. Human relationists assumed that the problems created by organizations were largely limited to the psychological consequences of poor interpersonal relations within them, rather than their impact on the environment. Could the organization really promote the psychological health of its members when by necessity it had to define psychological health in terms of the goals of the organization itself? The neo-Weberian model at least called manipulation 'manipulation' and was skeptical of claims about autonomy and self-realization.

But on one thing all the varied schools of organizational analysis now seemed to be agreed: organizations are systems – indeed, they are open systems. As the growth of the field has forced ever more variables into our consciousness, flat claims of predictive power are beginning to decrease and research has become bewilderingly complex. Even consulting groups need more than one or two tools in their kit-bag as the software multiplies.

The systems view is intuitively simple. Everything is related to everything else, though in uneven degrees of tension and reciprocity. Every unit, organization, department, or work group takes in resources, transforms them, and sends them out, and thus interacts with the larger system. The psychological, sociological, and cultural aspects of units interact. The systems view was explicit in the institutional work, since they tried to study whole organizations; it became explicit in the human relations school, because they were so concerned with the interactions of people. The political science and technology viewpoints also had to come to this realization, since they deal with parts affecting each other (sales affecting production; technology affecting structure).

But as intuitively simple as it is, the systems view has been difficult to put into practical use. We still find ourselves ignoring the tenets of the open-systems view, possibly because of the cognitive limits on our rationality. General systems theory itself had not lived up to its heady predictions; it remains rather nebulous. But at least there is a model for calling us to account and for stretching our minds, our research tools, and our troubled nostrums.

Some conclusions

Where does all this leave us? We might summarize the prescriptions and proscriptions for management very roughly as follows:

1 A great deal of the 'variance' in a firm's behavior depends on the environment. We have become more realistic about the limited range of change that can be induced through internal efforts. The goals of organizations, including those of profit and efficiency, vary greatly among industries and vary systematically by industries. This suggests that the impact of better management by itself will be limited, since so much will depend on market forces, competition, legislation, nature of the work force, available technologies and innovations, and so on. Another source of variation is, obviously, the history of the firm and its industry and its traditions.

2 A fair amount of variation in both firms and industries is due to the type of work done in the organization – the technology. We are now fairly confident in recommending that if work is predictable and routine, the necessary arrangement for getting the work done can be highly structured, and one can use a good deal of bureaucratic theory in accomplishing this. If it is not predictable, if it is nonroutine and there is a good deal of uncertainty as to how to do a job, then one had better utilize the theories that emphasize autonomy, temporary groups, multiple lines of authority and communications, and so on. We also know that this distinction is important when organizing different parts of an organization.

   We are also getting a grasp on the question of what is the most critical function in different types of organizations. For some organizations, it is production; for others, marketing; for still others, development. Furthermore, firms go through phases whereby the initial development of a market or a product or manufacturing process or accounting scheme may require a nonbureaucratic structure, but once it comes on stream, the structure should change to reflect the changed character of the work.

3 In keeping with this, management should be advised that the attempt to produce change in an organization through managerial grids, sensitivity training, and even job enrichment and job enlargement is likely to be fairly ineffective for all but a few organizations. The critical reviews of research in all these fields show that there is no scientific evidence to support the claims of the proponents of these various methods; that research has told us a great deal about social psychology, but little about how to apply the highly complex findings to actual situations. The key word is *selectivity:* We have no broad-spectrum antibiotics for interpersonal relations. Of course, managers should be sensitive, decent, kind, courteous, and courageous, but we have known that for some time now, and beyond a minimal threshold level the payoff is hard to measure. The various attempts to make work and interpersonal relations more humane and stimulating should be applauded,

but we should not confuse this with solving problems of structure, or as the equivalent of decentralization or participatory democracy.

4 The burning cry in all organizations is for 'good leadership,' but we have learned that beyond a threshold level of adequacy it is extremely difficult to know what good leadership is. The hundreds of scientific studies of this phenomenon come to one general conclusion: Leadership is highly variable or 'contingent' upon a large variety of important variables such as nature of task, size of the group, length of time the group has existed, type of personnel within the group and their relationships with each other, and amount of pressure the group is under. It does not seem likely that we'll be able to devise a way to select the best leader for a particular situation. Even if we could, that situation would probably change in a short time and thus would require a somewhat different type of leader.

Furthermore, we are beginning to realize that leadership involves more than smoothing the paths of human interaction. What has rarely been studied in this area is the wisdom or even the technical adequacy of a leader's decision. A leader does more than lead people; he also makes decisions about the allocation of resources, type of technology to be used, the nature of the market, and so on. This aspect of leadership remains very obscure, but it is obviously crucial.

5 If we cannot solve our problems through good human relations or through good leadership, what are we then left with? The literature suggests that changing the structures of organizations might be the most effective and certainly the quickest and cheapest method. However, we are now sophisticated enough to know that changing the formal structure by itself is not likely to produce the desired changes. In addition, one must be aware of a large range of subtle, unobtrusive, and even covert processes and change devices that exist. If inspection procedures are not working, we are now unlikely to rush in with sensitivity training, nor would we send down authoritative communications telling people to do a better job. We are more likely to find out where the authority really lies, whether the degree of specialization is adequate, what the rules and regulations are, and so on, but even this very likely will not be enough.

According to the neo-Weberian bureaucratic model – it has been influenced by work on decision making and behavioral psychology – we should find out how to manipulate the reward structure, change the premises of the decision makers through finer controls on the information received and the expectations generated, search for interdepartmental conflicts that prevent better inspection procedures from being followed, and after manipulating these variables, sit back and wait for two or three months for them to take hold. This is complicated and hardly as dramatic as many of the solutions currently being peddled, but I think the weight of organizational theory is in its favor.

We have probably learned more, over several decades of research and theory, about the things that do *not* work (even though some of them obviously *should* have worked) than we have about things that do work. On balance, this is an important gain and should not discourage us. As you know, organizations are extremely complicated. To have as much knowledge as we do have in a fledgling discipline that has had to borrow from the diverse tools and concepts of psychology, sociology, economics, engineering, biology, history, and even anthropology is not really so bad.

References

This paper is an adaptation of the discussion to be found in Charles Perrow, *Complex Organizations: A Critical Essay* (Glenview, Ill.: Scott, Foresman, 1972). All the points made in this paper are discussed thoroughly in that volume.

The best overview and discussion of classical management theory, and its changes over time is by Joseph Massie, 'Management Theory' in *Handbook of Organizations*, ed. James March (Chicago: Rand McNally, 1965), pp. 387–422.

The best discussion of the changing justifications for managerial rule and worker obedience as they are related to changes in technology, and the like, can be found in Reinhard Bendix's *Work and Authority in Industry* (New York: John Wiley & Sons, 1956). See especially the chapter on the American experience.

Some of the leading lights of the classical view – F. W. Taylor, Colonel Urwick, and Henri Fayol – are briefly discussed in *Writers on Organizations* by D. S. Pugh, D. J. Hickson, and C. R. Hinings (Baltimore: Penguin, 1971). This brief, readable, and useful book also contains selections from many other schools that I discuss, including Weber, Woodward, Cyert and March, Simon, the Hawthorne Investigations, and the Human Relations Movement as represented by Argyris, Herzberg, Likert, McGregor, and Blake and Mouton.

As good a place as any to start examining the human relations tradition is Rensis Likert, *The Human Organization* (New York: McGraw-Hill, 1967). See also his *New Patterns of Management* (New York: McGraw-Hill, 1961).

The Buck Rogers School of organizational theory is best represented by Warren Bennis. See his *Changing Organizations* (New York: McGraw-Hill, 1966), and his book with Philip Slater. *The Temporary Society* (New York: Harper & Row, 1968). Much of this work is linked into more general studies, e.g., Alvin Toffler's very popular paperback *Future Shock* (New York: Random House, 1970), and Bantam Paperbacks; or Zibigniew Brzezinksy's *Between Two Ages: America's Role in the Technitronic Era* (New York: Viking Press, 1970). One of the first intimations of the new type of environment and firm and still perhaps the most perceptive is to be found in the volume by Tom Burns and G. Stalker, *The Management of Innovation* (London: Tavistock, 1961), where they distinguished between 'organic' and 'mechanistic' systems. The introduction, which is not very long, is an excellent and very tight summary of the book.

The political science tradition came in through three important works. First, Herbert Simon's *Administrative Behavior* (New York: Macmillan, 1948), followed by the second half of James March and Herbert Simon's *Organizations* (New York: John Wiley & Sons, 1958), then Richard M. Cyert and James March's *A Behavioral Theory of the Firm* (Englewood Cliffs, N.J.: Prentice-Hall, 1963). All three of these books are fairly rough going, though chapters 1, 2, 3, and 6 of the last volume are fairly short and accessible. A quite interesting book in this tradition, though somewhat heavy-going, is Michael Crozier's *The Bureaucratic Phenomenon* (Chicago: University of Chicago, and London: Tavistock Publications, 1964). This is a striking description of power in organizations, though there is a somewhat dubious attempt to link organization processes in France to the cultural traits of the French people.

The book by Joan Woodward, *Industrial Organisation: Theory and Practice* (London: Oxford University Press, 1965), is still very much worth reading. A fairly popular attempt to discuss the implications for this for management can be found in my own book *Organizational Analysis: A Sociological View* (London: Tavistock, 1970), chaps. 2 and 3. The impact of technology on structure is still fairly controversial. A number of technical studies have found both support and nonsupport, largely because the concept is defined so differently, but there is general agreement that different structures and leadership techniques are needed for different situations. For studies that support and document this viewpoint see James Thompson, *Organizations in Action* (New York: McGraw-Hill, 1967), and Paul Lawrence and Jay Lorsch, *Organizations and Environment* (Cambridge, Mass.: Harvard University Press, 1967).

The best single work on the relation between the organization and the environment and one of the most readable books in the field is Philip Selznick's short volume *Leadership in Administration* (Evanston, Ill.: Row, Peterson, 1957). But the large number of these studies are scattered about. I have summarized several in my *Complex Organizations: A Critical Essay*.

Lastly, the most elaborate and persuasive argument for a systems view of organizations is found in the first 100 pages of the book by Daniel Katz and Robert Kahn, *The Social Psychology of Organizations* (New York: John Wiley & Sons, 1966). It is not easy reading, however.

the promise, the power, the flaws (1975)

'The behavioural sciences: their potential and limitations', by Patrick Sills, *Personnel Review*, vol. 4, no. 3, 1975, pp. 5–12.

Patrick Sills reminds us that 'behavioural science knowledge is power', and that knowledge can be used in responsible and irresponsible ways. One of his arguments, therefore, concerns the need to contain this power. This view seems to contradict those who would dismiss the social or behavioural sciences – the study of people – as soft, woolly, and of little scientific interest. The social sciences are easily dismissed, on at least two counts. First, because their subject matter and findings are regarded as indistinguishable from common sense. Second, because there is no credible 'social engineering' that helps us to fix human and organizational problems in the sense that science has enabled us to develop a range of technologies to address medical and material problems. Where is the power in discovering what we already know, in rediscovering common sense, in attempting to document the invisible and the unmeasurable, in producing unusable results?

learning objectives

Once you have read and understood this article, you should be able to:

1 Explain more clearly the reasons behind the criticism and scepticism surrounding the relevance of behavioural and social science to organizational settings.
2 Develop your own detailed and balanced assessment of the strengths and weaknesses of the social sciences, particularly with respect to organizational applications.

learning pre-requisites

You will find it useful to be familiar with the discussion about the nature of social science in Chapter 2 of the core text. Note that Sills uses the term 'behavioural sciences', but says that this is synonymous for his purposes with the term 'social sciences' which we use in our text. His argument, however, concerns much more than methodology, and his points about the development of knowledge, power, and the application of that knowledge are relevant to the whole subject matter of organizational behaviour.

learning activities

1 As you read the article, list as many reasons as you can find to criticize and dismiss the social sciences, concerning weaknesses in their aims, methods, concepts, stage of development, and applicability. Maybe you can add points of your own here.
2 As you read the article, list as many reasons as you can find to defend and support

the social sciences, with respect to aims, methods, concepts, stage of development, and applicability. Once again, you can perhaps add points from your own experience.

3 Use the matrix below to develop your own assessment of the promise and problems of social science.

Social or behavioural science: a balanced assessment

	Problems: *the case for the prosecution*	*Promises:* *the case for the defence*
Aims		
Methods		
Concepts		
Stage of development		
Applications		
Other		

READING 2

The behavioural sciences: their potential and limitations*
Patrick Sills

Introduction

There is widespread non-understanding of the nature, possibilities and limitations of behavioural science among managements and trade unions. There is also considerable misunderstanding – indeed suspicion – between the three parties to behavioural science-in-industry contracts – the behavioural scientist, the manager and the trade unionist – about the motives for conducting studies and the methods of managing both scientific work in progress and the implementation of results. This lack of clarity among industrialists, incidentally, is by no means only their fault; their confidence has been known to be tricked by behavioural scientists who, for instance, make excessive claims for their product or transgress agreements by failing to provide expected feedback or infringing the principle of confidentiality.

Further to these technical-cum-managerial non- or misunderstandings about behavioural science in industry, there has been a paucity of thought and discussion about its ethical implications. My belief is that behavioural science studies should be conducted, and their results applied, on a wider scale in industry, to the mutual benefit of each of the three parties; but that this is unlikely to occur until a clearer understanding of 'what it's all about' exists among, and is shared between, members of managements, trade unions and behavioural science organizations.

My aim in this article is to provide a condensed introduction to the behavioural sciences – to describe what they are, and to discuss what they are not. I would like to suggest what the behavioural sciences are under several headings: definition of terms; constituent subject disciplines; behavioural science aims, methods and concepts; and, finally, two aspects of their application in industry – techniques, and areas of industrial management and relations to which they seem particularly relevant. I will then outline some of my practical, methodological and ethical concerns about the contemporary practice of behavioural science in industry.

Definition of terms

Blanket definitions are unhelpful; such a definition of behavioural science could only summarize what follows. But in case uncertainty exists about the different terms often used to describe what is apparently the same phenomenon, it should be mentioned that in everyday language the terms behavioural science, social science and human science – and behavioural studies, social studies and human studies – can be used interchangeably. There are sometimes differences of emphasis: for example, human science or studies can incorporate anatomy or physiology which are not strictly behavioural; social science or studies can be rigorously defined to exclude psychology and other individual-based areas of enquiry; and behavioural science is sometimes interpreted to exclude economics, which does not directly investigate behaviour. But for the purposes of this discussion, the terms can be assumed synonymous; and we can go on to explore their substance.

Constituent subject disciplines

One way of describing behavioural science is to imitate those who have defined intelligence as what intelligence tests measure, and outline the disciplines which, at least

* Reprinted by permission of Patrick Sills, Department of Education, Canterbury Christchurch College, from *Personnel Review*, Vol. 4, No. 3, 1975.

for research purposes, are subsumed under the umbrella term. The following list comprises the academic specialisms currently sponsored by the Social Science Research Council:

Economics and Social History
Economics
Human Geography
Management and Industrial Relations
Planning
Political Science and International Relations
Psychology
Social Anthropology
Social Sciences and the Law
Sociology and Social Administration
Statistics
Educational Research
Area Studies

This list indicates the broad interest range of behavioural science and the scope of what it offers to industry and other 'consumers'. The segment with which industry has been particularly concerned to date is management and industrial relations, and those aspects of psychology, sociology and economics which have been involved in their study. Though it should be noted that the topical image conjured up by the phrase 'behavioural science in industry' excludes economics; and it is the application of psychology and sociology to human behaviour in industry to which specific comments in this discussion will principally refer.

Nevertheless, appreciation of the broad scope of behavioural science is important; not least because it is the basic characteristics shared by the listed disciplines which form the 'guts' of behavioural science. The use of the term behavioural science implies common denominators. It is these common denominators which need to be explored in order to understand what behavioural science is really all about.

Behavioural science aims

The first of these common denominators is the overall purpose of different disciplines' pursuits and activities. The clue to this lies in the word science. It seems inherent in human nature to observe and try to make sense of, and predictions about, the behavioural world around us. As Barbara Wootton has said,

All of us can probably forecast in a limited number of specific situations the behaviour of a few people whom we know intimately with a degree of probability which, while it falls short of that with which astronomers foretell the eclipses, yet easily surpasses the success with which the meteorologists prophesy tomorrow's weather [1].

We are all, in some sense, behavioural scientists. Scientific method incorporates, but also elaborates, a common sense, or lay behavioural science, approach to human behaviour. 'It aims at objectivity, order and the establishment of hypotheses which can be tested [2].' Through the sequential stages of systematic exploration, description and explanation, the purpose of scientific method is 'to order the particular example by articulating it on a skeleton of general law [3]'. It is to start with hypotheses, develop these through empirical testing into theories, and finally attain sufficient confidence that all eventualities have been covered so as to give an 'if..., then....' proposition the status of scientific law. Even such laws, it should be noted, are subject to Heisenberg's principle of uncertainty, and scientific development is possibly best seen as the progressive refinement of hypotheses. Nevertheless, the greater confidence which can successively be placed in increasingly refined hypotheses lends weight to the scientific assumption that 'more methodical and sophisticated observation enables us to make more accurate forecasts [4]'. The primary concern of behavioural scientists is, through the cyclical and inter-connected processes of observation, hypothesis formulation and testing, prediction, verification and generalization, to explore, describe and explain the individual and collective behaviour of human beings, and thereby provide the opportunity for more accurate prediction and informed planning of their future behaviour.

It is difficult to assess how far the term Science with a capital 'S' is validly applied to behavioural scientists' efforts. If a body of general law were the precondition of acceptability as a science, then behavioural science does not make it. But Professor Cherns has recently suggested different criteria,

> first that knowledge should be cumulative; second, that observations should be replicable, i.e. that if I give you the recipe whereby I obtain my results you should …. be able to produce a similar set of results; the third criterion is that the hypotheses which are proposed should be falsifiable, in principle, by empirical data and should lead to the search for such data. The fourth criterion is that the data should be quantifiable, and the fifth that the experimental technique be followed of controlling other variables in order to estimate or measure the effect of the one under study [5].

Cherns believes that the 'hard' end of behavioural science, experimental psychology, satisfies these criteria. Other disciplines go part-way towards satisfying them, though:

1 Knowledge, too much for comfort, seems random and accidental rather than cumulative.
2 Replicability is bugged by the difficulty of repeating similar conditions of data collection.
3 It has to be admitted that the temptation to prove hypotheses right rather than wrong is not always resisted.
4 The subject matter is not always susceptible to accurate quantification.
5 Experimental method is difficult to apply to human behaviour because of the large number and complex interrelationships of the variables at play; their constant mutations make the control of, for instance, variables B, C, D and E, while the interaction of A and F is measured, hazardous in the extreme.

The behavioural sciences have a long way to go before fully meeting these five criteria of scientific activity. But their scientific base should not, because of this, be dismissed. The fundamental aims of behavioural scientists are scientific. They are as concerned as natural scientists to pursue scientific rigour and exactitude.

Behavioural science methods

Whether or not behavioural science acquires full respectability as a science depends largely on its methods, the second of its disciplines' common denominators. There is a persistent conflict between watertightness of method and meaningfulness of interpretation (the more rigorous the method, the more limited the scope of enquiry); but in the last resort conclusions contain no more substance than is allowed by the appropriateness and accuracy of the methods of collecting and analyzing the data on which they are based.

As mentioned above, there are three levels of scientific enquiry – exploration, description and explanation – and the methods used in a study depend principally on which of these objectives is uppermost. Research concerned with exploration needs to 'gain familiarity with a phenomenon, achieve new insights and, often, to formulate a more precise research problem or develop hypotheses [6]'. The methods of investigation therefore need to be flexible, depth-probing and comprehensive in the ground they cover. The most common are:

1 Unstructured interviews, particularly with key individuals, for example staff occupying senior and junior positions, with long and short service, deviants and stereotypes.
2 'Holistic' case studies of a situation designed to identify all variables at play without prejudging their relative force.
3 Participant observation, in which a research worker becomes involved in the social behaviour which he is simultaneously observing.
4 Use of documentary sources, for example analysis of records and background statistics, and survey of literature.

These methods are less scientifically rigorous than those used to pursue the research objectives of description or explanation. But they are more systematic and objective than common sense, and frequently lead to the perception both of new phenomena and of familiar items in a new light.

The second main research objective is description. Behavioural scientists are interested in describing and enumerating four particular characteristics of people:

1 Background biographical, or demographic, details.
2 Attitudes, feelings and opinions.
3 Relatively unconscious factors, for example in personality make-up and development.
4 Behaviour.

The first type of information is gleaned from records, interviews (though records are usually more accurate!) and secondary sources like the census on society and manpower planning data in industry.

The second type of information, attitudes and opinions, is most appropriately derived from relatively structured interviews and the distribution and collection of self-completion questionnaires.

The main techniques for collecting data about unconscious processes are: psychological tests, broadly measuring individual aptitude and achievement; interest tests, which measure for example vocational bent, the significance to an individual of different values, and the strength of his need for different types of interpersonal relationships; personality inventories; situational tests, for example 'country house' election procedures and leaderless group discussions; and projective techniques, for example sentence/completion, word association and Rorschach Ink-Blot tests. Data about the fourth type of information, behaviour, is collected by two main techniques: systematic observation, for example activity sampling or the recording of interactions between people in a group; and self-recording of activities by the subjects of a study, for instance a manager keeping diary notes of his daily round.

For each of the four types of information the main aim of behavioural science description is quantification. If statistical sampling rules are adhered to, it is possible to estimate the degree of confidence with which it can be assumed that the results of a sample correspond to those of a total population. While some of the methods are not as foolproof as others, and all are subject to constant improvement, the objective and quantitative descriptions of human characteristics which they render possible are vastly more accurate and powerful than any subjective judgment or assumption.

The third main objective of research is explanation and the development of causal theories. One approach to this is to subject the data collected by the methods appropriate for description to multivariate analysis. This can establish degrees of association between different variables. But such statistical interrelationships do not necessarily imply a causal connection. Experimental method is required to ensure that A is not merely associated with B but 'varies' before B, that A is directly causing B's variation, rather than indirectly through an intervening variable (the equivalent of a third party), and that the principle of concomitant variation is satisfied – in J S Mill's words,

> whatever phenomenon varies in any manner whenever another phenomenon varies in some particular manner is either a cause or effect of that phenomenon or is connected with it through some fact of causation.

The methods used in experimental research designs are two-fold:

1 Systematic observation of variables under controlled conditions, either retrospectively when a current situation is traced back to historical causes, or projectively, when experimental and control groups are selected and standardized in the present and hypothesized associations between two factors analysed over a period of future time.
2 Direct recording of human behaviour by instrumentation. These methods achieve most fully the rigour intended for all behavioural science data collection techniques.

Even these, however, in common with the others, are subject to the vagaries of researcher-, researched-, or environment-bias.

A major part of ensuring scientific rigour is to recognize where it falls short. Sometimes nothing can be done about it, in which case the confidence which can be placed in results is reduced. Frequently, however, behavioural scientists can be helped by statisticians to eliminate, or at least reduce in the analysis stage, bias and error which have crept in during data collection. Through the application of statistical techniques behavioural scientists can ensure that data analysis, as well as collection, is as exhaustive and rigorous as man, at a particular point in time, is able to devise.

The methods of data collection and analysis adopted by behavioural science disciplines are therefore not only a common denominator between them, but form the basis of their scientific claims. Methodological rigour is the main contemporary proof of scientific intent. It also contains the major promise for the future fulfilment of scientific aims.

Behavioural science concepts

A further common factor between disciplines which can serve to clarify their real nature is their concepts. In the past the main emphasis in the behavioural sciences has been the dynamics of individual, or collective, behaviour as independent and isolated phenomena. More recently it has been realized that what happens at one level of human behaviour can only be understood if looked at in relation to other levels. Just as medical researchers accept a psychosomatic basis to much illness – body and soul, so to speak, are dynamically interrelated – so it is impossible to interpret an individual's industrial behaviour without exploring the group in which he works, the organization of which that group is a part, and the wider environment in which the organization itself operates (not to mention similar factors in an individual's non-work environment). Behavioural scientists of all disciplines are increasingly trying to look at the 'total system'.

The term 'system' has two main implications. The first is that, for instance, in the study of organizational behaviour, the organization is seen as a whole, the parts of which are in a state of interdependence so that changes in one part of the organization provoke consequential changes in other parts. These parts may be different parts of the 'social system' (for example work groups or departments) or other parts of the whole organization with which this social *sub*-system is itself in a state of interdependence. In a commercial organization the two other principal subsystems are the technical and the economic. The second implication of the term system is openness. It is a characteristic of all organisms that they receive stimuli, energy or materials in from their environment, process and convert them, and transport them out again in a different form. The organization, group or individual is in a continuous state of interaction and exchange with its environment and has to be open to it. Indeed it is only through this openness that an organism or organization can maintain the state of equilibrium between itself and its environment which is necessary for survival.

This overall systemic model of the individual in groups in organizations in environments is relevant to all levels of human behaviour and behavioural science enquiry. It is also increasingly serving as a catalytic integrative force between the different disciplines; it makes nonsense of the boundaries dividing them.

The application of behavioural science

Behavioural scientists of all disciplines have been concerned with the development, as well as the research bit of the research and development continuum. Application of their findings to practical situations is the fourth common denominator between the different disciplines. Indeed, many managers' and trade unionists' initiation into behavioural science is frequently through one or other of the techniques evolved for application in industry. Derived from both the psychology and sociology disciplines, the techniques which have been used in, and seem particularly relevant to, industry can be classified into three: *diagnostic tools, training programmes* and *strategies for facilitating change*. The *diagnostic techniques* developed from behavioural science include:

> records analysis and manpower forecasting
> human asset accounting
> aptitude, personality and vocational tests, not least the battery developed by
>   Standard Oil known as the Early Identification of Management Potential
>   systematic approaches to interviewing
> attitude and opinion surveys
> behavioural analysis
> ergonomics
> socio-technical systems analysis.

Among the *training techniques* are:

> T-groups
> the managerial grid (Blake)
> the practice of management principles (Coverdale)
> problem analysis and decision-making (Kepner and Tregoe)
> the 3-D organizational effectiveness programme (Reddin)
> training for leadership (Adair)
> achievement–motivation development (McClelland)
> the technology of training – a systematic approach to the overall training process.

Thirdly, *change-facilitation techniques* developed by behavioural scientists include:

job enrichment
planned change
participative management
management by objectives
action research
organizational development/learning [7].

Through concern with application, behavioural scientists have not just lived in a world of their own; indeed it would make nonsense of their scientific profession if they did not test their hypotheses in real-life situations. Application is integral to the behavioural science process. But it also provides an industrial *firm*, for instance, with a *quid* for a behavioural science *quo*. Increasing understanding and improved practice of industrial management and relations have resulted, and could further result, from behavioural science applications. This is particularly true in the fields of personnel selection, appraisal, training and development; the design of equipment and workspaces; managerial style; the formation of work groups; the management of change; the management of conflict; organizational design and development; and more integrated planning and management of the overall business process.

The behavioural sciences – their potential

This highly summarized discussion of behavioural science is one practitioner's attempt to unravel the reality which underlies, and seems frequently lost sight of in particular manifestations. Behavioural science is an ordered, systematic way of satisfying man's curiosity about himself. Its embryonic stage of development should not belie its potential significance for man's own development.

'What everybody knows' was normally not known until established by research. About many possible issues there are at least two common sense opinions, and when one is shown on investigation to be correct, there is an unjust tendency to condemn the investigation instead of commending it for its elimination of plausible error [8].

It is only by understanding behavioural processes that individuals, groups, organizations and societies can hope to master rather than be mastered 'Savoir pour prévoir', the commitment of Auguste Comte, the founder of sociology, remains the irresistible promise of behavioural science. Man has the responsibility for determining his own destiny. Behavioural science offers ever-increasing help in considering what that destiny could be, and how it might be fulfilled. Behavioural science represents a powerful tool for increasing man's own power over his present and future.

The behavioural sciences – their limitations

Power is double-edged. It is the power which can be unleashed by behavioural science which provokes excitement and commitment. But it also spells caution. Knowledge is subject to degrees of completeness. At the moment in behavioural science it is usually less rather than more so. Additionally, behavioural knowledge, no less than nuclear, can be used for destructive or creative ends.

Incomplete knowledge

Behavioural science knowledge is far from complete. Claims to the contrary are false. This is partly endemic. All scientific truth is uncertain and relative; and the nature of the beast whose taming is being attempted by behavioural science is particularly complex and intractable. But error also arises from common faults in the way behavioural science is practised, not least in industry.

The design and conducting of behavioural science research is frequently sloppy and unthought-out. What Pugh called the 'writing-up methodology' is often employed, when research results bear no relation to objectives; when hypotheses prove to have been vague and incompletely tested by collected data; when the overall research design turns out not to fit into any wider theoretical field or not to have taken account of its cumulated knowledge; when fact does not illuminate theory, or theory, in any case, goes its own way regardless (particularly common in sociology); when data are crude or invalid (i.e. do not portray what they were assumed to when collected); when methods of data collection are unreliable (i.e. they might not collect the same data on more than one occasion); when analysis is selective and random, not doing justice to the totality of data collected (it seems frequently forgotten that statistical non-significance is as substantively significant as statistical significance – as a statistician colleague said recently, 'You can't ignore certain bits of data because it doesn't suit you'; but many do); when the qualitative and quantitative data from a study do not marry up; or when through trying to do everything, a piece of research achieves nothing. Behavioural scientists are not immune – indeed seem all too prone – to human weakness and what a lavatory cleaner (the organizational know-all *par excellence*) colleague terms 'arrogance'. In a recent book(s) review, Rudolf Klein welcomed the opportunity

> to get an impression of how a research project actually worked out. Instead of the usual, utterly deceptive version – where only the neatly filleted and packaged results are presented, without any hint of abandoned aims, personal friction or methodological compromises – we are getting something approaching the full story of what research is really like: a messy business with very little resemblance to the text-book models [9].

It may be that 'social scientists are not greater offenders in this respect than other scientists [10]', or even industrialists. But the reality should be recognized. Results and recommendations can be misleading and dangerous, even when having the appearance of accuracy and relevance. Consumer (not least the industrialist) beware the instant behavioural science theories and half-baked applications which frequently emerge from such 'messy businesses'.

There are three aspects of research output, implicit in this account of human shortcomings in designing and conducting projects, against which consumers should be particularly on their guard. The first is the tendency to assume that past patterns can necessarily be transmuted into predicted future patterns. All data are collected at a certain point in time: and each point in time has unique characteristics; the circumstances surrounding data change; they will therefore be different both before and after data are collected than during this part of the scientific process. Indeed the very act of collecting data is a special feature of the nonrepeatable circumstances. As Anthony Harris has said of economics,

> the only form of experimental testing … is to measure the past and use the results in a carefully statistically tested equation, to predict the future … But since the tests of equations can only be those of statistical correlation, we are in trouble. To get a long enough series of figures to produce a statistically testable equation we must go back some years – where the statistics exist for a period of years.

But this involves going into a past which is in every important way totally different from the present.

Behavioural scientists of all disciplines are wading in just as deep water; and their predictions about future happenings should be treated with the caution implicitly recommended in Harris' 'surprise that the results of economic forecasting are not even worse than they are [11].' In the last resort, 'what we know of the future we can know only as speculation, however reasonable we consider the inferences made [12].'

The second form of scientific wool-pulling which consumers should beware is the thinking away or glossing over of complexity. Many simplistic conclusions are reached and canvassed which fail to grapple with data's total reality. As a psychologist colleague recently stated, 'things usually get more complicated the more you look at them.' That is patently true when data are examined in the fundamental scientific spirit of humility and concern for truth. But the practice is often the reverse. The complications are successively ironed out so that neat, tidy conclusions can be reached; a simple, 'practical' report written, or application technique recommended; and an article submitted to a journal which satisfies academics' craving for tying up loose ends. Nor are behavioural scientists the only offenders in this respect. Discussing management training, Philip Sadler has said that

> managers tend to pay most attention to the sorts of definitive research findings which can be expressed so simply and consistently that they could be printed on a postcard. More and more, the teacher's job will be to persuade students of management that if prescriptions are so simple that they can be printed on a postcard, then they are probably not worth having [13].

Industrialists should beware oversimplification; they should also try to reduce the pressure on behavioural scientists (which derives in part from their demands) to portray elaborate situations in 'Noddy' terms. Complexity is a fact of the life which behavioural scientists are exploring, and industrialists are trying to make work; it should be grappled with both in theory and practice.

The third warning about behavioural science 'products' derives from complexity. One factor which does not help behavioural scientists to face complexity is their internal lines of demarcation. Disciplinary boundaries are strong – as strong as the pull of academic kudos and career reward. The consequence is that each discipline funnels total reality into the bearing which 99% of it has on the 1% with which the discipline happens to be concerned. In the process the 100% is distorted,

> Nature is not organized in the same way that universities are; in organizational structure as well as in educational content the university should make it clear that the disciplines do not represent exclusive subdomains of Nature … because real problems are not disciplinary – only the ways they are approached are – an increasing number of problems in the real world are better tackled by interdisciplinary teams [14].

Disciplines have their place; they extend specialist knowledge and methods. But specialist knowledge should not be reified. The behavioural sciences' apparent paralysis in the face of many contemporary social and industrial issues stems largely from their being caught in the trap of narrow disciplinary perspective and conceptualization,

> Our problems are so varied and wide-reaching as to open up possibilities which are as splendid as the problems are daunting. We have an opportunity to do what has needed doing for two or three hundred years – to create a society where an integrated culture, scientific, moral and religious – gives to technology such a moral driving force as ensures the good of humanity. The way forward is by

multiple groups struggling cooperatively with problems which are beyond the power of any one of us to solve. Such multiple groups are the new feature of our social structures that technology needs and society must demand from Church and commerce, mass media and medicine, Government (local and national) and universities as we struggle with contemporary issues [15].

Ian Ramsey's dream is a challenge both to industrialists and behavioural scientists. Both should work along the lines he suggests. They should also work together along the same lines. They should take the gloves off between them. Behavioural scientists should be true to their scientific profession, not least by admitting their human and methodological limitations: predictions about the future should be proclaimed uncertain; conclusions should match data, however much this limits their scope; and the distortions of disciplinary dogma should be acknowledged, allowed for and over-come. Industrialists, for their part, should welcome what they can obtain from behavioural science – hard, objective data and evaluative feedback; new ideas and insights; new questions and ways of looking at things; and a more integrated approach to the overall management of their enterprises. They should not expect or demand anything more, or different. Their interest should be in truth rather than half-truth; in science rather than slickness. They should help themselves by helping behavioural scientists. Industrialists and behavioural scientists will then, together, be more able to promote 'the good of humanity', not least through the all-embracing multiple groups envisaged by Ramsey.

The direction and control of behavioural science knowledge

Greater adherence in practice to scientific principles and methods will do much to enhance the contribution of behavioural science to industry and society. But the ethics of science fall short of the ethics of life. Scientific values should be pre-eminent. But more than these are needed. Behavioural science work and results affect more than behavioural scientists; and its practitioners should not shirk responsibility for the consequences of their activities on those who participate in studies, both individuals and organizations; students and teachers; policy-makers in any sphere (not to mention those on the receiving end); and society at large. Behavioural scientists should also take responsibility for the consequences for their disciplines of accepting non-scientific constraints on their activities by any of these people or bodies.

The professional associations of behavioural scientists, notably the British Sociological Association, have drawn up 'statements of ethical principles and their application to sociological practice'. These represent the minimum required protection both to interested parties and from them to behavioural scientists. Unfortunately they are neither widely known about nor applied. Each individual behavioural scientist, and each organization concerned with its teaching or research, should apply the principles. They should also ensure that relevant clauses (for instance, 'when the behavioural scientist's subjects are individuals, he should explain how he came upon their name. He should at all times ensure that his subjects understand their right to refuse to cooperate with the research. He should leave with those who have cooperated a document which will identify him and his organization, and indicate how they may be communicated with') are incorporated into their agreements with industrial or other clients.

This would be an improvement on the sub-professional and sub-ethical standard of much behavioural science work. But it is questionable whether advancement in this field can be left just to the goodwill and sense of responsibility of behavioural scientists and their professional bodies.

Ethical principles often need to be enshrined in institutional arrangements to ensure that they are adhered to. The need for such structures seems particularly urgent in relation to two aspects of behavioural science work: determination of the issues into which research should be conducted; and the form of oversight of research which ensures the protection of all parties' interests.

The resounding silence (or non-useful utterance) of behavioural scientists on issues like industrial relations and democracy, national planning, the relationship between industry and government, and the social responsibilities of commerce reflects, *inter alia*, a failure to consider national social priorities, and to build their investigation into planned programmes of research.

This failure stems partly from 'Schon's law – that no idea in good currency is appropriate to the circumstances of its time. And since you can only get money on the basis of ideas in good currency, you can never get money to work on any problem that's real ... we must become publicly attentive to how we decide what the issues are that are worth working on [16].'

One approach to making such decisions (adapting Schon's own 'model of a social system displaying a flexibility that would permit government to function more effectively as a learning system') is two-pronged. Firstly, 'the independence of research councils matters ... because research findings should not be influenced by political and professional pressures [17]' and because 'pools of competence' should be scanning the future and projecting optimal scientific developments.

Research councils, like separate disciplines, should have the responsibility for pushing back the frontiers of scientific knowledge and method.

But, at the same time,

> in Britain there are far too few meeting-points between the scientists, the social scientists, and the politicians and civil servants who finally make the decisions ... we must have a clear notion of ... moral and social choices ... and the mechanism by which science can be guided without being stifled ... we need new machinery if we are to use science more wisely than we have done up to now [18].

At the very least, national and regional development councils should have a strong and explicit social, as well as economic, dimension and brief. The Social Science Research Council and individual behavioural scientists should be represented on these bodies. Moreover, research money should partially be channelled through such bodies to ensure that issues identified as critical for society's future receive commensurate investigation.

Similar structures should also be evolved at industrial and company level. Industries and their constituent firms need to become more effective learning systems, to encompass the social, as well as economic and technical, aspects of planning, to develop planned interdisciplinary research programmes, to enmesh the efforts of researchers/advisers and policy-makers, and to involve trade unions and other interested parties in future thinking. In addition, collaborative links should be forged between the industrial/company and government/development council learning systems to ensure that national social priorities are taken into account and that issues considered to have ethical and human importance are researched, even if not directly relevant to a particular industry or firm.

Only such a flexible and imaginative approach to the planning and funding of research will make possible, at industry and company level, the refuting of Coates' and Topham's charge: that,

> since it was discovered, during the industrial upheavals which affected every advanced power during the first world war, that there were advantages for

authority in the affirmation that 'labour is not a commodity', there has arisen a whole plethora of schools in human relations in industry, which have examined practically every possible industrial relationship *but* that of humanity [19].

Only such an approach at national and regional level, will turn Schon's law on its head and ensure that scientific and social concerns are pursued, separately but also jointly, by the nation and its behavioural science resources.

A significant feature of the machinery suggested for the identification of ethical/social issues into which research should be conducted is the equal representation of all parties. The same principle should be applied to the overall management of research. Coates' and Topham's criticism of behavioural science in industry is not only directed at the method of choosing research topics. It implicitly accuses behavioural scientists of kowtowing to the powers-that-be at every stage of research. The segment of the industrial world which has latched on to the potential of behavioural science research is management, and the overall oversight of particular projects has rested almost entirely in management's hands. Trade unions, on the whole, have either been indifferent, or neo-Luddite to the extent of refusing their or their members' cooperation, and behavioural scientists have frequently been browbeaten into abandoning their better judgment (and scientific principles) on industrially sponsored or located projects because he who pays the piper calls the tune, even if the payment is no more than provision of research facilities.

A large bulk of research has been conducted, managed and utilized to further the objectives of one side in industry. It is small wonder that the other side tends to view behavioural science as yet another manipulative device for bolstering up managerial power. It is also not surprising that research pay-off has been marginal. Science can hardly be independent when paid for or supervised by only one of three parties. For the sake both of research and industry the three interests should each be party to the direction (in both senses), from start to finish, of a research project. Ideally, each party (and certainly management and trade union) should also hold an equal financial stake.

The protection of all parties' interests is necessary at each stage of research; but it is particularly critical when the implications of results are being considered and acted on. Behavioural science knowledge represents power; as mentioned above, power can be used responsibly or irresponsibly. But the most effective way of channelling power to morally and socially acceptable ends – to the good of humanity – is to make it subject to some form of democratic control. Many spheres of industrial power-wielding are likely to become more democratically accountable. But the need for this development seems particularly urgent when the power being wielded is based on people's willingness to provide self-revealing information, and when its use will significantly affect their own future. A fundamental, though often unrecognized, assumption in behavioral science is that all subjects are equal. Behavioural scientists, as much as their subjects, should ensure that this is reflected in arrangements made to direct and control all aspects of research projects and their follow-up.

Though the influence of power, and the possibility of its abuse through faulty structures, is most obvious within a company, or on a particular project, the same principle of democratic accountability applies at all levels of research, and behavioural science fallout. Equivalent arrangements at national level are more difficult to envisage. But the public is increasingly concerned about the invasion of privacy by data-gathering agencies and the possible breach of this privilege, not least through the scale and accessibility of data processing facilities.

Observation of the behaviour of others, and particularly communication of what has been observed, are activities covered to an extent by existing law aimed at protecting the privacy of the individual … the relevant law deals mainly with libel, with slander, with professional contracts and conceivably with what is called trespass [20].

Unless behavioural scientists' professional bodies strengthen their statements of ethical principles – 'such an ethic is only effective where it is based on publicly recognized and accepted standards of professional behaviour [21]' – and enforce wider adherence to them by members, they will inevitably face reaction through subjects' unions, consumer protection bodies, political pressure and, in the last resort, further legal curtailment of the freedom which they currently enjoy. Subjects and others affected by behavioural science studies require institutional protection both from professional abuse of privilege and from political arbitrariness in follow-up decisions and actions.

Conclusion

The behavioural sciences are able to offer a lot; and they hold out the promise of a lot more. They generate knowledge, which in turn represents power. But flaws in their current claims to knowledge should be recognized; and any real power must be checked and channelled by society at all levels of relationships and organization. The behavioural sciences should be taken seriously; they could help man to more effectively master his environment. But not too seriously, 'There's nowt so queer as folk', one of their main peculiarities being the desire to prove others, particularly experts, wrong.

This paper has tried to clarify both the promise, and some of the problems, of behavioural science. It is hoped that it will promote both heightened commitment to, and more considered caution in, the application of behavioural science to industrial life.

References

1 Barbara Wootton, *Testament for Social Science*, George Allen and Unwin, 1950.
2 W. J. H. Sprott, *Sociology*, Hutchinson, 1959.
3 J. Bronowski, *The Common Sense of Science*, Pelican, 1960.
4 R. L. Silburn, 'The improper study of mankind?' *Davy Foundation Lecture*, University of Nottingham Union, 1963.
5 A. B. Cherns, 'The use of the social sciences', *Inaugural Lecture*, Loughborough University, 1967.
6 C. Selltiz, M. Jahoda, M. Deutsch, S. Cook, *Research Methods in Social Relations*, Holt, Rinehart and Winston, New York, 1966.
7 Patrick A. Sills. *The Behavioural Sciences: Techniques of Application*, Institute of Personnel Management, 1973.
8 D. Macrae, *Ideology and Society*, Heinemann, 1961.
9 Rudolf Klein, 'Honest failure', *New Society*, 30 March 1972.
10 Grapevine, 'Perpetual projects', *New Society*, 18 November 1971.
11 Anthony Harris, 'The gloomy scientists', *The Guardian*, 29 August 1972.
12 H. A. Williams, *True Resurrection*, Mitchell Beazley, 1972.
13 P. Sadler, 'Management training and research in organization behaviour', paper given to the Annual Conference of the *Association of Teachers of Management*, 1970.
14 Russell L. Ackoff, *Mission of the University*, W. W. Norton, New York, 1966.
15 I. T. Ramsey, 'The influence of technology on the social structure', *Journal of the Royal Society of Arts*, August 1971.

16 Donald Schon, 'Government as a learning system', *The Listener*, 17 December 1970.
17 Shirley Williams, 'The responsibility of science', *The Times*, 27 February 1971.
18 Ibid.
19 Ken Coates and Tony Topham, *Workers' Control*, Panther, 1970.
20 A. T. M. Wilson, 'A note on the social sanctions of social research', *Sociological Review*, Vol. 3, No. 1, July 1955.
21 Ibid.

part 1 the individual in the organization

perception – the basis of behaviour, the basis of management diagnosis (1962)

'Perception: some recent research and implications for administration', by Sheldon S. Zalkind and Timothy W. Costello, *Administrative Science Quarterly*, vol. 7, 1962, pp. 218–35.

This is a classic analysis of the relevance of the psychology of perception to management. Despite the title of the article, and of the journal in which this first appeared, Zalkind and Costello point their remarks towards the management practitioner. The term 'administrator', archaic and narrower in its meaning today, should simply be read as 'manager'. (Perceptions of political correctness have changed since 1962, when all administrators were assumed to be male.) It would be difficult to find consistent measures to demonstrate that the performance of a manager will be improved through the use of this area of psychology. However, Zalkind and Costello make a systematic and compelling case for the importance of this field.

learning objectives

Once you have read and understood this article, you should be able to:

1 Explain and illustrate the wide range of factors that can influence the way we see things – our perceptual process.
2 Explain how characteristics of the perceiver and of the perceived can influence person perception.
3 Explain and illustrate how features of the context or situation can affect perception.

learning pre-requisites

You will find it useful to read Chapter 3 in the core text, on communications and perception, before reading this article. However, this is not essential.

learning activities

1 In the first part of this article, Zalkind and Costello ask what are some of the factors influencing perception? It is a simple task to go through the article and to list these. So, let's get creative. Imagine you have to give a presentation on this topic. How would you illustrate this message? Prepare an interesting graphic summarizing the points that Zalkind and Costello identify as factors affecting perception.
2 Produce a second, creative, interesting graphic illustrating how characteristics of the perceiver and the perceived influence the perceptual process.
3 Produce a third creative graphic illustrating the effects of situational factors on perception.
4 The authors identify 'two principal suggestions' for administrators at the end of the article. But there are more points of practical interest than this, surely? Draw

up your own list of advice and action points for managers, general and specific, from the article.

READING 3

Perception: some recent research and implications for administration*
Sheldon S. Zalkind and Timothy W. Costello†

The administrator frequently bases decisions and actions on his perception of other people. Behavioral scientists have been systematically studying the process of perception, focusing in recent years on interpersonal perception. Although their work has been done largely in laboratory settings, their conclusions have relevance for the administrator. This paper examines some of the recent work on interpersonal perception and suggests some implications for administrative practice.[1] No easy means is proposed to make objective what is essentially a subjective process; nevertheless it is possible to indicate some guidelines and precautions to use in this complex aspect of interpersonal relations. Understanding the process of interpersonal perception is one means of trying to avoid gross errors in interpersonal judgments.

Management practice is being increasingly influenced by behavioral science research in the areas of group dynamics, problem solving and decision making, and motivation. One aspect of behavior which has not been fully or consistently emphasized is the process of perception, particularly the recent work on person perception.

In this paper we shall summarize some of the findings on perception as developed through both laboratory and organizational research and point out some of the administrative and managerial implications. We discuss first some basic factors in the nature of the perceptual process including need and set; second, some research on forming impressions; third, the characteristics of the perceiver and the perceived; fourth, situational and organizational influences on perception; and finally, perceptual influences on interpersonal adjustment.

Nature of the perceptual process

What are some of the factors influencing perception? In answering the question it is well to begin by putting aside the attitude of naive realism, which suggests that our perceptions simply register accurately what is 'out there.' It is necessary rather to consider what influences distort one's perceptions and judgments of the outside world. Some of the considerations identified in the literature up to the time of Johnson's 1944 review of the research on object perception (where distortion may be even less extreme than in person perception) led him to suggest the following about the perceiver:[2]

1 He may be influenced by considerations that he may not be able to identify, responding to cues that are below the threshold of his awareness. For example, a

* Reprinted by permission from *Administrative Science Quarterly*, Vol. 7 (1962), 218–35.
† Baruch College, City College of New York and Adelphi University, respectively.
[1] Portions of this article were originally presented at the Eighth Annual International Meeting of The Institute of Management Sciences in Brussels, August, 1961.
[2] D. M. Johnson. A systematic treatment of judgment. *Psychological Bulletin*, Vol. 42 (1945), 193–224.

judgment as to the size of an object may be influenced by its color even though the perceiver may not be attending to color.

2 When required to form difficult perceptual judgments, he may respond to irrelevant cues to arrive at a judgment. For example, in trying to assess honesty, it has been shown that the other person's smiling or not smiling is used as a cue to judge his honesty.

3 In making abstract or intellectual judgments, he may be influenced by emotional factors – what is liked is perceived as correct.

4 He will weigh perceptual evidence coming from respect (or favored) sources more heavily than that coming from other sources.

5 He may not be able to identify all the factors on which his judgments are based. Even if he is aware of these factors he is not likely to realize how much weight he gives to them.

These considerations do not imply that we respond only to the subtle or irrelevant cues or to emotional factors. We often perceive on the basis of the obvious, but we are quite likely to be responding as well to the less obvious or less objective.

In 1958, Bruner, citing a series of researches, described what he called the 'New Look' in perception as one in which personal determinants of the perceptual process were being stressed.[3] Bruner summarized earlier work and showed the importance of such subjective influences as needs, values, cultural background, and interests on the perceptual process. In his concept of 'perceptual readiness' he described the importance of the framework or category system that the perceiver himself brings to the perceiving process.

Tapping a different vein of research, Cantril described perceiving as a 'transaction' between the perceiver and the perceived, a process of negotiation in which the perceptual end product is a result both of influences within the perceiver and of characteristics of the perceived.[4]

One of the most important of the subjective factors that influence the way we perceive, identified by Bruner and others, is *set*. A study by Kelley illustrated the point.[5] He found that those who were previously led to expect to meet a 'warm' person, not only made different judgments about him, but also behaved differently toward him, than those who were expecting a 'cold' one. The fact was that they simultaneously were observing the same person in the same situation. Similarly, Strickland indicated the influence of set in determining how closely supervisors feel they must supervise their subordinates.[6] Because of prior expectation one person was trusted more than another and was thought to require less supervision than another, even though performance records were identical.

Forming impressions of others

The data on forming impressions is of particular importance in administration. An administrator is confronted many times with the task of forming an impression of another person – a new employee at his desk, a visiting member from the home office, a staff member he has not personally met before. His own values, needs, and

[3] J. S. Bruner. Social psychology and perception, in E. Maccoby, T. Newcomb and E. Hartley (eds.), *Readings in social psychology* (3d ed.: New York, 1958), pp. 85–94.

[4] H. Cantril. Perception and interpersonal relations. *American Journal of Psychiatry*, Vol. 114 (1957), 119–26.

[5] H. H. Kelley. The warm-cold variable in first impressions of persons. *Journal of Personality*, Vol. 18 (1950), 431–39.

[6] L. H. Strickland. Surveillance and trust. *Journal of Personality*, Vol. 26 (1958), 200–15.

expectations will play a part in the impression he forms. Are there other factors that typically operate in this area of administrative life? One of the more obvious influences is the physical appearance of the person being perceived. In a study of this point Mason was able to demonstrate that people agree on what a leader should look like and that there is no relationship between the facial characteristics agreed upon and those possessed by actual leaders.[7] In effect, we have ideas about what leaders look like and we can give examples, but we ignore the many exceptions that statistically cancel out the examples.

In the sometimes casual, always transitory situations in which one must form impressions of others it is a most natural tendency to jump to conclusions and form impressions without adequate evidence. Unfortunately, as Dailey showed, unless such impressions are based on important and relevant data, they are not likely to be accurate.[8] Too often in forming impressions the perceiver does not know what is relevant, important, or predictive of later behavior. Dailey's research furthermore supports the cliché that, accurate or not, first impressions are lasting.

Generalizing from other research in the field, Soskin described four limitations on the ability to form accurate impressions of others.[9] First, the impression is likely to be disproportionately affected by the type of situation or surroundings in which the impression is made and influenced too little by the person perceived. Thus the plush luncheon club in which one first meets a man will dominate the impression of the man himself. Secondly, although impressions are frequently based on a limited sample of the perceived person's behavior, the generalization that the perceiver makes will be sweeping. A third limitation is that the situation may not provide an opportunity for the person perceived to show behavior relevant to the traits about which impressions are formed. Casual conversation or questions, for example, provide few opportunities to demonstrate intelligence or work characteristics, yet the perceiver often draws conclusions about these from an interview. Finally, Soskin agrees with Bruner and Cantril that the impression of the person perceived may be distorted by some highly individualized reaction of the perceiver.

But the pitfalls are not yet all spelled out; it is possible to identify some other distorting influences on the process of forming impressions. Research has brought into sharp focus some typical errors, the more important being stereotyping, halo effect, projection, and perceptual defense.

Stereotyping

The word 'stereotyping' was first used by Walter Lippmann in 1922 to describe bias in perceiving peoples. He wrote of 'pictures in people's heads,' called stereotypes, which guided (distorted) their perceptions of others. The term has long been used to describe judgments made about people on the basis of their ethnic group membership. For example, some say 'Herman Schmidt [being German] is industrious.' Stereotyping also predisposes judgments in many other areas of interpersonal relations. Stereotypes have developed about many types of groups, and they help to prejudice many of our perceptions about their members. Examples of stereotypes of groups other than those based on ethnic identification are bankers, supervisors,

---

[7] D. J. Mason. Judgments of leadership based upon physiognomic cues. *Journal of Abnormal and Social Psychology*, Vol. 54 (1957), 273–74.

[8] C. A. Dailey. The effects of premature conclusion upon the acquisition of understanding of a person. *Journal of Psychology*, Vol. 33 (1952), 133–52.

[9] W. E. Soskin. Influence of information on bias in social perception. *Journal of Personality*, Vol. 22 (1953), 118–27.

union members, poor people, rich people, and administrators. Many unverified qualities are assigned to people principally because of such group memberships.

In a research demonstration of stereotyping, Haire found that labeling a photograph as that of a management representative caused an impression to be formed of the person, different from that formed when it was labeled as that of a union leader.[10] Management and labor formed different impressions, each seeing his opposite as less dependable than his own group. In addition each side saw his own group as being better able than the opposite group to understand a point of view different from its own. For example, managers felt that other managers were better able to appreciate labor's point of view, than labor was able to appreciate management's point of view. Each had similar stereotypes of his opposite and considered the thinking, emotional characteristics, and interpersonal relations of his opposite as inferior to his own. As Stagner points out, 'It is plain that unionists perceiving company officials in a stereotyped way are less efficient than would be desirable. Similarly, company executives who see all labor unions as identical are not showing good judgment or discrimination.'[11]

One of the troublesome aspects of stereotypes is that they are so widespread. Finding the same stereotypes to be widely held should not tempt one to accept their accuracy. It may only mean that many people are making the same mistake. Allport has demonstrated that there need not be a 'kernel of truth' in a widely held stereotype.[12] He has shown that while a prevalent stereotype of Armenians labeled them as dishonest, a credit reporting association gave them credit ratings as good as those given other ethnic groups.

Bruner and Perlmutter found that there is an international stereotype for 'businessmen' and 'teachers.'[13] They indicated that the more widespread one's experience with diverse members of a group, the less their group membership will affect the impression formed.

An additional illustration of stereotyping is provided by Luft.[14] His research suggests that perception of personality adjustment may be influenced by stereotypes, associating adjustment with high income and maladjustment with low income.

Halo effect

The term halo effect was first used in 1920 to describe a process in which a general impression which is favorable or unfavorable is used by judges to evaluate several specific traits. The 'halo' in such case serves as a screen keeping the perceiver from actually seeing the trait he is judging. It has received the most attention because of its effect on rating employee performance. In the rating situation, a supervisor may single out one trait, either good or bad, and use this as the basis for his judgment of all other traits. For example, an excellent attendance record causes judgments of productivity, high quality of work, and so forth. One study in the U.S. Army showed that officers who were liked were judged more intelligent than those who were disliked, even though they had the same scores on intelligence tests.

We examine halo effect here because of its general effect on forming impressions. Bruner and Taguiri suggest that it is likely to be most extreme when we are forming

[10] M. Haire. Role perceptions in labor-management relations. An experimental approach. *Industrial and Labor Relations Review*, Vol. 8 (1955), 204–16.

[11] R. Stagner. *Psychology of industrial conflict* (New York, 1956), p. 35.

[12] G. Allport. *Nature of prejudice* (Cambridge, Mass., 1954).

[13] J. S. Bruner and H. V. Perlmutter. Compatriot and foreigner: A study of impression formation in three countries. *Journal of Abnormal and Social Psychology*, Vol. 55 (1957), 253–60.

[14] J. Luft. Monetary value and the perception of persons. *Journal of Social Psychology*, Vol. 46 (1957), 245–51.

impressions of traits that provide minimal cues in the individual's behavior, when the traits have moral overtones, or when the perceiver must judge traits with which he has had little experience.[15] A rather disturbing conclusion is suggested by Symonds that halo effect is more marked the more we know the acquaintance.[16]

A somewhat different aspect of the halo effect is suggested by the research of Grove and Kerr.[17] They found that knowledge that the company was in receivership caused employees to devalue the higher pay and otherwise superior working conditions of their company as compared to those in a financially secure firm.

Psychologists have noted a tendency in perceivers to link certain traits. They assume, for example, that when a person is aggressive he will also have high energy or that when a person is 'warm' he will also be generous and have a good sense of humor. The logical error, as it has been called, is a special form of the halo effect and is best illustrated in the research of Asch.[18] In his study the addition of one trait to a list of traits produced a major change in the impression formed. Knowing that a person was intelligent, skilful, industrious, determined, practical, cautious and warm led a group to judge him to be also wise, humorous, popular, and imaginative. When warm was replaced by cold, a radically different impression (beyond the difference between warm and cold) was formed. Kelley's research illustrated the same type of error.[19] This tendency is not indiscriminate; with the pair 'polite–blunt,' less change was found than with the more central traits of 'warm–cold.'

In evaluating the effect of halo on perceptual distortion, we may take comfort from the work of Wishner, which showed that those traits that correlate more highly with each other are more likely to lead to a halo effect than those that are unrelated.[20]

Projection

A defense mechanism available to everyone is projection, in which one relieves one's feelings of guilt or failure by projecting blame onto someone else. Over the years the projection mechanism has been assigned various meanings. The original use of the term was concerned with the mechanism to defend oneself from unacceptable feelings. There has since been a tendency for the term to be used more broadly, meaning to ascribe or attribute any of one's own characteristics to other people. The projection mechanism concerns us here because it influences the perceptual process. An early study by Murray illustrates its effect.[21] After playing a dramatic game, 'Murder,' his subjects attributed much more maliciousness to people whose photographs were judged than did a control group which had not played the game. The current emotional state of the perceiver tended to influence his perceptions of others; i.e., frightened perceivers judged people to be frightening. More recently, Feshback and Singer revealed further dynamics of the process.[22] In their study, subjects who

---

[15] J. S. Bruner and A. Taguiri. The perception of people, ch. xvii in G. Lindzey (ed.), *Handbook of social psychology* (Cambridge, Mass., 1954).

[16] P. M. Symonds. Notes on rating. *Journal of Applied Psychology*, Vol. 7 (1925), 188–95.

[17] B. A. Grove and W. A. Kerr. Specific evidence on origin of halo effect in measurement of morale. *Journal of Social Psychology*, Vol. 34 (1951), 165–70.

[18] S. Asch. Forming impressions of persons. *Journal of Abnormal and Social Psychology*, Vol. 60 (1946), 258–90.

[19] Kelley, The warm–cold variable in first impressions of persons.

[20] J. Wishner. Reanalysis of 'Impressions of personality,' *Psychology Review*, Vol. 67 (1960), 96–112.

[21] H. A. Murray. The effect of fear upon estimates of the maliciousness of other personalities. *Journal of Social Psychology*, Vol. 4 (1933), 310–29.

[22] S. Feshback and R. D. Singer. The effects of fear arousal upon social perception. *Journal of Abnormal and Social Psychology*, Vol. 55 (1957), 283–88.

had been made fearful judged a stimulus person (presented in a moving picture) as both more fearful and more aggressive than did nonfearful perceivers. These authors were able to demonstrate further that the projection mechanism at work here was reduced when their subjects were encouraged to admit and talk about their fears.

Sears provides an illustration of a somewhat different type of projection and its effect on perception.[23] In his study projection is seeing our own undesirable personality characteristics in other people. He demonstrated that people high in such traits as stinginess, obstinacy, and disorderliness, tended to rate others much higher on these traits than did those who were low in these undesirable characteristics. The tendency to project was particularly marked among subjects who had the least insight into their own personalities.

Research thus suggests that our perceptions may characteristically be distorted by emotions we are experiencing or traits that we possess. Placed in the administrative setting, the research would suggest, for example, that a manager frightened by rumored organizational changes might not only judge others to be more frightened than they were, but also assess various policy decisions as more frightening than they were. Or a general foremen lacking insight into his own incapacity to delegate might be oversensitive to this trait in his superiors.

Perceptual defense

Another distorting influence, which has been called perceptual defense, has also been demonstrated by Haire and Grunes to be a source of error.[24] In their research they ask, in effect, 'Do we put blinders on to defend ourselves from seeing those events which might disturb us?' The concept of perceptual defense offers an excellent description of perceptual distortion at work and demonstrates that when confronted with a fact inconsistent with a stereotype already held by a person, the perceiver is able to distort the data in such a way as to eliminate the inconsistency. Thus, by perceiving inaccurately he defends himself from having to change his stereotypes.

Characteristics of perceiver and perceived

We have thus far been talking largely about influences on the perceptual process without specific regard to the perceiver and his characteristics. Much recent research has tried to identify some characteristics of the perceiver and their influence on the perception of other people.

The perceiver

A thread that would seem to tie together many current findings is the tendency to use oneself as the norm or standard by which one perceives or judges others. If we examine current research, certain conclusions are suggested:

1   *Knowing oneself makes it easier to see others accurately.* Norman showed that when one is aware of what his own personal characteristics are he makes fewer errors in perceiving others.[25] Weingarten has shown that people with insight are

---

[23] R. R. Sears. Experimental studies of perception, 1. Attribution of traits. *Journal of Social Psychology*, Vol. 7 (1936), 151–63.

[24] M. Haire and W. F. Grunes. Perceptual defenses: Processes protecting an original perception of another personality. *Human Relations*, Vol. 3 (1958), 403–12.

[25] R. D. Norman. The interrelationships among acceptance-rejection, self-other identity, insight into self, and realistic perception of others. *Journal of Social Psychology*, Vol. 37 (1953), 205–35.

less likely to view the world in black-and-white terms and to give extreme judgments about others.[26]

2 *One's own characteristics affect the characteristics he is likely to see in others.* Secure people (compared with insecure) tend to see others as warm rather than cold, as was shown by Bossom and Maslow.[27] The extent of one's own sociability influences the degree of importance one gives to the sociability of other people when one forms impressions of them.[28] The person with 'authoritarian' tendencies is more likely to view others in terms of power and is less sensitive to the psychological or personality characteristics of other people than is a nonauthoritarian.[29] The relatively few categories one uses in describing other people tend to be those one uses in describing oneself.[30] Thus traits which are important to the perceiver will be used more when he forms impressions of others. He has certain constant tendencies, both with regard to using certain categories in judging others and to the amount of weight given to these categories.[31]

3 *The person who accepts himself is more likely to be able to see favorable aspects of other people.*[32] This relates in part to the accuracy of his perceptions. If the perceiver accepts himself as he is, he widens his range of vision in seeing others; he can look at them and be less likely to be very negative or critical. In those areas in which he is more insecure, he sees more problems in other people.[33] We are more likely to like others who have traits we accept in ourselves and reject those who have the traits which we do not like in ourselves.[34]

4 *Accuracy in perceiving others is not a single skill.* While there have been some variations in the findings, as Gage has shown, some consistent results do occur.[35] The perceiver tends to interpret the feelings others have about him in terms of his feelings towards them.[36] One's ability to perceive others accurately may depend on how sensitive one is to differences between people and also to the norms (outside of oneself) for judging them.[37] Thus, as Taft has shown, the ability to judge others does not seem to be a single skill.[38]

[26] E. Weingarten. A study of selective perception in clinical judgment. *Journal of Personality*, Vol. 17 (1949), 369–400.

[27] J. Bossom and A. H. Maslow. Security of judges as a factor in impressions or a warmth in others. *Journal of Abnormal and Social Psychology*, Vol. 55 (1957), 147–48.

[28] D. T. Benedetti and J. G. Hill. A determiner of the centrality of a trait in impression formation. *Journal of Abnormal and Social Psychology*, Vol. 60 (1960), 278–79.

[29] E. E. Jones. Authoritarianism as a determinant of first-impressions formation. *Journal of Personality*, Vol. 23 (1954), 107–27.

[30] A. H. Hastorf, S. A. Richardson, and S. M. Dornbusch. The problem of relevance in the study of person perception, in R. Taguiri and L. Petrullo, *Person perception and interpretation behavior* (Stanford, Calif., 1958).

[31] L. J. Cronbach. Processes affecting scores on 'Understanding of others' and 'Assumed similarity,' *Psychological Bulletin*, Vol. 52 (1955), 177–93.

[32] K. T. Omwake. The relation between acceptance of self and acceptance of others shown by three personality inventories. *Journal of Consulting Psychology*, Vol. 18 (1954), 443–46.

[33] Weingarten, A study of selective perception in clinical judgment.

[34] R. M. Lundy, W. Katovsky, R. L. Cromwell, and D. J. Shoemaker. Self acceptability and descriptions of sociometric choices. *Journal of Abnormal and Social Psychology*, Vol. 51 (1955), 260–62.

[35] N. L. Gage. Accuracy of social perception and effectiveness in interpersonal relationships. *Journal of Personality*, Vol. 22 (1953), 128–41.

[36] R. Taguiri, J. S. Bruner, and R. Blake. On the relation between feelings and perceptions of feelings among members of small groups, in Maccoby *et al. Readings in social psychology.*

[37] U. Bronfenbrenner, J. Harding, and M. Gallway. The measurement of skill in social perception, in H. L. McClelland, D. C. Baldwin, U. Bronfenbrenner, and F. L. Strodtbeck (eds.), *Talent and society* (Princeton, N.J., 1958), pp. 29–111.

[38] R. Taft. The ability to judge people. *Psychological Bulletin*, Vol. 52 (1955), 1–21.

Possibly the results in these four aspects of person perception can be viewed most constructively in connection with earlier points on the process of perception. The administrator (or any other individual) who wishes to perceive someone else accurately must look at the other person, not at himself. The things that he looks at in someone else are influenced by his own traits. But if he knows his own traits, he can be aware that they provide a frame of reference for him. His own traits help to furnish the categories that he will use in perceiving others. His characteristics, needs, and values can partly limit his vision and his awareness of the differences between others. The question one could ask when viewing another is: 'Am I looking at him, and forming my impression of his behavior in the situation, or am I just comparing him with myself?'

There is the added problem of being set to observe the personality traits in another which the perceiver does not accept in himself, e.g., being somewhat autocratic. At the same time he may make undue allowances in others for those of his own deficiencies which do not disturb him but might concern some people, e.g., not following prescribed procedures.

The perceived

Lest we leave the impression that it is only the characteristics of the perceiver that stand between him and others in his efforts to know them, we turn now to some characteristics of the person being perceived which raise problems in perception. It is possible to demonstrate, for example, that the status of the person perceived is a variable influencing judgments about his behavior. Thibaut and Riecken have shown that even though two people behave in identical fashion, status differences between them cause a perceiver to assign different motivations for the behavior.[39] Concerning co-operativeness, they found that high status persons are judged as wanting to co-operate and low status persons as having to co-operate. In turn, more liking is shown for the person of high status than for the person of low status. Presumably, more credit is given when the boss says, 'Good morning,' to us than when a subordinate says the same thing.

Bruner indicated that we use categories to simplify our perceptual activities. In the administrative situation, status is one type of category, and role provides another. Thus the remarks of Mr. Jones in the sales department are perceived differently from those of Smith in the purchasing department, although both may say the same thing. Also, one who knows Jones's role in the organization will perceive his behavior differently from one who does not know Jones's role. The process of categorizing on the basis of roles is similar to, if not identical with, the stereotyping process described earlier.

Visibility of the traits judged is also an important variable influencing the accuracy of perception.[40] Visibility will depend, for example, on how free the other person feels to express the trait. It has been demonstrated that we are more accurate in judging people who like us than people who dislike us. The explanation suggested is that most people in our society feel constraint in showing their dislike, and therefore the cues are less visible.

Some traits are not visible simply because they provide few external cues for their presence. Loyalty, for example, as opposed to level of energy, provides few early signs for observation. Even honesty cannot be seen in the situations in which most

[39] J. W. Thibaut and H. W. Riecken. Some determinants and consequences of the perception of social causality. *Journal of Personality*, Vol. 24 (1955), 113–33.
[40] Bruner and Taguiri, The perception of people.

impressions are formed. As obvious as these comments might be, in forming impressions many of us nevertheless continue to judge the presence of traits which are not really visible. Frequently the practical situation demands judgments, but we should recognize the frail reeds upon which we are leaning and be prepared to observe further and revise our judgments with time and closer acquaintance.

Situational influences on perception

Some recent research clearly points to the conclusion that the whole process of interpersonal perception is, at least in part, a function of the *group* (or interpersonal) context in which the perception occurs. Much of the research has important theoretical implications for a psychology of interpersonal relations. In addition, there are some suggestions of value for administrators. It is possible to identify several characteristics of the interpersonal climate which have direct effect on perceptual accuracy. As will be noted, these are characteristics which can be known, and in some cases controlled, in administrative settings.

Bieri provides data for the suggestion that when people are given an opportunity to interact in a friendly situation, they tend to see others as similar to themselves.[41] Applying his suggestion to the administrative situation, we can rationalize as follows: Some difficulties of administrative practice grow out of beliefs that different interest groups in the organization are made up of different types of people. Obviously once we believe that people in other groups are different, we will be predisposed to see the differences. We can thus find, from Bieri's and from Rosenbaum's work, an administrative approach for attacking the problem.[42] If we can produce an interacting situation which is cooperative rather than competitive, the likelihood of seeing other people as similar to ourselves is increased.

Exline's study adds some other characteristics of the social context which may influence perception.[43] Paraphrasing his conclusions to adapt them to the administrative scene, we can suggest that when a committee group is made up of congenial members who are willing to continue work in the same group, their perceptions of the goal-directed behavior of fellow committee members will be more accurate, although observations of purely personal behavior (as distinguished from goal-directed behavior) may be less accurate.[44] The implications for setting up committees and presumably other interacting work groups seem clear: Do not place together those with a past history of major personal clashes. If they must be on the same committee, each must be helped to see that the other is working toward the same goal.

An interesting variation in this area of research is the suggestion from Ex's work that perceptions will be more influenced or swayed by relatively unfamiliar people in the group than by those who are intimates.[45] The concept needs further research, but it provides the interesting suggestion that we may give more credit to strangers for having knowledge, since we do not know, than we do to our intimates whose backgrounds and limitations we feel we do know.

[41] J. Bieri. Change in interpersonal perception following interaction. *Journal of Abnormal and Social Psychology*, Vol. 48 (1953), 61–66.

[42] M. E. Rosenbaum. Social perception and the motivational structure of interpersonal relations. *Journal of Abnormal and Social Psychology*, Vol. 59 (1959), 130–33.

[43] R. V. Exline. Interrelations among two dimensions of sociometric status, group congeniality and accuracy of social perception. *Sociometry*, Vol. 23 (1960), 85–101.

[44] R. V. Exline. Group climate as a factor in the relevance and accuracy of social perception. *Journal of Abnormal and Social Psychology*, Vol. 55 (1957), 382–88.

[45] J. Ex. The nature of the relation between two persons and the degree of their influence on each other. *Acta Psychologica*, Vol. 17 (1960), 39–54.

The *organization*, and one's place in it, may also be viewed as the context in which perceptions take place. A study by Dearborn and Simon illustrates this point.[46] Their data support the hypothesis that the administrator's perceptions will often be limited to those aspects of a situation which relate specifically to his own department, despite an attempt to influence him away from such selectivity.

Perception of self among populations at different levels in the hierarchy also offers an opportunity to judge the influence of organizational context on perceptual activity. Porter's study of the self-descriptions of managers and line workers indicated that both groups saw themselves in different terms, which corresponded to their positions in the organization's hierarchy.[47] He stated that managers used leadership-type traits (e.g., inventive) to describe themselves, while line workers used follower-type terms (e.g., co-operative). The question of which comes first must be asked: Does the manager see himself this way because of his current position in the organization? Or is this self-picture an expression of a more enduring personal characteristic that helped bring the manager to his present position? This study does not answer that question, but it does suggest to an administrator the need to be aware of the possibly critical relationship between one's hierarchical role and self-perception.

Perceptual influences on interpersonal adjustment

Throughout this paper, we have examined a variety of influences on the perceptual process. There has been at least the inference that the operations of such influences on perception would in turn affect behavior that would follow. Common-sense judgment suggests that being able to judge other people accurately facilitates smooth and effective interpersonal adjustments. Nevertheless, the relationship between perception and consequent behavior is itself in need of direct analysis. Two aspects may be identified: (1) the effect of accuracy of perception on subsequent behavior and (2) the effect of the duration of the relationship and the opportunity for experiencing additional cues.

First then, from the applied point of view, we can ask a crucial question: Is there a relationship between accuracy of social perception and adjustment to others? While the question might suggest a quick affirmative answer, research findings are inconsistent. Steiner attempted to resolve some of these inconsistencies by stating that accuracy may have an effect on interaction under the following conditions: when the interacting persons are co-operatively motivated, when the behavior which is accurately perceived is relevant to the activities of these persons, and when members are free to alter their behavior on the basis of their perceptions.[48]

Where the relationship provides opportunity only to form an impression, a large number of subjective factors, i.e., set, stereotypes, projections, etc., operate to create an early impression, which is frequently erroneous. In more enduring relationships a more balanced appraisal may result as increased interaction provides additional cues for judgment. In his study of the acquaintance process, Newcomb showed that while early perception of favorable traits caused attraction to the perceived person, over a

[46] D. C. Dearborn and H. A. Simon. Selective perception, A note on the departmental identifications of executives. *Sociometry*, Vol. 21 (1958), 140–44.

[47] L. W. Porter. Differential self-perceptions of management personnel and line workers. *Journal of Applied Psychology*, Vol. 42 (1958), 105–9.

[48] I. Steiner. Interpersonal behavior as influenced by accuracy of social perception. *Psychological Review*, Vol. 62 (1955), 268–75.

four-month period the early cues for judging favorable traits became less influential.[49] With time, a much broader basis was used which included comparisons with others with whom one had established relationships. Such findings suggest that the warnings about perceptual inaccuracies implicit in the earlier sections of this paper apply with more force to the short-term process of impression forming than to relatively extended acquaintance-building relationships. One could thus hope that rating an employee after a year of service would be a more objective performance than appraising him in a selection interview – a hope that would be fulfilled only when the rater had provided himself with opportunities for broadening the cues heeded in forming his first impressions.

Summary

Two principal suggestions which increase the probability of more effective administrative action emerge from the research data. One suggestion is that the administrator be continuously aware of the intricacies of the perceptual process and thus be warned to avoid arbitrary and categorical judgments and to seek reliable evidence before judgments are made. A second suggestion grows out of the first: increased accuracy in one's self-perception can make possible the flexibility to seek evidence and to shift position as time provides additional evidence.

Nevertheless, not every effort designed to improve perceptual accuracy will bring about such accuracy. The dangers of too complete reliance on formal training for perceptual accuracy are suggested in a study by Crow.[50] He found that a group of senior medical students were somewhat less accurate in their perceptions of others after a period of training in physician-patient relationships than were an untrained control group. The danger is that a little learning encourages the perceiver to respond with increased sensitivity to individual differences without making it possible for him to gauge the real meaning of the differences he has seen.

Without vigilance to perceive accurately and to minimize as far as possible the subjective approach in perceiving others, effective administration is handicapped. On the other hand, research would not support the conclusion that perceptual distortions will not occur simply because the administrator says he will try to be objective. The administrator or manager will have to work hard to avoid seeing only what he wants to see and to guard against fitting everything into what he is set to see.

We are not yet sure of the ways in which training for perceptual accuracy can best be accomplished, but such training cannot be ignored. In fact, one can say that one of the important tasks of administrative science is to design research to test various training procedures for increasing perceptual accuracy.

[49] T. M. Newcomb. The perception of interpersonal attraction. *American Psychologist*, Vol. 11 (1956), 575–86, and *The acquaintance process* (New York, 1961).

[50] W. J. Crow. Effect of training on interpersonal perception. *Journal of Abnormal and Social Psychology*, Vol. 55 (1957), 355–59.

just how many basic needs does Maslow's theory identify? (1943)

'A theory of human motivation', by Abraham H. Maslow, *Psychological Review*, vol. 50, no. 4, 1943, pp. 370–96.

This must be one of the most widely cited, and most frequently reproduced, articles in the history of organizational behaviour. This does not mean, however, that the piece has been widely read. Anyone who has attended a management course over the past half-century, where the topic of motivation was covered, will know that Maslow identified a hierarchy of five human needs. All organizational behaviour instructors have an overhead transparency in their 'motivation' file showing the five-step hierarchy. This overhead is good for a half-hour lecture at least. Is this an accurate statement of Maslow's theory? Let us find out.

learning objectives

Once you have read and understood this article, you should be able to:

1 Explain Maslow's need theory, with reference to its original source.
2 Identify human needs beyond the five that are normally attributed to Maslow, but which are clearly set out in this article.
3 Produce your own overhead transparency with which to explain Maslow's theory of human motivation – accurately.

learning pre-requisites

You should read Chapter 4 in the core text, on motivation, before tackling this article. You need to note, however, that the chapter relies on a number of other publications by Maslow, and not just on this article.

learning activities

1 How many human needs does Maslow identify in this article? List them as you read through this piece. Check your list against the article and Chapter 4 in the core text (which draws, as indicated, on other sources).
2 In his summary, Maslow mentions 'certain more intellectual desires', in addition to the basic needs. What are these 'intellectual desires'? Again, check your findings against Chapter 4.
3 How would you illustrate the theory explained in this article, on a single sheet of paper, or on a single overhead transparency? Forget the five-step 'pyramid' most lecturers will probably have shown you. Get creative, and produce your own version!

READING
4

A theory of human motivation *
Abraham H. Maslow

I Introduction

In a previous paper (13) various propositions were presented which would have to be included in any theory of human motivation that could lay claim to being definitive. These conclusions may be briefly summarized as follows:

1 The integrated wholeness of the organism must be one of the foundation stones of motivation theory.

2 The hunger drive (or any other physiological drive) was rejected as a centering point or model for a definitive theory of motivation. Any drive that is somatically based and localizable was shown to be atypical rather than typical in human motivation.

3 Such a theory should stress and center itself upon ultimate or basic goals rather than partial or superficial ones, upon ends rather than means to these ends. Such a stress would imply a more central place for unconscious than for conscious motivations.

4 There are usually available various cultural paths to the same goal. Therefore conscious, specific, local-cultural desires are not as fundamental in motivation theory as the more basic, unconscious goals.

5 Any motivated behavior, either preparatory or consummatory, must be understood to be a channel through which many basic needs may be simultaneously expressed or satisfied. Typically an act has more than one motivation.

6 Practically all organismic states are to be understood as motivated and as motivating.

7 Human needs arrange themselves in hierarchies of prepotency. That is to say, the appearance of one need usually rests on the prior satisfaction of another, more prepotent need. Man is a perpetually wanting animal. Also no need or drive can be treated as if it were isolated or discrete; every drive is related to the state of satisfaction or dissatisfaction of other drives.

8 *Lists* of drives will get us nowhere for various theoretical and practical reasons. Furthermore any classification of motivations must deal with the problem of levels of specificity or generalization of the motives to be classified.

9 Classifications of motivations must be based upon goals rather than upon instigating drives or motivated behavior.

10 Motivation theory should be human-centered rather than animal-centered.

11 The situation or the field in which the organism reacts must be taken into account but the field alone can rarely serve as an exclusive explanation for behavior. Furthermore the field itself must be interpreted in terms of the organism. Field theory cannot be a substitute for motivation theory.

12 Not only the integration of the organism must be taken into account, but also the possibility of isolated, specific, partial or segmental reactions.

It has since become necessary to add to these another affirmation.

13 Motivation theory is not synonymous with behavior theory. The motivations are only one class of determinants of behavior. While behavior is almost always

*Reprinted by permission from 'A Theory of Human Motivation,' by Abraham H. Maslow, *Psychological Review*, 50. Copyright 1943 by the American Psychological Association.

motivated, it is also almost always biologically, culturally and situationally determined as well.

The present paper is an attempt to formulate a positive theory of motivation which will satisfy these theoretical demands and at the same time conform to the known facts, clinical and observational as well as experimental. It derives most directly, however, from clinical experience. This theory is, I think, in the functionalist tradition of James and Dewey, and is fused with the holism of Wertheimer (19), Goldstein (6), and Gestalt Psychology, and with the dynamicism of Freud (4) and Adler (1). This fusion or synthesis may arbitrarily be called a 'general-dynamic' theory.

It is far easier to perceive and to criticize the aspects in motivation theory than to remedy them. Mostly this is because of the very serious lack of sound data in this area. I conceive this lack of sound facts to be due primarily to the absence of a valid theory of motivation. The present theory then must be considered to be a suggested program or framework for future research and must stand or fall, not so much on facts available or evidence presented, as upon researches yet to be done, researches suggested perhaps, by the questions raised in this paper.

II The basic needs

The 'physiological' needs

The needs that are usually taken as the starting point for motivation theory are the so-called physiological drives. Two recent lines of research make it necessary to revise our customary notions about these needs, first, the development of the concept of homeostasis, and second, the finding that appetites (preferential choices among foods) are a fairly efficient indication of actual needs or lacks in the body.

Homeostasis refers to the body's automatic efforts to maintain a constant, normal state of the blood stream. Cannon (2) has described this process for (1) the water content of the blood, (2) salt content, (3) sugar content, (4) protein content, (5) fat content, (6) calcium content, (7) oxygen content, (8) constant hydrogen-ion level (acid-base balance) and (9) constant temperature of the blood. Obviously this list can be extended to include other minerals, the hormones, vitamins, etc.

Young in a recent article (21) has summarized the work on appetite in its relation to body needs. If the body lacks some chemical, the individual will tend to develop a specific appetite or partial hunger for that food element.

Thus it seems impossible as well as useless to make any list of fundamental physiological needs for they can come to almost any number one might wish, depending on the degree of specificity of description. We can not identify all physiological needs as homeostatic. That sexual desire, sleepiness, sheer activity and maternal behavior in animals, are homeostatic, has not yet been demonstrated. Furthermore, this list would not include the various sensory pleasures (tastes, smells, tickling, stroking) which are probably physiological and which may become the goals of motivated behavior.

In a previous paper (13) it has been pointed out that these physiological drives or needs are to be considered unusual rather than typical because they are isolable, and because they are localizable somatically. That is to say, they are relatively independent of each other, of other motivations and of the organism as a whole, and secondly, in many cases, it is possible to demonstrate a localized, underlying somatic base for the drive. This is true less generally than has been thought (exceptions are fatigue, sleepiness, maternal responses) but it is still true in the classic instance of hunger, sex, and thirst.

It should be pointed out again that any of the physiological needs and the consummatory behavior involved with them serve as channels for all sorts of other needs as well. That is to say, the person who thinks he is hungry may actually be seeking more for comfort, or dependence, than for vitamins or proteins. Conversely, it is possible to satisfy the hunger need in part by other activities such as drinking water or smoking cigarettes. In other words, relatively isolable as these physiological needs are, they are not completely so.

Undoubtedly these physiological needs are the most prepotent of all needs. What this means specifically is, that in the human being who is missing everything in life in an extreme fashion, it is most likely that the major motivation would be the physiological needs rather than any others. A person who is lacking food, safety, love, and esteem would most probably hunger for food more strongly than for anything else.

If all the needs are unsatisfied, and the organism is then dominated by the physiological needs, all other needs may become simply nonexistent or be pushed into the background. It is then fair to characterize the whole organism by saying simply that it is hungry, for consciousness is almost completely preempted by hunger. All capacities are put into the service of hunger-satisfaction, and the organization of these capacities is almost entirely determined by the one purpose of satisfying hunger. The receptors and effectors, the intelligence, memory, habits, all may now be defined simply as hunger-gratifying tools. Capacities that are not useful for this purpose lie dormant, or are pushed into the background. The urge to write poetry, the desire to acquire an automobile, the interest in American history, the desire for a new pair of shoes are, in the extreme case, forgotten or become of secondary importance. For the man who is extremely and dangerously hungry, no other interests exist but food. He dreams food, he remembers food, he thinks about food, he emotes only about food, he perceives only food and he wants only food. The more subtle determinants that ordinarily fuse with the physiological drives in organizing even feeding, drinking or sexual behavior, may now be so completely overwhelmed as to allow us to speak at this time (but *only* at this time) of pure hunger drive and behavior, with the one unqualified aim of relief.

Another peculiar characteristic of the human organism when it is dominated by a certain need is that the whole philosophy of the future tends also to change. For our chronically and extremely hungry man, Utopia can be defined very simply as a place where there is plenty of food. He tends to think that, if only he is guaranteed food for the rest of his life, he will be perfectly happy and will never want anything more. Life itself tends to be defined in terms of eating. Anything else will be defined as unimportant. Freedom, love, community feeling, respect, philosophy, may all be waved aside as fripperies which are useless since they fail to fill the stomach. Such a man may fairly be said to live by bread alone.

It cannot possibly be denied that such things are true but their *generality* can be denied. Emergency conditions are, almost by definition, rare in the normally functioning peaceful society. That this truism can be forgotten is due mainly to two reasons. First, rats have few motivations other than physiological ones, and since so much of the research upon motivation has been made with these animals, it is easy to carry the rat-picture over to the human being. Secondly, it is too often not realized that culture itself is an adaptive tool, one of whose main functions is to make the physiological emergencies come less and less often. In most of the known societies, chronic extreme hunger of the emergency type is rare, rather than common. In any case, this is still true in the United States. The average American citizen is experiencing appetite rather than hunger when he says 'I am hungry.' He is apt to experience sheer life-and-death hunger only by accident and then only a few times through his entire life.

Obviously a good way to obscure the 'higher motivations, and to get a lopsided view of human capacities and human nature, is to make the organism extremely and chronically hungry or thirsty. Anyone who attempts to make an emergency picture into a typical one and who will measure all of man's goals and desires by his behavior during extreme physiological deprivation is certainly being blind to many things. It is quite true that man lives by bread alone – when there is no bread. But what happens to man's desires when there is plenty of bread and when his belly is chronically filled?

At once other (and 'higher') needs emerge and these, rather than physiological hungers, dominate the organism. And when these in turn are satisfied, again new (and still 'higher') needs emerge and so on. This is what we mean by saying that the basic human needs are organized into a hierarchy of relative prepotency.

One main implication of this phrasing is that gratification becomes as important a concept as deprivation in motivation theory, for it releases the organism from the domination of a relatively more physiological need, permitting thereby the emergence of other more social goals. The physiological needs, along with their partial goals, when chronically gratified cease to exist as active determinants or organizers of behavior. They now exist only in a potential fashion in the sense that they may emerge again to dominate the organism if they are thwarted. But a want that is satisfied is no longer a want. The organism is dominated and its behavior organized only by unsatisfied needs. If hunger is satisfied, it becomes unimportant in the current dynamics of the individual.

This statement is somewhat qualified by a hypothesis to be discussed more fully later, namely that it is precisely those individuals in whom a certain need has always been satisfied who are best equipped to tolerate deprivation of that need in the future, and that furthermore, those who have been deprived in the past will react differently to current satisfactions than the one who has never been deprived.

The safety needs

If the physiological needs are relatively well gratified, there then emerges a new set of needs, which we may categorize roughly as the safety needs. All that has been said of the physiological needs is equally true, although in lesser degree, of these desires. The organism may equally well be wholly dominated by them. They may serve as the almost exclusive organizers of behavior, recruiting all the capacities of the organism in their service, and we may then fairly describe the whole organism as a safety-seeking mechanism. Again we may say of the receptors, the effectors, of the intellect and the other capacities that they are primarily safety-seeking tools. Again, as in the hungry man, we find that the dominating goal is a strong determinant not only of his current world-outlook and philosophy but also of his philosophy of the future. Practically everything looks less important than safety, (even sometimes the physiological needs which being satisfied, are now underestimated). A man, in this state, if it is extreme enough and chronic enough, may be characterized as living almost for safety alone.

Although in this paper we are interested primarily in the needs of the adult, we can approach an understanding of his safety needs perhaps more efficiently by observation of infants and children, in whom these needs are much more simple and obvious. One reason for the clearer appearance of the threat or danger reaction in infants, is that they do not inhibit this reaction at all, whereas adults in our society have been taught to inhibit it at all costs. Thus even when adults do feel their safety to be threatened we may not be able to see this on the surface. Infants will react in a total fashion and as if they were endangered, if they are disturbed or dropped suddenly, startled by loud noises, flashing light, or other unusual sensory stimulation, by rough handling, by general loss of support in the mother's arms, or by inadequate support.[1]

In infants we can also see a much more direct reaction to bodily illnesses of various kinds. Sometimes these illnesses seem to be immediately and *per se* threatening and seem to make the child feel unsafe. For instance, vomiting, colic, or other sharp pains seem to make the child look at the whole world in a different way. At such a moment of pain, it may be postulated that, for the child, the appearance of the whole world suddenly changes from sunniness to darkness, so to speak, and becomes a place in which anything at all might happen, in which previously stable things have suddenly become unstable. Thus a child who because of some bad food is taken ill may, for a day or two, develop fear, nightmares, and a need for protection and reassurance never seen in him before his illness.

Another indication of the child's need for safety is his preference for some kind of undisrupted routine or rhythm. He seems to want a predictable, orderly world. For instance, injustice, unfairness, or inconsistency in the parents seems to make a child feel anxious and unsafe. This attitude may be not so much because of the injustice *per se* or any particular pains involved, but rather because this treatment threatens to make the world look unreliable, or unsafe, or unpredictable. Young children seem to thrive better under a system which has at least a skeletal outline of rigidity, in which there is a schedule of a kind, some sort of routine, something that can be counted upon, not only for the present but also far into the future. Perhaps one could express this more accurately by saying that the child needs an organized world rather than an unorganized or unstructured one.

The central role of the parents and the normal family setup are indisputable. Quarreling, physical assault, separation, divorce or death within the family may be particularly terrifying. Also parental outbursts of rage or threats of punishment directed to the child, calling him names, speaking to him harshly, shaking him, handling him roughly, or actual physical punishment sometimes elicit such total panic and terror in the child that we must assume more is involved than the physical pain alone. While it is true that in some children this terror may represent also a fear of loss of parental love, it can also occur in completely rejected children, who seem to cling to the hating parents more for sheer safety and protection than because of hope of love.

Confronting the average child with new, unfamiliar, strange, unmanageable stimuli or situations will too frequently elicit the danger or terror reaction, as for example, getting lost or even being separated from the parents for a short time, being confronted with new faces, new situations or new tasks, the sight of strange, unfamiliar or uncontrollable objects, illness or death. Particularly at such times, the child's frantic clinging to his parents is eloquent testimony to their role as protectors (quite apart from their roles as food-givers and love-givers).

From these and similar observations, we may generalize and say that the average child in our society generally prefers a safe, orderly, predictable, organized world, which he can count on and in which unexpected, unmanageable or other dangerous things do not happen, and in which, in any case, he has all-powerful parents who protect and shield him from harm.

That these reactions may so easily be observed in children is in a way a proof of the fact that children in our society feel too unsafe (or, in a word, are badly brought up). Children who are reared in an unthreatening, loving family do *not* ordinarily

---

[1] As the child grows up, sheer knowledge and familiarity as well as better motor development make these 'dangers' less and less dangerous and more and more manageable. Throughout life it may be said that one of the main conative functions of education is this neutralizing of apparent dangers through knowledge, *e.g.*, I am not afraid of thunder because I know something about it.

react as we have described above (17). In such children the danger reactions are apt to come mostly to objects or situations that adults too would consider dangerous.[2]

The healthy, normal, fortunate adult in our culture is largely satisfied in his safety needs. The peaceful, smoothly running, 'good' society ordinarily makes its members feel safe enough from wild animals, extremes of temperature, criminals, assault and murder, tyranny, etc. Therefore, in a very real sense, he no longer has any safety needs as active motivators. Just as a sated man no longer feels hungry, a safe man no longer feels endangered. If we wish to see these needs directly and clearly we must turn to neurotic or near-neurotic individuals, and to the economic and social underdogs. In between these extremes, we can perceive the expressions of safety needs only in such phenomena as, for instance, the common preference for a job with tenure and protection, the desire for a savings account, and for insurance of various kinds (medical, dental, unemployment, disability, old age).

Other broader aspects of the attempt to seek safety and stability in the world are seen in the very common preference for familiar rather than unfamiliar things, or for the known rather than the unknown. The tendency to have some religion or world-philosophy that organizes the universe and the men in it into some sort of satisfactorily coherent, meaningful whole is also in part motivated by safety-seeking. Here too we may list science and philosophy in general as partially motivated by the safety needs (we shall see later that there are also other motivations to scientific, philosophical or religious endeavor).

Otherwise the need for safety is seen as an active and dominant mobilizer of the organism's resources only in emergencies, *e.g.*, war, disease, natural catastrophes, crime waves, societal disorganization, neurosis, brain injury, chronically bad situation.

Some neurotic adults in our society are, in many ways, like the unsafe child in their desire for safety, although in the former it takes on a somewhat special appearance. Their reaction is often to unknown, psychological dangers in a world that is perceived to be hostile, overwhelming and threatening. Such a person behaves as if a great catastrophe were almost always impending, *i.e.*, he is usually responding as if to an emergency. His safety needs often find specific expression in a search for a protector, or a stronger person on whom he may depend, or perhaps, a Fuehrer.

The neurotic individual may be described in a slightly different way with some usefulness as a grown-up person who retains his childish attitudes toward the world. That is to say, a neurotic adult may be said to behave 'as if' he were actually afraid of a spanking, or of his mother's disapproval, or of being abandoned by his parents, or having his food taken away from him. It is as if his childish attitudes of fear and threat reaction to a dangerous world had gone underground, and untouched by the growing up and learning processes, were now ready to be called out by any stimulus that would make a child feel endangered and threatened.[3]

The neurosis in which the search for safety takes its clearest form is in the compulsive-obsessive neurosis. Compulsive-obsessives try frantically to order and stabilize the world so that no unmanageable, unexpected or unfamiliar dangers will ever appear (14). They hedge themselves about with all sorts of ceremonials, rules

[2] A 'test battery' for safety might be confronting the child with a small exploding firecracker, or with a bewhiskered face, having the mother leave the room, putting him upon a high ladder, a hypodermic injection, having a mouse crawl up to him, etc. Of course I cannot seriously recommend the deliberate use of such 'tests' for they might very well harm the child being tested. But these and similar situations come up by the score in the child's ordinary day-to-day living and may be observed. There is no reason why these stimuli should not be used with, for example, young chimpanzees.

[3] Not all neurotic individuals feel unsafe. Neurosis may have at its core a thwarting of the affection and esteem needs in a person who is generally safe.

and formulas so that every possible contingency may be provided for and so that no new contingencies may appear. They are much like the brain injured cases, described by Goldstein (6), who manage to maintain their equilibrium by avoiding everything unfamiliar and strange and by ordering their restricted world in such a neat, disciplined, orderly fashion that everything in the world can be counted upon. They try to arrange the world so that anything unexpected (dangers) cannot possibly occur. If, through no fault of their own, something unexpected does occur, they go into a panic reaction as if this unexpected occurrence constituted a grave danger. What we can see only as a none-too-strong preference in the healthy person, *e.g.*, preference for the familiar, becomes a life-and-death necessity in abnormal cases.

The love needs

If both the physiological and the safety needs are fairly well gratified, then there will emerge the love and affection and belongingness needs, and the whole cycle already described will repeat itself with this new center. Now the person will feel keenly, as never before, the absence of friends, or a sweetheart, or a wife, or children. He will hunger for affectionate relations with people in general, namely, for a place in his group, and he will strive with great intensity to achieve this goal. He will want to attain such a place more than anything else in the world and may even forget that once, when he was hungry, he sneered at love.

In our society the thwarting of these needs is the most commonly found core in cases of maladjustment and more severe psychopathology. Love and affection, as well as their possible expression in sexuality, are generally looked upon with ambivalence and are customarily hedged about with many restrictions and inhibitions. Practically all theorists of psychopathology have stressed thwarting of the love needs as basic in the picture of maladjustment. Many clinical studies have therefore been made of this need and we know more about it perhaps than any of the other needs except the physiological ones (14).

One thing that must be stressed at this point is that love is not synonymous with sex. Sex may be studied as a purely physiological need. Ordinarily sexual behavior is multi-determined, that is to say, determined not only by sexual but also by other needs, chief among which are the love and affection needs. Also not to be overlooked is the fact that the love needs involve both giving and receiving love.[4]

The esteem needs

All people in our society (with a few pathological exceptions) have a need or desire for a stable firmly based, (usually) high evaluation of themselves, for self-respect, or self-esteem, and for the esteem of others. By firmly based self-esteem, we mean that which is soundly based upon real capacity achievement and respect from others. These needs may be classified into two subsidiary sets. These are, first, the desire for strength, for achievement, for adequacy, for confidence in the face of the world, and for independence and freedom.[5] Secondly, we have what we may call the desire for

---

[4] For further details see (12) and (16, Chap. 5).

[5] Whether or not this particular desire is universal we do not know. The crucial question, especially important today, is 'Will men who are enslaved and dominated inevitably feel dissatisfied and rebellious?' We may assume on the basis of commonly known clinical data that a man who has known true freedom (not paid for by giving up safety and security but rather built on the basis of adequate safety and security) will not willingly or easily allow his freedom to be taken away from him. But we do not know that this is true for the person born into slavery. The events of the next decade should give us our answer. See discussion of this problem in (5).

reputation or prestige (defining it as respect or esteem from other people), recognition, attention, importance or appreciation.[6] These needs have been relatively stressed by Alfred Adler and his followers, and have been relatively neglected by Freud and the psychoanalysts. More and more today however there is appearing widespread appreciation of their central importance.

Satisfaction of the self-esteem need leads to feelings of self-confidence, worth, strength, capability and adequacy of being useful and necessary in the world. But thwarting of these needs produces feelings of inferiority, of weakness and of helplessness. These feelings in turn give rise to either basic discouragement or else compensatory or neurotic trends. An appreciation of the necessity of basic self-confidence and an understanding of how helpless people are without it, can be easily gained from a study of severe traumatic neurosis (8).[7]

The need for self-actualization

Even if all these needs are satisfied, we may still often (if not always) expect that a new discontent and restlessness will soon develop, unless the individual is doing what he is fitted for. A musician must make music, an artist must paint, a poet must write, if he is to be ultimately happy. What a man *can* be, he *must* be. This need we may call self-actualization.

This term, first coined by Kurt Goldstein, is being used in this paper in a much more specific and limited fashion. It refers to the desire for self-fulfillment, namely, to the tendency for him to become actualized in what he is potentially. This tendency might be phrased as the desire to become more and more what one is, to become everything that one is capable of becoming.

The specific form that these needs will take will of course vary greatly from person to person. In one individual it may take the form of the desire to be an ideal mother, in another it may be expressed athletically, and in still another it may be expressed in painting pictures or in inventions. It is not necessarily a creative urge although in people who have any capacities for creation it will take this form.

The clear emergence of these needs rests upon prior satisfaction of the physiological, safety, love and esteem needs. We shall call people who are satisfied in these needs, basically satisfied people and it is from these that we may expect the fullest (and healthiest) creativeness.[8] Since, in our society, basically satisfied people are the exception, we do not know much about self-actualization, either experimentally or clinically. It remains a challenging problem for research.

The preconditions for the basic need satisfactions

There are certain conditions which are immediate prerequisites for the basic need satisfactions. Danger to these is reacted to almost as if it were a direct danger to the basic needs themselves. Such conditions as freedom to speak, freedom to do what

---

[6] Perhaps the desire for prestige and respect from others is subsidiary to the desire for self-esteem or confidence in oneself. Observation of children seems to indicate that this is so, but clinical data give no clear support for such a conclusion.

[7] For more extensive discussion of normal self-esteem, as well as for reports of various researches, see (11).

[8] Clearly creative behavior, like painting, is like any other behavior in having multiple determinants. It may be seen in 'innately creative' people whether they are satisfied or not, happy or unhappy, hungry or sated. Also it is clear that creative activity may be compensatory, ameliorative or purely economic. It is my impression (as yet unconfirmed) that it is possible to distinguish the artistic and intellectual products of basically satisfied people from those of basically unsatisfied people by inspection alone. In any case, here too we must distinguish, in a dynamic fashion, the overt behavior itself from its various motivations or purposes.

one wishes so long as no harm is done to others, freedom to express one's self, freedom to investigate and seek for information, freedom to defend one's self, justice, fairness, honesty, orderliness in the group are examples of such preconditions for basic need satisfactions. Thwarting in these freedoms will be reacted to with a threat or emergency response. These conditions are not ends in themselves but they are almost so since they are so closely related to the basic needs, which are apparently the only ends in themselves. These conditions are defended because without them the basic satisfactions are quite impossible, or at least, very severely endangered.

If we remember that the cognitive capacities (perceptual, intellectual, learning) are a set of adjustive tools, which have, among other functions, that of satisfaction of our basic needs, then it is clear that any danger to them, any deprivation or blocking of their free use, must also be indirectly threatening to the basic needs themselves. Such a statement is a partial solution of the general problems of curiosity, the search for knowledge, truth and wisdom, and the ever-persistent urge to solve the cosmic mysteries.

We must therefore introduce another hypothesis and speak of degrees of closeness to the basic needs, for we have already pointed out that *any* conscious desires (partial goals) are more or less important as they are more or less close to the basic needs. The same statement may be made for various behavior acts. An act is psychologically important if it contributes directly to satisfaction of basic needs. The less directly it so contributes, or the weaker this contribution is, the less important this act must be conceived to be from the point of view of dynamic psychology. A similar statement may be made for the various defense or coping mechanisms. Some are very directly related to the protection or attainment of the basic needs, others are only weakly and distantly related. Indeed if we wished, we could speak of more basic and less basic defense mechanisms, and then affirm that danger to the more basic defenses (always remembering that this is so only because of their relationship to the basic needs).

The desires to know and to understand

So far, we have mentioned the cognitive needs only in passing. Acquiring knowledge and systematizing the universe have been considered as, in part, techniques for the achievement of basic safety in the world, or, for the intelligent man, expressions of self-actualization. Also freedom of inquiry and expression have been discussed as preconditions of satisfactions of the basic needs. True though these formulations may be, they do not constitute definitive answers to the question as to the motivation role of curiosity, learning, philosophizing, experimenting, etc. They are, at best, no more than partial answers.

This question is especially difficult because we know so little about the facts. Curiosity, exploration, desire for the facts, desire to know may certainly be observed easily enough. The fact that they often are pursued even at great cost to the individual's safety is an earnest of the partial character of our previous discussion. In addition, the writer must admit that, though he has sufficient clinical evidence to postulate the desire to know as a very strong drive in intelligent people, no data are available for unintelligent people. It may then be largely a function of relatively high intelligence. Rather tentatively, then, and largely in the hope of stimulating discussion and research, we shall postulate a basic desire to know, to be aware of reality, to get the facts, to satisfy curiosity, or as Wertheimer phrases it, to see rather than to be blind.

This postulation, however, is not enough. Even after we know, we are impelled to know more and more minutely and microscopically on the one hand, and on the other, more and more extensively in the direction of a world philosophy, religion, etc. The facts that we acquire, if they are isolated or atomistic, inevitably get theorized about, and either analyzed or organized or both. This process has been phrased by some as the search for 'meaning.' We shall then postulate a desire to understand, to systematize, to organize, to analyze, to look for relations and meanings.

Once these desires are accepted for discussion, we see that they too form themselves into a small hierarchy in which the desire to know is prepotent over the desire to understand. All the characteristics of a hierarchy of prepotency that we have described above, seem to hold for this one as well.

We must guard ourselves against the too easy tendency to separate these desires from the basic needs we have discussed above, *i.e.*, to make a sharp dichotomy between 'cognitive' and 'conative' needs. The desire to know and to understand are themselves conative, *i.e.*, have a striving character, and are as much personality needs as the 'basic needs' we have already discussed (19).

III Further characteristics of the basic needs

The degree of fixity of the hierarchy of basic needs

We have spoken so far as if this hierarchy were a fixed order but actually it is not nearly as rigid as we may have implied. It is true that most of the people with whom we have worked have seemed to have these basic needs in about the order that has been indicated. However, there have been a number of exceptions.

1 There are some people in whom, for instance, self-esteem seems to be more important than love. This most common reversal in the hierarchy is usually due to the development of the notion that the person who is most likely to be loved is a strong or powerful person, one who inspires respect or fear, and who is self confident or aggressive. Therefore such people who lack love and seek it, may try hard to put on a front of aggressive, confident behavior. But essentially they seek high self-esteem and its behavior expressions more as a means-to-an-end than for its own sake; they seek self-assertion for the sake of love rather than for self-esteem itself.

2 There are other, apparently innately creative people in whom the drive to creativeness seems to be more important than any other counter-determinant. Their creativeness might appear not as self-actualization released by basic satisfaction, but in spite of lack of basic satisfaction.

3 In certain people the level of aspiration may be permanently deadened or lowered. That is to say, the less prepotent goals may simply be lost, and may disappear forever, so that the person who has experienced life at a very low level, *i.e.*, chronic unemployment, may continue to be satisfied for the rest of his life if only he can get enough food.

4 The so-called 'psychopathic personality' is another example of permanent loss of the love needs. These are people who, according to the best data available (9), have been starved for love in the earliest months of their lives and have simply lost forever the desire and the ability to give and to receive affection (as animals lose sucking or pecking reflexes that are not exercised soon enough after birth).

5 Another cause of reversal of the hierarchy is that when a need has been satisfied for a long time, this need may be underevaluated. People who have never experienced chronic hunger are apt to underestimate its effects and to look upon food as a rather unimportant thing. If they are dominated by a higher need, this higher need will seem to be the most important of all. It then becomes possible, and indeed does actually happen, that they may, for the sake of this higher need, put

themselves into the position of being deprived in a more basic need. We may expect that after a long-time deprivation of the more basic need there will be a tendency to reevaluate both needs so that the more prepotent need will actually become consciously prepotent for the individual who may have given it up very lightly. Thus, a man who has given up his job rather than lose his self-respect, and who then starves for six months or so, may be willing to take his job back even at the price of losing his self-respect.

6 Another partial explanation of *apparent* reversals is seen in the fact that we have been talking about the hierarchy of prepotency in terms of consciously felt wants or desires rather than of behavior. Looking at behavior itself may give us the wrong impression. What we have claimed is that the person will *want* the more basic of two needs when deprived in both. There is no necessary implication here that he will act upon his desires. Let us say again that there are many determinants of behavior other than the needs and desires.

7 Perhaps more important than all these exceptions are the ones that involve ideals, high social standards, high values and the like. With such values people become martyrs; they will give up everything for the sake of a particular ideal, or value. These people may be understood, at least in part, by reference to one basic concept (or hypothesis) which may be called 'increased frustration-tolerance through early gratification.' People who have been satisfied in their basic needs throughout their lives, particularly in their earlier years, seem to develop exceptional power to withstand present or future thwarting of these needs simply because they have strong, healthy character structure as a result of basic satisfaction. They are the 'strong' people who can easily weather disagreement or opposition, who can swim against the stream of public opinion and who can stand up for the truth at great personal cost. It is just the ones who have loved and been well loved, and who have had many deep friendships who can hold out against hatred, rejection or persecution.

I say all this in spite of the fact that there is a certain amount of sheer habituation which is also involved in any full discussion of frustration tolerance. For instance, it is likely that those persons who have been accustomed to relative starvation for a long time, are partially enabled thereby to withstand food deprivation. What sort of balance must be made between these two tendencies, of habituation on the one hand, and of past satisfaction breeding present frustration tolerance on the other hand, remains to be worked out by further research. Meanwhile we may assume that they are both operative, side by side, since they do not contradict each other. In respect to this phenomenon of increased frustration tolerance, it seems probable that the most important gratifications come in the first two years of life. That is to say, people who have been made secure and strong in the earliest years, tend to remain secure and strong thereafter in the face of whatever threatens.

Degrees of relative satisfaction

So far our theoretical discussion may have given the impression that these five sets of needs are somehow in step-wise, all-or-none relationships to each other. We have spoken in such terms as the following: 'If one need is satisfied, then another emerges.' This statement might give the false impression that a need must be satisfied 100 per cent before the next need emerges. In actual fact, most members of our society who are normal, are partially satisfied in all their basic needs and partially unsatisfied in all their basic needs at the same time. A more realistic description of the hierarchy would be in terms of decreasing percentages of satisfaction as we go up the hierarchy of prepotency. For instance, if I may assign arbitrary figures for the sake of illustration, it is as if the average citizen is satisfied perhaps 85 per cent in his physiological needs, 70 per cent in his safety needs, 50 per cent in his love needs, 40 per cent in his self-esteem needs, and 10 per cent in his self-actualization needs.

As for the concept of emergence of a new need after satisfaction of the prepotent need, this emergence is not a sudden, saltatory phenomenon but rather a gradual emergence by slow degrees from nothingness. For instance, if prepotent need A is satisfied only 10 per cent then need B may not be visible at all. However, as this need A becomes satisfied 25 per cent, need B may emerge 5 per cent, as need A becomes satisfied 75 per cent need B may emerge 90 per cent, and so on.

Unconscious character of needs

These needs are neither necessarily conscious nor unconscious. On the whole, however, in the average person, they are more often unconscious rather than conscious. It is not necessary at this point to overhaul the tremendous mass of evidence which indicates the crucial importance of unconscious motivation. It would by now be expected, on a priori grounds alone, that unconscious motivations would on the whole be rather more important than the conscious motivations. What we have called the basic needs are very often largely unconscious although they may, with suitable techniques, and with sophisticated people become conscious.

Cultural specificity and generality of needs

This classification of basic needs makes some attempt to take account of the relative unity behind the superficial differences in specific desires from one culture to another. Certainly in any particular culture an individual's conscious motivational content will usually be extremely different from the conscious motivational content of an individual in another society. However, it is the common experience of anthropologists that people, even in different societies, are much more alike than we would think from our first contact with them, and that as we know them better we seem to find more and more of this commonness. We then recognize the most startling differences to be superficial rather than basic, *e.g.*, differences in style of hairdress, clothes, tastes in food, etc. Our classification of basic needs is in part an attempt to account for this unity behind the apparent diversity from culture to culture. No claim is made that it is ultimate or universal for all cultures. The claim is made only that it is relatively *more* ultimate, more universal, more basic, than the superficial conscious desires from culture to culture, and makes a somewhat closer approach to common-human characteristics. Basic needs are *more* common-human than superficial desires or behaviors.

Multiple motivations of behavior

These needs must be understood not to be *exclusive* or single determiners of certain kinds of behavior. An example may be found in any behavior that seems to be physiologically motivated, such as eating, or sexual play or the like. The clinical psychologists have long since found that any behavior may be a channel through which flow various determinants. Or to say it in another way, most behavior is multi-motivated. Within the sphere of motivational determinants any behavior tends to be determined by several or *all* of the basic needs simultaneously rather than by only one of them. The latter would be more an exception than the former. Eating may be partially for the sake of filling the stomach, and partially for the sake of comfort and amelioration of other needs. One may make love not only for pure sexual release, but also to convince one's self of one's masculinity, or to make a conquest, to feel powerful, or to win more basic affection. As an illustration, I may point out that it would be possible (theoretically if not practically) to analyze a single act of an individual and see in it the expression of his physiological needs, his safety needs, his love needs, his esteem needs and self-actualization. This contrasts sharply with the more naive brand of trait psychology in which one trait or one motive accounts for a certain kind of act, *i.e.*, an aggressive act is traced soley to a trait of aggressiveness.

Multiple determinants of behavior

Not all behavior is determined by the basic needs. We might even say that not all behavior is motivated. There are many determinants of behavior other than motives.[9] For instance, one other important class of determinants is the so-called 'field' determinants. Theoretically, at least, behavior may be determined completely by the field, or even by specific isolated external stimuli, as in association of ideas, or certain conditioned reflexes. If in response to the stimulus word 'table,' I immediately perceive a memory image of a table, this response certainly has nothing to do with my basic needs.

Secondly, we may call attention again to the concept of 'degree of closeness to the basic needs' or 'degree of motivation.' Some behavior is highly motivated, other behavior is only weakly motivated. Some is not motivated at all (but all behavior is determined).

Another important point[10] is that there is a basic difference between expressive behavior and coping behavior (functional striving, purposive goal seeking). An expressive behavior does not try to do anything; it is simply a reflection of the personality. A stupid man behaves stupidly, not because he wants to, or tries to, or is motivated to, but simply because he *is* what he is. The same is true when I speak in a bass voice rather than tenor or soprano. The random movements of a healthy child, the smile on the face of a happy man even when he is alone, the springiness of the healthy man's walk, and the erectness of his carriage are other examples of expressive, non-functional behavior. Also the *style* in which a man carries out almost all his behavior, motivated as well as unmotivated, is often expressive.

We may then ask, is *all* behavior expressive or reflective of the character structure? The answer is 'No.' Rote, habitual, automatized, or conventional behavior may or may not be expressive. The same is true for most 'stimulus-bound' behaviors.

It is finally necessary to stress that expressiveness of behavior, and goal-directedness of behavior are not mutually exclusive categories. Average behavior is usually both.

Goals as centering principle in motivation theory

It will be observed that the basic principle in our classification has been neither the instigation nor the motivated behavior but rather the functions, effects, purposes, or goals of the behavior. It has been proven sufficiently by various people that this is the most suitable point for centering in any motivation theory.[11]

---

[9] I am aware that many psychologists and psychoanalysts use the term 'motivated' and 'determined' synonymously, *e.g.*, Freud. But I consider this an obfuscating usage. Sharp distinctions are necessary for clarity of thought, and precision in experimentation.

[10] To be discussed fully in a subsequent publication.

[11] The interested reader is referred to the very excellent discussion of this point in Murray's *Explorations in Personality* (15).

Animal- and human-centering

This theory starts with the human being rather than any lower and presumably 'simpler' animal. Too many of the findings that have been made in animals have been proven to be true for animals but not for the human being. There is no reason whatsoever why we should start with animals in order to study human motivation. The logic or rather illogic behind this general fallacy of 'pseudo-simplicity' has been exposed often enough by philosophers and logicians as well as by scientists in each of the various fields. It is no more necessary to study animals before one can study man than it is to study mathematics before one can study geology or psychology or biology.

We may also reject the old, naive behaviorism which assumed that it was somehow necessary, or at least more 'scientific' to judge human beings by animal standards. One consequence of this belief was that the whole notion of purpose and goal was excluded from motivational psychology simply because one could not ask a white rat about his purposes. Tolman (18) has long since proven in animal studies themselves that this exclusion was not necessary.

Motivation and the theory of psychopathogenesis

The conscious motivational content of everyday life has, according to the foregoing, been conceived to be relatively important or unimportant accordingly as it is more or less closely related to the basic goals. A desire for an ice cream cone might actually be an indirect expression of a desire for love. If it is, then this desire for the ice cream cone becomes extremely important motivation. If however the ice cream is simply something to cool the mouth with, or a casual appetitive reaction, then the desire is relatively unimportant. Everyday conscious desires are to be regarded as symptoms, as *surface indicators of more basic needs*. If we were to take these superficial desires at their face value we would find ourselves in a state of complete confusion which could never be resolved, since we would be dealing seriously with symptoms rather than with what lay behind the symptoms.

Thwarting of unimportant desires produces no psychopathological results; thwarting of a basically important need does produce such results. Any theory of psychopathogenesis must then be based on a sound theory of motivation. A conflict or a frustration is not necessarily pathogenic. It becomes so only when it threatens or thwarts the basic needs, or partial needs that are closely related to the basic needs (10).

The role of gratified needs

It has been pointed out above several times that our needs usually emerge only when more prepotent needs have been gratified. Thus gratification has an important role in motivation theory. Apart from this, however, needs cease to play an active determining or organizing role as soon as they are gratified.

What this means is that, *e.g.*, a basically satisfied person no longer has the needs for esteem, love, safety, etc. The only sense in which he might be said to have them is in the almost metaphysical sense that a sated man has hunger, or a filled bottle has emptiness. If we are interested in what *actually* motivates us, and not in what has, will, or might motivate us, then a satisfied need is not a motivator. It must be considered for all practical purposes simply not to exist, to have disappeared. This point should be emphasized because it has been either overlooked or contradicted in every theory of motivation I know.[12] The perfectly healthy, normal, fortunate man has no sex

---

[12] Note that acceptance of this theory necessitates basic revision of the Freudian theory.

needs or hunger needs, or needs for safety, or for love, or for prestige, or self-esteem, except in stray moments of quickly passing threat. If we were to say otherwise, we should also have to aver that every man had all the pathological reflexes, *e.g.*, Babinski, etc., because if his nervous system were damaged, these would appear.

It is such considerations as these that suggest the bold postulation that a man who is thwarted in any of his basic needs may fairly be envisaged simply as a sick man. This is a fair parallel to our designation as 'sick' of the man who lacks vitamins or minerals. Who is to say that a lack of love is less important than a lack of vitamins? Since we know the pathogenic effects of love starvation, who is to say that we are invoking value-questions in an unscientific or illegitimate way, any more than the physician does who diagnoses and treats pellagra or scurvy? If I were permitted this usage, I should then say simply that a healthy man is primarily motivated by his needs to develop and actualize his fullest potentialities and capacities. If a man has any other basic needs in any active, chronic sense, then he is simply an unhealthy man. He is as surely sick as if he had suddenly developed a strong salt hunger or calcium hunger.[13]

If this statement seems unusual or paradoxical the reader may be assured that this is only one among many such paradoxes that will appear as we revise our ways of looking at man's deeper motivations. When we ask what man wants of life, we deal with his very essence.

IV Summary

1 There are at least five sets of goals, which we may call basic needs. These are briefly physiological, safety, love, esteem, and self-actualization. In addition, we are motivated by the desire to achieve or maintain the various conditions upon which these basic satisfactions rest and by certain more intellectual desires.

2 These basic goals are related to each other, being arranged in a hierarchy of pre-potency. This means that the most prepotent goal will monopolize consciousness and will tend of itself to organize the recruitment of the various capacities of the organism. The less prepotent needs are minimized, even forgotten or denied. But when a need is fairly well satisfied, the next prepotent ('higher') need emerges, in turn to dominate the conscious life and to serve as the center of organization of behavior, since gratified needs are not active motivators.

Thus man is a perpetually wanting animal. Ordinarily the satisfaction of these wants is not altogether mutually exclusive, but only tends to be. The average member of our society is most often partially satisfied and partially unsatisfied in all of his wants. The hierarchy principle is usually empirically observed in terms of increasing percentages of non-satisfaction as we go up the hierarchy. Reversals of the average order of the hierarchy are sometimes observed. Also it has been observed that an individual may permanently lose the higher wants in the hierarchy under special conditions. There are not only ordinarily multiple motivations for usual behavior, but in addition many determinants other than motives.

3 Any thwarting or possibility of thwarting of these basic human goals, or danger to the defenses which protect them, or to the conditions upon which they rest, is con-

---

[13] If we were to use the word 'sick' in this way, we should then also have to face squarely the relations of man to his society. One clear implication of our definition would be that (1) since a man is to be called sick who is basically thwarted, and (2) since such basic thwarting is made possible ultimately only by forces outside the individual, then (3) sickness in the individual must come ultimately from a sickness in the society. The 'good' or healthy society would then be defined as one that permitted man's highest purposes to emerge by satisfying all his prepotent basic needs.

sidered to be a psychological threat. With a few exceptions, all psychopathology may be partially traced to such threats. A basically thwarted man may actually be defined as a 'sick' man, if we wish.

4 It is such basic threats which bring about the general emergency reactions.

5 Certain other basic problems have not been dealt with because of limitations of space. Among these are *(a)* the problem of values in any definitive motivation theory, *(b)* the relation between appetites, desires, needs and what is 'good' for the organism, *(c)* the etiology of the basic needs and their possible derivation in early childhood, *(d)* redefinition of motivational concepts, *i.e.*, drive, desire, wish, need, goal, *(e)* implication of our theory for hedonistic theory, *(f)* the nature of the uncompleted act, of success and failure, and of aspiration-level, *(g)* the role of association, habit and conditioning, *(h)* relation to the theory of inter-personal relations, *(i)* implications for psychotherapy, *(j)* implication for theory of society, *(k)* the theory of selfishness, *(l)* the relation between needs and cultural patterns, *(m)* the relation between this theory and Allport's theory of functional autonomy. These as well as certain other less important questions must be considered as motivation theory attempts to become definitive.

References

1 Adler, A. *Social interest.* London: Faber & Faber, 1938.

2 Cannon, W. B. *Wisdom of the body.* New York: Norton, 1932.

3 Freud, A. *The ego and the mechanisms of defense.* London: Hogarth, 1937.

4 Freud, S. *New introductory lectures on psychoanalysis.* New York: Norton, 1933.

5 Fromm, E. *Escape from freedom.* New York: Farrar and Rinehart, 1941.

6 Goldstein, K. *The organism.* New York: American Book Co., 1939.

7 Horney, K. *The neurotic personality of our time.* New York: Norton, 1937.

8 Kardiner, A. *The traumatic neuroses of war.* New York: Hoeber, 1941.

9 Levy, D. M. Primary affect hunger. *Amer. J. Psychiat.*, 1937, 94, 643–652.

10 Maslow, A. H. Conflict, frustration, and the theory of threat. *J. Abnorm. (soc.) Psychol.*, 1943, 38, 81–86.

11 —— . Dominance, personality and social behavior in women. *J. Soc. Psychol.*, 1939, 10, 3–39.

12 —— . The dynamics of psychological security-insecurity. *Character & Pers.*, 1942, 10, 331–344.

13 —— . A preface to motivation theory. *Psychosomatic Med.*, 1943, 5, 85–92.

14 —— , & Mittelmann, B. *Principles of abnormal psychology.* New York: Harper & Bros., 1941.

15 Murray, H. A., *et al. Explorations in personality.* New York: Oxford University Press, 1938.

16 Plant, J. *Personality and the cultural pattern.* New York: Commonwealth Fund, 1937.

17 Shirley, M. Children's adjustments to a strange situation. *J. Abnorm. (soc.) Psychol.*, 1942, 37, 201–217.

18 Tolman. E. C. *Purposive behavior in animals and men.* New York: Century, 1932.

19 Wertheimer, M. Unpublished lectures at the New School for Social Research.

20 Young. P. T. *Motivation of behavior.* New York John Wiley & Sons, 1936.

21 —— . The experimental analysis of appetite. *Psychol. Bull*, 1941, 38, 129–164.

reading 5

the power of rewards (1970)

'Beyond the teaching machine: the neglected area of operant conditioning in the theory and practice of management', by Walter R. Nord, *Organizational Behavior and Human Performance*, vol. 4, no. 4, 1970, pp. 375–401.

Most of us like to think that we are in control of our behaviour and destiny, that we are not pawns pushed around the checkerboard of life by unseen environmental factors. Behavioural psychologists have argued otherwise, emphasizing the way in which our behaviour is shaped by patterns of reward and punishment. The advice of 'humanist' psychologists, such as Herzberg and Maslow, appears to contradict the recommendations of behaviourists, such as Watson and Skinner. In this article, Nord argues that these extreme positions are not as far apart as they appear. In most settings, people do change their behaviours to obtain desirable rewards. Nord argues that conditioning should not be ignored as a management technique.

learning objectives

Once you have read and understood this article, you should be able to:

1 Understand and explain the differences and similarities in the behaviourist and humanist approaches to learning.
2 Understand the benefits to be derived from the use of behavioural modification regimes involving positive reinforcement in specialized organizational settings, such as mental hospitals and schools for children with special needs.
3 Understand Nord's case for the use of conditioning techniques in organizations.

learning pre-requisites

You should first read Chapter 5 in the core text, on learning, particularly the sections explaining the behaviourist approach to learning, and behaviour modification techniques. Nord's article uses technical terms with which you need to be familiar. Warning: this is not an 'easy read'. Chapter 4, on motivation, is also relevant because Nord tries in this article to link the work of the behaviourists with the motivation theories of Douglas McGregor, Frederick Herzberg and Abraham Maslow. Skinner's view of behaviour sits awkwardly with the view that we are self-defining beings in search of self-actualization.

learning activities

1 Use the matrix on the following page to summarize the main points of similarity and contrast between the 'humanist' and the 'behaviourist' approaches according to Nord. Note points where Nord identifies agreement as well as disagreement.
2 List the problems Nord identifies in using punishment as a technique for behav-

iour control. Compare his argument with the case set out in Chapter 5 of the core text.

3 Nord identifies a number of useful applications for positive reinforcement techniques across a range of organizational settings. Make a list of these applications for yourself.

The 'humanist' school and the 'behaviourist' school: similarities and differences

Humanists say this:	*Behaviourists say this:*

READING
5

Beyond the teaching machine: the neglected area of operant conditioning in the theory and practice of management*
Walter R. Nord†

The work of B. F. Skinner and the operant conditioners has been neglected in management and organizational literature. The present paper is an attempt to eliminate this lacuna. When most students of management and personnel think of Skinner's work, they begin and end with programmed instruction. Skinner's ideas, however, have far greater implications for the design and operation of social systems and organizations than just the teaching machine. These additional ideas could be of great practical value.

While neglecting conditioning, writers in the administrative, management, and personnel literature have given extensive attention to the work of other behavioral scientists. McGregor and Maslow are perhaps the behavioral scientists best known to practitioners and students in the area of business and management. Since the major concern of managers of human resources is the prediction and control of the behavior of organizational participants, it is curious to find that people with such a need are extremely conversant with McGregor and Maslow and totally ignorant of Skinner. This condition is not surprising since leading scholars in the field, of what might be termed the applied behavioral sciences, have turned out book after book, article after article, and anthology after anthology with scarcely a mention of Skinner's contributions to the design of social systems. While many writers who deal with the social psychology of organizations are guilty of the omission, this paper will

* Reprinted by permission from *Organizational Behavior and Human Performance*, Vol. 4, No. 4, (November 1969), pp. 375–401. Copyright © 1970 Academic Press. Inc. *Printed in U.S.A.*

† School of Business and Public Administration, Washington University, St. Louis, Missouri 63130. The author wishes to acknowledge the helpful comments of Dr. Ann Nord, Dr Raymond Hilgert, and Mr. Timothy Parker.

focus primarily on the popular positions of Douglas McGregor, Abraham Maslow, and Frederick Herzberg to aid in exposition.

Almost every book in the field devotes considerable attention to Maslow and McGregor. These men have certainly contributed ideas which are easily understood and 'make sense' to practitioners. Also, many practitioners have implemented some of these ideas successfully. However, the belief in the Maslow–McGregor creed is not based on a great deal of evidence. This conclusion is not mine alone, but in fact closely parallels Maslow's (1965) own thoughts. He wrote:

> After all, if we take the whole thing from McGregor's point of view of a contrast between a Theory X view of human nature, a good deal of the evidence upon which he bases his conclusions comes from my researches and my papers on motivations, self-actualization, et cetera. But I of all people should know just how shaky this foundation is as a final foundation. My work on motivations came from the clinic, from a study of neurotic people. The carry-over of this theory to the industrial situation has some support from industrial studies, but certainly I would like to see a lot more studies of this kind before feeling finally convinced that this carry-over from the study of neurosis to the study of labor in factories is legitimate. The same thing is true of my studies of self-actualizing people – there is only this one study of mine available. There were many things wrong with the sampling, so many in fact that it must be considered to be, in the classical sense anyway, a bad or poor or inadequate experiment. I am quite willing to concede this – as a matter of fact, I am eager to concede it – because I'm a little worried about this stuff which I consider to be tentative being swallowed whole by all sorts of enthusiastic people, who really should be a little more tentative in the way that I am (pp. 55–56).

By contrast, the work of Skinner (1953) and his followers has been supported by millions of observations made on animals at all levels of the phylogenetic scale, including man. Over a wide variety of situations, behavior has been reliably predicted and controlled by operant and classical conditioning techniques.

Why then have the applied behavioral sciences followed the McGregor–Maslow approach and ignored Skinner? Several reasons can be suggested. First is the metaphysical issue. Modern Americans, especially of the managerial class, prefer to think of themselves and others as being self-actualizing creatures near the top of Maslow's need-hierarchy, rather than as animals being controlled and even 'manipulated' by their environment. McGregor (1960) developed his argument in terms of Maslow's hierarchy. Skinner's position is unattractive in the same way the Copernican theory was unattractive. Second, Skinner's work and stimulus-response psychology in general appear too limited to allow application to complex social situations. Certainly, this point has much merit. The application of *S–R* theory poses a terribly complex engineering problem, perhaps an insoluble one in some areas. Nevertheless, the designs of some experimental social systems, which will be discussed later in this paper, demonstrate the feasibility of the practical application of Skinnerian psychology to systems design. A third possible reason for the acceptance of the McGregor and Maslow school and rejection of Skinner may stem from the fact that the two approaches have considerable, although generally unrecognized overlap. As will be shown below, McGregor gave primary importance to the environment as the determinant of individual behavior. Similarly, although not as directly, so does Maslow's hierarchy of needs. The major issue between Skinner and McGregor–Maslow has to do with their models of man. Skinner focuses on man being totally shaped by his environment. Maslow–McGregor see man as having an essence or intrinsic nature which is only congruent with certain environments. The evidence for any one set of metaphysical assumptions is no better than for almost any other set. Empirically, little has been found which helps in choosing between Skinner's and McGregor's assumptions. Further, since most managers are concerned mainly with behavior, the sets of assumptions are of limited importance. It should be noted, however, that if McGregor's writings were stripped of Maslow's model of man, his conclusions on the descriptive and proscriptive levels would remain unchanged. Such a revision would also make McGregor's ideas almost identical with Skinner's. With more attention to contingencies of reinforcement and a broader view of the possibilities of administering reinforcement, the two sets of ideas as they apply to prediction and control of action would be virtually indistinguishable.

The remainder of this paper will be devoted to three areas. First, the similarities and differences between McGregor and Skinner will be discussed. Then, a summary of the Skinnerian position will be presented. Finally, the potential of the Skinnerian approach for modern organizations will be presented with supporting evidence from social systems in which it has already been applied.

McGregor and Skinner compared

The importance of environmental factors in determining behavior is the crucial and dominant similarity between Skinner and McGregor. As will be shown below, environmental determination of behavior is central to both men.

McGregor (1960) gave central importance to environmental factors in determining how a person behaves. For example, he saw employee behavior as a consequence of organizational factors which are influenced by managerial strategy. In a sense, Theory X management leads to people behaving in a way which confirms Theory X assumptions, almost as a self-fulfilling prophecy. In addition, McGregor's statement of Theory Y assumptions places stress on 'proper conditions,' rewards and punishments, and other environmental factors. Further, he recognized the importance of immediate feedback in changing behavior. Also, he noted that failure to achieve results is often due to inappropriate methods of control. These are the very terms a behaviorist such as Skinner uses in discussing human actions. Finally, McGregor (1966) noted stimulus-response psychology as a possible model for considering organizational behavior. However, he discarded the reinforcement approach because it did not permit intrinsic rewards to be dealt with. Such a view not only led him to discard a model which describes, by his own admission, important behaviors, but is based on an incomplete view of reinforcement.

McGregor's basic arguments could have been based on Skinner rather than Maslow. The major difference would be the assumption of fewer givens about human nature. In view of this similarity one need not choose either Skinner or McGregor. Rather, there is considerable overlap in that both focus on changing the environmental conditions to produce changes in behavior. Further, both writers place substantial emphasis on the goals of prediction and control. Both are quite explicit in suggesting that we often get undesired results because we use inappropriate methods of control. In fact, the emphasis that McGregor's (1960) first chapter gives to the role of environment in controlling behavior seems to place him clearly in the behavioral camp.

Certainly there are important differences between Skinner and McGregor as well as the marked similarities noted above. For example, McGregor's (1960) use of Maslow's hierarchy of needs implies a series of inborn needs as a focus of the causal factors of behavior whereas Skinner (1953) views environmental factors as the causes of behavior. This difference does not, however, suggest an unresolvable conflict on the applied level. Skinner too allows for satiation on certain reinforcers which will be subject to species' and individual differences. Proceeding from this premise Skinner focuses on the environmental control of behavior in a more rigorous and specific fashion than did McGregor. For example, McGregor (1960) advocated an agricultural approach to development which emphasizes the provision of the conditions for behavioral change as a management responsibility. He noted in a general way that features of the organization, such as a boss, will influence behavioral change. He added that the change would not be permanent unless the organizational environment reinforced the desired behavior pattern. Such a general approach is an assumed basis for Skinner, who proceeds to focus on the types of reinforcement, the details of the administration of reinforcement, and the outcomes which can be expected from the administration of various types of reinforcement. Thus, changes in behavior which are predicted and achieved by Skinnerian methods can be viewed as empirical support for the work of McGregor.

There are other commonalities in the thinking of the two men. Both assume that there are a wide number of desirable responses available to a person which he does not make, because the responses are not rewarded in the environment. Both suggest that many undesired responses are repeated because they are rewarded. Both are clearly advocating a search for alternatives to controlling behavior which will be more effective in developing desired responses.

At this same level of analysis, there seems to be one major difference which revolves around the issue of self-control. However, this difference may be more apparent than real. Skinner (1953) wrote 'It appears, therefore, that society is responsible for the larger part of the behavior of self-control. If this is correct, little ultimate control remains with the individual (p. 240).' Continuing on self-control, Skinner adds: 'But it is also behavior: and we account for it in terms of other variables in the environment and history of the individual. It is these variables which provide the ultimate control (p. 240).'

In apparent contrast, McGregor (1960) stated: 'Theory Y assumes that people will exercise self-direction and self-control in the achievement of organizational objectives *to the degree that they are committed to those objectives* (p. 56).' Seemingly this statement contradicts Skinner in placing the locus of control inside the individual. However, this conflict is reduced a few sentences later when McGregor (1960) added 'Managerial policies and practices materially affect this degree of commitment (p. 56).' Thus, both writers, Skinner far more unequivocally than McGregor, see the external environment as the primary factor in self-control. While McGregor polemicized against control by authority, he was not arguing that man is 'free.' Perhaps the more humanistic tone of McGregor's writing or his specific attention to managerial problems faced in business is responsible for his high esteem among students of management relative to that accorded Skinner. While metaphorically there is great difference, substantively there is little. It would seem, however, that metaphors have led practitioners and students of applied behavioral science to overlook some valuable data and some creative management possibilities.

One major substantive difference between the two approaches exists: it involves intrinsic rewards. McGregor (1966) saw a dichotomy in the effects of intrinsic and extrinsic rewards, noting research which has shown intrinsic ones to be more effective. He concludes the 'mechanical' view (reinforcement theory) is inadequate, because it does not explain the superior outcomes of the use of 'intrinsic' over 'extrinsic' rewards. Here, as will be discussed in more detail later in connection with Herzberg, the problem is McGregor's failure to consider scheduling of reinforcement. 'Intrinsic' rewards in existing organizations may be more effective because they occur on a more appropriate schedule for sustaining behavior than do 'extrinsic' rewards. Intrinsic rewards are given by the environment for task completion or a similar achievement, and often occur on a ratio schedule. The implications of this crucial fact will be discussed shortly in considering Skinner's emphasis on the scheduling of rewards. For the present, it is suggested that McGregor gave little attention to reinforcement schedules and made a qualitative distinction between external and internal rewards. He seems to agree with Skinner that achievement, task completion, and control of the environment are reinforcers in themselves. Skinner's work suggests, however, that these rewards have the same consequences as 'extrinsic' rewards, if they are given on the same schedule.

By way of summary to this point, it appears that more humanistic social scientists have been preferred by managers to behaviorists such as Skinner in their efforts to improve the management of human resources. Perhaps the oversight has been due to the congruence between their values and the metaphysics of people such as McGregor and Maslow. The differences between McGregor and Skinner do not appear to involve open conflict.

To the extent the two approaches agree, the major criterion in employing them would seem to be the degree to which they aid in predicting and controlling behavior toward organizational goals. The work of Skinner and his followers has much to offer in terms of the above criterion. In particular, McGregor's followers might find Skinner's work an asset in implementing Theory *Y*. The remainder of this paper will develop some of the major points of the Skinnerian approach and seek to explore their potential for industrial use.

Conditioning – a synthesis for organizational behavior

The behavioral psychology of Skinner assumes, like Theory *Y*, that rate of behavior is dependent on the external conditions in which the behavior takes place. Like Theory *X*, it stresses the importance of the administration of rewards and punishments. Unlike Theory *X*, Skinnerian psychology places an emphasis on rewards. Like Theory *Y* it emphasizes the role of interdependence between people in a social relationship and thus views the administration of rewards and punishments as an exchange. For those who are unfamiliar with the work of Skinner and his followers, a brief summary follows. Like any summary of an extensive body of work, this review omits a lot of important material. A more detailed, yet simple, introduction to conditioning can be found in Bijou and Baer (1961) and Skinner (1953). Extensions of this work by social exchange theorists such as Homans (1961) suggest that the conditioning model can be extended to a systems approach, contrary to McGregor's (1966) belief.

Generally, conditioned responses can be divided into two classes. Each class is acquired in a different fashion. The first class, generally known as respondent or classically conditioned behavior, describes the responses which are controlled by prior stimulation. These responses, generally thought of as being involuntary or reflexive, are usually made by the 'smooth muscles.' Common ones are salivation and emotional responses. Initially, the presentation of an unconditioned stimulus will elicit a specific response. For example, food placed on one's tongue will generally cause salivation. If a bell is sounded and then food is placed on the tongue, and this process is repeated several times, the sound of the bell by itself will elicit salivation. By this process, stimuli which previously did not control behavior such as the bell, can become a source of behavior control. Many of our likes and dislikes, our anxieties, our feelings of patriotism, and other emotions can be thought of as such involuntary responses. The implications of emotional responses are of major importance to the management of human resources and more will be said about them later. However, the second class of responses, the operants, are of even greater importance.

The rate of operant responses is influenced by events which follow them. These events are considered to be the consequences of behavior. The responses, generally thought to be voluntary, are usually made by striped muscles. All that is necessary for the development of an operant response is that the desired response has a probability of occurring which is greater than zero for the individual involved. Most rapid conditioning results when the desired response is 'reinforced' immediately (preferably about one-half second after the response). In other words, the desired response is followed directly by some consequence. In simple terms, if the outcome is pleasing to the individual, the probability of his repeating the response is apt to be increased. If the consequence is displeasing to the individual, the probability of his repeating the response is apt to be decreased. The process of inducing such change (usually an increase) in the response rate, is called operant conditioning. In general, the frequency of a behavior is said to be a function of its consequences.

The above description of operant conditioning is greatly simplified. The additional considerations which follow will only partially rectify this state. One crucial factor has to do with the frequency with which a given consequence follows a response. There are several possible patterns. Most obviously, the consequence can be continuous (for example, it follows the response every time the response is made). Alternatively a consequence might follow only some of the responses. There are two basic ways in which such partial reinforcement can be administered. First, the consequence can be made contingent on a certain number of responses. Two sub-patterns are possible. Every nth response may be reinforced or an average of $1/n$ of the responses may be reinforced in a random pattern. These two related patterns are called ratio schedules. The former is known as a fixed ratio and the latter is known as a variable ratio. Ratio schedules tend to generate a high rate of response, with the variable ratio schedule leading to a more durable response than both the fixed-ratio and continuous patterns. A second technique of partial reinforcement can be designed where the consequence follows the response only after a certain amount of time has elapsed. The first response made after a specified interval is then reinforced, but all other responses produce neutral stimulus outcomes. This pattern can also be either fixed or variable. Generally, interval schedules develop responses which are quite long lasting when reinforcement is no longer given, but do not yield as rapid a response rate as ratio schedules do. Obviously, mixed patterns of ratio and interval schedules can also be designed.

A second consideration about operant conditioning which deserves brief mention is the concept of a response hierarchy. All the responses which an individual could make under a given set of conditions can be placed in order according to probability that they will be made. In this view, there are two basic strategies for getting an individual to make the desired response. First, one could attempt to reduce the probability of all the more probable responses. Second, one could attempt to increase the probability of the desired response. Of course, some combination of these two approaches may often be used.

Strategies for changing the probability of a response can be implemented by punishment, extinction, and positive reinforcement. Generally punishment and extinction are used to decrease the occurrence of a response whereas positive reinforcement is used to increase its probability. An understanding of these three operations in behavior control is important, not only for knowing how to use them, but chiefly because of their unanticipated consequences or their side-effects.

Punishment is the most widely used technique in our society for behavior control. Perhaps, as Reese (1966) said, the widespread use of punishment is due to the immediate effects it has in stopping or preventing the undesired response. In this sense, the punisher is reinforced for punishing. Also, many of us seem to be influenced by some notion of what Homans (1961) called distributive justice. In order to reestablish what we believe to be equity, we may often be led to punish another person. This ancient assumption of '…an eye for an eye…' has been widely practiced in man's quest for equity and behavior control.

Whatever the reason for punishing, it can be done in two ways, both of which have unfortunate side-effects. First, punishment can be administered in the form of some aversive stimulus such as physical pain or social disapproval. Secondly, it can be administered by withdrawing a desired stimulus. The immediate effect is often the rapid drop in frequency of the punished response. The full effects, unfortunately, are often not clearly recognized. Many of these consequences are crucial for managers of organizations.

Punishment may be an inefficient technique for controlling behavior for a number of reasons. First, the probability of the response may be reduced only when the threat of punishment is perceived to exist. Thus, when the punishing agent is away, the undesired response may occur at its initial rate. Secondly, punishment only serves to reduce the probability of the one response. This outcome does not necessarily produce the desired response, unless that response is the next most probable one in the response hierarchy. Really, what punishment does is to get the individual to do something other than what he has been punished for. A third effect, is that the punishment may interfere with the response being made under desired circumstances. For example, if an organizational member attempts an innovation which is met with punishment by his superiors because they did not feel he had the authority to take the step, it is quite possible that his creative behavior will be reduced even in those areas where his superiors expect him to innovate.

In addition to these effects there are some other important by-products of punishment. Punishment may result in a person making responses which are incompatible with the punished response. Psychological tension, often manifested in emotional behavior such as fear or anxiety, is often the result. Secondly, punishment may lead to avoidance and dislike of the punishing agent. This effect can be especially important to managers who are attempting to build open, helping relationships with subordinates. The roles of punishing agent and helper are often incompatible. Many line-staff conflicts in organizations undoubtedly can be explained in these terms. Finally, punishment may generate counter-aggression. Either through a modeling effect or a justice effect, the punished person may respond with aggressive responses towards the punishing agent or towards some other stimulus.

The second technique for behavior change, commonly called extinction, also focuses primarily on reducing the probability of a response. Extinction arises from repeated trials where the response is followed by a neutral stimulus. This technique generates fewer by-products than punishment. However, like punishment it does not lead to the desired response being developed. Furthermore to the extent that one has built up an expectation of a reward for a certain response, a neutral consequence may be perceived as punishing. Thus, extinction may have some advantages over punishment, but has many of the same limitations.

Positive reinforcement is the final technique for changing behavior. Under conditions of positive reinforcement, the response produces a consequence that results in an increase in the frequency of the response. It is commonly stated that such a consequence is rewarding, pleasing, or drive reducing for the individual. The operant conditioners, however, avoid such inferences and define positive reinforcers, as stimuli which increase the probability of a preceding response. Positive reinforcement is efficient for several reasons. First, it increases the probable occurrence of the desired response. The process involves rewarding approximations to the direct response itself immediately after it is made. The desired behavior is being directly developed as opposed to successive suppression of undesired acts. Secondly, the adverse emotional responses associated with punishment and extinction are apt to be reduced and in fact favorable emotions may be developed. Since people tend to develop positive affect to others who reward them the 'trainer' is apt to become positively valenced in the eyes of the 'learner.'

By way of summary, Skinner's (1953) approach suggested that the control of behavior change involves a reduction in the probability of the most prepotent response and/or an increase in the probability of some desired response. Punishment and extinction may be used. These means can only reduce the probability of the unwanted response being made. Also, they may have undesired side-effects. The third technique, positive reinforcement, has the important advantage of developing the desired response rather than merely reducing the chances of an undesired one. Also, positive reinforcement is apt to produce favorable rather than unfavorable 'side-effects' on organizational relationships.

This approach seems to suggest that both or neither Theory X and Theory Y assumptions are useful. This section suggested that conditioning may be both Theory X and Theory Y. Perhaps since the operant view does not make either set of assumptions, it is neither Theory X nor Theory Y. Operant conditioning is consistent with Theory Y in suggesting that the limits on human beings are a function of the organizational setting, but Like Theory X, implies something about human nature; namely that deprivation or threat of some sort of deprivation is a precondition for behavior to be controlled. From the managerial perspective, however, the nomonological question is of little significance. The important thing to managers is behavior and the major point of this approach is that behavior is a function of its consequences. Good management is that which leads to the desired behavior by organizational members. Management must see to it that the consequences of behavior are such as to increase the frequency of desired behavior and decrease the frequency of undesired behaviors. The question becomes, how can managers develop a social system which provides the appropriate consequences? In many ways the answer to this question is similar to what Theory Y advocates have suggested. However, there are some new possibilities.

Applications of conditioning in organizations

The potential uses of the Skinnerian framework for social systems are increasing rapidly. The approach has far more applicability to complex social systems than has often been recognized. McGregor's rejection of the stimulus-response or the reward-punishment approach as inadequate for management because it does not allow for a systems approach is quite inconsistent with this general trend and his own environmentally based approach. Recent work in the field of behavioral control has begun to refute McGregor's position. The Skinnerian view can be and has been used to redesign social systems.

The most complete redesign was envisioned by Skinner (1948) in his novel, *Walden Two*. In this book, Skinner developed a society based on the use of positive reinforcement and experimental ethics geared to the goal of competition of a coordinated social unit with its environment. In other words, the system is designed to reward behaviors which are functional for the whole society. Social change is introduced on the basis of empirical data. A a result of the success of this system, man is enabled to pursue those activities which are rewarding in themselves. Although the book is a novel, it can be a valuable stimulus for thought about the design of social organization.

In addition, Skinner (1954) has taken a fresh look at teaching and learning in conventional educational systems. He noted that the school system depends heavily on aversive control or punishment. The use of low marks and ridicule have merely been substituted for the 'stick.' The teacher, in Skinner's view, is an out of date reinforcing mechanism. He suggested the need to examine the reinforcers which are available in the system and to apply them in a manner which is consistent with what is known about learning. For example, control over the environment itself may be rewarding. Perhaps grades reinforce the wrong behavior and are administered on a rather poor schedule. It would seem that a search for new reinforcers and better reinforcement schedules is appropriate for all modern organizations.

These speculations suggest the potential for great advances. *Walden Two* is in many ways an ideal society but has been a source of horror to many readers. The thoughts about changes in teaching methods are also a subject of controversy. However, the environment can be designed to aid in the attainment of desired ends. People resist the idea that they can be controlled by their environment. This resistance does not change the fact that they are under such control. Recently evidence has begun to accumulate that the Skinnerian approach can be employed to design social systems.

Much of this evidence was collected in settings far removed from modern work organizations. The reader's initial response is apt to be, 'What relevance do these studies have to my organization?' Obviously, the relationship is not direct. However, if, as the operant approach maintains, the conditioning process describes the acquisition and maintenance of behavior, the same principles can be applied to any social organization. The problem of application becomes merely that of engineering. The gains may well be limited only by an administrator's ingenuity and resources.

Much of the evidence comes from studies of hospitalized mental patients and autistic children, although some has been based on normal lower class children. A few examples from these studies will serve to document the great potential of the conditioning methods for social systems. Allyon and Azrin (1965) observed mental patients' behavior to determine what activities they engaged in when they had a chance. They then made tokens contingent on certain responses such as work on hospital tasks. These tokens could be exchanged for the activities the patients preferred to engage in. The results of this approach were amazing. In one experiment five schizophrenics and three mental defectives served as *S*s. They did jobs regularly and adequately when tokens were given for the job. Such performance was reported to be in sharp contrast to the erratic and inconsistent behavior characteristic of such patients. When the tokens were no longer contingent on the work, the performance dropped almost to zero. In a second experiment, a whole ward of 44 patients served as *S*s. A similar procedure was followed and 11 classes of tasks observed. When tokens were contingent upon the desired responses, the group spent an average of 45 hours on the tasks daily. When tokens were not contingent on responses, almost no time was spent on the tasks. The implications seem rather clear. When desired behavior is rewarded, it will be emitted, when it is not rewarded, it will not be emitted.

A great deal of related work has been reported. Allyon (1966) and Wolf, Risley, and Mees (1966) have shown how a reinforcement procedure can be effective in controlling the behavior of a psychotic patient and of an autistic child respectively. These are but a few of the many studies in a growing body of evidence.

More important for present purposes are the applications of this approach in more complex social situations. The work of Hamblin *et al.* (1967) shows some of the interesting possibilities of the conditioning approach for school classes and aggressive children. A token system was used to shape desired behavior. Through the application of the conditioning approach to the school system, gains may be made in educating children from deprived backgrounds. Two examples will illustrate these possibilities.

The first example comes from a recent newspaper story. A record shop owner in a Negro area of Chicago reported seeing the report card of a Negro boy. The owner thought the boy was bright, but the report card showed mostly unsatisfactory performance. He told the boy he would give him $5 worth of free records if he got all 'excellents' on the next report card. Ten weeks later the boy returned with such a card to collect his reward. The owner reported that similar offers to other children had a remarkable effect in getting them to study and do their homework. The anecdote demonstrates what everyone knows anyway: people will work for rewards. It also suggests the converse: people will not work if rewards do not exist. The problems of education in the ghetto and motivation to work in general, may be overcome by appropriate reinforcement. Further support for this statement comes from the work of Montrose Wolf.

Wolf (1966) ran a school for children, most of whom were sixth graders, in a lower class Negro area of Kansas City. The children attended this school for several hours after school each day and on Saturday. Rewards were given in the form of tickets which could be saved and turned in for different kinds of things like toys, food, movies, shopping trips, and other activities. Tickets were made contingent on academic performance within the remedial school itself, and on performance in the regular school system. The results were remarkable. The average regular school grade of the students was raised to C from D. The results on standard achievement tests showed the remedial group progressed over twice as much in one year as they had done the previous year. They showed twice as much progress as a control group. Other gains were also noted. Wolf reported that a severe punishment was not to let the children attend school. They expressed strong discontent when school was not held because of a holiday. He further noted that when reading was no longer rewarded with tickets, the students still continued to read more than before the training. Arithmetic and English did not maintain these increments. Thus, to some extent, reading appeared to be intrinsically rewarding.

A final point concerns the transferability of skills learned in such a school to society at large. Will the tasks that are not rewarding in themselves be continued? The answer is probably not, unless other rewards are provided. The task then becomes to develop skills and behavior which society itself will reward. If this method is applied to develop behavior which is rewarded by society, the behavior is apt to be maintained. The same argument holds for organizational behavior. It will be fruitless to develop behavior which is not rewarded in the organization.

In summary, evidence has been presented to show the relevance of the Skinnerian approach to complex social systems. Certainly the evidence is only suggestive of future possibilities. The rest of this paper attempts to suggest some of these implications for organizational management.

Management through positive reinforcement

The implications of the systematic use of positive reinforcement for management range over many traditional areas. Some of the more important areas include training and personnel development, compensation and alternative rewards, supervision and leadership, job design, organizational design, and organizational change.

Training and personnel development

The area of training has been the first to benefit from the application of conditioning principles with the use of programmed learning and the teaching machine. An example of future potential comes from the Northern Systems Company Training Method for assembly line work. In this system, the program objectives are broken down into subobjectives. The training employs a lattice which provides objective relationships between functions and objectives, indicates critical evaluation points, and presents a visual display of go-no-go functions. Progress through various steps is reinforced by rewards. To quote from a statement of the training method '... the trainee gains satisfaction only by demonstrated performance at the tool stations. Second, he quickly perceives that correct behaviors obtain for him the satisfaction of his needs, and that incorrect behaviors do not (p. 20).' Correct performance includes not only job skills, but also the performance of social interaction which is necessary in a factory setting. The skills taught are designed to allow for high mobility in the industrial world. The Northern System's method develops behavior which the economic and social system will normally reinforce and has been successful in training people in a wide variety of skills. Its potential in training such groups as the 'hard-core' unemployed seems to be limited only by the resources and creativity of program designers.

The Skinnerian approach seems to have potential for all areas of personnel development, not only for highly programmed tasks. Reinforcement theory may be useful in the development of such behaviors as creativity. The work of Maltzman, Simon, Roskin, and Licht (1960) demonstrated this possibility. After a series of experiments employing a standard experimental training procedure with free association materials, these investigators concluded that a highly reliable increase in uncommon responses could be produced through the use of reinforcement. The similarity of their results to those of operant experiments with respect to the persistance of the responses and the effect of repetitions, led them to conclude that originality is a form of operant behaviour. Positive reinforcement increased the rate at which original responses were emitted.

Support is also available for the efficacy of operant conditioning to more conventional personnel and leadership development. Three such contributions are discussed below. The first concerns the organizational environment as a shaper of behavior of which Fleishman's (1967) study is a case in point. He found that human relations training programs were only effective in producing on-the-job changes if the organizational climate was supportive of the content of the program. More generally it would appear that industrial behavior is a function of its consequences. Those responses which are rewarded will persist: those responses which are not rewarded or are punished will decrease in frequency. If the organizational environment does not reward responses developed in a training program, the program will be, at best, a total waste of time and money. As Sykes (1962) has shown, at worst, such a program may be highly disruptive. A second implication of operant conditioning concerns the content of personnel development programs in the area of human relations. If, as Homans (1961) and others have suggested, social interaction is also influenced by the same operant principles, then people in interaction are constantly 'shaping' or conditioning each other. The behavior of a subordinate is to some degree developed by his boss and vice-versa. What more sensible, practical point could be taught to organizational members than that they are teaching their fellow participants to behave in a certain manner? What more practical, sensible set of principles could be taught than that, due to latent dysfunctions generated, punishment and extinction procedures are less efficient ways to influence behavior than positive reinforcement? Clearly, the behavioral scientists who have contributed so greatly to organizational practice and personnel development have not put enough emphasis on these simple principles. The third implication for personnel development is added recognition that annual merit interviews and salary increments are very inefficient development techniques. The rewards or punishments are so delayed that they can be expected to have little feedback value for the employees involved. More frequent appraisals and distribution of rewards are apt to be far more effective, especially to the degree that they are related to specific tasks or units of work.

Job design

Recently, behavioral scientists have emphasized the social psychological factors which need to be attended to in job design. McGregor and others have suggested job enlargement. Herzberg (1968) has argued that job enlargement just allows an individual to do a greater variety of boring jobs and suggests that 'job enrichment' is needed. For present purposes, job enlargement and job enrichment will be lumped together. Both of these approaches are consistent with the conditioning view if two differences can be resolved. First, the definitions of motivation must be translated into common terms. Second, reinforcers operating in the newly designed jobs must be delineated and tested to see if the reinforcers postulated in the newly designed jobs are really responsible for behavioral changes or if there are other reinforcers operating.

With respect to the definitions of motivation, the two approaches are really similar in viewing the rate of behavior as the crucial factor. The major differences exist on the conceptual level. Both job enlargement and job enrichment are attempts to increase motivation. Conceptually, McGregor and Herzberg tend to view motivation as some internal state. The conditioning approach does not postulate internal states but rather deals with the manipulation of environmental factors which influence the rate of behavior. Actually, some combination of the two approaches may be most useful theoretically as Vinacke (1962) has suggested. However, if both approaches are viewed only at the operational level, it is quite probable that rates of behavior could be agreed on as an acceptable criterion. Certainly from the practitioners viewpoint, behavior is the crucial variable. When a manager talks about a motivated worker, he often means one who frequently makes desired responses at a high rate without external prompting from the boss. The traditional view of motivation as an inner-drive is of limited practical and theoretical value.

If both approaches could agree on the behavioral criterion, at least on an operational level, the operant approach could be employed to help resolve some practical and theoretical problems suggested by the work of McGregor and Herzberg. Since, generally speaking, the external conditions are most easily manipulated in an organization, attention can be focused on designing an environment which increases the frequency of the wanted responses. As a result, practitioners and students of organization could deal with motivation without searching for man's essence. We can avoid the metaphysical assumptions of Maslow and McGregor until they are better documented. The issue of a two-factor theory of motivation proposed by Herzberg which recently has been severely challenged by Lindsay, Marks, and Gorlow (1967) and Hulin and Smith (1967) among others can also be avoided. Attention can be confined to developing systems which produce high rates of desired behavior. Thus the conceptual differences about motivation do not cause unresolvable conflict at the present time.

The second area of difference between McGregor–Herzberg and the operant explanation of the effects of job enrichment stems from the failure of Herzberg and McGregor to recognize the great variety of possible rewards available in job design. The Skinnerian approach leads to the development of a more comprehensive discussion of the rewards from enriched or enlarged jobs. In terms of the operant approach, both job enrichment and job enlargement are apt to lead to what would generally be called greater motivation or what we will call higher rates of desired behavior. McGregor and Herzberg suggest feelings of achievement and responsibility explain these results. The reinforcement approach leads to a search for specific rewards in these newly designed jobs.

Job enlargement can be viewed simply as increasing the variety of tasks a person does. Recent research on self-stimulation and sensory deprivation has suggested that stimulation itself is reinforcing, especially when one has been deprived of it. The increased variety of tasks due to job enlargement may thus be intrinsically rewarding due to a host of reinforcers in the work itself rather than to any greater feeling of responsibility or achievement. These feelings may be a cause of greater productivity or merely correlates of the receipt of these intrinsic rewards from stimulation. The evidence is not clear, but the effects of job enlargement can at least be partially explained in operant terms.

Some additional support from this idea comes from Schultz's (1964) work on spontaneous alternation of behavior. Schultz suggested that spontaneous alternation of human behavior is facilitated (1) when responses are not reinforced and/or are not subjected to knowledge of correctness, (2) by the amount of prior exercise of one response alternative, and (3) by a short intertrial interval. Low feedback and reinforcement, short intervals between responses, and the frequent repetition of one response are all characteristic of many jobs which need enlargement. Merely making different responses may be rewarding to a worker, thereby explaining some of the benefits noted from job enlargement. It has also been noted that people create variation for themselves in performing monotonous tasks. For example, ritualized social interaction in the form of social 'games' is a form of such alternation workers developed noted by Roy (1964).

By way of summary, much of the current work on job enlargement and enrichment has attributed the effects to feelings of achievement or responsibility, without taking into account numerous other possible reinforcers which may be more basic. Further research to determine the efficacy of these various possibilities is needed before definite conclusions can be drawn. Do the feelings of achievement or responsibility operate as reinforcers in an operant manner? Do these feelings come from other more basic rewards as task variety? Present data does not permit answers to these questions.

With respect to the benefits noted from job enrichment, an operant model may provide further insights. Herzberg (1968) maintained that some jobs can not be 'enriched' or made more motivating in themselves. It is the contention of this paper that it is not the tasks which are the problem, but it is the reinforcement schedules. For example, what could be more boring, have less potential for achievement and realization of Herzberg's satisfiers, than the game of bingo. Yet people will sit for hours at bingo, often under punishing conditions (since the house takes in more than it pays out) and place tokens on numbers. Similar behavior is exhibited at slot-machines and other gambling devices. Most operational definitions of motivation would agree that these players are highly motivated. The reason is clear from the operant viewpoint. The reinforcement schedule employed in games of chance, the variable ratio schedule, is a very powerful device for maintaining a rapid rate of response. With respect to job design, the important requirement is that rewards follow performance on an effective schedule.

The type of rewards Herzberg (1968) called satisfiers may be important motivators because they are distributed on a variable ratio schedule. Herzberg's data does not rule out this explanation. Take achievement, for example. If a person is doing a job from which it is possible to get a feeling of achievement, there must be a reasonably large probability that a person will not succeed on the task. Often times, this condition means that some noncontinuous schedule of reinforcement is operating. An individual will succeed only on some variable ratio schedule. In addition, successful completion of the task is often the most important reward. The reward is, of course, immediate. A similar statement could be made about tasks which are said to yield intrinsic satisfaction, such as crossword puzzles or enriched jobs. Thus the factors Herzberg called motivators may derive their potency from the manner in which the rewards are administered. The task is immediately and positively reinforced by the environment on a variable ratio schedule. Often the schedule is one which rewards a very small fraction of a large number of responses. Since behavior is a function of its consequences, if jobs can be designed to reinforce desired behavior in the appropriate manner, 'motivated' workers are apt to result. Some of Herzberg's results may be explained without resort to a two-factor theory more parsimoniously in terms of schedules of reinforcement. Herzberg's (1966) finding that recognition is only a motivator if it is contingent on performance further documents the operant argument.

Another suggestion for job design from the operant tradition was suggested by Homans. He explored the relationship of the frequency of an activity and satisfaction to the amount of a reward. He concluded that satisfaction is generally positively related to the amount of reward whereas frequency of an activity is negatively related to the amount of reward the individual has received in the recent past. In order to have both high satisfaction and high activity, Homans (1961) suggested that tasks need to be designed in a manner such that repeated activities lead up to the accomplishment of some final result and get rewarded at a very low frequency until just before the final result is achieved. Then the reinforcement comes often. For example, consider the job of producing bottled soda. An optimal design would have the reward immediate on the completion of putting the caps on the bottles, but the task would be designed such that all the operations prior to capping were completed before any capping was done. Near the end of a work day, all the capping could be done. High output and satisfaction might then exist simultaneously. In general then, the operant approach suggests some interesting possibilities for designing jobs in ways which would maximize the power of reinforcers in the job itself.

A similar argument can be applied to some problems faced in administration and management. For example, it is commonly recognized that programmed tasks tend to be attended to before unprogrammed ones. It is quite obvious that programmed functions produce a product which is often tangible. The product itself is a reinforcer. An unprogrammed task often requires behavior which has not been reinforced in the past and will not produce a reward in the near future. It may be beneficial to provide rewards relatively early for behavior on unprogrammed tasks. This suggestion will be difficult to put into practice because of the very nature of unprogrammed tasks. Perhaps the best that can be done is to reward the working on such tasks.

Compensation and alternative rewards

Although whether money is a true 'generalized reinforcer' as Skinner suggests, has not been demonstrated conclusively, for years operant principles have been applied in the form of monetary incentive systems. Opsahl and Dunnette (1966) concluded that such programs generally do increase output. However, the restriction of output and other unanticipated consequences are associated with these programs. Many writers have attributed these consequences to social forces, such as the desire for approval from one's peers. Gewirtz and Baer (1958), for example, have shown that social approval has the same effects as other reinforcers in an operant situation.

Dalton's (1948) famous study on rate-busters may be interpreted to show that people who are more 'group-oriented' may place a higher value on social approval and hence are more apt to abide by group production norms than are less 'group-oriented' people. Thus, it is not that money in piece-rate systems is not a potential reinforcer, but rather other reinforcers are more effective, at least after a certain level of monetary reward.

The successful use of the Scanlon Plan demonstrates the value of combining both economic and social rewards. This plan rewards improved work with several types of reinforcers, and often more immediately and directly than many incentive systems. The Scanlon Plan combines economic rewards, often given monthly, with social rewards. The latter are given soon after an employee's idea has been submitted or used.

Related arguments can be made for other group incentive programs. Often jobs are interdependent. The appropriate reinforcement for such tasks should be contingent upon interdependent responses, not individual ones. Even if the jobs are independent, the workers are social-psychologically interdependent. Social rewards are often obtainable by restricting output. It is hardly surprising that individual incentive programs have produced the unanticipated consequences so often noted. Further, since rewards and punishments from the informal group are apt to be administered immediately and frequently they are apt to be very powerful in controlling behavior.

In general then, money and other rewards must be made contingent on the desired responses. Further, the importance of alternative rewards to money must be recognized and incorporated into the design of the work environment. The widely known path-goal to productivity model expresses a similar point.

Another problem of compensation in organizations is also apparent in an operant context. Often, means of compensation, especially fringe benefits, have the unanticipated consequence of reinforcing the wrong responses. Current programs of sick pay, recreation programs, employee lounges, work breaks, and numerous other personnel programs all have one point in common. They all reward the employee for not working or for staying away from the job. These programs are not 'bad,' since often they may act to reduce problems such as turnover. However, an employer who relies on them should realize what behavior he is developing by establishing these costly programs. Alternative expenditures must be considered. If some of the money that was allocated for these programs was used to redesign jobs so as to be more reinforcing in themselves, more productive effort could be obtained. This idea is certainly not new. A host of behavioral scientists have suggested that resources devoted to making performance of the job itself more attractive will pay social and/or economic dividends.

Another interesting application of conditioning principles has to to with the schedule on which pay is distributed. The conventional pay schedule is a fixed interval one. Further, pay often is not really contingent on one's performance. The response needed to be rewarded is often attending work on pay day. Not only is pay often not contingent upon performance, but the fixed interval schedule is not given to generating a high response rate. In a creative article, Aldis (1966) suggested an interesting compensation program employing a variable ratio schedule. Instead of an annual Christmas bonus or other types of such expected salary supplements, he suggested a lottery system. If an employee produced above an agreed upon standard, his name would be placed in a hat. A drawing would be held. The name(s) drawn would receive an amount of money proportionate to the number of units produced during that period of time. This system would approximate the desired variable ratio schedule.

In addition to the prosperity of the owners of gambling establishments, there is some direct evidence that variable ratio schedules will be of use to those charged with predicting and controlling human behavior. A leading St. Louis hardware company although apparently unaware of the work of the operant conditioners, has applied an approximate variable ratio schedule of reinforcement to reduce absenteeism and tardiness. Although the complete data is not available, the personnel department has reported surprising success. A brief description of the system will be presented below and a more detailed study will be written in the near future.

Under the lottery system, if a person is on time (that is, not so much as $\frac{1}{2}$ minute late) for work at the start of his day and after his breaks, he is eligible for a drawing at the end of the month. Prizes worth approximately $20 to $25 are awarded to the winners. One prize is available for each 25 eligible employees. At the end of six months, people who have had perfect attendance for the entire period are eligible for a drawing for a color television set. The names of all the winners and of those eligible are also printed in the company paper, such that social reinforcement may also be a factor. The plan was introduced because tardiness and absenteeism had become a very serious problem. In the words of the personnel manager, absenteeism and tardiness '…were lousy before.' Since the program was begun 16 months ago, conditions have improved greatly. Sick leave costs have been reduced about 62%. After the first month, 151 of approximately 530 employees were eligible for the drawing. This number has grown larger, although not at a steady rate to 219 for the most recent month. Although the comparable figures for the period before the program were unfortunately not available, management has noted great improvements. It would appear that desired behavior by organization participants in terms of tardiness and absenteeism can be readily and inexpensively developed by a variable ratio schedule of positive reinforcement. The possibilities for other areas are limited largely by the creativity of management.

The operant approach also has some additional implications for the use of money as a reward. First, many recent studies have shown money is not as important as other job factors in worker satisfaction. Herzberg, (1968) among others, has said explicitly that money will not promote worker satisfaction. Undoubtedly, in many situations, Herzberg is correct. However, crucial factors of reward contingencies and schedules have not been controlled in these studies. Again, it appears that the important distinction that can be made between Herzberg's motivators and hygiene factors is that the former set of rewards are contingent on an individual's responses and the latter are not. If a work situation were designed so that money was directly contingent on performance, the results might be different. A second point has to do with the perception of money as a reward. Opsahl and Dunnette (1966) have recently questioned pay secrecy policies. They maintained that pay secrecy leads to misperception of the amount of money that a promotion might mean. The value of the reinforcers are underestimated by the participants suggesting that they are less effective than they might otherwise be. Certainly, alternative rewards are likely to be 'over chosen.' By following policies of pay secrecy, organizations seem to be failing to utilize fully their available monetary rewards.

In addition to underutilization of money rewards, organizations seem to be almost totally unaware of alternative reinforcers, and in fact see punishment as the only viable method of control when existing reinforcers fail. What are some alternatives to a punishment centered bureaucracy? Some, such as job design, improved scheduling of reinforcement, and a search for new reinforcers have already been suggested. There are other possible reinforcers, a few of which are discussed below.

The important thing about reinforcers is that they be made immediately contingent on desired performance to the greatest degree possible. The potential reinforcers discussed here also require such a contingent relationship, although developing such relationships may be a severe test of an administrator's creativity.

One of the more promising reinforcers is leisure. It would seem possible in many jobs to establish an agreed upon standard output for a day's work. This level could be higher than the current average. Once this amount is reached, the group or individual could be allowed the alternative of going home. The result of experiments in this direction would be interesting to all concerned. Quite possibly, this method might lead to a fuller utilization of our labor force. The individual may be able to hold two four-hour jobs, doubling his current contribution. Such a tremendous increase in output is quite possible as Stagner and Rosen (1966) have noted, when the situation possesses appropriate contingencies. Certainly, the problems of industrial discipline, absenteeism, and grievances which result in lower productivity might be ameliorated. Another possible reinforcer is information. Guetzkow (1965) noted that people have a strong desire to receive communication. Rewarding desired performance with communication or feedback may be a relatively inexpensive reinforcer. Graphs, charts, or even tokens which show immediate and cumulative results may serve this function. Some of the widely accepted benefits from participative management may be due to the reinforcing effect of communication. Certainly the 'Hawthorne effect' can be described in these terms. In addition, social approval and status may be powerful reinforcers. Blau's classic study described by Homans (1961) on the exchange of approval and status for help is but one example. People will work for approval and status. If these are made contingent on a desired set of responses, the response rate can be increased. At present, often social approval is given by one's peers, but is contingent on behavior which is in conflict with organizational goals.

In addition to these reinforcers, there are certain social exchange concepts such as justice, equity, reciprocity, and indebtedness which deserve attention. Recent research has demonstrated that an unbalanced social exchange, such as one which is inequitable or leaves one person indebted to someone else, may be tension producing in such a way that individuals work to avoid them. In other words, unbalanced exchanges are a source of punishment. Relationships, such as those involving dependency, which result in such social imbalance can be expected to have the same latent consequences as punishment. Techniques which employ social imbalance to predict and control behavior can be expected to be less efficient in most respects than ones based on positive reinforcement.

The crucial variable in distributing any reward is contingency. Managers have been quick to point out that the problem with a 'welfare-state' is that rewards do not depend on desired behavior. This point is well taken. It is surprising that the same point has not been recognized in current management practices.

Organizational climate and design

Important aspects of human behavior can be attributed to the immediate environment in which people function. The potential then exists to structure and restructure formal organizations in a manner to promote the desired behavior. Once this point is recognized and accepted by managers, progress can begin. The reaction of managers to this approach is often, 'You mean my organization should reward people for what they ought to do anyway?' The answer is that people's behavior is largely determined by its outcomes. It is an empirical fact rather than a moral question. If you want a certain response and it does not occur, you had better change the reinforcement contingencies to increase its probable occurrence.

The first step in the direction of designing organizations on this basis involves defining explicitly the desired behaviors and the available reinforcers. The next step is to then make these rewards dependent on the emission of the desired responses. What are some of the implications of such reasoning for organizational design?

Already the importance of organizational climate has been discussed in connection with human development. Some additional implications merit brief consideration. A major one concerns conformity. Often today the degree to which people conform to a wide variety of norms is lamentably acknowledged and the question is asked, 'Why do people do it?' The reasons in the operant view are quite clear: conformity is rewarded, deviance is punished. People conform in organizations because conformity is profitable in terms of the outcomes the individual achieves. In fact, Nord (in press) and Walker and Heyns (1962) presented considerable evidence that conformity has the same properties as other operant responses. If managers are really worried about the costs of conformity in terms of creativity and innovation, they must look for ways to reward deviance, to avoid punishing nonconformity, and to avoid rewarding conformity. Furthermore, the way in which rewards are administered is important. Generally, if rewards are given by a person or group of people, a dependency relationship is created, with hostility, fear, anxiety, and other emotional outcomes being probable. Dependence itself may be a discomforting condition. It is therefore desirable to make the rewards come from the environment. Rewards which have previously been established for reaching certain agreed upon goals are one such means. Meaningful jobs, in which achievement in itself is rewarding are another way. In general, to the degree that competition is with the environment or forces outside the organization, and rewards come from achievement itself, the more effective the reinforcers are apt to be in achieving desired responses.

A final point concerns the actual operation of organizations. Increasingly it is recognized that a formal organization, which aims at the coordination of the efforts of its participants, is dependent on informal relationships for its operation. As Gross (1968) noted

> In administration, also, 'the play's the thing' and not the script. Many aspects of even the simplest operation can never be expressed in writing. They must be sensed and felt … Daily action is the key channel of operational definition. In supplying cues and suggestions, in voicing praise and blame, in issuing verbal instructions, administrators define or clarify operational goals in real life (p. 406).

More generally, what makes an organization 'tick' is the exchange of reinforcers within it and between it and its environment. The nature of these exchanges involves both economic and social reinforcers. Many of these are given and received without explicit recognition or even awareness on the part of the participants. The operant approach focuses attention on these exchange processes. As a result, it may prove to be an invaluable asset to both administrators and students of administration and organization.

A final advantage of the operant approach for current organizational theory and analysis may be the attention it focuses on planned and rational administration. Gouldner (1966) noted 'Modern organizational analysis by sociologists is overpreoccupied with the spontaneous and unplanned responses which organizations make to stress, and too little concerned with patterns of planned and rational administration (p. 397).' The Skinnerian approach leads to rational planning in order to control outcomes previously viewed as spontaneous consequences. This approach could expand the area of planning and rational action in administration.

References

Aldis, O. Of pigeons and men. In R. Ulrich, T. Stachnik and J. Mabry (eds.), *Control of human behavior*. Glenview, Ill.: Scott, Foresman, 1966, pp. 218–21.

Ayllon, T. Intensive treatment of psychotic behavior by stimulus satiation and food reinforcement. In R. Ulrich, T. Stachnik and T. Mabry (eds.), *Control of human behavior.* Glenview, Ill.: Scott, Foresman, 1966, pp. 170–76.

Ayllon, T. and Azrin, N. H. The measurement and reinforcement of behavior of psychotics. *Journal of the Experimental Analysis of Behavior,* 1965, 8, 357–83.

Bijou, S. W. and Baer, D. M. *Child development.* Vol. 1. New York: Appleton-Century-Crofts, 1961.

Dalton, M. The industrial 'rate-buster': A characterization. *Applied Anthropology,* 1948, 7, 5–18.

Fleishman, E. A. Leadership climate, human relations training, and supervisory behavior. In E. A. Fleishman, (ed.), *Studies in personnel and industrial psychology.* Homewood, Ill.: Dorsey, 1967, pp. 250–63.

Free records given for E's, pupils report cards improve. *St. Louis Post Dispatch,* December 3, 1967.

Gewirtz, J. L. and Baer, D. M. Deprivation and satiation of social reinforcers as drive conditions. *Journal of Abnormal and Social Psychology,* 1958, 57, 165–72.

Gouldner, A. W. Organizational analysis. In Bennis, W. G., Benne, K. D. and Chin, R. (eds.), *The planning of change.* New York: Holt, Rinehart, and Winston, 1966, pp. 393–99.

Gross, B. M. *Organizations and their managing.* New York: Free Press, 1968.

Guetzkow, H. Communications in organizations. In J. G. March (ed.), *Handbook of organizations.* Chicago: Rand McNally, 1965, pp. 534–73.

Hamblin, R. L., Bushell, O. B., Buckholdt, D., Ellis, D., Ferritor, D., Merritt, G., Pfeiffer, C., Shea, D., and Stoddard, D. Learning, problem children and a social exchange system. Annual Report of the Social Exchange Laboratories, Washington University, and Student Behavior Laboratory, Webster College, St. Louis, Mo. August, 1967.

Herzberg, F. One more time: How do you motivate employees? *Harvard Business Review,* January–February 1968, pp. 53–62.

Herzberg, F. *Work and the nature of man.* Cleveland: World, 1966.

Homans, G. C. *Social behavior: Its elementary forms.* New York: Harcourt, Brace & World, 1961.

Hulin, C. L. and Smith, P. A. An empirical investigation of two implications of the two-factor theory of job satisfaction. *Journal of Applied Psychology,* 1967, 51, 396–402.

Lindsay, C. A., Marks, E., and Gorlow, L. The Herzberg theory: A critique and reformulation. *Journal of Applied Psychology,* 1967, 51, 330–39.

Maltzman, I., Simon, S., Roskin, D., and Licht, L. Experimental studies in the training of originality. *Psychological Monographs: General and Applied,* 1960, 74 (6, Whole No. 493).

Maslow, A. *Eupsychian management.* Homewood, Ill.: Dorsey, 1965.

McGregor, D. *The human side of enterprise.* New York: McGraw-Hill, 1960.

McGregor, D. *Leadership and motivation.* Cambridge, Mass.: M. I. T. Press, 1966.

Nord, W. R. Social exchange theory: An integrative approach to social conformity. *Psychological Bulletin,* (in press).

Northern Systems Company, A proposal to the department of labor for development of a prototype project for the new industries program. Part one.

Opsahl, R. L. and Dunnette, M. D. The role of financial compensation in industrial motivation. *Psychological Bulletin,* 1966, 66, 94–118.

Reese, E. P. *The analysis of human operant behaviour.* Dubuque, La.: William C. Brown, 1966.

Roy, D. F. 'Banana time' Job satisfaction and informal interaction. In Bennis, W. G., Schein, E. H., Berlew, D. E., and Steele, F. I. (eds.), *Interpersonal dynamics.* Homewood, Ill.: Dorsey, 1964, 583–600.

Schultz, D. P. Spontaneous alteration behavior in humans, implications for psychological research. *Psychological Bulletin,* 1964, 62, 394–400.

Skinner, B. F. *Science and human behavior,* New York: Macmillan, 1953.

Skinner, B. F. The science of learning and the art of teaching. *Harvard Educational Review,* 1954, 24, 86–97.

Skinner, B. F. *Walden two.* New York: Macmillen, 1948.

Stagner, R. and Rosen, H. *Psychology of union-management relations.* Belmont, Cal.: Wadsworth, 1966.

Sykes, A. J. M. The effect of a supervisory training course in changing supervisors' perceptions and expectations of the role of management. *Human Relations*, 1962, 15, 227–43.

Vinacke, E. W. Motivation as a complex problem. *Nebraska symposium on motivation*, 1962, 10, 1–45.

Walker, E. L., and Heyns, R. W. *An anatomy of conformity*. Englewood Cliffs, N.J.: Prentice-Hall, 1962.

Wolf, M. M. Paper read at Sociology Colloquium, Washington University, December 5, 1966.

Wolf, M. M., Risley, T., and Mees, H. Application of operant conditioning procedures to the behavior problems of an autistic child. In R. Ulrich, T. Stachnik and T. Mabry (eds.), *Control of human behavior*. Glenview, Ill.: Scott, Foresman, 1966, pp. 187–93.

should personality assessment be a part of selection? (1994)

'Personality and personnel selection', by Ivan T. Robertson, in C. L. Cooper and D. M. Rousseau (eds), *Trends in Organizational Behavior*, John Wiley, London, 1994, pp. 75–89.

The debate surrounding the use of personality assessment in employee selection generated a lot of attention during the 1990s. The growth in use of such techniques is based on the belief that personality is related in some way to career and job success. However, the hard evidence reveals only limited links between measures of personality on the one hand and measures of job performance on the other. If a personality assessment cannot predict performance in a job, then that assessment can have only limited value as a selection tool. In this article, Ivan Roberston weighs the evidence, and makes a compelling case for the continued use and further development of these techniques as practical organizational tools.

learning objectives

Once you have read and understood this article, you should be able to:

1 Appreciate the difficulties in correlating personality measures with job performance.
2 Understand and apply the concept of 'reciprocal determinism'.
3 Apply Robertson's model of personality and job performance to your own work.

learning pre-requisites

You will find it useful first to read Chapter 6 in the core text, on personality. This article is cited in that chapter which also uses Robertson's summary figure, relating personality constructs to job performance.

learning activities

1 Using Bandura's framework of 'reciprocal determinism', construct an example from your own recent experience which illustrates: (a) how your behaviour is influenced by your predispositions and by your situation; and (b) how your experience has influenced your character, and affected your situation.
2 Draw up your own framework diagram listing the 'big five' personality factors, and the features of high and low scorers on each. Construct your own personality profile across these five factors, by indicating where you feel you would score high or low.
3 Draw Robertson's 'personality and job performance' figure as it applies to you, and to your work as a student. Enter your own profile in the 'personality constructs' box. Identify the ideal 'work competences' of an effective student. List what you regard as the main 'job demands' and 'situational factors'. Can this

approach predict your overall academic performance? Can you identify from this analysis actions – for you, for your instructor – that would improve your academic performance?

READING
6
Personality and personnel selection*
Ivan T. Robertson

Personality constructs and theoretical ideas from the personality domain have featured in the personnel selection research literature in only a limited number of ways. By far the most important and extensively researched theme involves the use of personality assessment in personnel selection decision-making. This chapter concentrates on this use of personality assessment.

Most psychologists divide human individual differences into two broad categories: intelligence (general mental ability) and personality. There is considerable evidence that scores on tests of general mental ability are closely linked to success in a wide variety of occupational areas (Hunter & Hunter, 1984). Some practitioners and researchers seem reluctant to accept and act on this finding. Certainly the use of ability testing is far less widespread than research evidence alone would lead one to expect. The use of such tests is complicated by various issues such as the relatively poor scores obtained by some subgroups of the population and the restricted range of scores obtained for some applicant groups (e.g. university graduates); nevertheless the scientific evidence is clear.

The position with personality assessment is rather different and if anything, the use of personality assessment procedures in organizations has been far more widespread than research evidence would support. It seems that many human resource practitioners feel that personality factors have an important role to play in determining job success. Hard, scientific evidence to support all of the uses to which personality measures are put is not available. As this chapter will show there is, however, evidence that personality characteristics are important in determining work behaviour and that there is a role for personality assessment in personnel selection. Personality assessment procedures are prominent in organizations and are used in selection decisions, placement and career development. By contrast with intelligence testing the research evidence to support the use of personality assessment has emerged only recently and is still much less extensive.

Approaches to personality

There is no single unifying theory of personality within psychology. Psychologists share an understanding that personality concerns the factors of temperament and disposition that are responsible for some of the differences between people and the cross-situational similarities in any individual's behaviour. Mischel (1993) identified five major approaches to personality: psychodynamic; trait and biological; phenomenological; behavioural and cognitive–social. One major way in which these approaches to personality differ is the extent to which they emphasize the role of external (situational) forces or that of stable psychological (person) forces. Early behavioural approaches stressed the role of the reinforcing or punishing aspects of

* Reprinted by permission from *Trends in Organizational Behavior*, Volume 1. Edited by C. L. Cooper and D. M. Rousseau © 1994 John Wiley & Sons Ltd.

the situation and placed little emphasis on internal, psychological factors. By contrast, psychodynamic approaches focus on the role of internal, often unconscious, psychological forces. Phenomenological approaches stress that the meaning of events is different for each individual and also focus attention on within-person factors. Another major way in which personality theories differ concerns the extent to which they provide procedures for measuring individual differences so that personalities of individuals may be examined and the personalities of different people compared. Although cognitive–social approaches incorporate roles for person and situational factors there is no unique system for personality measurement associated with this approach. Trait approaches to personality provide a set of dimensions that may be used to describe the characteristics of individuals. The associated tests and questionnaires that have been developed may be used to provide profiles of the personalities of different people and to make comparisons between them on a one to one basis or, with the aid of extensive normative data, to compare individuals with a relevant population or subgroup. The capability of trait/factor analytic approaches to measure, compare, classify and evaluate people has made them popular amongst personnel psychologists and human resource practitioners. Other theoretical views of human personality may have the potential to contribute to personnel selection decision-making but so far this potential, if it exists, has not been realized.

Personality in context

In recent years scholars in the organization behaviour field have debated the primacy of dispositional or situational factors in the determination of people's outlook and behaviour. On the one side interesting and important research, exemplified by the controversial article of Staw and Ross (1985), suggests that even qualities such as job satisfaction, which by definition seem to be situationally determined, may have a stable dispositional component. Staw and Ross (1985) found correlations of 0.24 for job satisfaction measures taken five years apart (1966–1971) for a sample of men who had changed both occupation and employer during the period. This compared with a correlation of 0.37 for men who had stayed in the same occupation with the same employer. Although subsequent research (Newton & Keenen, 1991) has questioned the methodology used by Staw and Ross (1985) it has also reinforced the finding that job and work attitudes show stability even when situations change. Another, related line of research has offered support for the view that job and work attitudes and values may have a genetic component. Most of this work has involved kinship studies in which the scores of individuals of varying genetic and environmental similarity (e.g. identical twins reared apart) are compared. In the first study of its kind focusing on job satisfaction Arvey et al (1989) found an intraclass correlation coefficient of 0.31 for the general job satisfaction scores of a set of identical twins reared apart. Clearly it is unlikely that job satisfaction is inherited directly. It may be, however, as Arvey et al (1989) theorize, that some stable personality characteristics are partly genetically determined and in turn influence job satisfaction scores. For example, if the tendency to construe events in a negative way (known as negative affect, Watson & Clark, 1984) is partly inherited this tendency would spill over into evaluations of various features of a person's life, including satisfaction with a job. In fact there is clear evidence to show that both negative affect and positive affect (Watson & Clark, 1984) exert some influence on a variety of variables, such as job satisfaction, that might, at face value, seem to be entirely situationally determined. Positive affect is not merely the antithesis of negative affect but refers to a distinct personality dimension that is independent of negative affectivity.

Positive affect reflects the extent to which a person is feeling a zest for life, feeling up versus down. High positive affect is most clearly defined by words such as active, excited, alert, enthusiastic and strong, whereas low positive affect is best characterized by terms reflecting fatigue such as sluggish and drowsy. Negative affect, in contrast, represents the extent to which a person feels upset or unpleasantly aroused versus peaceful. High negative affect includes a wide variety of unpleasant states (e.g. distressed, nervous, angry, guilty and scornful), whereas low negative affect is marked by terms such as calm and relaxed (Watson & Clark, 1984: p. 472).

Using alternative terminology negative affect is emotional stability or neuroticism and positive affect is extraversion (Eysenck, 1970). If dispositional characteristics such as positive and negative affect exert a pervasive influence this would be expected to show in both work and non-work areas of an individual's life. Research has indeed revealed links between work and non-work well-being (Warr, 1990). Research evidence has also shown that job satisfaction is related to measures of negative and positive affect in ways that would be expected (see Furnham & Zacherl, 1986; Levin & Stokes, 1989). This research offers convincing support for the pervasive influence of personality factors.

Research evidence in favour of situational effects is also compelling. A long and successful stream of work, based originally on the behavioural framework developed by Skinner and others (Luthans & Martinko, 1987), has shown that the manipulation of reinforcing and punishing features of the environment can exert a powerful influence on behaviour. Experiments involving the design of work to incorporate the job characteristics of skill variety, task identity, task significance, autonomy and feedback (Fried & Ferris, 1987) have revealed that changes in behaviour and outlook can be brought about.

An impartial reading of the available research leads to the inescapable conclusion that both situations and disposition are involved in the determination of behaviour. Bandura (1986) has provided the framework of 'reciprocal determinism' to illustrate the joint interacting effects of person (dispositional) and situational variables with behaviour (Figure 1).

In this framework behaviour is a function of both person and situational variables. In turn behaviour may exert an influence on situational and personal factors. For example, although a strong situation may exert a major influence on behaviour, it is also possible for a person to behave in a way that changes the situation. When this framework is applied to the elements involved in personnel selection it becomes very clear that it is impossible to predict anyone's future work behaviour from a knowledge of his or her personal qualities only. Although knowledge of the person (e.g. personality characteristics and mental ability) might provide a basis for partial understanding

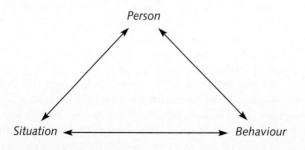

Figure 1 Reciprocal determinism

of future behaviour a knowledge of the situation is also important in providing a complete picture. This analysis shows quite clearly that there is likely to be a ceiling, determined by the extent to which situational factors have been taken into account, to the accuracy of any personnel selection method.

As yet there is no universal procedure for incorporating knowledge of situational factors into personnel selection processes. Many factors might be involved in determining the role of situational factors but at least two seem to be of particular importance when personality assessment is considered.

Job analysis is an often recommended first stage in the personnel selection process. Although most personnel selection texts do not highlight the fact, conducting a job analysis represents a systematic way of paying attention to some of the situational factors that may be important in determining a job holder's performance. Job analysis also provides a basis for drawing inferences about which personality characteristics or other psychological variables may be important for job success. It would be reasonable to expect that validity studies involving personality constructs would produce more positive results when the selection of personality constructs measured has been based on systematic job analysis.

Job performance criteria

The second important factor is the nature of the job performance criteria used. It is well recognized in the personnel selection literature that some performance criteria are more prone to contamination than others. Often this contamination is the result of situational factors. Raw sales figures, for example, reflect the performance of the salesperson and the area in which he or she works. This suggests that some criteria are likely to be more situationally dependent than others and thus less predictable from a knowledge of an individual's personal make-up. As noted earlier this impact of the situation is usually treated as contamination or error in the criterion measurement. At a more general level it reflects a need to incorporate some influence for situational variables in personnel selection research. The specificity of the criteria used is also an important issue. Successful overall job performance may be attained with a variety of different personality profiles; for example extroversion may be an asset only if combined with agreeableness. For most other selection procedures the scores for the component measures involved would be expected to combine positively to enhance overall job performance. High performance on all of the exercises in an assessment centre would be a much stronger signal of good job performance than some combination of high and low performance. For personality constructs the position is more complex. The theoretical sophistication of models linking personality constructs to job performance is not yet sufficient to provide clear predictions of how personal factors might combine to enhance or diminish overall performance. It is, however, realistic to make predictions, based on theory, about the links between personality constructs and specific job competences. This suggests that studies using personality constructs should not focus only on overall job performance but also at the more specific level of particular job competences.

Criterion-related validity

Since the late 1970s researchers' views of the validity of personnel selection methods have undergone significant change. Before this period the consensus view was that the validity of methods was inconsistent and generally rather meagre. What researchers had failed to take account of was that most validity studies were conducted on small samples, often with a restricted range of scores and unreliable measuring procedures. When corrections were made for these artefacts, with the aid of meta-analysis procedures (Hunter & Schmidt, 1990), the conclusion that validities for most methods were inconsistent and poor was shown to be false. Throughout the 1980s a series of meta-analyses were conducted to evaluate more accurately the validity of all of the major personnel selection procedures. Encouraging validity coefficients were found for many personnel selection procedures. Assessment centres (Gaugler et al, 1987), structured, job-related interviews (Wiesner & Cronshaw, 1988), work sample tests (Hunter & Hunter, 1984; Robertson & Downs, 1989) and mental ability tests (Schmitt et al, 1984) were all found to display good levels of criterion-related validity.

Personality constructs used in personnel selection

Historically a large number of different personality constructs have been utilized in personnel selection research. Often the constructs used have been drawn from general personality instruments, which measure a range of traits, such as the Sixteen PF (Cattell, Eber & Tatsuoka, 1970), the California Personality Inventory (Gough, 1987), the Minnesota Multiphasic Personality Inventory (Hathaway & McKinley, 1943) etc. More specific personality constructs such as locus of control (Rotter, 1966) or type A behaviour pattern (Friedman & Rosenman, 1974) have also been investigated. Until recently there were few generalizable findings and the prevailing climate of opinion amongst researchers was in line with the view expressed by Guion and Gottier (1965) that there was no evidential basis for recommending the use of personality testing in selection situations. Part of the difficulty in evaluating findings and organizing research into the criterion-related validity of personality constructs lay in the lack of a clear consensus concerning the nature of the major personality dimensions. For many years Eysenck (e.g. Eysenck, 1970; Eysenck & Eysenck, 1985) presented evidence and argued that two of the fundamental dimensions of personality were emotional stability and extraversion. More recent work has confirmed this view and added three other key dimensions to the personality psychologists' lexicon: conscientiousness; agreeableness and openness to experience. Low and high scorers on these characteristics are described below (from Costa & McCrae, 1985).

▶ Openness: high scorers are open to new experiences, have broad interests and are very imaginative; low scorers are down-to-earth, practical, traditional and pretty much set in their ways.
▶ Agreeableness: high scorers are compassionate, good-natured, and eager to cooperate and avoid conflict; low scorers are hardheaded, sceptical, proud and competitive. They tend to express anger directly.
▶ Conscientiousness: high scorers are conscientious and well-organized, have high standards and always strive to achieve goals; low scorers are easygoing, not very well-organized and sometimes careless. They prefer not to make plans.

Together with extraversion and emotional stability (mentioned earlier in this chapter) these factors make up the so-called 'big five' personality characteristics. The big five factors have been confirmed when using various data collection procedures and in several different languages, including English, Dutch, German and Japanese (John, 1990). They have also been shown to be stable over time (McCrae and Costa, 1990). Much of the more recent research on the criterion-related validity of personality has used the big five as an organizing framework or has focused on specific job-relevant factors such as integrity (see Ones, Viswesvaran & Schmidt, 1993) or service orientation (Hogan, Hogan & Busch, 1984).

The criterion-related validity of personality assessment

An early attempt to provide a quantifiable indication of the criterion-related validity of personality was reported by Ghiselli and Barthol (1953). Although some useful validities were found, Ghiselli and Barthol were not encouraging about the use of personality instruments in personnel selection. The first meta-analysis using the Schmidt–Hunter (Hunter & Schmidt, 1990) procedures to provide evidence on the criterion-related validity of personality assessment (Schmidt et al, 1984) found an overall validity of only 0.15 (uncorrected for unreliability or range restriction).

Although the initial meta-analysis results for personality assessment were not encouraging there are good reasons to believe that the results obtained were under-estimating the validity of personality constructs. These reasons are discussed more fully in Robertson (1993). Briefly, the meta-analytic procedures used to estimate the criterion-related validity of personality constructs need to be different from those used for other personnel selection methods. The essence of the difference is that hypothesis-driven procedures need to be used when personality constructs are being evaluated. With other personnel selection methods clear hypotheses are nearly always explicitly or implicitly used in the individual studies that are subjected to meta-analysis. For example the components of a work sample test will have been derived from job analysis and the scores produced on all aspects of the test will be expected to correlate with job performance. When personality measures are used in a validity study it is common for all of the dimensions measured by a particular test to be included, even when there is no strong expectation that every dimension will be linked with job performance. The averaging process used in meta-analysis to estimate criterion-related validity for a set of local validation studies on personality needs to ensure that only personality dimensions that are expected to relate to the criteria are included. More recent meta-analysis (e.g. Barrick & Mount, 1991; Tett, Jackson & Rothstein, 1991) have shown that when hypothesis driven procedures are used better results are obtained. The clearest demonstration of this is provided in some of the results obtained by Tett et al (1991). When a global averaging of all of the coefficients from the studies examined by Tett et al (1991) was conducted the resulting estimate of the population validity (0.16) was very close to that obtained by Schmitt et al (1984) using similar procedures (0.15). When Tett et al (1991) focused on studies in which confirmatory research strategies and job analysis had been used to select personality constructs the results were much better. For these studies the mean sample size weighted validity coefficient was 0.25 (0.38 when corrected for unreliability), though it should be noted that there were only seven studies in this category.

A study conducted by Robertson and Kinder (1993) examined links between personality constructs and specific competences using an hypothesis driven procedure. Robertson and Kinder used practitioners who were trained in the use of a specific personality instrument (the Occupational Personality Questionnaire (OPQ); Saville & Holdsworth, 1990) to generate hypotheses linking personality constructs with job competences. Meta-analytic procedures were then used to cumulate the results from a sample of studies to investigate the hypothesized relationships. The resulting mean sample-size weighted validity coefficients (uncorrected for unreliability or restriction of range) varied from 0.09 to 0.33. Robertson and Kinder also examined the extent to which personality variables provided incremental validity beyond that provided by measures of mental ability. Their results revealed very little overlap between the criterion variable correlated with ability and that associated with personality, suggesting that personality constructs provide unique information about potential performance at work. Further support for this conclusion has been given by Barrick, Mount and Strauss (1993) who also found that personality and ability variables contributed non-overlapping variance associated with performance measures.

As far as specific job-relevant scales are concerned good validities have been obtained for both integrity testing (Ones et al, 1993) and service orientation (Hogan et al, 1984).

It is worth noting that the studies mentioned above have focused on personality characteristics at fairly high levels of generality (the big five) and at more detailed levels of analysis. The criteria used have also varied in level, with some studies focusing on overall work performance and others concentrating on more specific criteria such as particular job competences. Both levels of analysis seem to be important in obtaining a better understanding of the role of personality in work performance. Obviously it is important to examine the extent to which overall performance may be dependent on personality. In reality though the links between overall performance and personality are likely to be mediated by specific competences. A conceptual framework linking personality to work performance thus needs to include several elements: personality constructs; work competences; situational variables; job demands; overall work performance and for completeness, genetic and environmental determinants of personality. Figure 2 illustrates this framework.

As the evidence reviewed briefly above reveals, personality is a function of both environmental and genetic factors. In turn, according to the framework in Figure 2, personality factors help to determine work competences. Depending upon the job demands and the work situation these competences then combine and interact to influence overall performance. The demands of the job determine the relative importance of each competence to overall performance. The specific competences act as mediators between the underlying personality variables and overall effectiveness. Barrick, Mount and Strauss (1993), for example, have shown how the setting of goals mediates the links between conscientiousness and overall job performance. To give substance to Figure 2, the big five personality characteristics have been included as personality factors and illustrative competences from those employed by Robertson and Kinder (1993) have been used. It is important to stress, however, that although there is some consensus amongst personality researchers on the big five, there is no such consensus on a set of generic work competences. Indeed, as work on

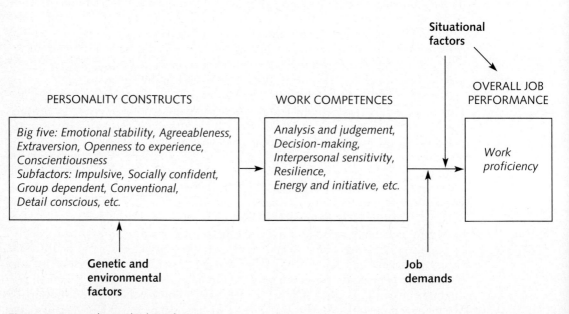

Figure 2 Personality and job performance

the measurement of such variables using assessment centre technology suggests (e.g. Bycio, Alvares & Hahn, 1987) there is considerable uncertainty about the extent to which discrete competences can be identified and measured. The influence of situational variables is also awkward to deal with. Again there is no commonly agreed framework or set of variables to use. Recent work is, however, beginning to provide some clarification of the role that situational variables can play. Barrick and Mount (1993) have shown that, for jobs that are high in autonomy, the links between personality constructs and performance are stronger than there are for lower autonomy jobs. This is very much in line with the more general theoretical proposition that individual difference variables, such as personality, will exert more influence when situations are weak and will be less important in strong, highly constraining settings (Adler & Weiss, 1988).

An agenda for future work

The results presented above show that there is a useful role for personality testing to play in personnel selection and Figure 2 gives a simple framework for looking at personality–performance links. When the personality constructs involved are clear and thought is given to the expected link between these constructs and work behaviour, it is likely that worthwhile information may be derived from personality measurement. In the last decade or so researchers have established links between criterion measures of work behaviour and personality constructs drawn from the big five. Links with criterion measures and personality constructs measured at a more detailed level than the big five have also been established. This information is helpful and has definite applied value but there is some way to go before the research base provides evidence to support the wide-ranging use of personality measurement. This lack of knowledge constrains the extent to which personality testing may be able to contribute to selection and other human resource decisions, such as team building. Everyday experience suggests that the effectiveness of individuals, teams and other organizational units is dependent, in part, upon the personality characteristics of the individuals involved. Research into personality and work performance supports this view and has uncovered linear relationships between various, specific personality constructs and indicators of either overall work performance or specific work-related competences. Unfortunately neither the problems of individual selection nor those of building successful work groups can be resolved with the aid of this knowledge.

First consider the selection of individuals. With the restricted number of personality traits measured in the big five framework there are still many different combinations that might occur in any individual profile. Even if a person's position on each individual characteristic is restricted to high, medium or low 125 (5 × 5 × 5) possible combinations are possible. If standard ten (sten) scores are used then nearly ten million combinations are possible. If personality is measured using a more detailed level of analysis the possible personality profiles become bewilderingly large (e.g. the 16 personality factors of the 16PF would give over a thousand billion different profiles). It is likely that different personality profiles can lead to equally effective work behaviour and performance since a person's behaviour pattern is a function of how his or her specific personality traits combine to help to determine behaviour in a particular setting. This suggests that for any given job several different combinations of personality characteristics may be effective. All of the recent research mentioned earlier in this chapter is limited to findings about the links between single characteristics and work behaviour. Further progress will be made if investigators begin to address the role of combinations of personality constructs in the determination of behaviour.

The problems involved in this kind of research are certainly difficult but may not be as overwhelming as they appear at first sight. Although many different personality profiles exist in principle not all combinations occur in practice; furthermore strong theoretical ideas can be used to limit the personality constructs and interactions of these constructs that will be relevant in any particular setting. There is also some potential in the development of expert system heuristics that are driven by theoretical ideas about how personality constructs combine and interact. In other words it is not necessary to explore the effect of every possible personality mix before being in a position to generate clear guidance, based on evidence. Such systems use theories to build predictions about the behaviour of people with specific profiles and it should be possible to validate the system (i.e. the theory) without the need to examine the behaviour derived from every possible personality profile.

In addition to the need to understand the combined effect of personality characteristics there is the need to understand the shape of the relationship between personality factors and aspects of work behaviour. For example there are work settings where an outgoing person will be more effective than someone who is more reserved (i.e. extroversion will be correlated with work success). It is nevertheless quite easy to imagine that someone who is at the extreme of the extroversion range, particularly if this is coupled with an extreme score on some other factor such as agreeableness, would be less effective than if he or she was less extreme. There is clear evidence that personality characteristics are sometimes related to behaviour in non-linear ways (e.g. Mueller, 1992), though this work is more or less exclusively confined to laboratory studies. Research designed to explore the role of personality in work behaviour, which recognizes and explores non-linear relationships, has the potential to make a significant contribution to both theory and practice.

The performance of anyone who is selected for a position in an organization is likely to be influenced, to some extent, by the situation that he or she works in. For many people the most salient features of the work situation are other people working in the same organization; these may be colleagues, subordinates, bosses or other team members. As shown above, there is considerable complexity in attempting to grasp the role of several personality constructs in relation to the behaviour of one person. Attempting to do this for the behaviour of people who interact at work is an even more challenging task. Relatively little is available in the scientific literature to assist with this task. There are some conceptual frameworks in existence but although these have found favour with some practitioners the scientific evaluation is generally not available or not supportive. Scientifically valid frameworks that help to explain and predict the behaviour of interacting personalities in particular settings would make a major contribution to knowledge and have a very important role to play in practical problem solving and human resource decision-making.

References

Adler, S. & Weiss, H. M. (1988) Recent developments in the study of personality and organizational behavior. In C. L. Cooper & I. T. Robertson (Eds.) *International Review of Industrial and Organizational Psychology, 1988.* Chichester: John Wiley.

Arvey, R. D., Bouchard, T. J., Segal, N. L. & Abraham, L. M. (1989) Job satisfaction: Environmental and genetic components. *Journal of Applied Psychology*, **74**, 187–192.

Bandura, A. (1986) *Social Foundations of Thought and Action: A Social Cognitive Theory.* Englewood Cliffs, NJ: Prentice Hall.

Barrick, M. R. & Mount, M. K. (1991) The big five personality dimensions and job performance: A meta-analysis. *Personnel Psychology*, **44**, 1–26.

Barrick, M. R. & Mount, M. K. (1993) Autonomy as a moderator of the relationship between the big five personality dimensions and job performance. *Journal of Applied Psychology,* **78,** 111–118.

Barrick, M. R., Mount, M. K. & Strauss, J. P. (1993) Conscientiousness and performance of sales representatives: Test of the mediating effects of goal setting. *Journal of Applied Psychology,* **78,** 715–722.

Bycio, P., Alvares, K. M. & Hahn, J. (1987) Situational specificity in assessment center ratings: A confirmatory factor analysis. *Journal of Applied Psychology,* **72,** 463–474.

Cattell, R. B., Eber, H. W. & Tatsuoka, M. M. (1970) *Handbook for the Sixteen Personality Factor Questionnaire (16PF).* Windsor: National Foundation for Educational Research.

Coasta, P. T. & McCrae, R. R. (1985) *Manual for the NEO Personality Inventory.* Odessa, Florida: Psychological Assessment Resources.

Eysenck, H. J. (1970) *The Structure of Human Personality.* London: Methuen.

Eysenck, H. J. & Eysenck, M. J. (1985) *Personality and Individual Differences: A Natural Science Approach.* New York: Plenum Press.

Fried, Y. & Ferris, G. R. (1987) The validity of the job characteristics model: A review and meta-analysis. *Personnel Psychology,* **40,** 287–322.

Friedman, M. D. & Rosenman, R. H. (1974) *Type A Behavior and Your Heart.* New York: Knopf.

Furnham, A. & Zacherl, M. (1986) Personality and job satisfaction. *Personality and Individual Differences,* **7,** 453–459.

Gaugler, B., Rosenthal, D. B., Thornton, G. C. and Bentson, C. (1987) Meta-analysis of assessment center validity. *Journal of Applied Psychology,* **72,** 493–511.

Ghiselli, E. E. & Barthol, R. P. (1953) The validity of personality inventories in the selection of employees. *Journal of Applied Psychology,* **37,** 18–20.

Gough, H. G. (1987) *Manual: The California Psychological Inventory.* Palo Alto, CA: Consulting Psychologists Press.

Guion, R. M. & Gottier, R. F. (1965) Validity of personality measures in personnel selection. *Personnel Psychology,* **18,** 135–164.

Hathaway, S. R. & McKinley, J. C. (1943) *Manual for the Minnesota Multiphasic Personality Inventory.* New York: Psychological Corporation.

Hogan, J., Hogan, R. & Busch, C. M. (1984) How to measure service orientation. *Journal of Applied Psychology,* **69,** 167–173.

Hunter, J. E. & Hunter, R. F. (1984) Validity and utility of alternative predictors of job performance. *Psychological Bulletin,* **96,** 72–98.

Hunter, J. E. & Schmidt, F. L. (1990) *Methods of Meta-Analysis.* Newbury Park: Sage.

John, O. P. (1990) The big five factor taxonomy: Dimensions of personality in natural language and in questionnaires. In L. A. Pervin (Ed.) *Handbook of Personality Theory and Research.* New York: Guilford Press.

Levin, I. & Stokes, J. P. (1989) Dispositional approach to job satisfaction: Role of negative affectivity. *Journal of Applied Psychology,* **74,** 752–758.

Luthans, F. & Martinko, M. (1987) Behavioral approaches to organizations. In C. L. Cooper & I. T. Robertson (Eds.) *International Review of Industrial and Organizational Psychology, 1987.* Chichester: John Wiley.

McCrae, R. R. & Costa, P. T. (1990) *Personality in Adulthood.* New York: Guilford.

Mischel, W. (1993) *Introduction to Personality,* 5th Edition. New York: Holt-Saunders.

Mueller, J. H. (1992) Anxiety and performance. In A. P. Smith & D. M. Jones (Eds.) *Handbook of Human Performance, Volume 3: State and Trait.* London: Academic Press.

Newton, T. & Keenan, T. (1991) Further analyses of the disposition argument in organizational behavior. *Journal of Applied Psychology,* **76,** 781–787.

Ones, D. S., Viswesvaran, C. & Schmidt, F. L. (1993) Comprehensive meta-analysis of integrity test validities: Findings and implications for personnel selection and theories of job performance. *Journal of Applied Psychology,* **78,** 679–703.

Robertson, I. T. (1993) Personality assessment and personnel selection. *European Review of Applied Psychology,* **43,** 187–194.

Robertson, I. T. & Downs, S. (1989) Work sample tests of trainability: A meta-analysis. *Journal of Applied Psychology,* **74,** 402–410.

Robertson, I. T. & Kinder, A. (1993). Personality and job competences: The criterion-related validity of some personality variables. *Journal of Occupational and Organizational Psychology*, **66**, 225–244.

Rotter, J. B. (1966) Generalized expectancies for internal vs external control of reinforcement. *Psychological Monographs*, **80** (Whole No. 609).

Saville and Holdsworth Ltd (1990) *Occupational Personality Questionnaire Manual*. Esher, Surrey: Saville and Holdsworth.

Schmitt, N., Gooding, R. Z., Noe, R. A. & Kirsch, M. (1984) Meta-analysis of validity studies published between 1964 and 1982 and the investigation of study characteristics. *Personnel Psychology*, **37**, 407–422.

Staw, B. M. & Ross, J. (1985) Stability in the midst of change: A dispositional approach to job attitudes. *Journal of Applied Psychology*, **70**, 469–525.

Tett, R. P., Jackson, D. N. & Rothstein, M. (1991) Personality measures as predictors of job performance: A meta-analytic review. *Personnel Psychology*, **44**, 703–742.

Warr, P. B. (1990) The measurement of well-being and other aspects of mental health. *Journal of Occupational Psychology*, **63**, 193–210.

Watson, D. & Clark, L. A. (1984) Negative affectivity: The disposition to experience aversive emotional states. *Psychological Bulletin*, **96**, 465–490.

Wiesner, W. H. & Cronshaw, S. F. (1988) A meta-analytic investigation of the impact of interview format and degree of structure on the validity of the employment interview. *Journal of Occupational Psychology*, **61**, 270–290.

part 2 # groups in the organization

what did Elton Mayo really say? (1949)

'The perspectives of Elton Mayo', by Reinhard Bendix and Lloyd H. Fisher, and 'Some corrections to . . .', by George C. Homans, *Review of Economics and Statistics*, vol. 31, 1949, pp. 312–19 and 319–21 respectively.

Everybody has heard of the Hawthorne studies and of Elton Mayo. However, few students know what Mayo actually said, and fewer still are aware of the response that his writings received from fellow academics of the time. In the last 30 years, there has been a great deal of criticism about the research design and research methods used, and the conclusions that were drawn from the data obtained. Before such criticisms can be evaluated, it is necessary to know what Mayo did say, and as importantly, what he did not say.

This article was written by a pair of leading professors of human relations at the time. It was published in 1949, the year of Mayo's death, and represents a contribution to the 'human relations debate' of the period. The points made by the writers, are responded to by George Homans, a member of Mayo's research team, and a writer who was to become a leading sociologist in the 1950s. At the time this article was published, human relations was the 'hot' topic of the day in business and management circles.

learning objectives

Once you have read and understood this article, you should be able to:

1 Explain how Elton Mayo's research and conclusions were viewed by some of the contemporary academics of the time.
2 Identify the areas of greatest contention between Mayo and other writers.
3 Assess Homans's response to the points made by Bendix and Fisher.

learning pre-requisites

Before attempting the activities described below, you should have read Chapter 7 of the core text, and the journal articles, 'The perspectives and Elton Mayo', by Reinhard Bendix and Lloyd H. Fisher, and 'Some corrections to . . .', by George C. Homans in *Review of Economics and Statistics*, vol. 31, 1949, pp. 312–19 and 319–21.

learning activities

There are two learning activities associated with this reading. First a short crossword testing your basic knowledge of the reading. Second, a short evaluation question.

1 Complete the crossword below.

Across

1 and 5 down. A justified social arrangement is based on what? (11, 11)
7 See 2 down.
8 Co-operation must be organized, but not artificially, thus it must be concerned with friends perhaps (6).
9 Mayo's co-operation theories grew into theories on groups, with the attitude that authority should be 'letting line' (anag., 11).

Down

2 and 7 across. Malinowski, it can be said, agrees with Mayo in that society's co-operation can be? (11, 9).
3 Co-operation should not concentrate on 'ecological money'? (8).
4 Prejudice and emotions are avoided, can this be organized through rail transport? (8).
5 See 1 across.
6 Mayo states that on-going conflict could push society back to what time? (6, 4).
10 The management —— has the opportunity and responsibility to work with employees towards a common goal (5).

2 Some critics would argue that Mayo underestimated the influence exerted by government on industry. Use your knowledge of this article to assess this viewpoint, raising two substantive issues.

READING
7

The perspectives of Elton Mayo*
Reinhard Bendix and Lloyd H. Fisher

The small number of Elton Mayo's writings[1] belies the extent of his influence since coming to Harvard in 1926. Many social scientists and businessmen in the United States are indebted to him. His ideas have stimulated both social science research and factory management.

The influence of Mr. Mayo has been notable in the work of those social scientists who apply to their study of modern society the techniques and concepts developed in the analyses of simpler cultures. He has imparted to this anthropology of the modern life his strong feeling for the necessity of the stable social relationships which characterize traditional societies[2] and are commonly so lacking in our own. However, the influence of Mayo's work has been greatest in the promotion of a sociological or anthropological approach to industrial management. Much of the content of those courses in the universities catalogued as 'Human Relations in Industry' consists of the work of Mayo, his colleagues, and his students. It is not yet possible to assess the effect of this approach on the personnel practices of factory managers. It may be that a later age will compare Mayo's work with that of Frederick W. Taylor, and indeed the 'human relations approach' and 'scientific management' are not unrelated. At any rate, Mayo's emphasis on the human side of worker–management relations has had a considerable effect upon the literature and perhaps the practices of personnel relations. This influence has already been substantial enough to warrant an attempt to consider its major tendencies. It is to this end that the present article is addressed.

Basic orientations

There is consistency in the writings of Mayo. From his earliest book in which he reviewed the social and political scene in Australia to the last of his trilogy on the problems of industrial society, a sense of imminent danger pervades his writing. It is not an unequivocal prophecy of doom, for escape from the cataclysm is open to those who are not too blind to see.

Spontaneous cooperation

What one must see in order to be saved is that the essence of a healthy society is a sound social organization. And the requirement of a sound social organization is the *spontaneous* cooperation of its members within the various enterprises in which they are organized. Conflict in human society, and especially political conflict, is always a symptom of social disease.

---

* Reprinted from *Review of Economics and Statistics*, 31 (1949), 312–319, by permission of Reinhard Bendix and the publisher, Cambridge, Mass., Harvard University Press. Copyright 1949 by the President and Fellows of Harvard College.

[1] The late Elton Mayo was Professor of Industrial Research at the Harvard University School of Business Administration. His written work consists of six books: *Democracy and Freedom, An Essay in Social Logic* (1919); *The Human Problems of an Industrial Civilization* (1933, new ed. 1946); *The Social Problems of an Industrial Civilization* (1945); *The Political Problem of Industrial Civilization* (1947); *Some Notes on the Psychology of Pierre Janet* (1948); and, together with George Lombard, *Teamwork and Labor Turnover in the Aircraft Industry of Southern California* (1944). In addition, Mayo has written some 30 articles and numerous forewords to the books of his colleagues, collaborators, and disciples.

[2] See the numerous writings of W. L. Warner, B. Gardner, S. Kimball, C. Arensberg, G. Homans, A. Davis, W. F. Whyte, and others.

An understanding of the term 'spontaneous' reveals the main drift of Mayo's work. Spontaneous does not mean voluntary. If Mayo gave to the term 'spontaneous' the meaning of voluntary he would belong in a different political current altogether. He would appear as one in a long line of liberal theorists who have attempted to find a reconciliation in industrial society between the function of authority and the liberal requirement of individual consent. But this would have raised problems which Mayo has shown no intention of dealing with—problems of agreement on the nature and the ends of industrial organization itself.

Man's conduct in society, according to Mayo, is primarily determined by tradition. It is this reliance upon tradition that distinguishes spontaneous behavior from voluntary behavior. For it is precisely traditional behavior which can be spontaneous without being voluntary.[3] Thus, individual happiness and the social 'growth and health' of society are dependent not upon freedom from unreasonable restraint nor upon any rational calculus of pleasure and pain, nor upon the opportunity for self-development, but upon whether or not the individual has a sense of 'social function.'

In his earliest book, *Democracy and Freedom, An Essay in Social Logic*, published in Australia in 1919, Mayo laid down the thesis which remained the core of his subsequent work.

Viewed from the standpoint of social science, society is composed of individuals organized in occupational groups, each group fulfilling some function of the society. Taking this fact into account, psychology . . . is able to make at least one general assertion as to the form a given society must take if it is to persist as a society. It must be possible for the individual to feel, as he works, that his work is socially necessary; he must be able to see beyond his group to the society. Failure in this respect will make disintegration inevitable. (p. 37.)[4]

As a diagnosis of the plight and problem of industrial man this is neither novel nor in itself politically revealing. This is indeed the sin of bourgeois society. Both socialists and fascists excoriate it. It is denounced by the agrarian and by the medievalist. It is the attack of Ruskin and Morris upon nineteenth century capitalism. It is the case for conservatism as Burke made it.

The decline of civilization

In the hands of Mayo the charge becomes really comprehensive. Australia as Mayo saw it in 1919 exhibited on all sides the growth of conflict and the decline of civilization. The belief that government could aid in the development of social cooperation he stigmatized as a dangerous illusion. Government can only 'record and enforce existing moral relationships,' it cannot initiate or change them. Those who think that social cooperation can be achieved by political means help to intensify class conflict and thus bring closer the disintegration of society. Hence party politics and democracy deserve to be condemned because they sanction the conception of a class society and thereby feed the forces of social disorder.

The recent growth of interest in political matters in Australia is by no means a sign of social health. (*Democracy and Freedom*, p. 43.)

Revolution or civil war is the only outcome of the present irreconcilable attitude of Australian political parties. The methods of 'democracy,' far from providing a

---

[3] Social behavior, to be sure, is not exclusively or even predominantly voluntary and rational. However, Mayo proposes the further cultivation and extension of traditional behavior as a positive social objective.

[4] For a similar comment see Mayo, *Human Problems*, p. 166.

means of solving the industrial problem, have proved entirely inadequate to the task. Political organization has been mistaken for political education; the party system has accentuated and added to our industrial difficulties. Democracy has done nothing to help society to unanimity, nothing to aid the individual to a sense of social function. Under its tutelage, social development has achieved a condition of perilous instability, a condition which democracy as such can apparently do little or nothing to cure. (*Ibid.*, p. 44.)

Government and industrial relations

All of this is most clearly seen in the field of industrial relations. Mayo deplores industrial conflict, but any government intervention to relieve it is an empty if not a dangerous delusion. The state cannot 'produce by regulation [the cooperation] which can only be the result of spontaneous growth.'[5]

The office of rules and regulations is to express a static relation; prohibition can do nothing to bring about a condition of wholehearted and spontaneous cooperation. Collaboration in the complex purposes of civilization is the mark of social health; any ideal which aims at less than this is dangerous. Civilization has passed beyond nineteenth century individualism to twentieth century class rivalry. Its capacity to survive depends upon its capacity to achieve a social condition that will subsume castes and classes under a community of interest and purpose. To achieve this, artificial restrictions must be eliminated and 'common rules' revoked—except where common rules undoubtedly express the social mind. Human nature may be trusted to work out a gradual solution once the attempt to find political nostrums and ad hoc remedies is abandoned. (*Ibid.*, pp. 49–50.)

The political devices which have been developed under democratic institutions to regulate industrial relations are but an 'artificial substitute for (the spontaneous growth of) human cooperation.' (*Ibid.*, pp. 51–52.)

These opinions of three decades ago are essentially similar to the views which Mayo has expressed in recent years. In his *Human Problems* he concludes a chapter on 'Government and Society' with the statement that

No form of political action can ever substitute for this loss (of social function). Political action in a given community presumes the desire and capacity of individuals to work together; the political function cannot operate in a community from which this capacity has disappeared. (p. 167.)

Again in his book of 1945 he quotes with approval the assertion of Figgis that the state has never created 'in any real sense' the social institutions of modern society. And he denounces with Figgis any thought of the constructive role which politics and government may play in our society as that monstrous idea of 'an omnipotent state facing an equally unreal aggregate of unrelated individuals.'[6] It is difficult to understand Mayo's work unless one realizes how much he abhors conflict, competition, or disagreement. Conflict is a 'social disease' and cooperation is 'social health.' But many forms of cooperation, especially those initiated or aided by political means (e.g., collective bargaining), are not cooperation after all, but artificial substitutes for it. In 1919 Mayo wrote that only 'spontaneous cooperation' is socially healthy,[7] and more

[5] *Democracy and Freedom*, p. 48.
[6] *Social Problems*, pp. 54–55.
[7] *Democracy and Freedom*, p. 49.

recently he has held that this ideal of social health can only be found in the Middle Ages, when society was characterized by a community of purpose among all its members.[8]

For Mayo the conditions necessary for a healthy social organism are present when each individual has a sense of social function and responsibility. Tradition assigns him his role in the group. Cooperation is assured because the purposes of each are the purposes of all. And this basic unanimity is the social foundation of all human collaboration. Unanimity and cooperation are traditional rather than deliberate, spontaneous rather than voluntary. Any effort to achieve cooperation deliberately in the absence of a basic identity of purpose (within the group) is the beginning of social disintegration. In his elaboration of this view, Mayo draws heavily on the work of the anthropologist.

On this basis, Mayo passes adverse judgment on many facets of contemporary life. He deplores competition as well as the class struggle, politicians as well as election campaigns, economic self-interest as well as interest in political affairs. He deplores them all because they do not contribute to 'spontaneous cooperation.' Cooperation is easy enough, he writes in a recent work, in the face of an emergency. However, 'the real problem is that of the maintenance of *spontaneous cooperation* in times of peace.'[9]

> The immense changes of the last two centuries have disturbed all the traditional social balances. Material and technical achievements have outpaced free communication between groups and the capacity for spontaneous cooperation. Study of the social facts is only now beginning—at a critical moment when the general ignorance of the facts of social organization has become alarming. Owing to this general ignorance, the political leaders in many countries have introduced another unfortunate complication by relapsing on the ancient idea of compulsion by central authority. This has affected even those countries that nominally retain the forms of democratic government. . . . Compulsion has never succeeded in rousing eager and spontaneous cooperation. [Under compulsion] the popular will to collaborate ultimately withers. . . . The will to survive and cooperate must come from within. (*Political Problem*, p. 24.)

Thus, government is nearly synonymous with 'compulsion by central authority.' In 1947, as in 1919, Mr. Mayo creates a dichotomy between the spontaneous cooperation which is inherent in society, and the dangerous and destructive effect which politics and governmental action have on the will of the people to cooperate. He acknowledges that in modern society cooperation must be deliberately organized, since the force of tradition has weakened in our day.[10] Yet that deliberate planning of cooperation, as Mayo sees it, is not to be achieved by governmental institutions, but rather through the development of administrative elites within the private, and more particularly the industrial, organizations of our society.

A great many scientists and citizens share Mr. Mayo's concern over the bitter and dangerous conflicts which beset modern society. But not only does Mayo misconceive the remedy, he misconceives the disease as well. Political conflicts do not necessarily cause a civilization to decline; they may as readily be the necessary condition of a free society, and except upon the radical hypothesis that freedom and civilization are

---

[8] *Political Problem*, p. 23. Whether the Middle Ages did in fact possess this community of purpose is open to serious doubt. The idealization and even falsification of the past appears to be a characteristic response to present discontents.

[9] *Political Problem*, p. 12.

[10] Cf. *Social Problems*, p. 9.

mutual enemies, the charge cannot be supported. Government for natural man may indeed be an artifice, but so is the industrial society in which he will be either slave or master. Competition, with its conflict of interest, lacks the order and discipline of a traditional society; but the more conventional complaint is that we have too little competition rather than too much. We know very little about the requirements of the 'social health' of an entire society to make pronouncements upon it—too little, in fact, to be sure that even the concept has meaning. To assert, as Mayo does, that competition, self-interest, and politics will destroy civilization, and that a society is doomed unless it can 'restore' to the individual a sense of his 'social function' is only to assert his preference for the social organization of the Middle Ages. Many will agree that important and difficult problems arise from the conflicts of modern society, but many will question that the solution lies with the re-establishment of the traditional society of the past. How, then, does Mayo propose to deal with the problem of cooperation in modern society?

Small work group

Mayo repeatedly criticizes social scientists, businessmen, and politicians for their failure to solve the problem of human cooperation. Their various attempts have come to naught (if in fact they have not made matters worse) because they have been based either upon insufficient evidence or upon political nostrums which have served to arouse human passions and make constructive solutions impossible. These errors may be avoided only by an insistence upon the need for a detailed investigation of the social and psychological structure of cooperation. Only empirical research into how men act in concert can lead to the basic 'knowledge-of-acquaintance' without which cooperation cannot be organized effectively. Social scientists have been satisfied with 'knowledge about' facts rather than of the facts at first hand. Impelled by these convictions, Mayo was occupied for many years with careful and painstaking research of the Hawthorne Plant of the Western Electric Company. This work led to the now famous conclusions that work output is a function of the degree of work-satisfaction, which in turn depends upon the informal social pattern of the work group.

It will be assumed that the Hawthorne studies are familiar to the reader in a general way. They have now become part of the established findings of industrial management. They concern us here only because of a certain looseness with which Mayo interprets his findings, and because of certain ambiguities and elisions which result.

The work groups which Mayo observed in the Hawthorne experiments were separated from the factory proper. To test the effect of separation itself, output records were taken for each member of the group before and after isolation. Since output did not change it was concluded that isolation in itself had no effect upon output.[11] It was not until the several workers under the sympathetic ministrations of skillful supervisors became a cohesive group that output rose. Thus the increased output was the fruit of spontaneous cooperation and the sense of social function its cause. In evaluating the experiment as a whole, Mayo concluded that a sense of personal futility pervaded the ordinary work situation and prevented the effective cooperation of workers with management.[12]

It is by no means clear that the conditions or supervision achieved for the isolated work group could ever be reproduced for the factory. Isolation, though perhaps in itself insufficient to produce increased output, may yet have been a necessary

[11] *Human Problems*, p. 59.
[12] *Ibid.*, p. 120.

condition for successful supervision. It is conceivable that the 'sense of social function' depended as much in the end upon separation from the common run of the factory as upon the non-invidious attachment of the group members to each other. In any event, there are opportunities for illusions on the part of a small work group that would not be possible for a factory as a whole. The isolation of the small work group, however essential for purposes of observation, disguises the interdependence of group with factory and the factory with the economy as a whole. To sever the ties which related the work group to the process of production may make observation of the group manageable. It will obscure the fact, however, that the worker is subject to the authority of the employer. If the factory were not in some measure an authoritarian institution, production would break down. The 'sense of social function,' however valuable in itself, will have a limited range of acceptable manifestations in the factory.

It would appear also that there is considerable ambiguity as to whether social cooperation and the sense of social function are always signs of 'social health.' Clearly Mayo regards cooperation for objectives defined by management, e.g., increased production, as a high order of self-fulfillment. But what may be an even more spontaneous form of cooperation, e.g., trade union activities, seems to stand on a different footing.[13]

Mayo's writings are open to the interpretation that the cooperation of workers with management is 'socially healthy,' while cooperation among workers for ends of their own is not. It is certainly true that the mechanization and routinizing of the working day is a basic source of discontent. A number of social scientists today are preoccupied with the manifold consequences of the problem. But in the entire literature of the nineteenth and twentieth centuries, only the proponents of the corporative state have suggested that work satisfaction can be regained only by integrating the worker into the plant-community under the leadership of management.

Elite of industrial managers

The implicit denial of the inevitably authoritarian aspects of a factory system plays a strategic role in Mr. Mayo's philosophy. He seeks to restore 'spontaneous cooperation.' The men he charges with this task of restoration are the industrial managers. According to Mayo, they have used their authority in the past in a manner which has created a widespread sense of futility. Can they now be expected to 'create a sense of social function'? The answer to this question takes the form of exhortation.

> The world over we are greatly in need of an administrative elite, who can assess and handle the concrete difficulties of human collaboration. As we lose the non-logic of a social code, we must substitute a logic of understanding. If at all the critical posts in communal activity we had intelligent persons capable of analyzing an individual or group attitude in terms of, first, the degree of logical understanding, second, the non-logic of social codes in action, and, third, the irrational exasperation symptomatic of conflict and baffled effort; if we had an elite capable of such analysis, very many of our difficulties would dwindle to vanishing point. (*Human Problems*, p. 185.)

This is indeed an ancient quest. It started with Plato's unsuccessful attempt to

---

[13] Trade unions are mentioned twice in Mayo's writings, once when he alludes to the resistance of trade unions to technological change (*Human Problems*, p. 181) and a second time when he states that trade unions repeat the mistake of management in organizing for industrial warfare rather than cooperation (*Political Problem*, p. 22).

persuade the tyrant Dionysius of the virtues of philosophy. It ends—for the time being—with the attempt to persuade businessmen that they are able and ought to be willing to rescue our civilization.

Mayo's confidence is this ability of our industrial managers derives from the evidence of the Hawthorne studies. He suggests to the managers that they adopt the Human Relations Approach, because the 'sense of social function,' which was created in the experimental work group without much exercise of authority, is to him the model solution. Whether industrial managers can run a whole factory on the model of a work group of five girls is a question Mayo has not faced. He simply assumes that managers can organize production with a minimum exercise of authority and a maximum attention to the individual's work-satisfaction. And since the cooperation of the workers in the experimental group was convincing evidence of 'spontaneous cooperation,' he calls upon the managers to organize the factory accordingly. In this manner Mayo has come to advocate an approach to industrial relations which overlooks the role of authority in the organization of production, It is unfair to charge an author with the use which other people make of his ideas. But it is not entirely fortuitous that managers, having adopted the Mayo approach but who nonetheless must exercise authority to meet production quotas, are often found to engage in verbalisms which disguise the exercise of authority in the vocabulary of the Human Relations Approach.

A good deal of Mayo's writings has been devoted to persuading industrial managers that the future of our civilization depends upon them. They are told that in modern society cooperation cannot be left to chance. They must organize cooperation, since most forms of organized cooperation so far tried are artificial, political, and part of the unfortunate legacy of the nineteenth century. To do so successfully, the managers must become aware 'that it is a human social and not economic problem which they face.'[14] Furthermore, the barriers between administrators and social scientists should be broken down. Administrators should have a knowledge of the social sciences, while social scientists should have an acquaintance with the facts.

> We have failed to train students in the study of social situations; we have thought that first-class technical training was sufficient in a modern and mechanical age. As a consequence we are technically competent as no other age in history has been; and we combine this with utter social incompetence. This defect of education and administration has of recent years become a menace to the whole future of civilization. (*Social Problems*, p. 120.)

The intense hostilities which modern society engenders demand 'intelligent attention.'

> The administrator of the future must be able to understand the human-social facts for what they actually are, unfettered by his own emotion or prejudice. He cannot achieve this ability except by careful training—a training that must include knowledge of the relevant technical skills, of the systematic ordering of operations and of the organization of cooperation. (*Ibid.*, p. 122.)

This knowledge of the 'human-social facts' will enable the factory manager, according to Mayo, to organize the 'spontaneous' cooperation of workers and in that way he may rescue our civilization.

We shall pass over the logical problem involved in organizing 'spontaneous' cooperation. In calling upon the industrial manager to organize cooperation, Mayo has

---

[14] *Human Problems*, p. 188.

in mind the type of cooperation which existed among men during the Middle Ages and in primitive societies.[15] In these societies, custom and tradition prompted men to agree on the goals of their actions. Tradition also gave them a feeling of their social function, in that the rights and duties which were theirs by birth established a meaningful relationship between the individual and his society.

This theme is applied to the problems of modern industry. Men of a primitive tribe cooperate 'spontaneously' because they do not question the authority of tradition. In an analogous way, Mr. Mayo appears to believe that workers cooperate only when they accept the objectives of management. How else can we account for his assertion that since the industrial revolution there has been no effective collaboration between managers and workers?[16] Once workers agree with the objectives of management it becomes the task of the latter to organize the plant in a cooperative manner. But here Mr. Mayo assumes what he has yet to prove: that there is a natural community between worker and manager. Where that is true, managers may well mitigate industrial discipline by attending to the job satisfaction of their workers; but if 'spontaneous cooperation' is *not* characteristic of industrial relations, as Mayo never tires of pointing out, then the human relations approach is only an embellishment of the antagonistic cooperation between workers and managers. As such it may serve its modest function, but as such it will not enable the elite of industrial managers to play the large role which Mayo assigns to them.

Assets of conflict and dangers of unanimity

In most fields of social science it is important that the writer's basic values be clearly stated. In the study of industrial relations it is essential. Mr. Mayo has not done that, although it is evident that he prefers cooperation to conflict. But one may share that preference without condemning all kinds of conflict. And the desire for cooperation should he limited by the recognition that a certain measure of conflict is the inescapable accompaniment of an individual's freedom of choice.

Mr. Mayo makes distinction between the established society of the Middle Ages and of primitive tribes, and the adaptive society of today. He speaks of the need to develop social skills to supplement our technical skills. He says that cooperation must be organized rather than be left to chance. These and similar statements are in themselves plausible; but they are made with a certain bent for overstatement. To demand spontaneous cooperation in a society in which cooperation must be organized is meaningless. To demand unanimity of purpose in a society in which voluntary associations abound is to ask too much. To say that the individual must have a sense of social function or our civilization will perish, is a play with dangerous symbols. We really do not know how happy mankind must be in order to preserve its civilization.[17] It is the fashion today, and Mayo has contributed his share to the vogue, to become transfixed by gazing at the pathologies of our age. But nothing is gained, it seems to us, by making the modern dilemma worse than it is. Much may be lost if alarmist views provoke alarming social and political 'remedies.'

Yet the modern dilemma *is* serious, cooperation *is* difficult to attain. Organized labor is pitted against organized capital, and their cooperation is interrupted from time to time by a peaceable or combative re-definition of organizational preroga-

---

[15] This idea had had an important influence on modern social science research. Cf. Mr. Mayo's comments on the study of Newburyport, Mass., by W. K. Warner and his colleagues, *Human Problems*, pp. 138–43.

[16] *Human Problems*, p. 179.

[17] In fact, we have the testimony of Dr. Freud, whom Mayo quotes approvingly in other connections, that any civilization leads to discontent.

tives. In this situation Mr. Mayo has offered us a political nostrum despite his own rather vehement denunciation of such remedies. His appeal is clearly directed to the elite of industrial managers, whom he charges with the task of organizing cooperation in their plants through the 'human relations approach.' From this Mayo apparently expects that workers would cooperate with management without organizing in trade unions and precipitating industrial conflicts. If the strongest need of industrial workers is to have a sense of their social function, and if the 'human relations approach' can provide this sense while membership in a trade union (at the price of intermittent industrial conflict) cannot, then Mayo would be correct in his diagnosis. But what evidence is there to prove this contention? The difficulty is that Mr. Mayo seeks to prove too much; he seeks to rescue our civilization as a whole by advocating remedies which might alleviate but not cure some of its ailments. He has shown that a good bit can be said for mitigating the harshness of industrial discipline by a more understanding cultivation of human relations within the plant. And his appeal is directed to the correct address, since it is the elite of industrial managers which is peculiarly equipped to act upon Mayo's insight. But the Goliath of industrial warfare cannot be slain by the David of human relations.

If we want rather to preserve the freedom of association, we must run the risk of industrial warfare. Mr. Mayo has indicated that many of our social and industrial conflicts would be avoided if managers, workers, and the people generally had more of a sense of social responsibility. But most people in modern society express their sense of social responsibility by their participation in such associations as the National Association of Manufacturers, the Chamber of Commerce or the Congress of Industrial Organizations. These and other associations will conflict. The crucial issue is not to avoid all conflict, but to contain that conflict within the limits of a broad pattern of common purposes—and that occurs daily in every industrial community of the land. It is the peculiar blindness of Mayo and others who have seen the medieval vision, that they do not understand that it is precisely the *freedom* to conflict which establishes the boundaries within which the actual conflicts can be contained.

An appeal to the leaders in unions and management to do their share is entirely appropriate. But Mr. Mayo forgets—in his appeal to the elite—that these leaders are both the servants and the masters of their respective organizations. *Their* success in helping our society and economy retain the middle ground between the enforced cooperation of dictatorship and a destructive frequency of conflicts, is a small although essential element. It is intimately related to a variety of factors such as the total productivity of a country, its security from outside attack, the 'temper' of a people in periods of acute crisis, the role of the military, and others. Such factors add up to a quality of flexibility in a society, which cannot easily be measured but which constitutes its capacity for enduring internal conflicts relatively unimpaired. The human relations approach, if it were purged of its false metaphysic and its tendency to become the empty slogan of the advertising man, might make a very modest contribution to that capacity. In his claims for this approach, Mr. Mayo suffers from a widespread delusion of modern intellectuals, who believe that knowledge is power in the direct sense that they can instruct a powerful elite and 'rescue' society.

Mr. Mayo has left no doubt that he regards the failure to achieve complete cooperation and a meaningful life for the individual as the outstanding failure of democracy. In this he ranges himself alongside other critics of democracy. These others, conservatives like Burke and revolutionaries like Marx, were usually at some pains to make clear the different standards according to which they found democracy and industrial society wanting, and to make plain the ethical platforms from which their criticisms were launched. Theirs were moral and ethical visions. Mr. Mayo is apt to try to pass as a technical prophet and to justify the ethical assumptions implicit in his prescription on an 'else we perish' basis. But if one should choose to regard the emergency as a trifle less critical than Mayo believes it to be, then the urgency of survival no longer is a justification in itself for the means adopted. The means of survival may be various, and there may be some grounds less imperative than survival which become relevant. If we can defer the cataclysm for a while, it will not be inappropriate to inquire rather deeply into the terms of this unanimity which Mayo believes to be the condition of survival itself, and into the objects of the cooperation which it is the function of industrial managers to organize. There is a question or two to be answered.

Mayo's failure as a social scientist arises in large measure from his failure to define sharply the ethical presuppositions of his scientific work. Without these presuppositions made clear, the knowledge and skill which Mayo finds so undervalued in democratic societies deserve no higher rating than they get. Knowledge and skill have no implicit direction, no necessary ethical content. With equal efficiency and dispatch they may take us where we do or where we do not want to go. Until the ethical credentials pass critical scrutiny, democratic societies do well to keep their powder dry.

Some corrections to 'The perspectives of Elton Mayo'[*]
George C. Homans

'The Perspectives of Elton Mayo' has left out the foreground: the concrete research in industry that Mayo did and that others did with him. This research brought to the light of explicit understanding some—not all—of the determinants of workers' behavior, the importance of which had been appreciated only intuitively before his time. Later research, even in fields somewhat different from the one in which he worked, has abundantly confirmed his findings.[1] If this is 'failure as a social scientist,' then most of us would be happy to fail.

No rounded appraisal of Mayo's work can neglect the concrete research findings. Bendix and Fisher are not talking about them but about their broader 'interpretation.' This brings up two kinds of questions: (1) Are the findings applicable for action in situations other than the ones in which they were reached? (2) How did Mayo himself interpret his findings? The first question can, I think, be answered only by further research. The second can easily be answered wrong. A man is always able, if he wishes, to find in another's statements a meaning that the other, himself, did not place in them.

On the first point, I shall take just one example. Bendix and Fisher rightly point out that most of the Western Electric researches concerned small, isolated groups, and they go on to say: 'It is by no means clear that the conditions or supervision achieved for the isolated work group could ever be reproduced for the factory.' Of course it is not clear, and the question can be answered, not by debate, but by trying the experiment. It literally never has been tried, at least in a big factory. Mayo only asserted that it ought to be tried. Whatever its result we could not fail to learn by it, but if we do not try we shall never learn.

There is, by the way, in Mayo's work no implication that he studied all the problems

---

[*] Reprinted from *Review of Economics and Statistics*, 31 (1949), 319–321, by permission of the author and the publisher.
[1] See, for example, W. F. Whyte, *Human Relations in the Restaurant Industry*.

and has all the answers. He did not study the social relationships within labor unions or between unions and management. It is often forgotten that there was nothing more than a company union at Hawthorne in the years when the research was being carried on. Some of his students are now working on labor relations. We also need, for example, a study of top management as a small work group. 'There is a question or two to be answered'; so let us get to work.

On the second point, anyone is at liberty to disagree with Mayo's own interpretation of his findings. As a former student of Mayo's I am only concerned here with making clear what that interpretation was, as it came out in his conversation and his writings. Bendix and Fisher are mistaken about it at certain crucial points.

Mayo is interested in discovering how spontaneous cooperation can be achieved. But Bendix and Fisher say that for him 'spontaneous does not mean voluntary.' I wholly disagree. That is just exactly what it does mean, and a description, such as Malinowski's, of a primitive society shows that cooperation can be both traditional *and* voluntary in the highest degree.

But it is, again, a misreading of Mayo to attribute to him a 'preference for the social order of the Middle Ages.' In making his distinction between an 'established' and an 'adaptive' society, he was careful to point out that any society we can look forward to at present is one in rapid change. The problem, he argued, is that of achieving spontaneous cooperation in a society that cannot leave cooperation to tradition. Failure to solve the problem will in fact take us back to an 'established' society like that of the Middle Ages. He was always interested in studies of traditional cooperation, but it was not his model for our society, which he hoped could become 'adaptive.'[2]

Nor can Mayo be exposed as an anarchist—someone who believes in 'the dangerous and destructive effects which politics and governmental action have on the will of the people.' Bendix and Fisher put him in the position of opposing government when faced with the simple question, 'Are you for government or against it?' But this is not the question, and Mayo would say that such an 'all or nothing' choice is characteristic of obsessive thinking. His real position is well stated in a remark that Bendix and Fisher quote without seeing its significance: 'Political action in a given community presumes the desire and capacity of individuals to work together; the political function cannot operate in a community from which this capacity has disappeared.' This does not imply that political conflict is inevitably destructive; it does imply that politics cannot work for growth in a society unless certain conditions hold, among others, a range of consensus among the members of the society. If the consensus does not exist, Mayo certainly holds that enforced cooperation, ultimately by dictatorship, destroys the capacity for spontaneous cooperation on which, he feels, the maintenance of civilization rests. But this view is not the same thing as opposition to governmental action. Since his retirement from Harvard, Mayo has found nothing in his convictions to prevent his working, as a consultant on industrial problems, with the labor government of Great Britain.[3]

As for the elite of industrial managers, Mayo did his work in industry, and it was natural for him to address himself to its leaders, especially as industry is obviously a key sector of modern society. He does not, one way or the other, express 'confidence in the ability of our industrial managers,' except to underline their competence in the merely technological field. He does point out that they, among others, have a responsibility and an opportunity. He feels that legislation is not going to help us out of our

---

[2] See especially *The Social Problems of an Industrial Civilization* (1945), p. 12.
[3] Elton Mayo died while this article was in press.

difficulties if it is not accompanied by an increased capacity for and a new conception of administration. He wants 'intelligent persons capable of analysing an individual or group attitude' at 'all the critical posts of communal activity.' The emphasis is on the *all*. Here again he is not in the position of opposing political action but of stating its necessary concomitants. And as for authority, Mayo would hold that authority, far from being necessarily in conflict with spontaneous cooperation, can exist at a high level only if spontaneous cooperation is achieved. And it is too often forgotten, among the existing conflicts of our industrial life, that, after all, workers and management do share one common activity: both together are producing goods and services for the use of the public.

Mayo never 'condemns all kinds of conflict.' He does not think in absolute but in relative values. He feels that there is, quantitatively, enough unresolved conflict in our civilization to put it in danger of a collapse backward to the Middle Ages he is supposed to admire so much. This belief is certainly not hard to hold nor original with Mayo. Indeed, concern about our social and international conflicts is so widely shared that, if Bendix and Fisher do not share it, perhaps it is they who ought to make their 'ethical presuppositions' clear.

individual member role performance for group task achievement (1953)

'The specialist', by Robert Sheckley, in *The SF Collection*, Chancellor Press, 1994, pp. 240–55; first published by the Galaxy Publishing Corporation, 1953.

It is sometimes easier to understand a topic or an issue by standing back from it. This reading consists of a science fiction short story written by Robert Sheckley. Although set in outer space, it reinforces the inter-galactic need for group effectiveness if a task is to be successfully accomplished, and it stresses the importance of the individual, complementary contributions of all members in achieving the group objective. We hope that you enjoy learning from it.

learning objectives

Once you have read and understood the prescribed materials, you should be able to:

1 Assess your knowledge of the concepts and ideas in Chapters 8 and 10 of the core text.
2 Analyze aspects of group structure, team member roles and group effectiveness within a work context.
3 Understand and apply the above in a new organizational setting.

learning pre-requisites

Before proceeding, you should read Chapter 8 and Chapter 10 of the core text, and the short story, 'The Specialist', by Robert Sheckley that follows.

learning activities

1 Every character in the short story played at least one of the team roles described by Meredith Belbin. Fill in the gaps to match the character to their team role.

Team role(s)	*Character*
1. Co-ordinator	(a) _____
2. _____	(b) Eye
3. Team Worker	(c) Doctor
4. _____	(d) Walls
5. Shaper	(e) _____
6. Monitor-Evaluator, Plant, Completer-Finisher	(f) _____
7. Monitor-Evaluator	(g) _____

2 Provide brief answers to the following questions.

▶ In one sentence, explain what Meredith Belbin's theory attempts to do.
▶ Imagine that you conducted a sociometric test on the Ship's crew. Which of its members would be revealed as a *mutual pair*?

▶ 'As with all groups, the team roles of the crew members in this story are not necessarily associated with their functional roles'. Is this statement true or false? Explain.

▶ In order to distinguish which factors affect group behaviour, researchers manipulate different variables, such as group size, task to be performed, and so on. The variable which is manipulated is called the _____ variable.

▶ All the members of the Ship have one and the same type of power. What is it?

▶ The diffusion of responsibility hypothesis, and cultural value hypothesis are two of the explanations offered to explain the *risky shift phenomenon*. What is the third?

▶ The Ship has a very effective communication structure. This is essential because all of its crew members depend on the information provided by the others. Shaw studied five communication networks – chain, wheel, 'Y', com-con and circle. (a) Draw the communication network which most accurately represents that found on this Ship, and (b) explain your diagram.

▶ The sequence in which information is transferred to allow Pusher to do his job is: Eye to Thinker, Thinker to Accumulator, Accumulator to Pusher. (a) Is this sequence correct? (b) Explain.

3 Fill in the blanks in the short summary that follows by selecting the appropriate words from the wordlist. There are more words in the list than fit into the summary.

Wordlist:

Doctor	Walls	democratic
Engine	ambiguity	effectiveness
Eye	conflict	functional
Feeder	cohesion	inspiration
Pusher	command	productivity
Talker	communication	satisfaction
Thinker	co-operative	specialists

Story summary

The Ship is composed of a crew who are all _____ (1). Each member depends on all the others forming a _____ (2) unit. Unlike human group roles, the team roles of each of the crew members are exactly the same as their _____ (3) roles. Through Eye, for example, _____ (4) was able to watch the storm and give Engine directions. As a Monitor-Evaluator, Engine is sober and unemotional, and lacks _____ (6). When faced with the problem of Pusher's death, _____ (6) came up with a range of possibilities which were then voted on. An agreement was easily reached which reflects strong group _____ (7). All members were united, illustrating the positive relationship between group cohesiveness, group _____ (8) and _____ (9). Talker appears to lead the crew because he forms the _____ (10) structure. His _____ (11) leadership style is necessitated by the fact that expertise in all tasks is always limited to only one crew member. Information exchange does not create a distorted message because there is no chain of _____ (12). All group roles are inter-linked. As the loss of_____ (13) revealed, if one crew member is lost, the Ship cannot function effectively.

READING

8

*The Specialist**
Robert Sheckley

The photon storm struck without warning, pouncing upon the Ship from behind a bank of giant red stars. Eye barely had time to flash a last-second warning through Talker before it was upon them.

It was Talker's third journey into deep space, and his first light-pressure storm. He felt a sudden pang of fear as the Ship yawed violently, caught the force of the wave-front and careened end for end. Then the fear was gone, replaced by a strong pulse of excitement.

Why should he be afraid, he asked himself – hadn't he been trained for just this sort of emergency?

He had been talking to Feeder when the storm hit, but he cut off the conversation abruptly. He hoped Feeder would be all right. It was the youngster's first deep-space trip.

The wire-like filaments that made up most of Talker's body were extended throughout the Ship. Quickly he withdrew all except the ones linking him to Eye, Engine, and the Walls. This was strictly their job now. The rest of the Crew would have to shift for themselves until the storm was over.

Eye had flattened his disc-like body against a Wall, and had one seeing organ extended outside the Ship. For greater concentration, the rest of his seeing organs were collapsed, clustered against his body.

Through Eye's seeing organ, Talker watched the storm. He translated Eye's purely visual image into a direction for Engine, who shoved the Ship around to meet the waves. At appreciably the same time, Talker translated direction into velocity for the Walls who stiffened to meet the shocks.

The coordination was swift and sure – Eye measuring the waves, Talker relaying the messages to Engine and Walls, Engine driving the Ship nose-first into the waves, and Walls bracing to meet the shock.

Talker forgot any fear he might have had in the swiftly functioning teamwork. He had no time to think. As the Ship's communication system, he had to translate and flash his messages at top speed, coordinating information and directing action.

In a matter of minutes, the storm was over.

'All right,' Talker said. 'Let's see if there was any damage!' His filaments had become tangled during the storm, but he untwisted and extended them through the Ship, plugging everyone into circuit. 'Engine?'

'I'm fine,' Engine said. The tremendous old fellow had dampened his plates during the storm, easing down the atomic explosions in his stomach. No storm could catch an experienced spacer like Engine unaware.

'Walls?'

The Walls reported one by one, and this took a long time. There were almost a thousand of them, thin, rectangular fellows making up the entire skin of the Ship. Naturally, they had reinforced their edges during the storm, giving the whole Ship resiliency. But one or two were dented badly.

Doctor announced that he was all right. He removed Talker's filament from his head, taking himself out of circuit, and went to work on the dented Walls. Made mostly of hands, Doctor had clung to an Accumulator during the storm.

'Let's go a little faster now!' Talker said, remembering that there still was the

* Reprinted by permission.

problem of determining where they were. He opened the circuit to the four Accumulators. 'How are you?' he asked.

There was no answer. The Accumulators were asleep. They had had their receptors open during the storm and were bloated on energy. Talker twitched his filaments around them, but they didn't stir.

'Let me!' Feeder said. Feeder had taken quite a beating before planting his suction cups to a Wall, but his cockiness was intact. He was the only member of the Crew who never needed Doctor's attention; his body was quite capable of repairing itself.

He scuttled across the floor on a dozen or so tentacles, and booted the nearest Accumulator. The big, conical storage unit opened one eye, then closed it again. Feeder kicked him again, getting no response. He reached for the Accumlator's safety valve and drained off some energy.

'Stop that!' the Accumulator said.

'Then wake up and report!' Talker told him.

The Accumulators said testily that they were all right, as any fool could see. They had been anchored to the floor during the storm.

The rest of the inspection went quickly. Thinker was fine, and Eye was ecstatic over the beauty of the storm. There was only one casualty.

Pusher was dead. Bipedal, he didn't have the stability of the rest of the Crew. The storm had caught him in the middle of a floor, thrown him against a stiffened Wall, and broken several of his important bones. He was beyond Doctor's skill to repair.

They were silent for a while. It was always serious when a part of the Ship died. The Ship was a cooperative unit, composed entirely of the Crew. The loss of any member was a blow to all the rest.

It was especially serious now. They had just delivered a cargo to a port several thousand light years from Galactic Centre. There was no telling where they might be.

Eye crawled to a Wall and extended a seeing organ outside. The Walls let it through, then sealed around it. Eye's organ pushed out, far enough from the Ship so he could view the entire sphere of stars. The picture travelled through Talker, who gave it to Thinker.

Thinker lay in one corner of the room, a great shapeless blob of protoplasm. Within him were all the memories of his space-going ancestors. He considered the picture, compared it rapidly with others stored in his cells, and said, 'No galactic planets within reach.'

Talker automatically translated for everyone. It was what they had feared.

Eye, with Thinker's help, calculated that they were several hundred light years off their course, on the galactic periphery.

Every Crew member knew what that meant. Without a Pusher to boost the Ship to a multiple of the speed of light, they would never get home. The trip back, without a Pusher, would take longer than most of their lifetimes.

'What would you suggest?' Talker asked Thinker.

This was too vague a question for the literal-minded Thinker. He asked to have it rephrased.

'What would be our best line of action,' Talker asked, 'to get back to a galactic planet?'

Thinker needed several minutes to go through all the possibilities stored in his cells. In the meantime, Doctor had patched the Walls and was asking to be given something to eat.

'In a little while we'll all eat,' Talker said, twitching his tendrils nervously. Even though he was the second youngest Crew member – only Feeder was younger – the responsibility was largely on him. This was still an emergency; he had to coordinate information and direct action.

One of the Walls suggested that they get good and drunk. This unrealistic solution was vetoed at once. It was typical of the Walls' attitude, however. They were fine workers and good shipmates, but happy-go-lucky fellows at best. When they returned to their home planets, they would probably blow all their wages on a spree.

'Loss of the Ship's Pusher cripples the Ship for sustained faster-than-light speeds,' Thinker began without preamble. 'The nearest galactic planet is four hundred and five light years off.'

Talker translated all this instantly along his wave-packet body.

'Two courses of action are open. First, the Ship can proceed to the nearest galactic planet under atomic power from Engine. This will take approximately two hundred years. Engine might still be alive at this time, although no one else will.

'Second, locate a primitive planet in this region, upon which are latent Pushers. Find one and train him. Have him push the Ship back to galactic territory.'

Thinker was silent, having given all the possibilities he could find in the memories of his ancestors.

They held a quick vote and decided upon Thinker's second alternative. There was no choice, really. It was the only one which offered them any hope of getting back to their homes.

'All right,' Talker said. 'Let's eat! I think we all deserve it.'

The body of the dead Pusher was shoved into the mouth of Engine, who consumed it at once, breaking down the atoms to energy. Engine was the only member of the Crew who lived on atomic energy.

For the rest, Feeder dashed up and loaded himself from the nearest Accumulator. Then he transformed the food within him into the substances each member ate. His body chemistry changed, altered, adapted, making the different foods for the Crew.

Eye lived entirely on a complex chlorophyll chain. Feeder reproduced this for him, then went over to give Talker his hydrocarbons, and the Walls their chlorine compound. For Doctor he made a facsimile of a silicate fruit that grew on Doctor's native planet.

Finally, feeding was over and the Ship back in order. The Accumulators were stacked in a corner, blissfully sleeping again. Eye was extending his vision as far as he could, shaping his main seeing organ for high-powered telescopic reception. Even in this emergency, Eye couldn't resist making verses. He announced that he was at work on a new narrative poem, called *Peripheral Glow*. No one wanted to hear it, so Eye fed it to Thinker, who stored everything, good or bad, right or wrong.

Engine never slept. Filled to the brim on Pusher, he shoved the Ship along at several times the speed of light.

The Walls were arguing among themselves about who had been the drunkest during their last leave.

Talker decided to make himself comfortable. He released his hold on the Walls and swung in the air, his small round body suspended by his criss-crossed network of filaments.

He thought briefly about Pusher. It was strange. Pusher had been everyone's friend and now he was forgotten. That wasn't because of indifference; it was because the Ship was a unit. The loss of a member was regretted, but the important thing was for the unit to go on.

The Ship raced through the suns of the periphery.

Thinker laid out a search spiral, calculating their odds on finding a Pusher planet at roughly four to one. In a week they found a planet of primitive Walls. Dropping low, they could see the leathery, rectangular fellows basking in the sun, crawling over rocks, stretching themselves thin in order to float in the breeze.

All the Ship's Walls heaved a sigh of nostalgia. It was just like home.

These Walls on the planet hadn't been contacted by a galactic team yet, and were still unaware of their great destiny – to join in the vast Cooperation of the Galaxy.

There were plenty of dead worlds in the spiral, and worlds too young to bear life. They found a planet of Talkers. The Talkers had extended their spidery communication lines across half a continent.

Talker looked at them eagerly, through Eye. A wave of self-pity washed over him. He remembered home, his family, his friends. He thought of the tree he was going to buy when he got back.

For a moment, Talker wondered what he was doing here, part of a Ship in a far corner of the Galaxy.

He shrugged off the mood. They were bound to find a Pusher planet, if they looked long enough.

At least, he hoped so.

There was a long stretch of arid worlds as the Ship sped through the unexplored periphery. Then a planetful of primeval Engines, swimming in a radioactive ocean.

'This is rich territory,' Feeder said to Talker. 'Galactic should send a Contact party here.'

'They probably will, after we get back,' Talker said.

They were good friends, above and beyond the all-enveloping friendship of the Crew. It wasn't only because they were the youngest Crew members, although that had something to do with it. They both had the same kind of functions and that made for a certain rapport. Talker translated languages; Feeder transformed foods. Also, they looked somewhat alike. Talker was a central core with radiating filaments; Feeder was a central core with radiating tentacles.

Talker thought that Feeder was the next most aware being on the Ship. He was never really able to understand how some of the others carried on the processes of consciousness.

More suns, more planets! Engine started to overheat. Usually, Engine was used only for taking off and landing, and for fine manoeuvring in a planetary group. Now he had been running continuously for weeks, both over and under the speed of light. The strain was telling on him.

Feeder, with Doctor's help, rigged a cooling system for him. It was crude, but it had to suffice. Feeder rearranged nitrogen, oxygen and hydrogen atoms to make a coolant for the system. Doctor diagnosed a long rest for Engine. He said that the gallant old fellow couldn't stand the strain for more than a week.

The search continued, with the Crew's spirits gradually dropping. They all realized that Pushers were rather rare in the Galaxy, as compared to the fertile Walls and Engines.

The Walls were getting pock-marked from interstellar dust. They complained that they would need a full beauty treatment when they got home. Talker assured them that the company would pay for it.

Even Eye was getting bloodshot from staring into space so continuously.

They dipped over another planet. Its characteristics were flashed to Thinker, who mulled over them.

Closer, and they could make out the forms.

Pushers! Primitive Pushers!

They zoomed back into space to make plans. Feeder produced twenty-three different kinds of intoxicants for a celebration.

The Ship wasn't fit to function for three days.

'Everyone ready now?' Talker asked, a bit fuzzily. He had a hangover that bumped all along his nerve ends. What a drunk he had thrown! He had a vague recollection of embracing Engine, and inviting him to share his tree when they got home.

He shuddered at the idea.

The rest of the Crew were pretty shaky, too. The Walls were letting air leak into space; they were just too wobbly to seal their edges properly. Doctor had passed out.

But the worst off was Feeder. Since his system could adapt to any type of fuel except atomic, he had been sampling every batch he made, whether it was an unbalanced iodine, pure oxygen or a supercharged ester. He was really miserable. His tentacles, usually a healthy aqua, were shot through with orange streaks. His system was working furiously, purging itself of everything, and Feeder was suffering the effects of the purge.

The only sober ones were Thinker and Engine. Thinker didn't drink, which was unusual for a spacer, though typical of Thinker, and Engine couldn't.

They listened while Thinker reeled off some astounding facts. From Eye's pictures of the planet's surface, Thinker had detected the presence of metallic construction. He put forth the alarming suggestion that these Pushers had constructed a mechanical civilization.

'That's impossible,' three of the Walls said flatly, and most of the Crew were inclined to agree with them. All the metal they had ever seen had been buried in the ground or lying around in worthless oxidized chunks.

'Do you mean that they make things out of metal?' Talker demanded. 'Out of just plain dead metal? What could they make?'

'They couldn't make anything,' Feeder said positively. 'It would break down constantly. I mean metal doesn't *know* when it's weakening.'

But it seemed to be true. Eye magnified his pictures, and everyone could see that the Pushers had made vast shelters, vehicles, and other articles from inanimate material.

The reason for this was not readily apparent, but it wasn't a good sign. However, the really hard part was over. The Pusher planet had been found. All that remained was the relatively easy job of convincing a native Pusher.

That shouldn't be too difficult. Talker knew that cooperation was the keystone of the Galaxy, even among primitive peoples.

The Crew decided not to land in a populated region. Of course, there was no reason not to expect a friendly greeting, but it was the job of a Contact Team to get in touch with them as a race. All they wanted was an individual.

Accordingly, they picked out a sparsely populated land-mass, drifting in while that side of the planet was dark.

They were able to locate a solitary Pusher almost at once.

Eye adapted his vision to see in the dark, and they followed the Pusher's movements. He lay down, after a while, beside a small fire. Thinker told them that this was a well-known resting habit of Pushers.

Just before dawn, the Walls opened, and Feeder, Talker and Doctor came out.

Feeder dashed forward and tapped the creature on the shoulder. Talker followed with a communication tendril.

The Pusher opened his seeing organs, blinked them, and made a movement with his eating organ. Then he leaped to his feet and started to run.

The three Crew members were amazed. The Pusher hadn't even waited to find out what the three of them wanted!

Talker extended a filament rapidly, and caught the Pusher, fifty feet away, by a limb. The Pusher fell.

'Treat him gently!' Feeder said. 'He might be startled by our appearance.' He twitched his tendrils at the idea of a Pusher – one of the strangest sights in the Galaxy, with his multiple organs – being startled at someone else's appearance.

Feeder and Doctor scurried to the fallen Pusher, picked him up and carried him back to the Ship.

The Walls sealed again. They released the Pusher and prepared to talk.

As soon as he was free, the Pusher sprang to his limbs and ran at the place where the Walls had sealed. He pounded against them frantically, his eating organ open and vibrating.

'Stop that!' the Wall said. He bulged, and the Pusher tumbled to the floor. Instantly, he jumped up and started to run forward.

'Stop him!' Talker said. 'He might hurt himself.'

One of the Accumulators woke up enough to roll into the Pusher's path. The Pusher fell, got up again, and ran on.

Talker had his filaments in the front of the Ship also, and he caught the Pusher in the bow. The Pusher started to tear at his tendrils, and Talker let go hastily.

'Plug him into the communication system!' Feeder shouted. 'Maybe we can reason with him.'

Talker advanced a filament towards the Pusher's head, waving it in the universal sign of communication. But the Pusher continued his amazing behaviour, jumping out of the way. He had a piece of metal in his hand and he was waving it frantically.

'What do you think he's going to do with that?' Feeder asked. The Pusher started to attack the side of the Ship, pounding at one of the Walls. The Wall stiffened instinctively and the metal snapped.

'Leave him alone,' Talker said. 'Give him a chance to calm down.'

Talker consulted with Thinker, but they couldn't decide what to do about the Pusher. He wouldn't accept communication. Every time Talker extended a filament, the Pusher showed all the signs of violent panic. Temporarily, it was an impasse.

Thinker vetoed the plan of finding another Pusher on the planet. He considered this Pusher's behaviour typical; nothing would be gained by approaching another. Also, a planet was supposed to be contacted only by a Contact Team.

If they couldn't communicate with this Pusher, they never would with another on the planet.

'I think I know what the trouble is,' Eye said. He crawled up on an Accumulator. 'These Pushers have evolved a mechanical civilization. Consider for a minute how they went about it. They developed the use of their fingers, like Doctor, to shape metal. They utilized their seeing organs, like myself. And probably countless other organs.' He paused for effect.

'These Pushers have become unspecialized.'

They argued over it for several hours. The Walls maintained that no intelligent creature could be unspecialized. It was unknown in the Galaxy. But the evidence was before them – the Pusher cities, their vehicles. This Pusher, exemplifying the rest, seemed capable of a multitude of things.

He was able to do everything except Push.

Thinker supplied a partial explanation. 'This is not a primitive planet. It is relatively old and should have been in the Cooperation thousands of years ago. Since it was not, the Pushers upon it were robbed of their birthright. Their ability, their speciality was to Push, but there was nothing *to* Push. Naturally, they have developed a deviant culture.

'Exactly what this culture is, we can only guess. But on the basis of the evidence, there is reason to believe that these Pushers are – uncooperative.'

Thinker had a habit of uttering the most shattering statement in the quietest possible way.

'It is entirely possible,' Thinker went on inexorably, 'that these Pushers will have nothing to do with us. In which case, our chances are approximately two hundred and eight-three to one against finding another Pusher planet.'

'We can't be sure he won't cooperate,' Talker said, 'until we get him into communication.' He found it almost impossible to believe that any intelligent creature would refuse to cooperate willingly.

'But how?' Feeder asked. They decided upon a course of action. Doctor walked slowly up to the Pusher, who backed away from him. In the meantime, Talker extended a filament outside the Ship, around, and in again, behind the Pusher.

The Pusher backed against a Wall – and Talker shoved the filament through the Pusher's head, into the communication socket in the centre of his brain.

The Pusher collapsed.

When he came to, Feeder and Doctor had to hold the Pusher's limbs, or he would have ripped out the communication line. Talker exercised his skill in learning the Pusher's language.

It wasn't too hard. All Pusher languages were of the same family, and this was no exception. Talker was able to catch enough surface thoughts to form a pattern.

He tried to communicate with the Pusher.

The Pusher was silent.

'I think he needs food,' Feeder said. They remembered that it had been almost two days since they had taken the Pusher on board. Feeder worked up some standard Pusher food and offered it.

'My God! A steak!' the Pusher said.

The Crew cheered along Talker's communication circuits. The Pusher had said his first words.

Talker examined the words and searched his memory. He knew about two hundred Pusher languages and many more simple variations. He found that this Pusher was speaking a cross between two Pusher tongues.

After the Pusher had eaten, he looked around. Talker caught his thoughts and broadcast them to the Crew.

The Pusher had a queer way of looking at the Ship. He saw it as a riot of colours. The walls undulated. In front of him was something resembling a gigantic spider, coloured black and green, with his web running all over the Ship and into the heads of all the creatures. He saw Eye as a strange, naked little animal, something between a skinned rabbit and an egg yolk – whatever those things were.

Talker was fascinated by the new perspective the Pusher's mind gave him. He had never seen things that way before. But now that the Pusher was pointing it out, Eye *was* a pretty funny-looking creature.

They settled down to communication.

'What in hell *are* you things?' the Pusher asked, much calmer now than he had been during the two days. 'Why did you grab me? Have I gone nuts?'

'No,' Talker said, 'you are not psychotic. We are a galactic trading ship. We were blown off our course by a storm and our Pusher was killed.'

'Well, what does that have to do with me?'

'We would like you to join our crew,' Talker said, 'to be our new Pusher.'

The Pusher thought it over after the situation was explained to him. Talker could catch the feeling of conflict in the Pusher's thoughts. He hadn't decided whether to accept this as a real situation or not. Finally, the Pusher decided that he wasn't crazy.

'Look, boys,' he said, 'I don't know what you are or how this makes sense. I have to get out of here. I'm on a furlough, and if I don't get back soon, the US Army's going to be very interested.'

Talker asked the Pusher to give him more information about 'army', and he fed it to Thinker.

'These Pushers engage in personal combat,' was Thinker's conclusion.

'But *why?*' Talker asked. Sadly he admitted to himself that Thinker might have been right; the Pusher didn't show many signs of willingness to cooperate.

'I'd like to help you lads out,' Pusher said,' but I don't know where you get the idea that I could push anything this size. You'd need a whole division of tanks just to budge it.'

'Do you approve of these wars?' Talker asked, getting a suggestion from Thinker.

'Nobody likes war – not those who have to do the dying at least.'

'Then why do you fight them?'

The Pusher made a gesture with his eating organ, which Eye picked up and sent to Thinker. 'It's kill or be killed. You guys know what war is, don't you?'

'We don't have any wars,' Talker said.

'You're lucky,' the Pusher said bitterly. 'We do. Plenty of them.'

'Of course,' Talker said. He had the full explanation from Thinker now. 'Would you like to end them?'

'Of course I would.'

'Then come with us! Be our Pusher!'

The Pusher stood up and walked up to an Accumulator. He sat down on it and doubled the ends of his upper limbs.

'How the hell can I stop all wars?' the Pusher demanded. 'Even if I went to the big shots and told them – '

'You won't have to,' Talker said. 'All you have to do is come with us. Push us to our base. Galactic will send a Contact Team to your planet. That will end your wars.'

'The hell you say,' the Pusher replied. 'You boys are stranded here, huh? Good enough! No monsters are going to take over Earth.'

Bewildered, Talker tried to understand the reasoning. Had he said something wrong? Was it possible that the Pusher didn't understand him?

'I thought you wanted to end wars,' Talker said.

'Sure I do. But I don't want anyone *making* us stop. I'm no traitor. I'd rather fight.'

'No one will make you stop. You will just stop because there will be no further need for fighting.'

'Do you know why we're fighting?'

'It's obvious.'

'Yeah? What's your explanation?'

'You Pushers have been separated from the main stream of the Galaxy,' Talker explained. 'You have your speciality – pushing – but nothing to push. Accordingly, you have no real jobs. You play with things – metal, inanimate objects – but find no real satisfaction. Robbed of your true vocation, you fight from sheer frustration.

'Once you find your place in the galactic Cooperation – and I assure you that it is an important place – your fighting will stop. Why should you fight, which is an unnatural occupation, when you can push? Also, your mechanical civilization will end, since there will be no need for it.'

The Pusher shook his head in what Talker guessed was a gesture of confusion. 'What is this pushing?'

Talker told him as best he could. Since the job was out of his scope, he had only a general idea of what a Pusher did.

'You mean to say that *that* is what every Earthman should be doing?'

'Of course,' Talker said. 'It is your great speciality.'

The Pusher thought about it for several minutes. 'I think you want a physicist or a mentalist or something. I could never do anything like that. I'm a junior architect.

And besides – well, it's difficult to explain.'

But Talker had already caught Pusher's objection. He saw a Pusher female in his thoughts. No, two, three. And he caught a feeling of loneliness, strangeness. The Pusher was filled with doubts. He was afraid.

'When we reach Galactic,' Talker said, hoping it was the right thing, 'you can meet other Pushers. Pusher females, too. All you Pushers look alike, so you should become friends with them. As far as loneliness in the Ship goes – it just doesn't exist. You don't understand the Cooperation yet. No one is lonely in the Cooperation.'

The Pusher was still considering the idea of there being other Pushers. Talker couldn't understand why he was so startled at that. The Galaxy was filled with Pushers, Feeders, Talkers, and many other species, endlessly duplicated.

'I can't believe that anybody could end all war,' Pusher said. 'How do I know you're not lying?'

Talker felt as if he had been struck in the core. Thinker must have been right when he said these Pushers would be uncooperative. Was this going to be the end of Talker's career? Were he and the rest of the Crew going to spend the rest of their lives in space, because of the stupidity of a bunch of Pushers?

Even thinking this, Talker was able to feel sorry for the Pusher. It must be terrible, he thought. Doubting, uncertain, never trusting anyone. If these Pushers didn't find their place in the Galaxy, they would exterminate themselves. Their place in the Cooperation was long overdue.

"What can I do to convince you?' Talker asked.

In despair, he opened all the circuits to the Pusher. He let the Pusher see Engine's good-natured gruffness, the devil-may-care humour of the Walls; he showed him Eye's poetic attempts, and Feeder's cocky good nature. He opened his own mind and showed the Pusher a picture of his home planet, his family, the tree he was planning to buy when he got home.

The pictures told the story of all of them, from different planets, representing different ethics, united by a common bond – the galactic Cooperation.

The Pusher watched it all in silence.

After a while, he shook his head. The thought accompanying the gesture was uncertain, weak – but negative.

Talker told the Walls to open. They did, and the Pusher stared in amazement.

'You may leave,' Talker said. 'Just remove the communication line and go.'

'What will you do?'

'We will look for another Pusher planet.'

'Where? Mars? Venus?'

'We don't know. All we can do is hope there is another in this region.'

The Pusher looked at the opening, then back at the Crew. He hesitated and his face screwed up in a grimace of indecision.

'All that you showed me was true?'

No answer was necessary.

'All right,' the Pusher said suddenly, 'I'll go. I'm a damned fool, but I'll go. If this means what you say – it *must* mean what you say!'

Talker saw that the agony of the Pusher's decision had forced him out of contact with reality. He believed that he was in a dream, where decisions are easy and unimportant.

'There's just one little trouble,' Pusher said with the lightness of hysteria. 'Boys, I'll be damned if I know how to push. You said something about faster-than-light? I can't even run the mile in an hour.'

'Of course you can push,' Talker assured him, hoping he was right. He knew what a Pusher's abilities were; but this one –

'Just try it.'

'Sure,' Pusher agreed. 'I'll probably wake up out of this, anyhow.'

They sealed the ship for take-off while Pusher talked to himself.

'Funny,' Pusher said. 'I thought a camping trip would be a nice way to spend a furlough and all I do is get nightmares!'

Engine boosted the Ship into the air. The Walls were sealed and Eye was guiding them away from the planet.

'We're in open space now,' Talker said. Listening to Pusher, he hoped his mind hadn't cracked. 'Eye and Thinker will give a direction, I'll transmit it to you, and you push along it.'

'You're crazy,' Pusher mumbled. 'You must have the wrong planet. I wish you nightmares would go away.'

'You're in the Cooperation now,' Talker said desperately. 'There's the direction. Push!'

The Pusher didn't do anything for a moment. He was slowly emerging from his fantasy, realizing that he wasn't in a dream, after all. He felt the Cooperation. Eye to Thinker, Thinker to Talker, Talker to Pusher, all inter-coordinated with Walls, and with each other.

'What is this?' Pusher asked. He felt the oneness of the Ship, the great warmth, the closeness achieved only in the Cooperation.

He pushed.

Nothing happened.

'Try again,' Talker begged.

Pusher searched his mind. He found a deep well of doubt and fear. Staring into it, he saw his own tortured face.

Thinker illuminated it for him.

Pushers had lived with this doubt and fear for centuries. Pushers had fought through fear, killed through doubt.

That was where the Pusher organ was!

Human – specialist – Pusher – he entered fully into the Crew, merged with them, threw mental arms around the shoulders of Thinker and Talker.

Suddenly, the Ship shot forward at eight times the speed of light. It continued to accelerate.

resisting and succumbing to group pressure (1955)

'Opinions and social pressure', by Solomon E. Asch, *Scientific American*, vol. 193, no. 5, 1955, pp. 31–5 (offprint no. 450).

Social control, that is, overt and covert pressure applied by members of groups, is at the heart of understanding much of the behaviour that occurs within organizations. Some of the earliest laboratory studies on the subject of group conformity were carried out by the psychologist, Solomon Asch. They concerned the psychology of groups, and the influence that they exerted over individuals. His work has been built upon by many other researchers, but remains the foundation stone for our knowledge of social control.

learning objectives

Once you have read and understood the prescribed material, you should be able to:

1 Assess your knowledge of the concepts contained in Chapter 9 of the core text.
2 Understand the theory, procedures and findings reported in Solomon Asch's article, 'Opinions and social pressure'.

learning pre-requisites

Before proceeding, you should read Chapter 9 of the core text, 'Group control', and the article, 'Opinions and social pressure' that follows.

learning activity

This learning activity invites you to test your knowledge. The following questions relate to the journal article. Write T [= true] or F [= false] in the space on the left of the number, for each of the 33 statements, to indicate whether you believe it be true or false.

1 An individual is more likely to conform if there is a unanimity of 3 as opposed to 1.
2 The presence of a truthful partner decreases the power of the majority by a third.
3 The presence of a Moderate Dissenter would produce the most accurate results for the subjects.
4 The effect of a truthful partner switching to the majority would cause an increase in subject errors.
5 In Asch's experiment, Desertion is defined as a truthful partner simply leaving the group.
6 When an overall majority gradually breaks away, eventually leaving the subject alone, the subject is independent up until the time no one is supporting him or her.
7 When opposition against a subject was increased to two people, the subjects accepted the wrong answer 15.6 per cent of the time.

8 The study showed that the experience of having had a partner, and braving the majority opposition with them, strengthened the subject's independence when that partner left.

9 Asch found that when the discrepancy between the standard line and the other lines became grossly manifest, every subject repudiated it and chose independently.

10 If a Moderate Dissenter is present, the power of the majority decreases by a third.

11 All the yielding subjects underestimated the frequency with which they conformed.

12 Towards the end of the nineteenth century, the view that only hysterical patients could be fully hypnotized was challenged by Hyppollyte Bernheim and Jean Martin Charcot.

13 A Yielding Person could be described as someone who had the capacity to recover from doubt and re-establish their equilibrium.

14 If a Truthful Partner left instead of a Deserter, their effect on the subject outlasted their presence.

15 In the presence of a Moderate Dissenter, the majority of errors the subjects made were moderate, rather than flagrant.

16 The values and beliefs that we hold are not innate, and can be influenced by social forces.

17 Gabriel Tarde believed that social man lived in a hypnotic trance.

18 Conformity is shown to increase as group size increases.

19 The degree of conformity decreases when group members have a higher status than the subject.

20 The results of Asch's experiments can be explained, in part, by subjects' innate need for a satisfying response from their peers.

21 The evidence of a person's senses cannot be contradicted by social pressures.

22 Asch conducted his experiment using an optical illusion.

23 Distortion-of-action yielding involves a subject not perceiving themselves to be incorrect, but yielding, nevertheless, because of an overriding need not to appear different from, or inferior to, others.

24 The weight of pressure to conform increases proportionally with the size of the majority.

25 The unanimity of the majority can affect the pressure on a subject to conform.

26 The presence of a Dissenter can affect the degree of influence that the majority is able to exert over a subject.

27 The effect of the majority on the subject is greatest when a Moderate, rather than when an Extremist Dissenter, is present.

28 Asch distinguished several different types of yielding.

29 When a subject is isolated, the tendency to conform increases dramatically.

30 The confidence gained by having a partner remains, even when that same Partner defects to the majority.

31 Charcot proposed that hypnosis was an extreme form of a normal psychological process known as suggestibility.

32 All the individuals who did not succumb to the pressure of the group were characterized by an inability to recover from doubt, which all the yielding subjects lacked.

33 Asch's experiments illustrate the way in which a person's viewpoint will shift to come into line with that of a consensus.

READING
9 *Opinions and social pressure**
Solomon E. Asch

Exactly what is the effect of the opinions of others on our own? In other words, how strong is the urge toward social conformity? The question is approached by means of some unusual experiments.

That social influences shape every person's practices, judgments and beliefs is a truism to which anyone will readily assent. A child masters his 'native' dialect down to the finest nuances; a member of a tribe of cannibals accepts cannibalism as altogether fitting and proper. All the social sciences take their departure from the observation of the profound effects that groups exert on their members. For psychologists, group pressure upon the minds of individuals raises a host of questions they would like to investigate in detail.

How, and to what extent, do social forces constrain people's opinions and attitudes? This question is especially pertinent in our day. The same epoch that has witnessed the unprecedented technical extension of communication as also brought into existence the deliberate manipulation of opinion and the 'engineering of consent.' There are many good reasons why, as citizens and as scientists, we should be concerned with studying the ways in which human beings form their opinions and the role that social conditions play.

Studies of these questions began with the interest in hypnosis aroused by the French physician Jean Martin Charcot (a teacher of Sigmund Freud) toward the end of the 19th century. Charcot believed that only hysterical patients could be fully hypnotized, but this view was soon challenged by two other physicians, Hyppolyte Bernheim and A. A. Liébault, who demonstrated that they could put most people under the hypnotic spell. Bernheim proposed that hypnosis was but an extreme form of a normal psychological process which became known as 'suggestibility.' It was shown that monotonous reiteration of instructions could induce in normal persons in the waking state involuntary bodily changes such as swaying or rigidity of the arms, and sensations such as warmth and odor.

It was not long before social thinkers seized upon these discoveries as a basis for explaining numerous social phenomena, from the spread of opinion to the formation of crowds and the following of leaders. The sociologist Gabriel Tarde summed it all up in the aphorism: 'Social man is a somnambulist.'

When the new discipline of social psychology was born at the beginning of this century, its first experiments were essentially adaptations of the suggestion demonstration. The technique generally followed a simple plan. The subjects, usually college students, were asked to give their opinions or preferences concerning various matters; some time later they were again asked to state their choices, but now they were also informed of the opinions held by authorities or large groups of their peers on the same matters. (Often the alleged consensus was fictitious.) Most of these studies had substantially the same result: confronted with opinions contrary to their own, many subjects apparently shifted their judgments in the direction of the views of the majorities or the experts. The late psychologist Edward L. Thorndike reported that he had succeeded in modifying the esthetic preferences of adults by this procedure. Other psychologists reported that people's evaluations of the merit of a literary passage could be raised or lowered by ascribing the passage to different authors. Apparently the sheer weight of numbers or authority sufficed to change opinions, even when no arguments for the opinions themselves were provided.

Now the very ease of success in these experiments arouses suspicion. Did the subjects actually change their opinions, or were the experimental victories scored only on paper? On grounds of common sense, one must question whether opinions are generally as watery as these studies indicate. There is some reason to wonder whether it was not the investigators who, in their enthusiasm for a theory, were suggestible, and whether the ostensibly gullible subjects were not providing answers which they thought good subjects were expected to give.

The investigations were guided by certain underlying assumptions, which today are common currency and account for much that is thought and said about the operations of propaganda and public opinion. The assumptions are that people submit uncritically and painlessly to external manipulation by suggestion or prestige, and that any given idea or value can be 'sold' or 'unsold' without reference to its merits. We should be skeptical, however, of the supposition that the power of social pressure necessarily implies uncritical submission to it: independence and the capacity to rise above group passion are also open to human beings. Further, one may question on psychological grounds whether it is possible as a rule to change a person's judgment of a situation or an object without first changing his knowledge or assumptions about it.

In what follows I shall describe some experiments in an investigation of the effects of group pressure which was carried out recently with the help of a number of my

Figure 1 The experiment is repeated in the Laboratory of Social Relations at Harvard University. Seven student subjects are asked by the experimenter (*right*) to compare the length of lines (*see Figure 2*). Six of the subjects have been coached beforehand to give unanimously wrong answers. The seventh (*sixth from the left*) has merely been told that it is an experiment in perception

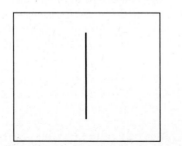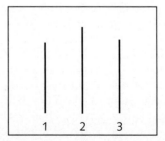

Figure 2 Subjects were shown two cards. One bore a standard line. The other bore three lines, one of which was the same length as the standard. The subjects were asked to choose this line.

associates. The tests not only demonstrate the operations of group pressure upon individuals but also illustrate a new kind of attack on the problem and some of the more subtle questions that it raises.

A group of seven to nine young men, all college students, are assembled in a class-room for a 'psychological experiment' in visual judgement. The experimenter informs them that they will be comparing the lengths of lines. He shows two large white cards. On one is a single vertical black line—the standard whose length is to be matched. On the other card are three vertical lines of various lengths. The subjects are to choose the one that is of the same length as the line on the other card. One of the three actually is of the same length; the other two are substantially different, the difference ranging from three quarters of an inch to an inch and three quarters.

The experiment opens uneventfully. The subjects announce their answers in the order in which they have been seated in the room, and on the first round every person chooses the same matching line. Then a second set of cards is exposed; again the group is unanimous. The members appear ready to endure politely another boring experiment. On the third trial there is an unexpected disturbance. One person near the end of the group disagrees with all the others in his selection of the matching line. He looks surprised, indeed incredulous, about the disagreement. On the following trial he disagrees again, while the others remain unanimous in their choice. The dissenter becomes more and more worried and hesitant as the disagreement continues in succeeding trials; he may pause before announcing his answer and speak in a low voice, or he may smile in an embarrassed way.

What the dissenter does not know is that all the other members of the group were instructed by the experimenter beforehand to give incorrect answers in unanimity at certain points. The single individual who is not a party to this prearrangement is the focal subject of our experiment. He is placed in a position in which, while he is actually giving the correct answers, he finds himself unexpectedly in a minority of one, opposed by a unanimous and arbitrary majority with respect to a clear and simple fact. Upon him we have brought to bear two opposed forces: the evidence of his senses and the unanimous opinion of a group of his peers. Also, he must declare his judgments in public, before a majority which has also stated its position publicly.

The instructed majority occasionally reports correctly in order to reduce the possibility that the naive subject will suspect collusion against him. (In only a few cases did the subject actually show suspicion; when this happened, the experiment was stopped and the results were not counted.) There are 18 trials in each series, and on 12 of these the majority responds erroneously.

How do people respond to group pressure in this situation? I shall report first the statistical results of a series in which a total of 123 subjects from three institutions of higher learning (not including my own, Swarthmore College) were placed in the minority situation described above.

Two alternatives were open to the subject: he could act independently, repudiating the majority, or he could go along with the majority, repudiating the evidence of his senses. Of the 123 put to the test, a considerable percentage yielded to the majority. Whereas in ordinary circumstances individuals matching the lines will make mistakes less than 1 per cent of the time, under group pressure the minority subjects swung to acceptance of the misleading majority's wrong judgments in 36.8 per cent of the selections.

Of course individuals differed in response. At one extreme, about one quarter of the subjects were completely independent and never agreed with the erroneous judgments of the majority. At the other extreme, some individuals went with the majority nearly all the time. The performances of individuals in this experiment tend to be highly consistent. Those who strike out on the path of independence do not, as a

Figure 3 The experiment proceeds as follows. In the top picture the subject (*center*) hears rules of the experiment for the first time. In the second picture he makes his first judgment of a pair of cards, disagreeing with the unanimous judgment of the others. In the third he leans forward to look at another pair of cards. In the fourth he shows the strain of repeatedly disagreeing with the majority. In the fifth, after 12 pairs of cards have been shown, he explains that 'he has to call them as he sees them.' This subject disagreed with the majority on all 12 trials. Seventy-five per cent of experimental subjects agree with the majority in varying degrees

rule, succumb to the majority even over an extended series of trials, while those who choose the path of compliance are unable to free themselves as the ordeal is prolonged.

The reasons for the startling individual differences have not yet been investigated in detail. At this point we can only report some tentative generalizations from talks with the subjects, each of whom was interviewed at the end of the experiment. Among the independent individuals were many who held fast because of staunch confidence in their own judgment. The most significant fact about them was not absence of responsiveness to the majority but a capacity to recover from doubt and to re-establish their equilibrium. Others who acted independently came to believe that the majority was correct in its answers, but they continued their dissent on the simple ground that it was their obligation to call the play as they saw it.

Among the extremely yielding persons we found a group who quickly reached the conclusion: 'I am wrong, they are right.' Others yielded in order 'not to spoil your results.' Many of the individuals who went along suspected that the majority were 'sheep' following the first responder, or that the majority were victims of an optical illusion; nevertheless, these suspicions failed to free them at the moment of decision. More disquieting were the reactions of subjects who construed their difference from the majority as a sign of some general deficiency in themselves, which at all costs they must hide. On this basis they desperately tried to merge with the majority, not realizing the longer-range consequences to themselves. All the yielding subjects underestimated the frequency with which they conformed.

Which aspect of the influence of a majority is more important—the size of the majority or its unanimity? The experiment was modified to examine this question. In one series the size of the opposition was varied from one to 15 persons. The results showed a clear trend. When a subject was confronted with only a single individual who contradicted his answers, he was swayed little: he continued to answer independently and correctly in nearly all trials. When the opposition was increased to two, the pressure became substantial: minority subjects now accepted the wrong answer 13.6 per cent of the time. Under the pressure of a majority of three, the subjects' errors jumped to 31.8 per cent. But further increases in the size of the majority apparently did not increase the weight of the pressure substantially. Clearly the size of the opposition is important only up to a point.

Disturbance of the majority's unanimity had a striking effect. In this experiment the subject was given the support of a truthful partner—either another individual who did not know of the prearranged agreement among the rest of the group, or a person who was instructed to give correct answers throughout.

The presence of a supporting partner depleted the majority of much of its power. Its pressure on the dissenting individual was reduced to one fourth: that is, subjects answered incorrectly only one fourth as often as under the pressure of a unanimous majority (see *Figure 6*). The weakest persons did not yield as readily. Most interesting were the reactions to the partner. Generally the feeling toward him was one of warmth and closeness; he was credited with inspiring confidence. However, the subjects repudiated the suggestion that the partner decided them to be independent.

Was the partner's effect a consequence of his dissent, or was it related to his accuracy? We now introduced into the experimental group a person who was instructed to dissent from the majority but also to disagree with the subject. In some experiments the majority was always to choose the worst of the comparison lines and the instructed dissenter to pick the line that was closer to the length of the standard one; in others the majority was consistently intermediate and the dissenter most in error. In this manner we were able to study the relative influence of 'compromising' and 'extremist' dissenters.

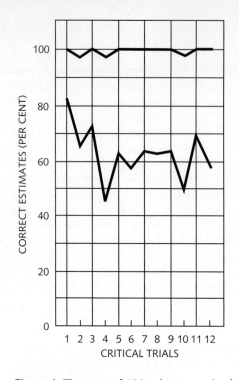

Figure 4 The error of 123 subjects, each of whom compared lines in the presence of six to eight opponents, is plotted in the lower curve. The accuracy of judgments not under pressure is indicated in the upper curve

Again the results are clear. When a moderate dissenter is present, the effect of the majority on the subject decreases by approximately one third, and extremes of yielding disappear. Moreover, most of the errors the subjects do make are moderate, rather than flagrant. In short, the dissenter largely controls the choice of errors. To this extent the subjects broke away from the majority even while bending to it.

On the other hand, when the dissenter always chose the line that was more flagrantly different from the standard, the results were of quite a different kind. The extremist dissenter produced a remarkable freeing of the subjects; their errors dropped to only 9 per cent. Furthermore, all the errors were of the moderate variety. We were able to conclude that dissent *per se* increased independence and moderated the errors that occurred, and that the direction of dissent exerted consistent effects.

In all the foregoing experiments each subject was observed only in a single setting. We now turned to studying the effects upon a given individual of a change in the situation to which he was exposed. The first experiment examined the consequences of losing or gaining a partner. The instructed partner began by answering correctly on the first six trials. With his support the subject usually resisted pressure from the majority: 18 of 27 subjects were completely independent. But after six trials the partner joined the majority. As soon as he did so, there was an abrupt rise in the subjects' errors. Their submission to the majority was just about as frequent as when the minority subject was opposed by a unanimous majority throughout.

It was surprising to find that the experience of having had a partner and of having braved the majority opposition with him had failed to strengthen the individuals' independence. Questioning at the conclusion of the experiment suggested that we had overlooked an important circumstance; namely, the strong specific effect of 'desertion'

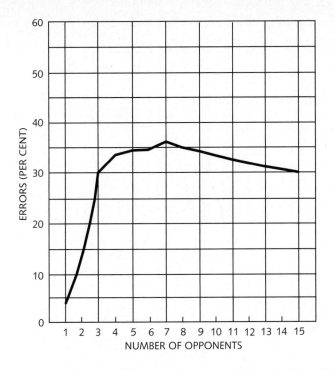

Figure 5 The size of majority which opposed them had an effect on the subjects. With a single opponent the subject erred only 3.6 per cent of the time; with two opponents he erred 13.6 per cent; three, 31.8 per cent; four, 35.1 per cent; six, 35.2 per cent; seven, 37.1 per cent; nine, 35.1 per cent; 15, 31.2 per cent

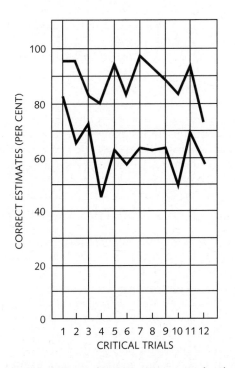

Figure 6 Two subjects supporting each other against a majority made fewer errors (*upper curve*) than one subject did against a majority (*lower curve*)

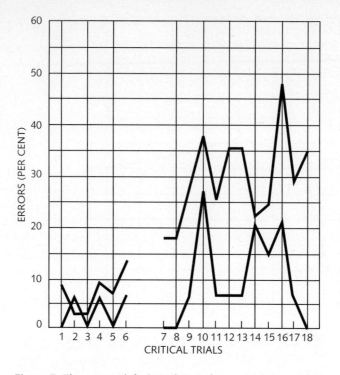

Figure 7 The partner left the subject after six trials in a single experiment. The upper curve shows the error of the subject when the partner 'deserted' to the majority. The lower curve shows the error when the partner merely left the room

by the partner to the other side. We therefore changed the conditions so that the partner would simply leave the group at the proper point. (To allay suspicion it was announced in advance that he had an appointment with the dean.) In this form of the experiment, the partner's effect outlasted his presence. The errors increased after his departure, but less markedly than after a partner switched to the majority.

In a variant of this procedure the trials began with the majority unanimously giving correct answers. Then they gradually broke away until on the sixth trial the naive subject was alone and the group unanimously against him. As long as the subject had anyone on his side, he was almost invariably independent, but as soon as he found himself alone, the tendency to conform to the majority rose abruptly.

As might be expected, an individual's resistance to group pressure in these experiments depends to a considerable degree on how wrong the majority is. We varied the discrepancy between the standard line and the other lines systematically, with the hope of reaching a point where the error of the majority would be so glaring that every subject would repudiate it and choose independently. In this we regretfully did not succeed. Even when the difference between the lines was seven inches, there were still some who yielded to the error of the majority.

The study provides clear answers to a few relatively simple questions, and it raises many others that await investigation. We would like to know the degree of consistency of persons in situations which differ in content and structure. If consistency of independence or conformity in behavior is shown to be a fact, how is it functionally related to qualities of character and personality? In what ways is independence related to sociological or cultural conditions? Are leaders more independent than other people, or are they adept at following their followers? These and many other questions may perhaps be answerable by investigations of the type described here.

Life in society requires consensus as an indispensable condition. But consensus, to be productive, requires that each individual contribute independently out of his experience and insight. When consensus comes under the dominance of conformity, the social process is polluted and the individual at the same time surrenders the powers on which his functioning as a feeling and thinking being depends. That we have found the tendency to conformity in our society so strong that reasonably intelligent and well-meaning young people are willing to call white black is a matter of concern. It raises questions about our ways of education and about the values that guide our conduct.

Yet anyone inclined to draw too pessimistic conclusions from this report would do well to remind himself that the capacities for independence are not to be underestimated. He may also draw some consolation from a further observation: those who participated in this challenging experiment agreed nearly without exception that independence was preferable to conformity.

excessive group cohesion impedes task performance (1971)

'Groupthink', by Irving L. Janis, *Psychology Today magazine*, November 1971, pp. 43–6.

The idea that the more cohesive a group or team is, then the more effective it is, is a tenet which underlies much of the team-building activities performed by organization development consultants and trainers. Yet research has shown that a group can become too cohesive, and as a result, can make wrong decisions. The dangers posed by over-cohesive groups were first discovered in the late 1960s by Irving Janis, a psychologist working at Yale University. The label he gave to the tunnel thinking that resulted in faulty group decision-making was *groupthink*. Janis went on to help groups recognize their own deficiencies by listing various symptoms of groupthink, and also suggested a number of remedies to counteract its effects.

learning objectives

Once you have read and understood the prescribed material, you should be able to:

1 Identify the causes, symptoms and consequences of groupthink, and remedies to counter it.
2 Relate the causes of groupthink to earlier research on individual conformity and group pressure and control.
3 Relate the various symptoms of groupthink in a systematic and sequential way.
4 Provide examples of groupthink-infected speech and thought.
5 Suggest the likely difficulties in implementing Janis's suggested remedies to counter groupthink.

learning pre-requisites

Before proceeding, you should read Chapters 9 and 10 of the core text, and the following article, 'Groupthink', by Irving L. Janis.

learning activity

Janis's article on groupthink deals with the topic under four main headings – its causes, symptoms, products (or consequences) and remedies. The four learning activities address each of these.

1 *Causes*: Compared with his discussion of the symptoms of groupthink, Janis's explanation of its causes is somewhat superficial. Nevertheless, he does briefly indicate what these may be. Use your knowledge of Chapter 9, to identify three causes of groupthink mentioned in the article, and explain briefly how each contributes to create the phenomenon.

2 *Symptoms*: A large part of Janis's article deals with a description of each of the eight

Causes of groupthink→	Overestimation by the group→	Closed mindedness→	Reinforcement of conformity
Factors encouraging	Develops faulty expectations of the consequences of group action	Members close their minds exactly when decision-making requires open minds. Leads to faulty consensus	Conformity that was previously established is now reinforced

symptoms of groupthink. These can be found in Chapter 10 of the core text as well. Use the table below to first identify the causes (or antecedent conditions) which encourage groupthink. Insert these in the first column. Then, classify the eight symptoms of groupthink under the three headings, according to the definition provided. Each column will have between 2 and 4 symptoms.

3 *Products*: The products or consequences of groupthink ultimately translate into what people think and say (or don't say) within the group. The New Yorker cartoon in the the core text (p. 285) captures this idea rather neatly. Devise a mental thought or verbal statement which encapsulates each of the six products described by Janis. For example, the first might be typified by the verbal statement 'Look, let's not get distracted by all these possibilities. Let's stick to considering this one, and get a decision.'

4 *Remedies*: Janis recommends nine possible remedies for countering groupthink, before going on to identify four problems in implementing them. Review all of the remedies that he suggests, and for each of the nine, identify a possible implementation problem. These problems may relate to the remedy's practicality, feasibility, timeliness, cost or other similar dimensions.

READING
10
groupthink: the desperate drive for consensus at any cost*
Irving L. Janis

'How could we have been so stupid?' President John F. Kennedy asked after he and a close group of advisers had blundered into the Bay of Pigs invasion. For the last two years I have been studying that question, as it applies not only to the Bay of Pigs decision-makers but also to those who led the United States into such other major fiascos as the failure to be prepared for the attack on Pearl Harbor, the Korean War stalemate and the escalation of the Vietnam War.

Stupidity certainly is not the explanation. The men who participated in making the Bay of Pigs decision, for instance, comprised one of the greatest arrays of intellectual talent in the history of American Government—Dean Rusk, Robert McNamara, Douglas Dillon, Robert Kennedy, McGeorge Bundy, Arthur Schlesinger Jr., Allen Dulles and others.

It also seemed to me that explanations were incomplete if they concentrated only on disturbances in the behavior of each individual within a decision-making body: temporary emotional states of elation, fear, or anger that reduce a man's mental efficiency, for example, or chronic blind spots arising from a man's social prejudices or idiosyncratic biases.

I preferred to broaden the picture by looking at the fiascos from the stand point of group dynamics as it has been explored over the past three decades, first by the great social psychologist Kurt Lewin and later in many experimental situations by myself and other behavioral scientists. My conclusion after poring over hundreds of relevant documents—historical reports about formal group meetings and informal conversations among the members—is that the groups that committed the fiascos were victims of what I call 'groupthink.'

Groupy. In each case study, I was surprised to discover the extent to which each group displayed the typical phenomena of social conformity that are regularly encountered in studies of group dynamics among ordinary citizens. For example, some of the phenomena appear to be completely in line with findings from social psychological experiments showing that powerful social pressures are brought to bear by the members of a cohesive group whenever a dissident begins to voice his objections to a group consensus. Other phenomena are reminiscent of the shared illusions observed in encounter groups and friendship cliques when the members simultaneously reach a peak of 'groupy' feelings.

Above all, there are numerous indications pointing to the development of group norms that bolster morale at the expense of critical thinking. One of the most common norms appears to be that of remaining loyal to the group by sticking with the policies to which the group has already committed itself, even when those policies are obviously working out badly and have unintended consequences that disturb the conscience of each member. This is one of the key characteristics of groupthink.

1984. I use the term groupthink as a quick and easy way to refer to the mode of thinking that persons engage in when *concurrence-seeking* becomes so dominant in a cohesive ingroup that it tends to override realistic appraisal of alternative courses of action. Groupthink is a term of the same order as the words in the newspeak vocabulary George Orwell used in his dismaying world of *1984*. In that context, groupthink takes on an invidious connotation. Exactly such a connotation is intended, since the term refers to a deterioration in mental efficiency, reality testing and moral judgments as a result of group pressures.

The symptoms of groupthink arise when the members of decision-making groups become motivated to avoid being too harsh in their judgments of their leaders' or their colleagues' ideas. They adopt a soft line of criticism, even in their own thinking. At their meetings, all the members are amiable and seek complete concurrence on every important issue, with no bickering or conflict to spoil the cozy, 'we-feeling' atmosphere.

Kill. Paradoxically, soft-headed groups are often hard-hearted when it comes to dealing with outgroups or enemies. They find it relatively easy to resort to dehumanizing solutions—they will readily authorize bombing attacks that kill large numbers of civilians in the name of the noble cause of persuading an unfriendly government to negotiate at the peace table. They are unlikely to pursue the more difficult and controversial issues that arise when alternatives to a harsh military solution come up for discussion. Nor are they inclined to raise ethical issues that carry the implication that this *fine group of ours, with its humanitarianism and its highmind-ed principles, might be capable of adopting a course of action that is inhumane and immoral.*

Norms. There is evidence from a number of social-psychological studies that as the members of a group feel more accepted by the others, which is a central feature of increased group cohesiveness, they display less overt conformity to group norms. Thus we would expect that the more cohesive a group becomes, the less the members will feel constrained to censor what they say out of fear of being socially punished for antagonizing the leader or any of their fellow members.

In contrast, the groupthink type of conformity tends to increase as group cohesiveness increases. Groupthink involves nondeliberate suppression of critical thoughts as a result of internalization of the group's norms, which is quite different from deliberate suppression on the basis of external threats of social punishment. The more cohesive the group, the greater the inner compulsion on the part of each member to avoid creating disunity, which inclines him to believe in the soundness of whatever proposals are promoted by the leader or by a majority of the group's members.

In a cohesive group, the danger is not so much that each individual will fail to reveal his objections to what the others propose but that he will think the proposal is a good one, without attempting to carry out a careful, critical scrutiny of the pros and cons of the alternatives. When groupthink becomes dominant, there also is considerable suppression of deviant thoughts, but it takes the form of each person's deciding that his misgivings are not relevant and should be set aside, that the benefit of the doubt regarding any lingering uncertainties should be given to the group consensus.

Stress. I do not mean to imply that all cohesive groups necessarily suffer from groupthink. All ingroups may have a mild tendency toward groupthink, displaying one or another of the symptoms from time to time, but it need not be so dominant as to influence the quality of the group's final decision. Neither do I mean to imply that there is anything necessarily inefficient or harmful about group decisions in general. On the contrary, a group whose members have properly defined roles, with traditions concerning the procedures to follow in pursuing a critical inquiry, probably is capable of making better decisions than any individual group member working alone.

The problem is that the advantages of having decisions made by groups are often lost because of powerful psychological pressures that arise where the members work closely together, share the same set of values and, above all, face a crisis situation that puts everyone under intense stress.

The main principle of groupthink, which I offer in the spirit of Parkinson's Law, is this: *The more amiability and esprit de corps there is among the members of a policy-making ingroup, the greater the danger that independent critical thinking will be replaced by groupthink, which is likely to result in irrational and dehumanising actions directed against outgroups.*

Symptoms. In my studies of high-level governmental decision-makers, both civilian and military, I have found eight main symptoms of groupthink.

1 **Invulnerability**. Most or all of the members of the ingroup share an illusion of invulnerability that provides for them some degree of reassurance about obvious dangers and leads them to become over-optimistic and willing to take extraordinary risks. It also causes them to fail to respond to clear warnings of danger.

The Kennedy ingroup, which uncritically accepted the Central Intelligence

Agency's disastrous Bay of Pigs plan, operated on the false assumption that they could keep secret the fact that the United States was responsible for the invasion of Cuba. Even after news of the plan began to leak out, their belief remained unshaken. They failed even to consider the danger that awaited them: a worldwide revulsion against the U.S.

A similar attitude appeared among the members of President Lyndon B. Johnson's ingroup, the 'Tuesday Cabinet,' which kept escalating the Vietnam War despite repeated setbacks and failures. 'There was a belief,' Bill Moyers commented after he resigned, 'that if we indicated a willingness to use our power, they [the North Vietnamese] would get the message and back away from an all-out confrontation. . . . There was a confidence—it was never bragged about, it was just there—that when the chips were really down, the other people would fold.'

A most poignant example of an illusion of invulnerability involves the ingroup around Admiral H. E. Kimmel, which failed to prepare for the possibility of a Japanese attack on Pearl Harbor despite repeated warnings. Informed by his intelligence chief that radio contact with Japanese aircraft carriers had been lost, Kimmel joked about it: 'What, you don't know where the carriers are? Do you mean to say that they could be rounding Diamond Head (at Honolulu) and you wouldn't know it?' The carriers were in fact moving full-steam toward Kimmel's command post at the time. Laughing together about a danger signal, which labels it as a purely laughing matter, is a characteristic manifestation of groupthink.

2 **Rationale**. As we see, victims of groupthink ignore warnings; they also collectively construct rationalizations in order to discount warnings and other forms of negative feedback that, taken seriously, might lead the group members to reconsider their assumptions each time they recommit themselves to past decisions. Why did the Johnson ingroup avoid reconsidering its escalation policy when time and again the expectations on which they based their decisions turned out to be wrong? James C. Thompson, Jr., a Harvard historian who spent five years as an observing participant in both the State Department and the White House, tells us that the policymakers avoided critical discussion of their prior decisions and continually invented new rationalizations so that they could sincerely recommit themselves to defeating the North Vietnamese.

In the fall of 1964, before the bombing of North Vietnam began, some of the policymakers predicted that six weeks of air strikes would induce the North Vietnamese to seek peace talks. When someone asked, 'What if they don't?' the answer was that another four weeks certainly would do the trick.

Later, after each setback, the ingroup agreed that by investing just a bit more effort (by stepping up the bomb tonnage a bit, for instance), their course of action would prove to be right. The *Pentagon Papers* bear out those observations.

In *The Limits of Intervention*, Townsend Hoopes, who was acting Secretary of the Air Force under Johnson, says that Wait W. Rostow in particular showed a remarkable capacity for what has been called 'instant rationalization.' According to Hoopes, Rostow buttressed the group's optimism about being on the road to victory by culling selected scraps of evidence from news reports or, if necessary, by inventing 'plausible' forecasts that had no basis in evidence at all.

Admiral Kimmel's group rationalized away their warnings, too. Right up to December 7, 1941, they convinced themselves that the Japanese would never dare attempt a full-scale surprise assault against Hawaii because Japan's leaders would realize that it would precipitate an all-out war which the United States would surely win. They made no attempt to look at the situation through the eyes of the Japanese leaders—another manifestation of groupthink.

3 **Morality**. Victims of groupthink believe unquestioningly in the inherent morality of their ingroup; this belief inclines the members to ignore the ethical or moral consequences of their decisions.

Evidence that this symptom is at work usually is of a negative kind—the things that are left unsaid in group meetings. At least two influential persons had doubts about the morality of the Bay of Pigs adventure. One of them, Arthur Schlesinger, Jr., presented his strong objections in a memorandum to President Kennedy and Secretary of State Rusk but suppressed them when he attended meetings of the Kennedy team. The other, Senator J. William Fulbright, was not a member of the group, but the President invited him to express his misgivings in a speech to the policymakers. However, when Fulbright finished speaking the President moved on to other agenda items without asking for reactions of the group.

David Kraslow and Stuart H. Loory, in *The Secret Search for Peace in Vietnam*, report that during 1966 President Johnson's ingroup was concerned primarily with selecting bomb targets in North Vietnam. They based their selections on four factors—the military advantage, the risk to American aircraft and pilots, the danger of forcing other countries into the fighting, and the danger of heavy civilian casualties. At their regular Tuesday luncheons, they weighed these factors the way school teachers grade examination papers, averaging them out. Though evidence on this point is scant, I suspect that the group's ritualistic adherence to a standardized procedure induced the members to feel morally justified in their destructive way of dealing with the Vietnamese people—after all, the danger of heavy civilian casualties from U.S. air strikes was taken into account on their checklists.

4 **Stereotypes**. Victims of groupthink hold stereotyped views of the leaders of enemy groups: they are so evil that genuine attempts at negotiating differences with them are unwarranted, or they are too weak or too stupid to deal effectively with whatever attempts the ingroup makes to defeat their purposes, no matter how risky the attempts are.

Kennedy's groupthinkers believed that Premier Fidel Castro's air force was so ineffectual that obsolete B-26s could knock it out completely in a surprise attack before the invasion began. They also believed that Castro's army was so weak that a small Cuban-exile brigade could establish a well-protected beachhead at the Bay of Pigs. In addition, they believed that Castro was not smart enough to put down any possible internal uprisings in support of the exiles. They were wrong on all three assumptions. Though much of the blame was attributable to faulty intelligence, the point is that none of Kennedy's advisers even questioned the CIA planners about these assumptions.

The Johnson advisers' sloganistic thinking about 'the Communist apparatus' that was 'working all around the world' (as Dean Rusk put it) led them to overlook the powerful nationalistic strivings of the North Vietnamese government and its efforts to ward off Chinese domination. The crudest of all stereotypes used by Johnson's inner circle to justify their policies was the domino theory ('If we don't stop the Reds in South Vietnam, tomorrow they will be in Hawaii and next week they will be in San Francisco,' Johnson once said). The group so firmly accepted this stereotype that it became almost impossible for any adviser to introduce a more sophisticated viewpoint.

In the documents on Pearl Harbor, it is clear to see that the Navy commanders stationed in Hawaii had a naive image of Japan as a midget that would not dare to strike a blow against a powerful giant.

5 **Pressure**. Victims of groupthink apply direct pressure to any individual who momentarily expresses doubts about any of the group's shared illusions or who

questions the validity of the arguments supporting a policy alternative favored by the majority. This gambit reinforces the concurrence-seeking norm that loyal members are expected to maintain.

President Kennedy probably was more active than anyone else in raising skeptical questions during the Bay of Pigs meetings, and yet he seems to have encouraged the group's docile, uncritical acceptance of defective arguments in favor of the CIA's plan. At every meeting, he allowed the CIA representatives to dominate the discussion. He permitted them to give their immediate refutations in response to each tentative doubt that one of the others expressed, instead of asking whether anyone shared the doubt or wanted to pursue the implications of the new worrisome issue that had just been raised. And at the most crucial meeting, when he was calling on each member to give his vote for or against the plan, he did not call on Arthur Schlesinger, the one man there who was known by the President to have serious misgivings.

Historian Thomson informs us that whenever a member of Johnson's ingroup began to express doubts, the group used subtle social pressures to 'domesticate' him. To start with, the dissenter was made to feel at home provided that he lived up to two restrictions: 1) that he did not voice his doubts to outsiders, which would play into the hands of the opposition; and 2) that he kept his criticisms within the bounds of acceptable deviation, which meant not challenging any of the fundamental assumptions that went into the group's prior commitments. One such 'domesticated dissenter' was Bill Moyers. When Moyers arrived at a meeting, Thomson tells us, the President greeted him with, 'Well, here comes Mr. Stop-the-Bombing.'

6 **Self-censorship**. Victims of groupthink avoid deviating from what appears to be group consensus; they keep silent about their misgivings and even minimize to themselves the importance of their doubts.

As we have seen, Schlesinger was not at all hesitant about presenting his strong objections to the Bay of Pigs plan in a memorandum to the President and the Secretary of State. But he became keenly aware of his tendency to suppress objections at the White House meetings. 'In the months after the Bay of Pigs, I bitterly reproached myself for having kept so silent during those crucial discussions in the cabinet room,' Schlesinger writes in *A Thousand Days*, 'I can only explain my failure to do more than raise a few timid questions by reporting that one's impulse to blow the whistle on this nonsense was simply undone by the circumstances of the discussion.'

7 **Unanimity.** Victims of groupthink share an illusion of unanimity within the group concerning almost all judgments expressed by members who speak in favor of the majority view. This symptom results partly from the preceding one, whose effects are augmented by the false assumption that any individual who remains silent during any part of the discussion is in full accord with what the others are saying.

When a group of persons who respect each other's opinions arrives at a unanimous view, each member is likely to feel that the belief must be true. This reliance on consensual validation within the group tends to replace individual critical thinking and reality testing, unless there are clear-cut disagreements among the members. In contemplating a course of action such as the invasion of Cuba, it is painful for the members to confront disagreements within their group, particularly if it becomes apparent that there are widely divergent views about whether the preferred course of action is too risky to undertake at all. Such disagreements are likely to arouse anxieties about making a serious error. Once the sense of unanimity is shattered, the members no longer can feel complacently confident about the decision they are inclined to make. Each man must then face the annoying realization that there are troublesome uncertainties and he must diligently seek out the best information he can get in order to decide for himself exactly how serious the risks might be. This is one of the unpleasant consequences of being in a group of hardheaded, critical thinkers.

To avoid such an unpleasant state, the members often become inclined, without quite realizing it, to prevent latent disagreements from surfacing when they are about to initiate a risky, course of action. The group leader and the members support each other in playing up the areas of convergence in their thinking, at the expense of fully exploring divergencies that might reveal unsettled issues.

'Our meetings took place in a curious atmosphere of assumed consensus,' Schlesinger writes. His additional comments clearly show that, curiously, the consensus was an illusion—an illusion that could be maintained only because the major participants did not reveal their own reasoning or discuss their idiosyncratic assumptions and vague reservations. Evidence from several sources makes it clear that even the three principals—President Kennedy, Rusk and McNamara—had widely differing assumptions about the invasion plan.

8 **Mindguards**. Victims of groupthink sometimes appoint themselves as mindguards to protect the leader and fellow members from adverse information that might break the complacency they shared about the effectiveness and morality of past decisions. At a large birthday party for his wife, Attorney General Robert F. Kennedy, who had been constantly informed about the Cuban invasion plan, took Schlesinger aside and asked him why he was opposed. Kennedy listened coldly and said, 'You may be right or you may be wrong, but the President has made his mind up. Don't push it any further. Now is the time for everyone to help him all they can.'

Rusk also functioned as a highly effective mindguard by failing to transmit to the group the strong objections of three 'outsiders' who had learned of the invasion plan—Undersecretary of State Chester Bowles, USIA Director Edward R. Murrow, and Rusk's intelligence chief, Roger Hilsman. Had Rusk done so, their warnings might have reinforced Schlesinger's memorandum and jolted some of Kennedy's ingroup, if not the President himself, into reconsidering the decision.

Products. When a group of executives frequently displays most or all of these interrelated symptoms, a detailed study of their deliberations is likely to reveal a number of immediate consequences. These consequences are, in effect, products of poor decision-making practices because they lead to inadequate solutions to the problems under discussion.

First, the group limits its discussions to a few alternative courses of action (often only two) without an initial survey of all the alternatives that might be worthy of consideration.

Second, the group fails to reexamine the course of action initially preferred by the majority after they learn of risks and drawbacks they had not considered originally.

Third, the members spend little or no time discussing whether there are nonobvious gains they may have overlooked or ways of reducing the seemingly prohibitive costs that made rejected alternatives appear undesirable to them.

Fourth, members make little or no attempt to obtain information from experts within their own organizations who might be able to supply more precise estimates of potential losses and gains.

Fifth, members show positive interest in facts and opinions that support their preferred policy, they tend to ignore facts and opinions that do not.

Sixth, members spend little time deliberating about how the chosen policy might be hindered by bureaucratic inertia, sabotaged by political opponents, or temporarily derailed by common accidents. Consequently, they fail to work out contingency plans to cope with foreseeable setbacks that could endanger the overall success of their chosen course.

Support. The search for an explanation of why groupthink occurs has led me through a quagmire of complicated theoretical issues in the murky area of human motivation. My belief, based on recent social psychological research, is that we can best understand the various symptoms of groupthink as a mutual effort among the group members to maintain self-esteem and emotional equanimity by providing social support to each other, especially at times when they share responsibility for making vital decisions.

Even when no important decision is pending, the typical administrator will begin to doubt the wisdom and morality of his past decisions each time he receives information about setbacks, particularly if the information is accompanied by negative feedback from prominent men who originally had been his supporters. It should not be surprising, therefore, to find that individual members strive to develop unanimity and esprit de corps that will help bolster each other's morale, to create an optimistic outlook about the success of pending decisions, and to reaffirm the positive value of past policies to which all of them are committed.

Pride. Shared illusions of invulnerability, for example, can reduce anxiety about taking risks. Rationalizations help members believe that the risks are really not so bad after all. The assumption of inherent morality helps the members to avoid feelings of shame or guilt. Negative stereotypes function as stress-reducing devices to enhance a sense of moral righteousness as well as pride in a lofty mission.

The mutual enhancement of self-esteem and morale may have functional value in enabling the members to maintain their capacity to take action, but it has maladaptive consequences insofar as concurrence-seeking tendencies interfere with critical, rational capacities and lead to serious errors of judgment.

While I have limited my study to decision-making bodies in government, groupthink symptoms appear in business, industry and any other field where small, cohesive groups make the decisions. It is vital, then, for all sorts of people—and especially group leaders—to know what steps they can take to prevent groupthink.

Remedies. To counterpoint my case studies of the major fiascos, I have also investigated two highly successful group enterprises, the formulation of the Marshall Plan in the Truman Administration and the handling of the Cuban missile crisis by President Kennedy and his advisers. I have found it instructive to examine the steps Kennedy took to change his group's decision-making processes. These changes ensured that the mistakes made by his Bay of Pigs ingroup were not repeated by the missile crisis ingroup, even though the membership of both groups was essentially the same.

The following recommendations for preventing groupthink incorporate many of the good practices I discovered to be characteristic of the Marshall Plan and missile crisis groups:

1 The leader of a policy-forming group should assign the role of critical evaluator to each member, encouraging the group to give high priority to open airing of objections and doubts. This practice needs to be reinforced by the reader's acceptance of criticism of his own judgments in order to discourage members from soft-pedaling their disagreements and from allowing their striving for concurrence to inhibit critical thinking.
2 When the key members of a hierarchy assign a policy-planning mission to any group within their organization, they should adopt an impartial stance instead of stating preferences and expectations at the beginning. This will encourage open inquiry and impartial probing of a wide range of policy alternatives.

3   The organization routinely should set up several outside policy planning and evaluation groups to work on the same policy question, each deliberating under a different leader. This can prevent the insulation of an ingroup.

4   At intervals before the group reaches a final consensus, the leader should require each member to discuss the group's deliberations with associates in his own unit of the organization—assuming that those associates can be trusted to adhere to the same security regulations that govern the policy-makers—and then to report back their reactions to the group.

5   The group should invite one or more outside experts to each meeting on a staggered basis and encourage the experts to challenge the views of the core members.

6   At every general meeting of the group, whenever the agenda calls for an evaluation of policy alternatives, at least one member should play devil's advocate, functioning as a good lawyer in challenging the testimony of those who advocate the majority position.

7   Whenever the policy issue involves valued relations with a rival nation or organization, the group should devote a sizable block of time, perhaps an entire session, to a survey of all warning signals from the rivals and should write alternative scenarios on the rivals' intentions.

8   When the group is surveying policy alternatives for feasibility and effectiveness, it should from time to time divide into two or more subgroups to meet separately, under different chairmen, and then come back together to hammer out differences.

9   After reaching a preliminary consensus about what seems to be the best policy, the group should hold a 'second-chance' meeting at which every member expresses as vividly as he can all his residual doubts, and rethinks the entire issue before making a definitive choice.

How. These recommendations have their disadvantages. To encourage the open airing of objections, for instance, might lead to prolonged and costly debates when a rapidly growing crisis requires immediate solution. It also could cause rejection, depression and anger. A leader's failure to set a norm might create cleavage between leader and members that could develop into a disruptive power struggle if the leader looks on the emerging consensus as anathema. Setting up outside evaluation groups might increase the risk of security leakage. Still, inventive executives who know their way around the organizational maze probably can figure out how to apply one or another of the prescriptions successfully, without harmful side effects.

They also could benefit from the advice of outside experts in the administrative and behavioral sciences. Though these experts have much to offer, they have had few chances to work on policy-making machinery within large organizations. As matters now stand, executives innovate only when they need new procedures to avoid repeating serious errors that have deflated their self-images.

In this era of atomic warheads, urban disorganization and ecocatastrophes, it seems to me that policymakers should collaborate with behavioral scientists and give top priority to preventing groupthink and its attendant fiascos.

organization structures

what's the point of organization structure? (1974)

'Organizational design: an information processing view', by Jay R. Galbraith, *Interfaces*, vol. 4, no. 3, May 1974, pp. 28–36.

At first glance, the question of, 'what is the point of organization structure?' appears to be on a par with the question, 'why are we alive?' In both cases, students accept the existence of organization structure and life, and go on to study its manifestations and modes of operation. However, to be able to explain the different forms that an organization's structure can take, and to be able to comment on its appropriateness, it is necessary to understand its function.

In the 1970s, first Jay Galbraith and then Robert Duncan, argued that the purpose of structure in every organization is twofold. First, it facilitates the flow of information within the firm, in order to reduce the uncertainty in decision-making which is caused by information deficiency. The characteristics of a company's tasks, people and environments, all affect the level of uncertainty, and consequently, the information-processing requirements. Companies experience different levels and forms of uncertainty, and hence different information deficiencies. They therefore create different structures to meet their particular informational needs.

The second purpose of structure is to co-ordinate the different task activities performed by the different individuals, teams, departments and divisions that make up the organization. The more of these there are, and the more interdependent each is with the next, the more complex is this job of co-ordination. Such co-ordination is achieved through information transfer: 'Telling the left hand what the right hand is doing'. To deal with uncertainty, organizations either seek to reduce their information-processing needs, or to enhance their information-processing abilities; and frequently both. To co-ordinate diverse activities, they create integrator and liaison roles, establish committees and project groups, and issue books of rules and procedures.

learning objectives

Once you have read and understood the prescribed material, you should be able to:

1 Define the concepts of information processing, uncertainty reduction, and co-ordination.
2 Understand how the structure of an organization seeks to meet its particular requirements for information processing, uncertainty reduction and co-ordination, and how these are affected by its task, environment and people.
3 Appreciate how a company can have an 'inappropriate' structure and hence possibly become ineffective and unprofitable.

learning pre-requisites

Before proceeding, you should read Chapter 11 of the core text, and the article, 'Organizational design: an information processing view', by Jay R. Galbraith.

learning activity

Read the following scenario, and respond to the questions that follow it.

Imagine that you are a member of a ten-strong group of students who are competing with other teams to prepare an advertising poster for a local shop. Your client requires that your team's poster should contain at least three colours, some artwork; and an impactful phrase or caption that catches the attention of passers-by, and stays with them. Your team has one hour in which to complete this task. Your instructor recommends that your 'organization' should structure itself along functional lines. Dividing into three, equal-sized subgroups, each will specialize in different aspects of poster production The first will deal with poster layout (selection of poster size, shape, layout, colours, general arrangement); the second will focus on artwork (executing the drawings and lettering); while the third will decide on the choice of the written content. To avoid confusion about the different roles and responsibilities, and also distractions, the instructor further recommends that the three subgroups be placed in separate but adjacent rooms. The final suggestion is that each subgroup should appoint a leader, and that the entire group should also have an overall co-ordinator – the tenth person.

Questions:

1 Draw an organizational chart showing the instructor's proposed 'organization structure' for your group.
2 Consider the relationship between the nature of the task (poster production) and instructor's proposed structure. Where does it match or mismatch? State its strengths and weaknesses.
3 Does the time pressure make the instructor's proposed structure more or less appropriate? Why?
4 Should the three sets of activities described be performed sequentially or concurrently? Give your reasons.
5 Is the hierarchical structure of the organization (three levels of co-ordinator, subgroup leader and workers), and the physical separation of the three subgroups, likely to help or hinder the achievement of the task? Explain.
6 What inter-group communication needs must be met for the task to be achieved?
7 What is likely to be the role of the three subgroup leaders?
8 What aspects of the task contribute to its uncertainty?
9 What are the implications of such task uncertainty for the co-ordination of activities?
10 What are the possible trade-offs between task specialization by subgroup, and the co-ordination of the activities between them?
11 What are the implications of time pressure/task urgency, on the type of organization structure adopted?

These activities are adapted from J.W. French, 1993, 'Simulating organizational design issues', *Journal of Management Education*, vol. 17, no. 1, pp. 110–13.

Organization design: an information processing view*
Jay R. Galbraith

The information processing model

A basic proposition is that the greater the uncertainty of the task, the greater the amount of information that has to be processed between decision makers during the execution of the task. If the task is well understood prior to performing it, much of the activity can be preplanned. If it is not understood, then during the actual task execution more knowledge is acquired which leads to changes in resource allocations, schedules, and priorities. All these changes require information processing *during* task performance. Therefore *the greater the task uncertainty, the greater the amount of information that must be processed among decision makers during task execution in order to achieve a given level of performance.* The basic effect of uncertainty is to limit the ability of the organization to preplan or to make decisions about activities in advance of their execution. Therefore it is hypothesized that the observed variations in organizational forms are variations in the strategies of organizations to (1) increase their ability to preplan, (2) increase their flexibility to adapt to their inability to preplan, or (3) to decrease the level of performance required for continued viability. Which strategy is chosen depends on the relative costs of the strategies. The function of the framework is to identify these strategies and their costs.

The mechanistic model

This framework is best developed by keeping in mind a hypothetical organization. Assume it is large and employs a number of specialist groups and resources in providing the output. After the task has been divided into specialist subtasks, the problem is to integrate the subtasks around the completion of the global task. This is the problem of organization design. The behaviors that occur in one subtask cannot be judged as good or bad per se. The behaviors are more effective or ineffective depending upon the behaviors of the other subtask performers. There is a design problem because the executors of the behaviors cannot communicate with all the roles with whom they are interdependent. Therefore the design problem is to create mechanisms that permit coordinated action across large numbers of interdependent roles. Each of these mechanisms, however, has a limited range over which it is effective at handling the information requirements necessary to coordinate the interdependent roles. As the amount of uncertainty increases, and therefore information processing increases, the organization must adopt integrating mechanisms which increase its information processing capabilities.

1 Coordination by rules or programs

For routine predictable tasks March and Simon have identified the use of rules or programs to coordinate behavior between interdependent subtasks (March and Simon, 1958, chap. 6). To the extent that job related situations can be predicted in advance, and behaviors specified for these situations, programs allow an interdependent set of

---

* Reprinted from 'Organizational Design: An Information Processing View,' by Jay R. Galbraith, *Interfaces* 4, no. 3 (May 1974): 28–36, published by the Institute of Management Sciences.

activities to be performed without the need for interunit communication. Each role occupant simply executes the behavior which is appropriate for the task related situation with which he is faced.

2 Hierarchy

As the organization faces greater uncertainty its participants face situations for which they have no rules. At this point the hierarchy is employed on an exception basis. The recurring job situations are programmed with rules while infrequent situations are referred to that level in the hierarchy where a global perspective exists for all affected subunits. However, the hierarchy also has a limited range. As uncertainty increases the number of exceptions increases until the hierarchy becomes overloaded.

3 Coordination by targets or goals

As the uncertainty of the organization's task increases, coordination increasingly takes place by specifying outputs, goals, or targets (March and Simon, 1958, p. 145). Instead of specifying specific behaviors to be enacted, the organization undertakes processes to set goals to be achieved and the employees select the behaviors which lead to goal accomplishment. Planning reduces the amount of information processing in the hierarchy by increasing the amount of discretion exercised at lower levels. Like the use of rules, planning achieves integrated action and also eliminates the need for continuous communication among interdependent subunits as long as task performance stays within the planned task specifications, budget limits and within targeted completion dates. If it does not, the hierarchy is again employed on an exception basis.

   The ability of an organization to coordinate interdependent tasks depends on its ability to compute meaningful subgoals to guide subunit action. When uncertainty increases because of introducing new products, entering new markets, or employing new technologies these subgoals are incorrect. The result is more exceptions, more information processing, and an overloaded hierarchy.

Design strategies

The ability of an organization to successfully utilize coordination by goal setting, hierarchy, and rules depends on the combination of the frequency of exceptions and the capacity of the hierarchy to handle them. As the task uncertainty increases, the organization must again take organization design action. It can proceed in either of two general ways. First, it can act in two ways to reduce the amount of information that is processed. And second, the organization can act in two ways to increase its capacity to handle more information. The two methods for reducing the need for information and the two methods for increasing processing capacity are shown schematically in Figure 1. The effect of all these actions is to reduce the number of exceptional cases referred upward into the organization through hierarchical channels. The assumption is that the critical limiting factor of an organizational form is its ability to handle the nonroutine, consequential events that cannot be anticipated and planned for in advance. The nonprogrammed events place the greatest communication load on the organization.

1 Creation of slack resources

As the number of exceptions begin to overload the hierarchy, one response is to increase the planning targets so that fewer exceptions occur. For example, completion

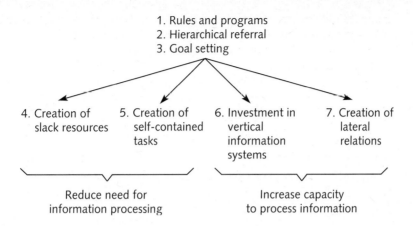

Figure 1 Organization design strategies

dates can be extended until the number of exceptions that occur are within the existing information processing capacity of the organization. This has been the practice in solving job shop scheduling problems (Pounds, 1963). Job shops quote delivery times that are long enough to keep the scheduling problem within the computational and information processing limits of the organization. Since every job shop has the same problem, standard lead times evolve in the industry. Similarly, budget targets could be raised, buffer inventories employed, and so on. The greater the uncertainty, the greater the magnitude of the inventory, lead time or budget needed to reduce an overload.

All of these examples have a similar effect. They represent the use of slack resources to reduce the amount of interdependence between subunits (March and Simon, 1958, Cyert and March, 1963). This keeps the required amount of information within the capacity of the organization to process it. Information processing is reduced because an exception is less likely to occur and reduced interdependence means that fewer factors need to be considered simultaneously when an exception does occur.

The strategy of using slack resources has its costs. Relaxing budget targets has the obvious cost of requiring more budget. Increasing the time to completion date has the effect of delaying the customer. Inventories require the investment of capital funds which could be used elsewhere. Reduction of design optimization reduces the performance of the article being designed. Whether slack resources are used to reduce information or not depends on the relative cost of the other alternatives.

The design choices are: (1) among which factors to change (lead time, overtime, machine utilization, and the like) to create the slack, and (2) by what amount should the factor be changed. Many operations research models are useful in choosing factors and amounts. The time-cost trade-off problem in project networks is a good example.

2 Creation of self-contained tasks

The second method of reducing the amount of information processed is to change the subtask groupings from resource (input) based to output based categories and give each group the resources it needs to supply the output. For example, the functional organization could be changed to product groups. Each group would have its own product engineers, process engineers, fabricating and assembly operations, and marketing activities. In other situations, groups can be created around product lines, geographical areas, projects, client groups, markets, and so on, each of which would contain the input resources necessary for creation of the output.

The strategy of self-containment shifts the basis of the authority structure from one based on input, resource skill, or occupational categories to one based on output or geographical categories. The shift reduces the amount of information processing through several mechanisms. First, it reduces the amount of output diversity faced by a single collection of resources. For example, a professional organization with multiple skill specialties providing service to three different client groups must schedule the use of these specialties across three demands for their services and determine priorities when conflicts occur. But, if the organization changed to three groups, one for each client category, each with its own full complement of specialties, the schedule conflicts across client groups disappear and there is no need to process information to determine priorities.

The second source of information reduction occurs through a reduced division of labor. The functional or resource specialized structure pools the demand for skills across all output categories. In the example above each client generates approximately one third of the demand for each skill. Since the division of labor is limited by the extent of the market, the division of labor must decrease as the demand decreases. In the professional organization, each client group may have generated a need for one third of a computer programmer. The functional organization would have hired one programmer and shared him across the groups. In the self-contained structure there is insufficient demand in each group for a programmer so the professionals must do their own programming. Specialization is reduced but there is no problem of scheduling the programmer's time across the three possible uses for it.

The cost of the self-containment strategy is the loss of resource specialization. In the example, the organization forgoes the benefit of specialist in computer programming. If there is physical equipment, there is a loss of economies of scale. The professional organization would require three machines in the self-contained form but only a large time-shared machine in the functional form. But those resources which have large economies of scale or for which specialization is necessary may remain centralized. Thus, it is the degree of self-containment that is the variable. The greater the degree of uncertainty, other things equal, the greater the degree of self-containment.

The design choices are the basis for the self-contained structure and the number of resources to be contained in the groups. No groups are completely self-contained or they would not be part of the same organization. But one product divisionalized firm may have 8 of 15 functions in the division while another may have 12 of 15 in the division. Usually accounting, finance, and legal services are centralized and shared. Those functions which have economies of scale, require specialization or are necessary for control remain centralized and not part of the self-contained group.

The first two strategies reduced the amount of information by lower performance standards and creating small autonomous groups to provide the output. Information is reduced because an exception is less likely to occur and fewer factors need to be considered when an exception does occur. The next two strategies accept the performance standards and division of labor as given and adapt the organization so as to process the new information which is created during task performance.

3 Investment in vertical information systems

The organization can invest in mechanisms which allow it to process information acquired during task performance without overloading the hierarchical communication channels. The investment occurs according to the following logic. After the organization has created its plan or set of targets for inventories, labor utilization, budgets, and schedules, unanticipated events occur which generate exceptions requiring adjustments to the original plan. At some point when the number of exceptions becomes substantial, it is preferable to generate a new plan rather than make incremental changes with each exception. The issue is then how frequently should plans be revised—yearly, quarterly, or monthly? The greater the frequency of replanning the greater the resources, such as clerks, computer time, input-output devices, and the like, required to process information about relevant factors.

The cost of information processing resources can be minimized if the language is formalized. Formalization of a decision-making language simply means that more information is transmitted with the same number of symbols. It is assumed that information processing resources are consumed in proportion to the number of symbols transmitted. The accounting system is an example of a formalized language.

Providing more information, more often, may simply overload the decision maker. Investment may be required to increase the capacity of the decision maker by employing computers, various man-machine combinations, assistants-to, and so on. The cost of this strategy is the cost of the information processing resources consumed in transmitting and processing data.

The design variables of this strategy are the decision frequency, the degree of formalization of language, and the type of decision mechanism which will make the choice. This strategy is usually operationalized by creating redundant information channels which transmit data from the point of origination upward in the hierarchy where the point of decision rests. If data is formalized and quantifiable, this strategy is effective. If the relevant data are qualitative and ambiguous, then it may prove easier to bring the decision down to where the information exists.

4 Creation of lateral relationships

The best strategy is to employ selectively joint decision processes which cut across lines of authority. This strategy moves the level of decision making down in the organization to where the information exists but does so without reorganizing around self-contained groups. There are several types of lateral decision processes. Some processes are usually referred to as the informal organization. However, these informal processes do not always arise spontaneously out of the needs of the task. This is particularly true in multinational organizations in which participants are separated by physical barriers, language differences, and cultural differences. Under these circumstances lateral processes need to be designed. The lateral processes evolve as follows with increases in uncertainty.

4.1 Direct contact

Between managers who share a problem. If a problem arises on the shop floor, the foreman can simply call the design engineer, and they can jointly agree upon a solution. From an information processing view, the joint decision prevents an upward referral and unloads the hierarchy.

4.2 Liaison roles

When the volume of contacts between any two departments grows, it becomes economical to set up a specialized role to handle this communication. Liaison men are typical examples of specialized roles designed to facilitate communication between two interdependent departments and to bypass the long lines of communcation involved in upward referral. Liaison roles arise at lower and middle levels of management.

4.3 Task forces

Direct contact and liaison roles, like the integration mechanisms before them, have a limited range of usefulness. They work when two managers or functions are involved. When problems arise involving seven or eight departments, the decision-making capacity of direct contacts is exceeded. Then these problems must be referred upward. For uncertain, interdependent tasks such situations arise frequently. Task forces are a form of horizontal contact which is designed for problems of multiple departments.

The task force is made up of representatives from each of the affected departments. Some are full-time members, others may be part-time. The task force is a temporary group. It exists only as long as the problem remains. When a solution is reached, each participant returns to his normal tasks.

To the extent that they are successful, task forces remove problems from higher levels of the hierarchy. The decisions are made at lower levels in the organization. In order to guarantee integration, a group problem-solving approach is taken. Each affected subunit contributes a member and therefore provides the information necessary to judge the impact on all units.

4.4 Teams

The next extension is to incorporate the group decision process into the permanent decision processes. That is, as certain decisions consistently arise, the task forces become permanent. These groups are labeled teams. There are many design issues concerned in team decision making such as at what level do they operate, who participates, and so on (Galbraith, 1973, chaps. 6 and 7). One design decision is particularly critical. This is the choice of leadership. Sometimes a problem exists largely in one department so that the department manager is the leader. Sometimes the leadership passes from one manager to another. As a new product moves to the market place, the leader of the new product team is first the technical manager followed by the production and then the marketing manager. The result is that, if the team cannot reach a consensus decision and the leader decides, the goals of the leader are consistent with the goals of the organization for the decision in question. But quite often obvious leaders cannot be found. Another mechanism must be introduced.

4.5 Integrating roles

The leadership issue is solved by creating a new role – an integrating role (Lawrence and Lorsch, 1967, chap. 3). These roles carry the labels of product managers, program managers, project managers, unit managers (hospitals), materials managers, and the like. After the role is created, the design problem is to create enough power in the role to influence the decision process. These roles have power even when no one reports directly to them. They have some power because they report to the general manager. But if they are selected so as to be unbiased with respect to the groups they integrate and to have technical competence, they have expert power. They collect information and equalize power differences due to preferential access to knowledge and information. The power equalization increases trust and the quality of the joint decision process. But power equalization occurs only if the integrating role is staffed with someone who can exercise expert power in the form of persuasion and informal influences rather than exert the power of rank or authority.

4.6 Managerial linking roles

As tasks become more uncertain, it is more difficult to exercise expert power. The role must get more power of the formal authority type in order to be effective at coordinating the joint decisions which occur at lower levels of the organization. This position power changes the nature of the role which for lack of a better name is labeled a managerial linking role. It is not like the integrating role because it possesses formal position power but is different from line managerial roles in that participants do not report to the linking manager. The power is added by the following successive changes:

▶ The integrator receives approval power of budgets formulated in the departments to be integrated.
▶ The planning and budgeting process starts with the integrator making his initiation in budgeting legitimate.
▶ Linking manager receives the budget for the area of responsibility and buys resources from the specialist groups.

These mechanisms permit the manager to exercise influence even though no one works directly for him. The role is concerned with integration but exercises power through the formal power of the position. If this power is insufficient to integrate the subtasks and creation of self-contained groups is not feasible, there is one last step.

4.7 Matrix organization
The last step is to create the dual authority relationship and the matrix organization (Galbraith, 1971). At some point in the organization some roles have two superiors. The design issue is to select the locus of these roles. The result is a balance of power between the managerial linking roles and the normal line organization roles. Figure 2 depicts the pure matrix design.

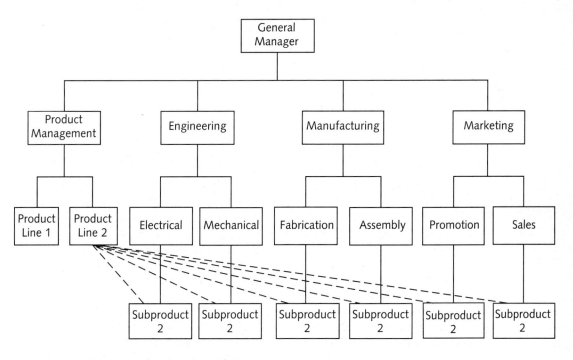

```
---- = Technical authority over product
____ = Formal authority over product (in product
       organization, these relationships may be reversed)
```

Figure 2 A pure matrix organization

Table 1

	Plastics	Food	Container
Percent new products in last ten years	35%	20%	0%
Integrating devices	Rules	Rules	Rules
	Hierarchy	Hierarchy	Hierarchy
	Planning	Planning	Planning
	Direct contact	Direct contact	Direct contact
	Teams at 3 levels	Task forces	
	Integrating department	Integrators	
Percent integrators/managers	22%	17%	0%

Source: Adopted from Lawrence and Lorsch, 1967, pp. 86–138 and Lorsch and Lawrence, 1968

The work of Lawrence and Lorsch is highly consistent with the assertions concerning lateral relations (Lawrence and Lorsch, 1967, Lorsch and Lawrence, 1968). They compared the types of lateral relations undertaken by the most successful firm in three different industries. Their data are summarized in Table 1. The plastics firm has the greatest rate of new product introduction (uncertainty) and the greatest utilization of lateral processes. The container firm was also very successful but utilized only standard practices because its information processing task is much less formidable. Thus, the greater the uncertainty the lower the level of decision making and the integration is maintained by lateral relations.

Table 1 points out the cost of using lateral relations. The plastics firm has 22 percent of its managers in integration roles. Thus, the greater the use of lateral relations the greater the managerial intensity. This cost must be balanced against the cost of slack resources, self-contained groups, and information systems.

Choice of strategy

Each of the four strategies has been briefly presented. The organization can follow one or some combination of several if it chooses. It will choose that strategy which has the least cost in its environmental context. (For an example, see Galbraith, 1970.) However, what may be lost in all of the explanations is that the four strategies are hypothesized to be an exhaustive set of alternatives. That is, if the organization is faced with greater uncertainty due to technological change, higher performance standards due to increased competition, or diversifies its product line to reduce dependence, the amount of information processing is increased. *The organization must adopt at least one of the four strategies when faced with greater uncertainty.* If it does not consciously choose one of the four, then the first, reduced performance standards, will happen automatically. The task information requirements and the capacity of the organization to process information are always matched. If the organization does not consciously match them, reduced performance through budget and schedule overruns will occur in order to bring about equality. Thus the organization should be planned and designed simultaneously with the planning of the strategy and resource allocations. But if the strategy involves introducing new products, entering new markets, and so on, then some provision for increased information must be made. Not to decide is to decide, and it is to decide upon slack resources as the strategy to remove hierarchical overload.

There is probably a fifth strategy which is not articulated here. Instead of changing the organization in response to task uncertainty, the organization can operate on its environment to reduce uncertainty. The organization through strategic decisions, long-term contracts, coalitions, and the like, can control its environment. But these maneuvers have costs also. They should be compared with costs of the four design strategies presented above.

Summary

The purpose of this paper has been to explain why task uncertainty is related to organizational form. In so doing the cognitive limits theory of Herbert Simon was the guiding influence. As the consequences of cognitive limits were traced through the framework, various organization design strategies were articulated. The framework provides a basis for integrating organizational interventions, such as information systems and group problem solving, which have been treated separately before.

Bibliography

Cyert, Richard, and James March. *The Behavioral Theory of the Firm.* Englewood Cliffs, N.J.: Prentice-Hall, 1963.

Galbraith, Jay. 'Environmental and Technological Determinants of Organization Design: A Case Study.' In *Studies in Organization Design*, edited by Lawrence and Lorsch. Homewood, Ill.: Richard D. Irwin, 1970.

Galbraith, Jay. 'Designing Matrix Organizations.' *Business Horizons*, February 1971, pp. 29–40.

Galbraith, Jay. *Organization Design.* Reading, Mass.: Addison-Wesley Publishing, 1973.

Lawrence, Paul, and Jay Lorsch. *Organization and Environment.* Boston: Division of Research, Harvard Business School, 1967.

Lorsch, Jay, and Paul Lawrence. 'Environmental Factors and Organization Integration.' Paper read at the Annual Meeting of the American Sociological Association, August 27, 1967, Boston, Mass.

March, James, and Herbert Simon. *Organizations.* New York: John Wiley & Sons, 1958.

Pounds, William. 'The Scheduling Environment.' In *Industrial Scheduling*, edited by Muth and Thompson. Englewood Cliffs, N.J.: Prentice-Hall, 1963.

Simon, Herbert. *Models of Man.* New York: John Wiley & Sons, 1957.

the continuing impact of scientific management on contemporary Japanese manufacturing (1993)

'Taylorism, new technology and just-in-time systems in Japanese manufacturing', by Robert F. Conti and Malcolm Warner, *New Technology, Work and Employment*, vol. 8, no. 1, 1993, pp. 31–42.

Scientific management techniques, and the Taylorist principles upon which they are based, are often considered to be only of historical interest. That they somehow represent a past era, and are either no longer used or are not relevant to today's organizations. Both are wrong conclusions. Chapter 12 in the core text on scientific management discussed how Taylorist principles are being applied to office contexts and to knowledge workers. Moreover, a glance around the cooking area of any fast food, hamburger restaurant, will reveal that scientific management techniques have been transferred from the car assembly line to the hamburger assembly line.

However, the purpose of this reading is to illustrate another point. Popular descriptions of Japanese manufacturing techniques which were so successful during the 1980s, have given the impression that they are totally new, and somehow the antithesis of those developed first by Frederick Taylor and then by Henry Ford. In order to challenge another misconception, this article traces the history and development of well known manufacturing techniques such as TQM and JIT. It emphasizes two points. First, that as with other processes and ideas, the Japanese companies adopted and then adapted Taylorism. Second, it illustrates the pervasive influence of scientific management through to the present day.

learning objectives

Once you have read and understood the prescribed material, you should be able to:

1 Identify the application of Taylorist principles in contemporary Japanese manufacturing practices.
2 Understand how Japanese manufacturers have modified scientific management techniques to meet their own requirements.
3 Assess to what extent Japanese management's high control techniques can co-exist with their encouragement of a high employee commitment strategy.

learning pre-requisites

Before proceeding, you should read Chapter 12 of the core text and the article, 'Taylorism, new technology and just-in-time systems in Japenese manufacturing', by Robert F. Conti and Malcolm Warner that follows.

learning activity

This short answer quiz consists of 25 questions and tests your knowledge of the article.

1 Conti and Warner's article contrasts Taylorist (scientific management) concepts and techniques, with 'state-of-the-art' Japanese ones like TQM and JIT. The argument that these authors propose is that:

(circle one of the following)

(a) Scientific management and Japanese techniques are related.   1

(b) Japanese techniques are based on, and are an extension of Taylorist ones.   2

(b) Japanese techniques depend on Taylorist ones for their effectiveness.   3

(d) Japanese techniques selectively employ Taylorist principles.   4

2 In the context of the article, explain the meaning of (a) exogenous; (b) indigenous.

3 According to the authors, what is the key mediating factor that determines how innovations such as scientific management are moulded?

4 Give five examples of any two scientific management *concepts*, and any two scientific management *techniques*.

5 List any two ways in which Frederick Taylor's ideas were disseminated through Japanese industry.

6 Name any three companies which used scientific management techniques before 1914.

7 List any six devices used in the JIT/TQM system.

8 Name one objective of the Kanban system.

9 Explain how the Ford manufacturing system achieves continuity and consistency of flow.

10 How does the JIT philosophy's view buffer stocks?

11 In the Japanese experience, list one effect of removing personal discretion from work tasks.

12 How does Toyota's mixed model scheduling differ from traditional mass production?

13 List two benefits that Toyota's mixed model scheduling has for the company?

14 From Toyota's experience, state two things that a mixed model scheduling system requires in order for it to achieve high quality and consistent output.

15 In Japanese companies, how does the *job design process*, used to create Taylorist-type jobs, differ from that originally used by Taylor?

16 In what ways does Japanese 'Taylorist' techniques, differ from Taylor's 'Taylorist' techniques?

17 Give an example of any three Japanese *high commitment* practices.

18 The article lists five different *high control practices*, and reports practices at six different company sites. For each site below, label the practice with the appropriate high control label.

Site	Product	This is an example of high control practice number:
1.	Walk-in refrigerators	_____
2.	Ice makers	_____
3.	Reach-in refrigerators	_____
4.	Beverage dispensers	_____
5.	Water purifiers	_____
6.	Kitchen equipment	_____

19 List the three elements that constitute an employee involvement programme.

20 *Teach yourself Japanese.* Correctly match the English translation in the left-hand column, with the Japanese word in the right-hand column.

(a)	lifetime employment	1.	shuskin koyo
(b)	card	2.	nenko
(c)	enterprise unionism	3.	poka yoke
(d)	seniority system	4.	kaizen
(e)	creative thinking	5.	kigyobetsu rodo kumiai
(f)	continuing improvement	6.	kanban
(g)	fool proof	7.	soikufu

21 What three elements constitute Hill's work content model?

22 Explain how the responsibility for the execution of the three elements, differs between Taylorist and Japanese approaches.

23 To achieve which three job designs objectives, do Japanese companies use Taylorist principles?

24 What do the following abbreviations stand for?

(a)	TQM	(d)	TQC
(b)	JIT	(e)	ZD
(c)	HRM	(f)	QC

25 What is your view about the Japanese application of Taylorist principles? Here are two positions. To which do you subscribe on the basis of your reading of the article?

Position 1: The managers are 'conning' their workers. Instead of management designing and imposing work designs that lead to the creation of boring, repetitive tasks, they are getting their own workers to de-skill their own jobs under the guise of participation. Because they were involved in the creation of mindless tasks, these same workers then feel committed to perform them.

Position 2: This a creative application of Taylorism. Given the need for continuity, consistency and efficiency of performance, the Japanese system does a good job. While the tasks may be designed to the 'idiot proof', workers are continually involved in improvements which stimulate them, are continually trained in a number of different skills, are challenged to produce different skills when manufacturing different products.

READING 12

Taylorism, new technology and just-in-time systems in Japanese manufacturing*

Robert F. Conti and Malcolm Warner†

This article attempts to examine what is believed to be a significant overall Taylorist influence in Japanese manufacturing as well as a specific manifestation of this phenomenon, namely the unique flow requirements of the generic Toyota system (JIT). The use of unbuffered flow, it is argued, is feasible only with consistent quality, thus making non-discretionary Taylorist job design a necessary condition.

* Reprinted by permission from Blackwell Publishers. *New Technology, Work and Employment*, Vol. 8 (1993), 31–42.
† Robert Conti is Assistant Professor of Management, Bryant College, Rhode Island, USA. Malcolm Warner is Professor and a Faculty member of the Judge Institute of Management Studies, University of Cambridge.

In this article we first present an *evolutionary* model of Japanese management which stresses *continuity* and links technological, economic and cultural variables to conditions of environmental change. In doing so, we hope to later demonstrate how the absorption of an *exogenous* set of management concepts and practices, namely Taylorism, gradually leads into what may be generally perceived as a later distinctly *indigenous* (that is, Japanese) set of developments and might be seen, for this reason, as incongruent with them or even contradictory. Clearly, any final view depends on both *historical* as well as *conceptual* interpretations of such organizational innovations [1].

At first sight, it might appear paradoxical that managerial importations in the period immediately before the First World War, such as time and motion studies as applied to older technologies might be ultimately connected with contemporary organizational software linked to new technologies. It seems a long time ago, around eighty years or so, since 'Scientific Management' was imported into Japan from the West, something which now seems conceptually distant from what in today's terminology we call the 'state of the art' management practice of total quality management (TQM), just-in-time (JIT) and associated techniques.

In the light of Urabe's model, we can see how the adaptation of Taylorism can proceed and how in turn TQM/JIT can be synthesized [2]. Such an evolutionary approach helps us see the way such *exogenous* innovations can be transformed into *indigenous* ones, with culture as an intervening variable in the process, mediating as it does, between choice of strategy and implementation (see Figure 1). Culture may thus be seen as the key to the explanation of how the organizational innovations are moulded and adapted to different work-environments. In the model, *exogenous* management theories and practices, as well as technology transfer may be seen as playing an important role. Whilst we concentrate on the specific contribution of Scientific Management in this paper, it should be seen as part of a broader process of the shaping of organizational innovation as Japan opened its doors to Western influence from the mid-nineteenth century onwards. Japan's modernization may be seen as starting with the Meiji Restoration in 1868, due to the inability of the old regime to keep control of internal economic and social change-processes. The new Meiji leadership set out to forge new goals based on both industrialization and modernization.

The main thrust of the paper, which tries to deal with this process is as follows. First, we argue that Taylorism was a greater influence in Japanese industry than is generally believed, although its impact was mediated by specifically Japanese cultural factors. As absorbed into Japanese industrial practices, Taylorism we therefore believe became an important ingredient of what has been held by many observers to be a uniquely Japanese system of organization and management, involving such practices as seniority (*nenko*) wages, lifetime employment (*shushin koyo*), enterprise unionism (*kigyobetsu rodo kumiai*) [3]. This model of management has deep roots in the Japanese past [4]. The argument we put forward in this paper is that Taylorism directly and indirectly moulded this process but was nonetheless enhanced by Japanese norms.

After this, we go on to show how the nature of Japanese 'Human Resource Management' (HRM) did not negate the earlier influence of Taylorism, but rather that the two proceeded together and interacted. At first sight, the Japanese management system appears to be essentially unlike the generally perceived Taylorist stereotype. This view is expressed by Konosuke Matsushita, founder of Matsushita Electric, in comparing Japanese and American manufacturing:

> Yes, we will win and you will lose. For you are not able to rid your minds of the obsolete Taylorisms that we never had [5].

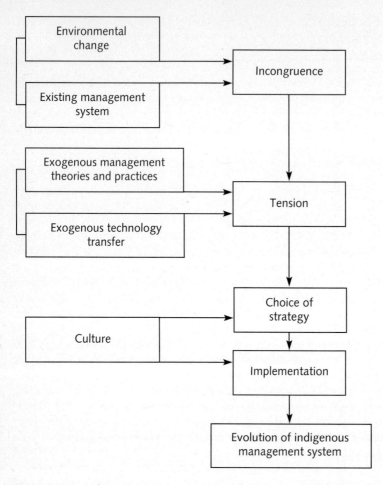

Figure 1 An evolutionary management model. *Source*: Adapted from Urabe 1988: 9

The validity of his statement, we believe, depends upon an overly narrow definition of Taylorism. A closer examination will reveal a more complex relationship. Here we can hypothesize that some features of distinctive systems for organizing economic activities may be translatable to other societies, even if the recipe may not be transferred *en bloc* [6]. The dominant institutions of Japanese business greatly affected the adaptation of Taylorism and appropriately modified it to suit their goals. We go on to argue that this influence extends in the post-war period, as seen in practices such as TQM/JIT and so on. The persistent 'societal effect' influences the way in which both managerial systems can be transferred and modified [7]. The coexistence and interplay of 'Scientific Management' with the evolution of an 'organization-oriented' employment system, not only in the inter-war years but also in the post-1945 period, must be recognized [8].

Last, evidence of the use of Taylorist principles in medium-volume, just-in-time production systems is presented as the main substance of the article, based on a study of six Japanese factories. Japanese personal names are presented in the Japanese ordering, with the family name first. Anglicized versions of company names are given where they are commonly used, and the titles of organizations will also be added in phonetic Japanese where possible.

The diffusion of Taylorism in Japan

The impact of Scientific Management on Japanese industry was felt by, first, the dissemination of Taylor's concepts and methods as a result of knowledge of, and translations of, his works; second, by books based on his ideas; and third, through the work of consultants who had knowledge of his theories and/or experience of his procedures. Figure 2 summarizes the chronology involved. We will now very briefly describe the importation of such exogenous theories and practices, as factors influencing the reconciliation of the tensions indicated, in the model of management evolution we have set out. We will argue that the crucial determinants of this process were largely in place by the end of the inter-war period, having started even earlier. We hope to place TQM/JIT developments in a broader setting, as part of a long-term process related to the introduction of *exogenous* management theories and practices.

To briefly summarize how Scientific Management arrived in Japan: Taylorism took root there just before the First World War. A Japanese branch of the *Taylor Society* was soon set up, one of the first outside the USA. *The Principles of Scientific*

1856	Birth of Frederick Winslow Taylor in Philadelphia, Pennsylvania
1878	Taylor starts work as sourcer at Midvale Steel Works
1898	Appointed management consultant at Bethlehem Steel
1903	*Shop Management* published
1906	*The Art of Cutting Metals* follows
1908	Nippon Electric apply standard motion studies
1911	*The Principles of Scientific Management* published
1912	*The Secret of Saving Lost Motion* (Japanese translation of above)
1912	Japanese followers of Taylor publish their books
1913	National Railways and leading textile firms adopt Taylorist techniques
1915	Yusukawa Electric introduce a Taylorist-influenced bonus-system
1915	Port Arthur (now Dallas) School of Technology first to teach Taylorist courses
1915	Death of Taylor
1915	*Toyobo* launches motion-study program
1919	State subsidy for the *Industrial Efficiency Institute*
1923	Araki sets up his own Efficiency Institute
1929	Gilbreth, Emerson and other Taylorists visit Japan
1929	Ishida initiates statistical process control experiments in Tokyo Electric
1929	Industrial Rationalization Program launched
1929	Shibaura introduce 'job wage' incentive system
1931	Japan invades Manchuria
1932	Above Shibaura incentive system modified and expanded; continues unchanged until 1945
1933	Organized (unionized) proportion of the Japanese labour force declines
1937	*Industrial Rationalization Bureau* renamed *Control Bureau*
1938	Mitsubishi Electric and Shibaura Electric begin to abandon time-study techniques
1939	Attempts at more regular wages and job practices
1942	Japan Management Association founded from miscellaneous constituent organizations
1945	End of Pacific War

Figure 2 Chronology of Taylorism and its impact on Japanese industry up to 1945

Management was translated into Japanese in 1912, as *The Secret of Saving Lost Motion*, selling over one and a half million copies. Hoshino Yukinori published his text, *A Report on Observations* in Japanese in 1912, based on Taylor's work which he had seen at first hand. Ikeda Toshiro brought out *Secrets for Eliminating Futile Work and Increasing Production*, selling over a million copies. The President of Mitsubishi purchased 20,000 for his employees and the head of Kawasaki Shipbuilding 50,000 for his workforce [9]. From 1913 onwards, the National Railways and the textile industry were seed-beds of Taylorism, although as early as 1908, Iwatare Junihoko of Nippon Electric, an early joint venture, had applied standard motion studies after studying abroad at Western Electric. Scientific Management was thus chosen as the route to industrial efficiency, as it offered a managerial solution to the growing labour and personnel problems facing Japanese business [10].

Taylorism was first introduced in the Japanese cotton textile industry during the First World War, as it resorted to 'rationalization' on a substantial scale [11]. Management sought to control work standards directly and to rely less on older workers for training. Cost-accounting and time and motion study were introduced as well as stricter quality-control, anticipating later innovations. Formal training programmes, brought in as 'rationalization', led to standardized job-classifications and promotion hierarchies, for which training was made specific [12]. In the next phase of Japanese industrialization, heavy industries were to the fore. The Mitsubishi Heavy Electric Company tried to enter the market but was constrained by 'the meagre level of our technological competence' [13]. State protection of heavy industry was to help, with selective use of foreign collaborators. Recruiting and selection became more systematic, based on the advice of US management consultants. Ford set up car-production in Yokohama in 1925 to assemble from knock-down kits; General Motors a year later introduced an assembly plant in Osaka, and providing expertise on Taylorist and Fordist methods.

The origins of just-in-time

Taylorism did not, however, have a major impact on the Japanese car industry until the late 1940s. Cusumano points out that work factor-analysis methods adopted were a refinement of the time and motion studies that Frederick Taylor and Frank Gilbreth had pioneered [14]. Engineers at both Nissan and Toyota did not, however, receive details of the new cameras or measuring instruments of analyzing worker's motions and cycle times until after the Second World War. Nissan actively sought links with General Motors in the 1930s, using US engineers and even bought an American plant to set up in Japan; whereas Toyota endeavoured to develop its own methods, build up its R & D and recruit the most able Japanese engineers.

As Francks points out:

> Toyoda Kiichiro, the founder of Toyota, resembled Aikawa (the founder of Nissan) in being a qualified mechanical engineer, but he retained much more of an interest in the practice of science and engineering than did the business-empire-building Aikawa. With the engineering resources of the Toyoda Loom Company behind him, he decided that the route to the achievement of his father's goal of a Japanese car industry lay not in the wholesale transfer of complete technologies from abroad, but rather in the development of his company's own capacity to select and adapt from the range of what was available. He believed that Toyota had access to the necessary engineering skills, augmented by the recruitment of Japanese-trained experts, including academics and former employees of the Ford and General Motors Japanese subsidiaries, and that the technology of

car production was sufficiently widely known to be acquired without the purchase of patents or licensing rights. Toyota therefore followed a strategy of buying what its engineers believed to be the best machine for the job and then dismantling, studying and copying it in-house [15].

The Toyota system involving techniques developed by Ohno Taiichi, who was Vice-President at Toyota, formerly in charge of its mechanical engineering section, was based on a 'just-in-time' formula which relied on a stringent policy of sub-contracting. Employees were to become the 'objects of labour-inventory control' according to one commentator [16]. It resulted in a fluctuating workforce, mostly situated beyond the company itself principally in sub-contractor firms, where employment was relatively insecure under 'the new Toyota version of Taylorism' [17]. The mass production Toyota system as developed by Ohno Taiichi has seldom been exactly replicated. However, the Toyota principles embodied in the generic form of just-in-time manufacturing (JIT) have been widely diffused, in Japan and throughout the industrialized world [18]. As will be shown, the unique product-flow requirements of JIT production generate an additional form of 'Toyota Taylorism'.

Japanese manufacturers had sought flexibility within the mass-production system. The reason for this was the need to cope with market segmentation and uncertainty, but is was also to achieve production increases, productivity gains and cost reductions. Such a flexible mass-production system was called just-in-time (JIT). It was a product of incremental process innovations, combining hardware and software and constituted a breakthrough in production management, working hand-in-hand with total quality management (TQM) systems.

To some commentators, JIT and TQM are seen as 'complementary' philosophies or 'tool-boxes' of techniques [19]. They are said to represent the aim to perfectly match the production process and the marketplace, that is, supply and demand. Quality must be 'built into' the product or service, with no buffer-stocks and therefore less capital cost. The new systems involve 'a whole paraphernalia of devices such as work flow simplification, set-up time reduction, cellular organization, job rotation, stock reduction, *kanban* controls, line balancing, statistical process control, quality circles' and so on [20]. '*Kanban*' involves the use of a small plastic plate, originally paper (about $3\frac{1}{2}" \times 9"$) which gives the information to operatives at each production station. Two kinds of *kanban* cards are used. Each worker takes from the parts box of existing stock to the stock point of the earlier stage. The production-*kanban* is then deposited at the stock point and is signed to replace inventory used. 'The two *kanban* cards act as a real-time information system indicating production capacity, stock usage, and manpower utilization' [21]. The idea was to produce finished products 'just-in-time' to satisfy customers' orders, making sure the constitutent parts are ready at hand when needed. '*Kanban*' being quite literally the Japanese word for card, or record, to let workers know what parts were needed and when. It was the route to working without sizeable inventories, and to reduce batch sizes. It also made sure the Toyota worker was in tune with his group's working goals, and vice-versa. The ultimate aim was to move towards what is referred to as Zero Defects (ZD).

As Whitehill points out:

> The most obvious result of the *kanban* system is the drastic reduction of investment in inventories all down the line. Suppliers deliver just in time to meet the current demand for materials and parts. This most-publicized advantage alone of the JIT process would make it a major contributor to cost reduction and to organizational effectiveness. But it does much more. By streamlining the production flow

and injecting more flexibility in scheduling, changeover time and the costs associated with a varied product mix can be reduced dramatically.

It was the need to produce many models of Toyotas in small 'batches' that induced the company to pioneer the JIT system several decades ago. Today the concept is spreading throughout Japanese industry and is even spilling over to General Motors and other American companies feeling the hot breath of Japanese competition [22].

While some see JIT as the reversal of Taylorism and Fordism, others claim that it is not an alternative at all, but rather a complementary system helping rationalization. One view admits that 'the Japanese out-Taylor us all' [23]. It is thus said to increase value added with the same amount of labour, eliminate waste, and hence promote greater efficiency. How distinctly Japanese this process-innovation is remains debatable. As McMillan points out:

> As it turns out, the Toyota system has theoretical origins in scientific management. More than fifty years ago, Taylor's student and assistant Henry Gantt, developed planning tools which today look at the total production sequence in an attempt to develop assembly balancing techniques. The *kanban* system requires higher levels of fixed costs for additional tooling, materials handling, and factory layout, but operating costs are substantially lowered [24].

The impact of just-in-time production

JIT manufacturing has been applied to a variety of industries for both medium and high volume production in Japan. Such JIT systems utilize continuous product-flow and as Chandler points out, the success of any capital-intensive flow system, whether Ford/Mass Production or Toyota/JIT, requires 'Economies of Speed'—high velocity output that transforms the high fixed costs into low unit cost [25]. High velocity output is especially important in Japanese JIT, since the fixed labour costs of lifetime employment for core workers are added to the usual fixed capital costs. As will be seen, this creates an interplay between the lifetime employment requirement of an 'organization-oriented' employment system and the ability of 'Scientific Management' techniques to help meet that requirement.

Achieving high output levels here requires both continuity and consistency of product flow. The Ford mass-production model achieves continuity by using large buffer-stocks to ensure continued flow in the face of interruptions such as quality problems [26]. Consistency of flow is achieved by the use of a powered moving assembly-line, with defective units diverted to rework areas. The result is a constant output, variable, quality-system.

The JIT philosophy rejects buffers as a form of 'waste', requiring large capital investments in inventory, and masking the need to identify and eliminate underlying problems. Sequential flow of small product-quantities between work-stations is used, without 'just-in-case' inventory buffers. Product movement between work-stations tends to be either manual or by asynchronous 'power and free' conveyors that disengage the product while at a work-station, giving workers control over the cycle time. Workers stop the line when quality-problems are encountered [27]. Achieving economies of speed in a JIT system depends on both consistent quality, to avoid line shut downs; and consistent work station times, to maximize output. These conditions, in turn, require the systematic elimination of operating variability at all work-stations. As Klein points out,

> the reform process that ushers in JIT and SPC is meant to eliminate all variations within production and therefore requires strict adherence to rigid methods and procedures.

A major factor in reducing variability is the widespread use of 'fool-proof' (*poka yoke*) job design, supported by product and process design, aimed at removing personal discretion from work tasks [29]. As a result, Japanese JIT factories tend to operate with very Taylorist job designs as a necessary condition for this type of production. The need for an absence of operator-discretion is emphasized in the International Motor Vehicle program study. It concluded that all vestiges of craftsmanship in automotive production should be 'stamped out' in order to achieve consistently high production reliability [30]. Taylorist job designs, with their lack of worker discretion, can also contribute to a high level of JIT product flexibility as compared to traditional mass production [31]. This increased flexibility is achieved by the use of mixed model scheduling. Cusumano describes the Toyota mixed model system of scheduling sedans, hardtops and station wagons for daily production, on the same assembly line, in the ratios of their relative market demands. If, for instance, the relative demands are 2:1:12, a repeating sequence of a sedan, a hardtop, a sedan and a station wagon would be scheduled. In traditional mass production, only sedans would be built during the first two weeks of the month, followed by a week of hardtops and 12 weeks of station wagons. The Toyota approach has several advantages over traditional scheduling. Finished goods inventories are reduced, factory work loads are levelled, and customer service is greatly improved since all models are produced daily; instead of every two or four weeks, considerably reducing the average delivery time. The result is described by Lazonick as 'flexible mass production' [32].

The drawback of mixed model scheduling is the need for workers to continually adapt to the work-tasks required for the different models. This requires a well-trained committed workforce and job designs that yield a high level of 'fool proof' Taylorist tasks, to ensure high quality levels and consistent output. The lack of this approach to job design was a major factor in the failure of Winnebago, the leading American manufacturer of recreational vehicles, in implementing mixed model scheduling in 1988 [33]. Their vehicles were previously built in sequential batches of 50 or 100 of a given model. The change to mixed-model scheduling sent a daily stream of different models down the assembly line. In the absence of adequate training and 'fool proof' job designs, this daily profusion of models made it impossible for even the most dedicated workers to adapt. The resulting chaos created severe quality, output and cost problems and led to the firing of the two top executives.

While Japanese manufacturers use Taylorist job designs, the design process they employ is very un-Taylorist. The stereotypical Taylorist prescription of management determination and monopoly control of the 'one best method' is not followed. Instead, there is a high level of employee involvement in job design, supported by extensive workforce training in methods analysis, as described by Whittaker:

> It might seem that Bravermanian deskilling as the result of management intervention and replacement of craft skills by 'scientific, technical and engineering knowledge' is characteristic of Japanese factories. The objective, however, is primarily one of increased predictability and thence efficiency rather than deskilling workers. Furthermore, workers are not being excluded from this 'scientific, technical and engineering knowledge' but are being urged to acquire it [34].

Characteristics of Japanese manufacturing sites visited

In order to investigate the implementation of JIT systems, an empirical survey of six Japanese factories was carried out.

1 Sites

Six JIT applications were visited. Four of the factory sites were in western Japan, in Shimane Prefecture, and two were in the Nagoya metropolitan area:

Number	Location	Production workers	Trade Union
1	Shimane	300	Yes
2	Shimane	150	Yes
3	Shimane	175	Yes
4	Shimane	200	Yes
5	Nagoya	400	Yes
6	Nagoya	225	Yes

2 Methods of observations

(a) Plant tours
 1. Tour of each site, beginning at incoming raw materials and components storage, progressing along the product flow paths through finished goods storage, and ending with the major support activities such as engineering.
 2. Recording of observations was by 8 mm videotaping, 35 mm still photography and notes.

(b) Interviews

The executive vice-president, plant managers and foremen were interviewed. The interviews were both structured, using a prepared questionaire, and unstructured, primarily to clarify issues raised during the plant tours.

3 Production systems and products

All the sites produce commercial appliances, assembled from discrete parts. In-house manufactured parts are fabricated from raw materials e.g., stainless steel or galvanized steel, machined from bar stock e.g., brass or stainless steel, or formed from plastic sheets. A variety of components e.g., motors, electrical controls and fasteners are purchased from outside suppliers. All sites use a repetitive flow, JIT production system for assembly, operating to daily or weekly schedules of finished products. In-house production of parts is both in large-batches at selected sites, acting as 'parts feeders' for the other sites and in small ones made just-in-time for assembly requirements at each site. The Shimane sites tend to be more focused, producing primarily one product line or range, in a variety of models. The Nagoya sites produce both multiple lines and multiple models. The products manufactured and the production systems utilized are as follows:

Site no.	Product lines	Production systems
1	Walk-in refrigerators	Batch parts production JIT assembly
2	Ice Makers	JIT assembly
3	Reach-in Refrigerators	JIT assembly
4	Beverage Dispenser	JIT assembly
5	Water purifiers, Ice makers Ice dispensers	Batch parts production JIT assembly
6	Beverage dispensers, Vending machines, Kitchen equipment	JIT assembly

4 Summary of field results

A high degree of uniformity of practices was observed at the six factories. Common to all the sites are a number of practices designed to promote high level of management control and a high degree of employment commitment:

High control practices
1 Pervasive use of non-discretionary, Taylorist job design
2 Synchronized, JIT product flow
3 Regular feedback on flow rates and actual versus schedule production
4 Virtually no movement of workers away from their work-stations except during breaks
5 Highly visible displays of efficencies

High commitment practices
1 Quarterly improvement goals pursued by production workers
2 Regular training of workers in process improvement techniques
3 Two hours of paid time twice a month to work on improvement projects
4 Posting of improvement ideas
5 Lifetime employment for permanent workers

Noteworthy examples of some of the above practices were observed at each of the sites:

Site	Products	Observed examples
1	Walk-in refrigerators	All part drawings encapsulated in plastic to retain legibility and prevent errors
2	Ice makers	Sports-type electric scoreboard for real time display of actual versus scheduled production. Central graphic display of product flow rates at key work-stations to highlight problems
3	Reach-in refrigerators	Counter/alarm to ensure correct number of installed rivets; idea copied to ensure correct number of packed items
4	Beverage dispensers	Worker lunch room training area with displays of efficiency formulas
5	Water purifiers	Worker signals for replenishment of supplies without leaving work-station. Station number displayed in supply area for proper delivery
6	Kitchen equipment	Welding fixtures with pins that register with locating holes in sheet metal parts to allow only correct orientation of parts

The factories which varied in size from 150 to 400 production employees, are divisions of a major manufacturer of commercial appliances, and all use medium-volume JIT production. A typical example of 'fool-proof' job-design was observed at a work-station at one of the sites where brackets were installed inside a cabinet using a rivet-gun. As each rivet was set a counter stepped down, reaching zero when the last rivet was installed. As the operator moved the cabinet along the floor conveyor to the next station, a limit switch was dropped, resetting the counter to the total number of rivets. If the transfer of a cabinet with any missing rivets (counter not reading zero) was attempted, the limit switch would trigger an alarm, signalling the need for corrective action.

The example illustrates the mediated form of Taylorism used throughout the factories visited. The installation of the counter made the job more 'fool-proof' and hence more Taylorist. However, the idea was developed by the operator, as part of her improvement project for the prior quarter. An adaptation of her idea was seen later in the packing department, where it was used to ensure that the correct number of components were packed. The operator's development of the riveting counter system and its subsequent diffusion to another application were part of a company-wide employee involvement program. In all of the visited plants, employees pursued quarterly improvement goals; supported by training in methods and process analysis, assistance from engineers when requested, and two hours of paid time on Friday afternoons twice a month to work on projects. This continuing improvement, *kaizen* (*ky'zen*) type process generated a steady stream of implemented ideas and their diffusion was encouraged by the posting of sketches and descriptions of the ideas on bulletin boards in all company plants.

Both process-oriented and results-oriented performance measures were emphasized at the visited Japanese factories, consistent with the mixture of Taylorist and non-Taylorist activities at the sites. Process measures such as charts tracking the number of improvement projects and listing the participants were very prominently displayed. Also prominent, however, were displays of operating results. At the newest site, a large electric sports-type scoreboard, visible throughout the plant, continuously compared the cumulative real-time production schedule to the actual output achieved. In the chief foreman's office, a graphical display of the product flow paths indicated the flow rates at key points, to signal the need for corrective action before any operator was forced to shut down the line. In the lunch rooms of all plants, graphs of several efficiency measures were displayed. At virtually all work-stations, posters described both the qualitative and quantitative objectives for the current individual quarterly improvement projects.

The labour process at the visited sites is contradictory, with employees working four hours a month in a very non-Taylorist manner to make their work for the rest of the month even more Taylor-like. This contradiction can be addressed by using the 'work-content model' of Hill [35]. He characterizes work as having three phases: planning, doing and control. In the classical Taylorist model, the first and third phases are subsumed by management. Workers are responsible only for 'doing' what management has defined, and meeting the standards of the quality control inspectors. In the Japanese model observed at the plant sites, however, workers are involved in all three phases. They participate in planning as part of their improvement programs, and they exercise control since most quality control is delegated to the operators, including the authority to shut down the line. Therefore, only the 'doing' portions of the jobs are Taylorist. While traditional 'Scientific Management' job design incorporates as many Taylor principles as possible, the Japanese model appears to use only those necessary to meet the needs of variability reduction and consistent quality and output. In the terminology of Penrose, the goal seems to be the achievement of an optimum balance between the use of 'objective' and 'experiential' knowledge [36]. This goal is consistent with the requirements of the Japanese approach to total quality management (TQM).

An effective TQM program, we would argue, is a necessary condition for JIT production, and the two terms are increasingly linked to define TQM/JIT production [37]. A primary focus of TQM is on meeting the needs of internal 'clients' and external customers [38]. All JIT work stations face a very demanding set of 'clients', namely the downstream work-stations. These stations require an uninterrupted supply of high quality parts, arriving 'just-in-time'—conditions consistent with the low variability, non-discretionary Taylorist job tasks observed at the visited sites. The cumulative effect of meeting these internal 'client' needs is the production of high quality products that meet the expectations of the external customers. An equally important focus of TQM is achieving continuous improvement in meeting 'client' and customer needs.

This is made possible at the Japanese sites by the high level of worker commitment to their quarterly improvement projects. Utilizing the creativity and 'experiential' knowledge of the workforce makes it practical to continuously improve the hundreds of processes at the sites despite the relatively small number of professional manufacturing engineers employed. The improvements generated by the employees are formally implemented by the engineers who convert the primarily 'experiential' inputs of the workers into improved 'objective' job designs. This collaboration very effectively supports the TQM/JIT manufacturing system objective of continuously improving product quality levels. It also appears to be consistent with the conclusions of Klein [39]. She recommends that workers in a JIT environment should 'focus on task design, not execution' to balance the needs for worker autonomy and management control.

Sewell and Wilkinson however argue that:

> JIT/TQC regimes . . . are premised on more direct and detailed control (ideally 'total' control) and are characterised by a low degree of trust and strong management discipline. In these latter regards, JIT/TQC sounds like a reassertion of scientific management and the classic bureaucracy; it is not, however, for the organisational form is quite different. However, JIT/TQC does represent a reassertion of managerial prerogatives and for workers used to Volvo-style working may be experienced as such [40].

The distinguishing feature of the JIT-based factory is held to be 'visibility', with the implication of enhanced 'surveillance', likened by critics to Jeremy Bentham's classic *Panopticon*, envisaged by that nineteenth century utilitarian social philosopher as the ideal design for penal institutions. It thus is held to pre-empt workers enjoying 'idle' time or to 'hide' work, thus imposing 'management by stress'. It devolves responsibility in the workplace 'tactically', but increases 'strategic' control [41].

Rather than enhancing autonomy, however, JQM/JIT is therefore held 'to intensify the labour process as a result of increased surveillance and monitoring of workers' activities, heightened accountability, the harnessing of peer pressure within "teams" and via "customers" and the fostering of "involvement" in "waste elimination" and the continuous improvement of the production process' [42]. In sum, TQM/JIT stands accused of pushing back the frontiers of control.

Concluding remarks

Several important points have been clarified in this paper. First, we have tried to show how 'Scientific Management' was more widely diffused in Japanese industry in the inter-war years than most texts reveal. Second, we have set out the evolution of HRM in Japan as parallel to Taylorist developments. Third, we have pointed out that this link with Taylorism has continued into the post-war years, principally with the diffusion of JIT manufacturing and in the development of Total Quality Control (TQC), Zero Defect (ZD) and Quality Circles (QC), often subsumed under the rubric of TQM and regarded as pivotal to Japanese productivity enhancement.

To pull the final strands of our arguments together: the concept of *kaizen* (*ky'zen*) meaning continuous improvement, we feel, sums up the features we associated with Japanese management (TQM/JIT and so on). It epitomizes a process-oriented, as opposed to the Western results-based way of thinking and calls for an organizational culture where no day should go by without some improvement being made somewhere in the enterprise. *Kaizen* seeks to build the design approach, earlier associated with Taylorist industrial engineering, into contemporary systems. Japan's adaptation of Western technology and 'know-how' may therefore be seen as one of the most successful cases of transfer in modem times. Straightforward reproduction did not, however, take place; the Japanese fast improved on the techniques imported. This conclusion is not only true of technical 'hardware' but also managerial 'software'. It is therefore our contention that TQM/JIT systems may be seen as a legacy of Scientific Management, both directly and indirectly. If this initially seemed an apparent paradox, we hope we have made the case for its empirical resolution.

The development of the Toyota Production System, and its diffusion as generic JIT production has in fact extended the application of 'Scientific Management' into post-war Japanese manufacturing. The flow requirements for successful JIT production make the use of Taylorist job designs a necessary condition for achieving consistent quality through variability reduction. The job design process employed, however, conflicts with 'Scientific Management', since it features a degree of worker participation. This '*soikufu*' (creative thinking) approach to job design in Japan is described by Heiko:

> Scientific Management, where experts define what is to be done, how it is to be performed and how much time it should take, is replaced by continuous improvement, where all personnel participate in a continuous search for improvements [43].

The result is a mediated form of 'Scientific Management', with Taylorist job designs developed in a very non-Taylorist manner.

The '*soikufu*' policy and the key 'pillars' of Japanese industrial relations tend to generate high levels of worker commitment. Such commitment, combined with the management control inherent in JIT production makes possible the consistent delivery of high quality, competitively priced products. The result is a mutually reinforcing system. The 'pillars' contribute to the achievement of competitive advantage on the shop floor, which in turn yields profits levels that make it possible for the firm to continue to fund these supports. Last, but not least, the characteristics of the JIT production system that lead to its success in the marketplace raise a question about its impact at the work place on the quality of work life: specifically. 'Do the advantages of lifetime employment and "off-line" opportunities for exercising judgement and creativity compensate for the "on-line" pressures of the high intensity, "Scientific Management" environment of the JIT shop floor?' It is an important question, that is, we hope, increasingly being addressed [44].

References

1 For a fuller extended discussion of this theme and several other points, see Warner, M., 'Japanese culture, western management: Taylorism and Human Resources in Japan', *Organization Studies*, 1993, in press.

2 Urabe, K., 'Innovation and the Japanese management system', in Urabe, K., Child, I. and Kagono, T. (eds), *Innovation and Management: International Comparisons*, Berlin: de Gruyter, 1988, pp. 3–26.

3 See, for example, Morishima, M., *Why has Japan 'Succeeded'? Western Technology and the Japanese Ethos*, Cambridge University Press, 1982.

4 Smith, T. C., *Native Sources of Japanese Industrialisation, 1750–1920*, Berkeley: University of California Press, 1988.

5 Matsushita, K., 'The secret is shared', *Manufacturing Engineering*, Volume 100, No. 2, February, 1988.

6 Whitley, R. D., 'Eastern Asian enterprise structures and the comparative analysis of forms of business organization', *Organization Studies*, Vol. 1, 1990, pp. 47–74.

7 Maurice, M., Sorge, A. and Warner, M., 'Societal differences in organizing manufacturing units: a comparison of France, West Germany and Great Britain', *Organization Studies*, Vol. 1, No. 1, 1980, pp. 59–80.

8 See Dore, R. P., *British Factory—Japanese Factory*, London: Allen & Unwin, 1973. Dore, R.

P., *Flexible Rigidities*, Stanford University Press, 1986; Dare, R. P. and Sakmo, M., *How the Japanese Learn to Work*, Routledge, 1989.

9 McMillan, C. J., *The Japanese Industrial System*, Berlin: de Gruyter, 1985.

10 Kinzley, W. D., *Industrial Harmony in Modern Japan: The Invention of a Tradition*, Routledge, 1991.

11 Levine, S. B. and Kawada, H., *Human Resources in Japanese Industrial Development*, Princeton University Press, 1980.

12 See Okuda, K., 'Managerial evolution in Japan—I', *Management Japan*, Vol. 5, No. 1, 1971, pp. 13–19; Okuda, K., 'Management evolution in Japan—II', *Management Japan*, Vol. 5, No. 2, 1972, pp. 16–23; Okuda, K., *Hito to Keiei (Men and Management)*, Tokyo: Manejimento, 1985.

13 Yamamura, K., 'Japan's Deus Ex Machina: Western technology in the 1920s', *Journal of Japanese Studies*, Vol. 12, No. 1, 1986, pp. 65–94.

14 Cusumano, M. A., *The Japanese Automobile Industry: Technology and Management at Nissan and Toyota*, Harvard University Press, 1985.

15 Francks, P., *Japanese Economic Development*, Routledge, 1992.

16 Chalmers, N. J., *Industrial Relations in Japan: The Peripheral Workforce*, Routledge, 1989.

17 Ibid., p. 127.

18 Schonberger, R., *World Class Manufacturing*, Glencoe, Ill.: The Free Press, 1984.

19 Sewell, C. and Wilkinson, B., 'Someone to watch over me': Surveillance, discipline and the Just-in-Time labour process', *Sociology*, Vol. 26, No. 2, 1992, pp. 271–290.

20 Ibid., p. 278.

21 Macmillan, op. cit., p. 214.

22 Whitehill, A. M., *Japanese Management: Tradition and Transition*, London: Routledge, 1991.

23 Schonberger, R., *Japanese Manufacturing Techniques*, Glencoe, Ill.: The Free Press, 1982, p. 193.

24 McMillan, op cit., pp. 213–214.

25 Chandler, A. D. Jr, *The Visible Hand: The Managerial Revolution in American Business*, Cambridge, Mass.: Harvard University Press, 1977, p. 281.

26 Cusumano, M. A., op. cit., p. 264.

27 Schonberger, R., *World Class Manufacturing*, Glencoe, Ill.: The Free Press, 1984, p. 22.

28 Klein, J. A., 'The human costs of manufacturing reform', *Harvard Business Review*, March–April, 1989, p. 61.

29 Suzaki, K., *The New Manufacturing Challenge*, Glencoe, Ill.: The Free Press, 1987, p. 20.

30 Womack, J., Jones, D., and Roose, D., *The Machine That Changed the World*, New York: Rawson Associates, 1990, p. 91.

31 Cusumano, op. cit., p. 281.

32 Lazonick, W., *Competitive Advantage on the Shop Floor*, Harvard University Press, 1990, p. 270.

33 'Maybe Winnebago just wasn't ready for big city bosses', *Wall Street Journal*, October 17, 1988.

34 Whittaker, D. H, *Managing Innovation: A Study of Scottish and Japanese Factories*, Cambridge University Press, 1990, p. 161.

35 Hill, T., *Manufacturing Strategy*, New York: Richard Irwin, 1989, p. 167.

36 Penrose. E. T., *The Theory of the Growth of the Firm*, London: M. E. Shapiro, 1980, (Originally published 1959), p. 53.

37 Delbridge, R., Turnbull, P., and Wilkinson, B., 'Pushing back the frontiers: management control and work intensification under JIT/TQM factory regimes', *New Technology, Work and Employment*, Vol. 7, No. 2, 1992, p. 67.

38 Ciampa, D., *Total Quality*, Reading, Mass.: Addison-Wesley, 1991.

39 Klein, op. cit., p. 66.

40 Sewell and Wilkinson, op. cit., pp. 276–277.

41 Ibid., p. 279.

42 Delbridge et al., op cit., pp. 97–98.

43 Heiko, L., 'The conceptual foundation of Just-In-Time', in *Just-In-Time Manufacturing Systems*, A. Satir (ed.), New York: Elsevier, 1991, p. 9.

44 Delbridge et al., op. cit., p. 97 and Klein, J. A., op. cit., p. 60.

the ease with which people slip into pre-defined roles (1973)

'A study of prisoners and guards in a simulated prison', by Craig Haney, Curtis Banks and Philip Zimbardo, *Naval Research Reviews*, Office of Naval Research, Department of the Navy, Washington DC, September 1973.

A large part of how we behave, whether inside or outside organizations, is affected by our understanding of roles. Some roles, such as daughter, son, student or manager, we may be familiar with, due to our direct, first-hand experience. For other roles, we learn about them in indirect, second-hand ways. For example by reading books, watching TV or the movies, or listening to those who carry them out.

From the individual perspective, an understanding of a role allows us to behave appropriately in a particular social or work setting. From the organizational perspective, role definitions and role socialization are ways in which a company can control the behaviour of its individual members, and integrate their activities with one another. Philip Zimbardo's experiment, which is described in this reading, shows this more vividly than perhaps any other in recent times.

learning objectives

Once you have read and understood the prescribed material, you should be able to:

1 Assess your knowledge of Zimbardo's experiment.
2 Check your understanding of the key terms and concepts introduced in Zimbardo's experiment.
3 Analyze the research methodology used in Zimbardo's experiment, and place abstract conceptual variables into practice.
4 Apply your knowledge of organizational behaviour to suggest practices to improve the performance of prisons.

learning pre-requisites

Before proceeding, you should read Chapter 13 of the core text and the article, 'A study of prisoners and guards in a simulated prison', by Craig Haney, Curtis Banks and Philip Zimbardo that follows.

learning activities

Complete the crossword.

▶ Fit in the answers to the questions into the grid below. The appropriate number of words/letters for each answer is indicated in brackets.
▶ The missing word begins, down or across, at the box location indicated by the letter-number, for example, box E3.
▶ Complete the quotation from Zimbardo's study by inserting the correct letters in

the spaces provided below the grid. One co-ordinate (e.g. A14) equals one letter (e.g. = S).

▶ Two of the letters of the quotation's author's surname have already been inserted.

Down

E3   What treatment of prisoners was not permitted? (8, 5)

H10   The instruction given to the guards were ___ (7) guidelines.

L6   On which day of the study was the experiment terminated prematurely? (5)

K11   In private conversations, which topics did prisoners and guards rarely refer to? (8)

N4   Zimbardo claimed that there was abundant evidence that subjects went beyond this (4, 7).

A5   In the course of the study, prisoner's rights turned to ___ (10).

D13   What title did the undergraduate research assistant in the experiment have? (6)

C6   Who developed the rules for the mock prison? (6, 6)

Across

B15   During the ___ (11)-meeting, the guards had their tasks explained to them.

D11   Which response mode did the prisoners adopt? (7)

E7   The guards demonstrated ___ (10) in all interactions.

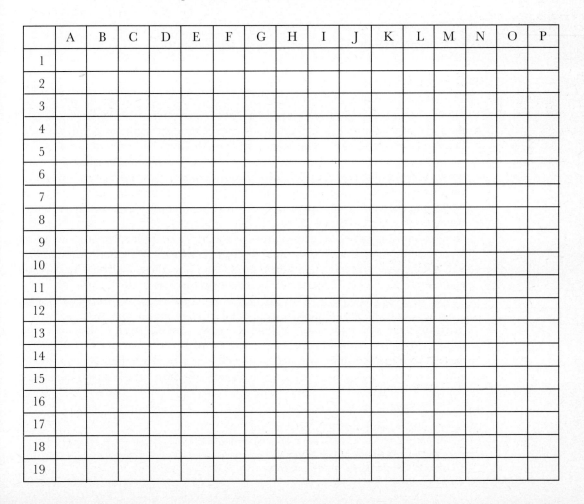

B4   As a result of which psychosomatic reaction was the fifth subject released? (4)

A1   The behaviour of some guards towards prisoners (5, 3, 4).

E3   In real prisons, informing, sexual control, and the development of cliques, are a means to gain this (5).

G5   Who was the superintendent of the mock prison? (8)

B19   The most hostile guards on each shift, took on this role (10).

Quotation

ONE WHO	A-l4	G-1	N-4	C-1	H-5	I-11	N-7	E-14
THE	E-1	N-5	G-19	C-15	B-15	C-9	E-14	
OF	N-8	L-5	E-7	E-14	K-15	K-16		
LIFE IS A	E-8	C-15	N-7	N-10	I-15	G-1	L-1	N-7
WHO COULD	C-13	J-19	I-15	E-1	E-14	A-1	J-1	F-15 E-19
ANYTHING.								

Author

E19   N5   E6   A1   K15   N7   V   K14   K   E5

READING 13

A study of prisoners and guards in a simulated prison*
Craig Haney, Curtis Banks and Philip Zimbardo†

The research reported in this article is part of a larger project sponsored by the Office of Naval Research which is designed to develop a better understanding of the basic psychological mechanisms underlying human aggression. In this study. Dr. Zimbardo fabricated a simulation of the essential characteristics of a prison environment. From a highly selected group of college students, Dr. Zimbardo randomly assigned half as 'guards' (with all attendant powers) and half as 'prisoners' (under the complete subjugation of the the 'guards'). Essentially then, a group of intelligent, 'normal' young men were put into a situation which demanded close contact over a period of several days. There was a well-defined authority/subordinate relationship between 'guards' and 'prisoners.' The 'prison' environment was further manipulated to promote anonymity, depersonalization, and dehumanization among the subjects. The study demonstrates how these variables combine to increase the incidence of aggressive behavior on the part of the 'guards' and submissive and docile conformity on the part of the 'prisoners.'

Studies such as this one help to identify and isolate the various processes which motivate aggressive/submissive behavior within a 'total institution' such as a prison. The Navy and Marine Corps have a direct interest in the conclusions drawn from this study in as much as parallels can be made between the forces which operated within Dr. Zimbardo's 'prison' and those which spawn disruptive

* Reprinted by permission from *Naval Research Reviews*, Office of Naval Research, Department of the Navy, Washington DC, September 1973.

† Dr. Zimbardo is Professor of Psychology at Stanford. In the field of social psychology, Dr. Zimbardo has done important work in the areas of dehumanization, criminal behavior, and criminal justice systems. Mr. Haney and Mr. Banks are graduate assistants.

interpersonal conflict in Naval prisons. More importantly, however, this study identifies some of the conditions which are likely to promote unrest when men are placed in situations which demand close contact for protracted periods of time. Such research increases the Navy's capability to develop effective training designs to eliminate conditions which elicit counter-productive conflict.

Introduction

After he had spent four years in a Siberian prison the great Russian novelist Dostoevsky commented surprisingly that his time in prison had created in him a deep optimism about the ultimate future of mankind because, as he put it, 'if man could survive the horrors of life he must surely be a creature who could withstand anything.' The cruel irony which Dostoevsky overlooked is that the reality of prison bears witness not only to the resiliency and adaptiveness of the men who tolerate life within its walls, but as well to the 'ingenuity' and tenacity of those who devised and still maintain our correctional and reformatory systems.

Nevertheless, in the century which has passed since Dostoevsky's imprisonment, little has changed to render the main thrust of his statement less relevant. Although we have passed through periods of enlightened humanitarian reform, in which physical conditions within prisons have improved somewhat, and the rhetoric of rehabilitation has replaced the language of punitive incarceration, the social institution of prison has continued to fail. On purely pragmatic grounds, there is substantial evidence that prisons really neither 'rehabilitate' nor act as a deterrent to future crime – in America, recidivism rates upwards of 75 per cent speak quite decisively to these criteria. And, to perpetuate what is also an economic failure, American taxpayers alone must provide an expenditure for 'corrections' of 1.5 billion dollars annually. On humanitarian grounds as well, prisons have failed: our mass media are increasingly filled with accounts of atrocities committed daily, man against man, in reaction to the penal system or in the name of it. The experience of prison creates undeniably, almost to the point of cliche, an intense hatred and disrespect in most inmates for the authority and the established order of society into which they will eventually return. And the toll it takes in the deterioration of human spirit for those who must administer it, as well as for those upon whom it is inflicted, is incalculable.

Attempts to provide an explanation of the deplorable condition of our penal system and its dehumanizing effects upon prisoners and guards, often focus upon what might be called the *dispositional hypothesis*. While this explanation is rarely expressed explicitly, it is central to a prevalent nonconscious ideology: that the state of the social institution of prison is due to the 'nature' of the people who administrate it, or the 'nature' of the people who populate it, or both. That is, a major contributing cause to despicable conditions, violence, brutality, dehumanization and degradation existing within any prison can be traced to some innate or acquired characteristic of the correctional and inmate population. Thus on the one hand, there is the contention that violence and brutality exist within prison because guards are sadistic, uneducated, and insensitive people. It is the 'guard mentality,' a unique syndrome of negative traits which they bring into the situation, that engenders the inhumane treatment of prisoners. On the other hand, there is the argument that prison violence and brutality are the logical and predictable results of the involuntary confinement of a collective of individuals whose life histories are, by definition, characterized by disregard for law, order and social convention and a concurrent propensity for impulsivity and aggression. In seeming logic, it follows that these individuals, having proven themselves incapable of functioning satisfactorily within the 'normal' structure of society, cannot do so either inside the structure provided by prisons. To control such men, the argument continues, whose basic orientation to any conflict situation is to react with physical power or deception, force must be met with force, and a certain number of violent encounters must be expected and tolerated by the public.

The dispositional hypothesis has been embraced by the proponents of the prison *status quo* (blaming conditions on the evil in the prisoners), as well as by its critics (attributing the evil to guards and staff with their evil motives and deficient personality structures). The appealing simplicity of this proposition localizes the source of prison riots, recidivism and corruption in these 'bad seeds' and not in the conditions of the 'prison soil.' Such an analysis directs attention away from the complex matrix of social, economic and political forces that combine to make prisons what they are – and that would require complex, expensive, revolutionary actions to bring about any meaningful change. Instead, rioting prisoners are identified, punished, transferred to maximum security institutions or shot, outside agitators sought, and corrupt officials suspended – while the system itself goes on essentially unchanged, its basic structure unexamined and unchallenged.

However, the dispositional hypothesis cannot be critically evaluated directly through observation in existing prison settings, because such naturalistic observation necessarily confounds the acute effects of the environment with the chronic characteristics of the inmate and guard populations. To separate the effects of the prison environment *per se* from those attributable to *a priori* dispositions of its inhabitants requires a research strategy in which a 'new' prison is constructed, comparable in its fundamental social-psychological milieu to existing prison systems, but entirely populated by individuals who are undifferentiated in all essential dimensions from the rest of society.

Such was the approach taken in the present empirical study, namely, to create a prison-like situation in which the guards and inmates were initially comparable and characterized as being 'normal-average,' and then to observe the patterns of behavior which resulted, as well as the cognitive, emotional and attitudinal reactions which emerged. Thus we began our experiment with a sample of individuals who were in the normal range of the general population on a variety of dimensions we were able to measure. Half were randomly assigned to the role of 'prisoner,' the others to that of 'guard,' neither group having any history of crime, emotional disability, physical handicap or even intellectual or social disadvantage.

The environment created was that of a 'mock' prison which physically constrained the prisoners in barred cells and psychologically conveyed the sense of imprisonment to all participants. Our intention was not to create a *literal* simulation of an American prison, but rather a functional representation of one. For ethical, moral and pragmatic reasons we could not detain our subjects for extended or indefinite periods of time, we could not exercise the threat and promise of severe physical punishment, we could not allow homosexual or racist practices to flourish, nor could we duplicate certain other specific aspects of prison life. Nevertheless, we believed that we could create a situation with sufficient mundane realism to allow the role-playing participants to go beyond the superficial demands of their assignment into the deep structure of the characters they represented. To do so, we established functional equivalents for the activities and experiences of actual prison life which were expected to produce qualitatively similar psychological reactions in our subjects – feelings of power and powerlessness, of control and oppression, of satisfaction and frustration, of arbitrary rule and resistance to authority, of status and anonymity, of machismo and emasculation. In the conventional terminology of experimental social psychology, we first identified a number of relevant conceptual variables through analysis of existing prison situations, then designed a setting in which these variables were operationalized. No specific hypotheses were advanced other than the general one that assignment to the treatment of 'guard' or 'prisoner' would result in significantly different reactions on behavioral measures of interaction, emotional measures of mood state and pathology, attitudes towards self, as well as other indices of coping and adaptation to this novel situation. What follows is a discussion of how we created and peopled our prison, what we observed, what our subjects reported, and finally, what we can conclude about the nature of the prison environment and the psychology of imprisonment which can account for the failure of our prisons.

Method

Overview

The effects of playing the role of 'guard' or 'prisoner' were studied in the context of an experimental simulation of a prison environment. The research design was a relatively simple one, involving as it did only a single treatment variable, the random assignment to either a 'guard' or 'prisoner' conditions. These roles were enacted over an extended period of time (nearly one week) within an environment that was physically constructed to resemble a prison. Central to the methodology of creating and maintaining a psychological state of imprisonment was the functional simulation of significant properties of 'real prison life' (established through information from former inmates, correctional personnel and texts).

The 'guards' were free within certain limits to implement the procedures of induction into the prison setting and maintenance of custodial retention of the 'prisoners.' These inmates, having voluntarily submitted to the conditions of this total institution in which they now lived, coped in various ways with its stresses and its challenges. The behavior of both groups of subjects was observed, recorded, and analyzed. The dependent measures were of two general types: (1) transactions between and within each group of subjects, recorded on video and audio tape as well as directly observed; (2) individual reactions on questionnaires, mood inventories, personality tests, daily guard shift reports, and post experimental interviews.

Subjects

The 22 subjects who participated in the experiment were selected from an initial pool of 75 respondents, who answered a newspaper ad asking for male volunteers to participate in a psychological study of 'prison life' in return for payment of $15 per day. Each respondent completed an extensive questionnaire concerning his family background, physical and mental health history, prior experience and attitudinal propensities with respect to sources of psychopathology (including their involvements in crime). Each respondent also was interviewed by one of two experimenters. Finally, the 24 subjects who were judged to be most stable (physically and mentally), most mature, and least involved in anti-social behaviors were selected to participate in the study. On a random basis, half of the subjects were assigned the role of 'guard,' half were assigned to the role of 'prisoner.'

The subjects were normal, healthy, male college students who were in the Stanford area during the summer. They were largely of middle class socio-economic status and Caucasians (with the exception of one Oriental subject). Initially they were strangers to each other, a selection precaution taken to avoid the disruption of any pre-existing friendship patterns and to mitigate any transfer into the experimental situation of previously established relationships or patterns of behavior.

This final sample of subjects was administered a battery of psychological tests on the day prior to the start of the simulation, but to avoid any selective bias on the part of the experimenter-observers, scores were not tabulated until the study was completed.

Two subjects who were assigned to be a 'stand-by' in case an additional 'prisoner' was needed were not called, and one assigned to be a 'stand-by' guard decided against participating just before the simulation phase began – thus, our data analysis is based upon ten prisoners and eleven guards in our experimental conditions.

Procedure

Physical aspects of the prison

The prison was built in a 35-foot section of a basement corridor in the psychology building at Stanford University. It was partitioned by two fabricated walls; one was fitted with the only entrance door to the cell block and the other contained a small observation screen. Three small cells (6 × 9 ft.) were made from converted laboratory rooms by replacing the usual doors with steel barred, black painted ones, and removing all furniture.

A cot (with mattress, sheet and pillow) for each prisoner was the only furniture in the cells. A small closet across from the cells served as a solitary confinement facility: its dimensions were extremely small (2 × 2 × 7 ft.), and it was unlighted.

In addition, several rooms in an adjacent wing of the building were used as guard's quarters (to change in and out of uniform or for rest and relaxation), a bedroom for the 'warden' and 'superintendent,' and an interview-testing room. Behind the observation screen at one end of the 'yard' (small enclosed room representing the fenced prison grounds) was video recording equipment and sufficient space for several observers.

Operational details

The 'prisoner' subjects remained in the mock-prison 24 hours per day for the duration of the study. Three were arbitrarily assigned to each of the three cells; the others were on stand-by call at their homes. The 'guard' subjects worked on three-man, eight-hour shifts; remaining in the prison environment only during their work shift and going about their usual lives at other times.

Role instructions

All subjects had been told that they would be assigned either the guard or the prisoner role on a completely random basis and all had voluntarily agreed to play either role for $15.00 per day for up to two weeks. They signed a contract guaranteeing a minimally adequate diet, clothing, housing and medical care as well as the financial remuneration in return for their stated 'intention' of serving in the assigned role for the duration of the study.

It was made explicit in the contract that those assigned to be prisoners should expect to be under surveillance (have little or no privacy) and to have some of their basic civil rights suspended during their imprisonment, excluding physical abuse. They were given no other information about what to expect nor instructions about behavior appropriate for a prisoner role. Those actually assigned to this treatment were informed by phone to be available at their place of residence on a given Sunday when we would start the experiment.

The subjects assigned to be guards attended an orientation meeting on the day prior to the induction of the prisoners. At this time they were introduced to the principal investigators, the 'Superintendent' of the prison (the author) and an undergraduate research assistant who assumed the administrative role of 'Warden.' They were told that we wanted to try to simulate a prison environment within the limits imposed by pragmatic and ethical considerations. Their assigned task was to 'maintain the reasonable degree of order within the prison necessary for its effective functioning,' although the specifics of how this duty might be implemented were not explicitly detailed. They were made aware of the fact that, while many of the contingencies with which they might be confronted were essentially unpredictable (e.g., prisoner escape attempts), part of their task was to be prepared for such eventualties and to be able to deal appropriately with the variety of situations that might arise. The 'Warden' instructed the guards in the administrative details, including: the work-shifts, the mandatory daily completion of shift reports concerning the activity of guards and prisoners, the completion of 'critical incident' reports which detailed unusual occurrences, and the administration of meals, work and recreation programs for the prisoners. In order to begin to involve these subjects in their roles even before the first prisoner was incarcerated, the guards assisted in the final phases of completing the prison complex – putting the cots in the cells, signs on the walls, setting up the guards' quarters, moving furniture, water coolers, refrigerators, etc.

The guards generally believed that we were primarily interested in studying the behavior of the prisoners. Of course, we were as interested in the effects which enacting the role of guard in this environment would have on their behavior and subjective states.

To optimize the extent to which their behavior would reflect their genuine reactions to the experimental prison situation and not simply their ability to follow instructions, they were intentionally given only minimal guidelines for what it meant to be a guard. An explicit and categorical prohibition against the use of physical punishment or physical aggression was, however, emphasized by the experimenters. Thus, with this single notable exception, their roles were relatively unstructured initially, requiring each 'guard' to carry out activities necessary for interacting with a group of 'prisoners' as well as with other 'guards' and the 'correctional staff.'

Uniforms

In order to promote feelings of anonymity in the subjects each group was issued identical uniforms. For the guards, the uniform consisted of: plain khaki shirts and trousers, a whistle, a police night stick (wooden batons), and reflecting sunglasses which made eye contact impossible. The prisoners' uniform consisted of a loose fitting muslin smock with an identification number on front and back, no underclothes, a light chain and lock around one ankle, rubber sandals and a cap made from a nylon stocking. Each prisoner also was issued a toothbrush, soap, soapdish, towel and bed linen. No personal belongings were allowed in the cells.

The outfitting of both prisoners and guards in this manner served to enhance group identity and reduce individual uniqueness within the two groups. The khaki uniforms were intended to convey a military attitude, while the whistle and nightstick were carried as symbols of control and power. The prisoners' uniforms were designed not only to deindividuate the prisoners but to be humiliating and serve as symbols of their dependence and subservience. The ankle chain was a constant reminder (even during their sleep when it hit the other ankle) of the oppressiveness of the environment. The stocking cap removed any distinctiveness associated with hair length, color or style (as does shaving of heads in some 'real' prisons and the military). The ill-fitting uniforms made the prisoners feel awkward in their movements; since these 'dresses' were worn without undergarments, the uniforms forced them to assume unfamiliar postures, more like those of a woman than a man – another part of the emasculating process of becoming a prisoner.

Induction procedure

With the cooperation of the Palo Alto City Police Department all of the subjects assigned to the prisoner treatment were unexpectedly 'arrested' at their residences. A police officer charged them with suspicion of burglary or armed robbery, advised them of their legal rights, handcuffed them, thoroughly searched them (often as curious neighbors looked on) and carried them off to the police station in the rear of the police car. At the station they went through the standard routines of being fingerprinted, having an identification file prepared and then being placed in a detention cell. Each prisoner was blindfolded and subsequently driven by one of the experimenters and a subject-guard to our mock prison. Throughout the entire arrest procedure, the police officers involved maintained a formal, serious attitude, avoiding answering any questions of clarification as to the relation of this 'arrest' to the mock prison study.

Upon arrival at our experimental prison, each prisoner was stripped, sprayed with a delousing preparation (a deodorant spray) and made to stand alone naked for a while in the cell yard. After being given the uniform described previously and having an I.D. picture taken ('mug shot'), the prisoner was put in his cell and ordered to remain silent.

Administrative routine

When all the cells were occupied, the warden greeted the prisoners and read them the rules of the institution (developed by the guards and the warden). They were to be memorized and to be followed. Prisoners were to be referred to only by the number on their uniforms, also in an effort to depersonalize them.

The prisoners were to be served three bland meals per day, were allowed three supervised toilet visits, and given two hours daily for the privilege of reading or letterwriting. Work assignments were issued for which the prisoners were to receive an hourly wage to constitute their $15 daily payment. Two visiting periods per week were scheduled, as were movie rights and exercise periods. Three times a day all prisoners were lined up for a 'count' (one on each guard work-shift). The initial purpose of the 'count' was to ascertain that all prisoners were present, and to test them on their knowledge of the rules and their I.D. numbers. The first perfunctory counts lasted only about ten minutes, but on each successive day (or night) they were spontaneously increased in duration until some lasted several hours. Many of the pre-established features of administrative routine were modified or abandoned by the guards, and some privileges were forgotten by the staff over the course of study.

Results

Overview

Although it is difficult to anticipate exactly what the influence of incarceration will be upon the individuals who are subjected to it and those charged with its maintenance, especially in a simulated reproduction, the results of the present experiment support many commonly held conceptions of prison life and validate anecdotal evidence supplied by articulate ex-convicts. The environment of arbitrary custody had great impact upon the affective states of both guards and prisoners as well as upon the interpersonal processes taking place between and within those role-groups.

In general, guards and prisoners showed a marked tendency toward increased negativity of affect, and their overall outlook became increasingly negative. As the experiment progressed, prisoners expressed intentions to do harm to others more frequently. For both prisoners and guards self-evaluations were more deprecating as the experience of the prison environment became internalized.

Overt behavior was generally consistent with the subjective self-reports and affective expressions of the subjects. Despite the fact that guards and prisoners were essentially free to engage in any form of interaction (positive or negative, supportive or affrontive, etc.), the characteristic nature of their encounters tended to be negative, hostile, affrontive and dehumanizing. Prisoners immediately adopted a generally passive response mode while guards assumed a very active initiative role in all interactions. Throughout the experiment, commands were the most frequent form of verbal behavior and, generally, verbal exchanges were strikingly impersonal, with few references to individual identity. Although it was clear to all subjects that the experimenters would not permit physical violence to take place, varieties of less direct aggressive behavior were observed frequently (especially on the part of guards). In lieu of physical violence, verbal affronts were used as one of the most frequent forms of interpersonal contact between guards and prisoners.

The most dramatic evidence of the impact of this situation upon the participants was seen in the gross reactions of five prisoners who had to be released because of extreme emotional depression, crying, rage and acute anxiety. The pattern of symptoms was quite similar in four of the subjects and began as early as the second day of imprisonment. The fifth subject was released after being treated for a psychosomatic rash which covered portions of his body. Of the remaining prisoners, only two said they were not willing to forfeit the money they had earned in return for being 'paroled.' When the experiment was terminated prematurely after only six days, all the remaining prisoners were delighted by their unexpected good fortune. In contrast, most of the guards seemed to be distressed by the decision to stop the experiment and it appeared to us that they had become sufficiently involved in their roles that they now enjoyed the extreme control and power which they exercised and were reluctant to give it up. One guard did report being personally upset at the suffering of the prisoners, and claimed to have considered asking to change his role to become one of them – but never did so. None of the guards ever failed to come to work on time for their shift, and indeed, on several occasions guards remained on duty voluntarily and uncomplaining for extra hours – without additional pay.

The extremely pathological reactions which emerged in both groups of subjects testify to the power of the social forces operating, but still there were individual differences seen in styles of coping with this novel experience and in degrees of successful adaptation to it. Half the prisoners did endure the oppressive atmosphere, and not all the guards resorted to hostility. Some guards were tough but fair ('played by the rules'), some went far beyond their roles to engage in creative cruelty and harassment, while a few were passive and rarely instigated any coercive control over the prisoners.

Reality of the simulation

At this point it seems necessary to confront the critical question of 'reality' in the simulated prison environment: were the behaviors observed more than the mere acting out assigned roles convincingly? To be sure, ethical, legal and practical considerations set limits upon the degree to which this situation could approach the conditions existing in actual prisons and penitentiaries. Necessarily absent were some of the most salient aspects of prison life reported by criminologists and documented in the writing of prisoners. There was no involuntary homosexuality, no racism, no physical beatings, no threat to life by prisoners against each other or the guards. Moreover, the maximum anticipated 'sentence' was only two weeks and, unlike some prison systems, could not be extended indefinitely for infractions of the internal operating rules of the prison.

In one sense, the profound psychological effects we observed under the relatively minimal prison-like conditions which existed in our mock prison made the results even more significant, and force us to wonder about the devastating impact of chronic incarceration in real prisons. Nevertheless, we must contend with the criticism that our conditions were too minimal to provide a meaningful analogue to existing prisons. It is necessary to demonstrate that the participants in this experiment transcended the conscious limits of their preconceived stereotyped roles and their awareness of the artificiality and limited duration of imprisonment. We feel there is abundant evidence that virtually all of the subjects at one time or another experienced reactions which went well beyond the surface demands of role-playing and penetrated the deep structure of the psychology of imprisonment.

Although instructions about how to behave in the roles of guard or prisoner were not explicitly defined, demand characteristics in the experiment obviously exerted some directing influence. Therefore, it is enlightening to look to circumstances where role demands were minimal, where the subjects believed they were not being observed, or where they should not have been behaving under the constraints imposed by their roles (as in 'private' situations), in order to assess whether the role behaviors reflected anything more than public conformity or good acting.

When the private conversations of the prisoners were monitored, we learned that almost all (a full 90 per cent) of what they talked about was directly related to immediate prison conditions, that is, food, privileges, punishment, guard harassment, *etc.* Only one-tenth of the time did their conversations deal with their life outside the prison. Consequently, although they had lived together under such intense conditions, the prisoners knew surprisingly little about each other's past history or future plans. This excessive concentration on the vicissitudes of their current situation helped to make the prison experience more oppressive for the prisoners because, instead of escaping from it when they had a chance to do so in the privacy of their cells, the prisoners continued to allow it to dominate their thoughts and social relations. The guards too, rarely exchanged personal information during their relaxation breaks. They either talked about 'problem prisoners,' other prison topics, or did not talk at all. There were few instances of any personal communication across the two role groups. Moreover, when prisoners referred to other prisoners during interviews, they typically deprecated each other, seemingly adopting the guards' negative attitude.

From post experimental data, we discovered that when individual guards were alone with solitary prisoners and out of range of any recording equipment, as on the way to or in the toilet, harassment often was greater than it was on the 'Yard.' Similarly, video-taped analyses of total guard aggression showed a daily escalation even after most prisoners had ceased resisting and prisoner deterioration had become visibly obvious to them. Thus, guard aggression was no longer elicited as it was initially in response to perceived threats, but was emitted simply as a 'natural' consequence of being in the uniform of a 'guard' and asserting the power inherent in that role. In specific instances we noted cases of a guard (who did not know he was being observed) in the early morning hours pacing the Yard as the prisoners slept – vigorously pounding his night stick into his hand while he 'kept watch' over his captives. Or another guard who detained an 'incorrigible' prisoner in solitary confinement beyond the duration set by the guards' own rules, and then he conspired to keep him in the hole all night while attempting to conceal this information from the experimenters who were thought to be too soft on the prisoners.

In passing we may note in additional point about the nature of role-playing and the extent to which dual behavior is 'explained away' by reference to it. It will be recalled that many guards continued to intensify their harassment and aggressive behavior even after the second day of the study, when prisoner deterioration became marked and visible and emotional breakdowns began to occur (in the presence of the guards). When questioned after the study about their persistent affrontive and harassing behavior in the face of prisoner emotional trauma, most guards replied that they were 'just playing the role' of a tough guard, although none ever doubted the magnitude or validity of the prisoners' emotional response. The reader may wish to consider to what extremes an individual may go, how great must be the consequences of his behavior for others, before he can no longer rightfully attribute his actions to 'playing a role' and thereby abdicate responsibility.

When introduced to a Catholic priest, many of the role-playing prisoners referred to themselves by their prison number rather than their Christian names. Some even asked him to get a lawyer to help them get out. When a public defender was summoned to interview those prisoners who had not yet been released, almost all of them strenuously demanded that he 'bail' them out immediately.

One of the most remarkable incidents of the study occured during a parole board hearing when each of five prisoners eligible for parole was asked by the senior author whether he would be willing to forfeit all the money earned as a prisoner if he were to be paroled (released from the study). Three of the five prisoners said, 'yes,' they would be willing to do this. Notice that the original incentive for participating in the study had been the promise of money, and they were, after only four days, prepared to give this up completely. And, more surprisingly, when told that this possibility would have to be discussed with the members of the staff before a decision could be made, each prisoner got up quietly and was escorted by a guard back to his cell. If they regarded themselves simply as 'subjects' participating in an experiment for money, there was no longer any incentive to remain in the study and they could have easily escaped this situation which had so clearly become aversive for them by quitting. Yet, so powerful was the control which the situation had come to have over them, so much a reality had this simulated environment become, that they were unable to see that their original and singular motive for remaining no longer obtained, and they returned to their cells to await a 'parole' decision by their captors.

The reality of the prison was also attested to by our prison consultant who had spent over 16 years in prison, as well as the priest who had been a prison chaplain and the public defender, all of whom were brought into direct contact with our simulated prison environment. Further, the depressed affect of the prisoners, the guards' willingness to work overtime for no additional pay, the spontaneous use of prison titles and ID numbers in non role-related situations all point to a level of reality as real as any other in the lives of all those who shared this experience.

To understand how an illusion of imprisonment could have become so real, we need now to consider the uses of power by the guards as well as the effects of such power in shaping the prisoner mentality.

Pathology of power

Being a guard carried with it social status within the prison, a group identity (when wearing the uniform), and above all, the freedom to exercise an unprecedented degree of control over the lives of other human beings. This control was invariably expressed in terms of sanctions, punishment, demands, and with the threat of manifest physical power. There was no need for the guards to rationally justify a request as they did in their ordinary life, and merely to make a demand was sufficient to have it carried out. Many of the guards showed in their behavior and revealed in post experimental statements that this sense of power was exhilarating.

The use of power was self-aggrandizing and self-perpetuating. The guard power, derived initially from an arbitrary and randomly assigned label, was intensified whenever there was any perceived threat by the prisoners and this new level subsequently became the baseline from which further hostility and harassment would begin. The most hostile guards on each shift moved spontaneously into the leadership roles of giving orders and deciding on punishments. They became role models whose behavior was emulated by other members of the shift. Despite minimal contact between the three separate guard shifts and nearly 16 hours a day spent away from the prison, the absolute level of aggression, as well as more subtle and 'creative' forms of aggression manifested, increased in a spiralling function. Not to be tough and arrogant was to be seen as a sign of weakness by the guards, and even those 'good' guards who did not get as drawn into the power syndrome as the others respected the implicit norm of *never* contradicting or even interferring with an action of a more hostile guard on their shift.

After the first day of the study, practically all prisoner rights (even such things as the time and conditions of sleeping and eating) came to be redefined by the guards as 'privileges' which were to be earned by obedient behavior. Constructive activities such as watching movies or reading (previously planned and suggested by the experimenters) were arbitrarily cancelled until further notice by the guards – and were subsequently never allowed. 'Reward,' then became granting approval for prisoners to eat, sleep, go to the toilet, talk, smoke a cigarette, wear eyeglasses, or the temporary dimunition of harassment. One wonders about the conceptual nature of 'positive' reinforcement when subjects are in such conditions of deprivation, and the extent to which even minimally acceptable conditions become rewarding when experienced in the context of such an impoverished environment.

We might also question whether there are meaningful non-violent alternatives as models for behavior modification in real prisons. In a world where men are either powerful or powerless, everyone learns to despise the lack of power in others and in oneself. It seems to us, that prisoners learn to admire power for its own sake – power becoming the ultimate reward. Real prisoners soon learn the means to gain power whether through ingratiation, informing, sexual control of other prisoners or development of powerful cliques. When they are released from prison, it is likely they will never want to feel so powerless again and will take action to establish and assert a sense of power.

The pathological prisoner syndrome

Various coping strategies were employed by our prisoners as they began to react to their perceived loss of personal identity and the arbitrary control of their lives. At first they exhibited disbelief at the total invasion of their privacy, constant surveillance, and atmosphere of oppression in which they were living. Their next response was rebellion, first by the use of direct force, and later with subtle divisive tactics designed to foster distrust among the prisoners. They then tried to work within the system by setting up an elected grievance committee. When that collective action failed to produce meaningful changes in their existence, individual self-interests emerged. The breakdown in prisoner cohesion was the start of social disintegration which gave rise not only to feelings of isolation, but deprecation of other prisoners as well. As noted before, half the prisoners coped with the prison situation by becoming 'sick' –

extremely disturbed emotionally – as a passive way demanding attention and help. Others became excessively obedient in trying to be 'good' prisoners. They sided with the guards against a solitary fellow prisoner who coped with his situation by refusing to eat. Instead of supporting this final and major act of rebellion, the prisoners treated him as a trouble-maker who deserved to be punished for his disobedience. It is likely that the negative self-regard among the prisoners noted by the end of the study was the product of their coming to believe that the continued hostility toward all of them was justified because they 'deserved it' (following Walster, 1966). As the days wore on, the model prisoner reaction was one of passivity, dependence, and flattened affect.

Let us briefly consider some of the relevant processes involved in bringing about these reactions.

Loss of personal identity
For most people identity is conferred by social recognition of one's uniqueness, and established through one's name, dress, appearance, behavior style and history. Living among strangers who do not know your name or history (who refer to you only by number), dressed in a uniform exactly like all other prisoners, not wanting to call attention to one's self because of the unpredictable consequencies it might provoke – all led to a weakening of self identify among the prisoners. As they began to lose initiative and emotional responsivity, while acting ever more compliantly, indeed, the prisoners became deindividuated not only to the guards and the observers, but also to themselves.

Arbitrary control
On post-experimental questionnaires, the most frequently mentioned aversive aspect of the prison experience was that of being subjugated to the patently arbitrary, capricious decisions and rules of the guards. A question by a prisoner as often elicited derogation and aggression as it did a rational answer. Smiling at a joke could be punished in the same way that failing to smile might be. An individual acting in defiance of the rules could bring punishment to innocent cell partners (who became, in effect, 'mutually yoked controls'), to himself, or to all.

As the environment became more unpredictable, and previously learned assumptions about a just and orderly world were no longer functional, prisoners ceased to initiate any action. They moved about on orders and when in their cells rarely engaged in any purposeful activity. Their zombie-like reaction was the functional equivalent of the learned helplessness phenomenon reported by Seligman & Grove (1970). Since their behavior did not seem to have any contingent relationship to environmental consequences, the prisoners essentially gave up and stopped behaving. Thus the subjective magnitude of aversiveness was manipulated by the guards not in terms of physical punishment but rather by controlling the psychological dimension of environmental predictability (Singer & Glass, 1972).

Dependency and emasculation
The network of dependency relations established by the guards not only promoted helplessness in the prisoners but served to emasculate them as well. The arbitrary control by the guards put the prisoners at their mercy for even the daily, commonplace functions like going to the toilet. To do so, required publicly obtained permission (not always granted) and then a personal escort to the toilet while blindfolded and handcuffed. The same was true for many other activities ordinarily practiced spontaneously without thought, such as lighting a cigarette, reading a novel, writing a letter, drinking a glass of water, or brushing one's teeth. These were all privileged

activities requiring permission and necessitating a prior show of good behavior. These low level dependencies engendered a regressive orientation in the prisoners. Their dependency was defined in terms of the extent of the domain of control over all aspects of their lives which they allowed other individuals (the guards and prison staff) to exercise.

As in real prisons, the assertive independent, aggressive nature of male prisoners posed a threat which was overcome by a variety of tactics. The prisoner uniforms resembled smocks or dresses, which made them look silly and enabled the guards to refer to them as 'sissies' or 'girls.' Wearing these uniforms without any underclothes forced the prisoners to move and sit in unfamiliar, feminine postures. Any sign of individual rebellion was labelled as indicative of 'incorrigibility' and resulted in loss of privileges, solitary confinement, humiliation or punishment of cell mates. Physically smaller guards were able to induce stronger prisoners to act foolishly and obediently. Prisoners were encouraged to belittle each other publicly during the counts. These and other tactics all served to engender in the prisoners a lessened sense of their masculinity (as defined by their external culture). It followed then, that although the prisoners usually outnumbered the guards during line-ups and counts (nine vs. three) there never was an attempt to directly overpower them. (Interestingly, after the study was terminated, the prisoners expressed the belief that the basis for assignment to guard and prisoner groups was physical size. They perceived the guards were 'bigger,' when, in fact, there was no difference in average height or weight between these randomly determined groups.)

In conclusion, we believe this demonstration reveals new dimensions in the social psychology of imprisonment worth pursuing in future research. In addition, this research provides a paradigm and information base for studying alternatives to existing guard training, as well as for questioning the basic operating principles on which penal institutions rest. If our mock prison could generate the extent of pathology it did in such a short time, then the punishment of being imprisoned in a real prison does not 'fit the crime' for most prisoners – indeed, it far exceeds it! Moreover, since both prisoners and guards are locked into a dynamic, symbiotic relationship which is destructive to their human nature, guards are also society's prisoners.

References

Adorno, T. W., Frenkel-Brunswik, E., Levinson, D. J., and Sanford, R. N., *The Authoritarian Personality*, New York: Harper, 1950.

Charriere, H., *Papillion*, Robert Laffont, 1969.

Christie, R. and Geis, F. L. (Eds.), *Studies in Machiavellianism*, New York: Academic Press, 1970.

Comrey, A. L., *Comrey Personality Scales*, San Diego: Educational and Industrial Testing Service, 1970.

Glass, D. C. and Singer, J. E., 'Behavioral After Effects of Unpredictable and Uncontrollable Aversive Events,' *American Scientist*, 6 (4), 457–465, 1972.

Jackson, G., *Soledad Brother: the Prison Letters of George Jackson*, New York: Bantam Books, 1970.

Milgram, S., 'Some Conditions of Obedience and Disobedience to Authority,' *Human Relations*, 18 (1), 57–76, 1965.

Mischel, W., *Personality and Assessment*, New York: Wiley, 1968.

Schein, E., *Coercive Persuasion*, New York: Norton, 1961.

Seligman, M. E. and Groves, D. P., 'Nontransient Learned Helplessness,' *Psychonomic Science*, 19 (3), 191–192, 1970.

Walster, E., 'Assignment of Responsibility for an Accident,' *Journal of Personality and Social Psychology*, 3 (1), 73–79, 1966.

how valid are classical management principles? (1993)

'Principles of management: valid or vacuous?', by Alan B. Thomas, *Controversies in Management*, Routledge, London, 1993, pp. 156–84.

As a body of knowledge, the principles of management, continue to guide management choices and organizational design. Principles are associated with the writings of practising managers and consultants. As such, their content can be distinguished from that of the findings produced by academic researchers working in the field of management. The originators of management principles were Henri Fayol, Luther Gulick and Lyndall Urwick who wrote in the first third of the twentieth century. They established a tradition of management knowledge that has continued to this day. Successful managers, usually at the end of their careers, and with the aid of ghost writers, have rushed to distil their experiences, and set these down on paper. Their books have sold in their millions. The question remains of how valid and useful their pronouncements are in guiding management practice in the future.

learning objectives

Once you have read and understood the prescribed material, you should be able to:

1 Assess your view concerning the value of management principles.
2 Understand why such principles have been both welcomed and viewed with scepticism.

learning pre-requisites

Before proceeding, you should read Chapter 14 of the core text and the reading, 'Principles of management: valid or vacuous?', by A. B. Thomas that follows.

learning activities

1 In the quiz that follows, write T [= true] or F [= false] after each number, beside each of the nine statements, to indicate whether you believe it be true or false, with respect to the article.
    1 According to Copeman, 'management laws' are descriptions of how organizations and business executives behave.
    2 Classical management principles can be applied to all organizations, irrespective of the technology that they employ.
    3 Fayol's classical management principles were based upon extensive empirical research.
    4 According to Urwick, specialization, unity of command, and span-of-control, are all examples of classical management principles.

5 Classical management principles encourage the nurturing of individual creativity, decentralization, and the use of varied job skills by the individual.

6 The contingency theory of organizations, works on the principle that there is no 'one best way' to structure an organization, or its management practices.

7 According to Copeman, 'management principles' are guides to actions.

8 The contingency theory of organizations rejects all classical management principles as being inapplicable to modern organizations and their management practices.

9 According to Tom Peters, the advantage of the social science approach over that of the classicists, is that it offers the student and manager less complexity and uncertainty, and more security.

2 Make a list of any six classical management principles mentioned in the article. For each one, explain (a) how it can operate to increase the performance of the organization and the job satisfaction of its employees, and then (b) how that same principle can act to do the exact opposite.

READING

14   *Principles of management: valid or vacuous?**
Alan B. Thomas

Without principles one is in darkness and chaos.   Fayol (1916)

The currently accepted 'principles of administration' are little more than ambiguous and mutually contradictory proverbs.   Simon (1947)

Some years ago, I was involved in a project that was concerned with the preparation of training materials for a group of professional employees. Amongst other things, we had to decide the content of the training: what sorts of information should we aim to communicate to our trainees? During discussions with the project director, whose knowledge and experience of the field was extensive, I made the suggestion that our problem would be readily solved if we simply taught the principles of the job. What could be simpler? Naively expecting this idea to be welcomed with open arms I was taken aback to hear his reply: 'We can't do that because there aren't any!'

At the time I found this mildly shocking. After all, there was nothing new about this profession. Indeed, it had been practised for hundreds, if not thousands, of years. Could it really be that in this field, one of the oldest of all, there were still no well-recognized principles which could be taught to newcomers?

Anyone approaching management for the first time might well be tempted to ask much the same question of it as I did – of teaching. Given at least a century of collective experience of industrial management, it seems reasonable to expect that there should be general principles upon which its practice can be based. Surely we must have learned something! Yet my colleague's scepticism about the existence of principles of teaching could as well have been applied to the occupation of management. If there aren't any principles of teaching can the same be said for management?

The controversy in brief

The idea of there being principles which might be used to guide human affairs has a long history, stretching back at least to the Biblical story of Moses and the Ten Commandments. But the search for principles of management is a relatively recent development. Even though the problems of administering even quite large organizations, such as the military and government officialdom, were well known in, for example, ancient Egypt (Breasted, 1909; James, 1985) and in early imperial China (Loewe, 1968), systematic reflection on management is largely a product of the nineteenth and twentieth centuries. None the less, the quest for management principles in modern times continues an age-old tradition and reflects an equally ancient human interest in reducing the uncertainties which are a perennial feature of human life. The identification of principles holds out the promise of control over events in a capricious and uncertain world.

The controversy over management principles is closely bound up with more general debates concerning the nature of science and in particular with the nature of social science. We will be going more deeply into those issues in the next chapter but for the moment we can note that science has come to be thought of as the best and perhaps the only way to obtain reliable knowledge of how the world works. Managers clearly need to know how people and organizations work, so a scientific approach to those problems has an obvious appeal. Thus the idea of developing a science of management has gained considerable prominence with the expansion of the social sciences in the post-war years and with the growing need to find more effective ways of managing in a more hostile and competitive environment. Just as the natural sciences, like physics, have provided sound laws which enable us to act effectively on the natural world, so it has been hoped that social science might yield similar if less powerful laws which might constitute an effective and rational basis for the practice of management.

It was to this end or something like it that some of the best known 'classical' writers on management aspired. People such as Taylor and especially Fayol attempted to construct sets of scientific principles and techniques for the management of enterprises which, they hoped, would provide a better basis for managerial practice than mere custom and habit. But with the growing involvement of professional social scientists in the study of management, these early attempts to provide a science of management came under fierce attack with the result that they were virtually discredited.

The 1980s, however, saw a potent revival of interest in management principles among managers if not among management scientists. The publication of Peters and Waterman's *In Search of Excellence* (1982) offered a 'new' set of principles which seemingly offered the key to managing for excellence. Partly because of the enormous popularity of this book in management circles the debate over the existence and validity of general rules for successful management sparked into life once more.

What we find, then, is two contending camps, one committed to the view that management principles are valid and the other that they are vacuous. Although this might seem like an arcane issue, mainly of interest to scholars and philosophers of science, it is an important problem for managers too. For if management principles do exist, knowing what they are and using them as a basis for the process of managing seems essential. After all, it would be a pretty bad engineer who chose to ignore the laws of physics, so can a manager who pays no heed to the principles of management hope to be effective? If, on the other hand, there are no real management principles to speak of, those who act as if there were seem to be in much the same position as the medieval alchemists, believing that they can turn water into wine by applying meaningless formulae. Were this so we are still left with the question of how management can proceed otherwise. In the absence of principles must the 'darkness and chaos' envisaged by Fayol inevitably follow?

The idea of principles

You may have noticed that so far I have talked about principles in a rather vague way, so some attention to the alternative meanings of the term seems appropriate. This is particularly necessary because controversies often involve disagreements on the meaning of terms, sometimes to the extent that disputes seem to be about little more than this. It is therefore important to be aware of some of the ways in which the key word 'principles' can be understood before we pursue the management principles debate.

There are at least four shades of meaning which are associated with the term 'principles'. One of these is the idea of fundamentals, foundations or basics. Someone claiming to know the principles of management might be taken to mean, at least in part, that they know its essentials and in making this claim they are also saying that they know important things about it. This idea is expressed in the titles of introductory textbooks in many fields, such as Principles of Chemistry, Principles of Physical Geography, or whatever, which point to the intention of presenting the basic building-blocks of a discipline. An example in the management field is Carnall and Maxwell's *Management Principles and Policy* (1988).

A second meaning of 'principles' refers to ethics, morals or rules of right conduct. So to be 'unprincipled' or 'without principles' is to invite opprobrium whereas to 'act in accordance with one's principles' is a sign of moral probity. Management principles might therefore be understood as the moral rules which make up a code of ethics to which managers ought to adhere.

Thirdly, 'principles' might be thought of as scientific laws or as generalizations based on scientific knowledge, as in 'the principles of thermodynamics' or 'biological principles'. In this case, to speak of management principles might be to imply that management can be understood scientifically.

Finally, we might think of principles as rules, as in the 'principles of chess'. In the case of management, this might imply that there are certain rules which managers ought to follow if they are to be effective players in the game of management.

Copeman's *Laws of Business Management and the Executive Way of Life* (1962) is an example of a text that combines the second and third meanings of 'principles'. It also illustrates some of the semantic confusion surrounding this concept. The first part of this book presents ten 'laws of business management' which are defined as statements describing how a business organization and business executives behave. So, for example, we have the law of economic authority, the law of business strategy, and so on. Copeman is careful to distinguish these 'laws' from 'principles' because, he suggests, management principles are typically regarded as guides to action rather than the descriptions of how organizations and executives actually behave that he intends to discuss.

In the second part of the book Copeman deals with 'the executive way of life'. Unlike the descriptive 'laws' offered earlier, here he is concerned with 'manners and customs which are good in themselves' and with 'desirable standards of management conduct', that is to say with moral or normative rules. Copeman clearly separates this material from the 'laws', recognizing that these prescriptive standards are different in kind from law-like generalizations about business operations. Even so, it would be easy to treat both types of statement as kinds of principles.

Contributors to the controversy over management principles have not always been clear about which of these meanings they are using. Indeed, the vague and inconsistent way in which some management thinkers have used the word has been a source of confusion and a valid point of criticism (Mouzelis, 1967). None the less, the debate revolves largely around principles in the third and last meanings: are there scientific laws of management and can those laws be translated into rules for the conduct of managerial affairs?

To begin our exploration of these questions we must first examine the ideas of some of the early proponents of management principles who laid the basis for what has become known as 'classical management theory'.

The classical principles

The basic ideas of classical management theory were developed by writers in Europe and North America during the first half of this century. Among the best known of these contributors to management thought are Henri Fayol and Lyndall Urwick (both of whom we met in Chapter 2) and the Americans James Mooney and Alan Reiley.

A much less well-known figure, at least for his contribution to management thinking, is P. T. Barnum (1810–1891), the famous showman and entrepreneur. So far as I know Barnum never wrote a management book, yet his 'Rules for success in business' (Figure 1) published as an appendix to an early practical business book (Freedley, 1853), anticipated both in style and purpose the sets of principles that were to be produced much later by his more renowned successors. While the language and the content of Barnum's rules may seem quaint, at least one of them has recently been reproduced in modern guise in a world best-seller! (I leave it to you to work out which one.) Furthermore, by the end of his career, Barnum had amassed a fortune of over five million dollars.

'a few rules that I am convinced, from experience and observation, must be observed in order to ensure success in business.'

 1 Select the kind of business that suits your inclinations and temperament.
 2 Let your pledged word ever be sacred.
 3 Whatever you do, do it with all your might.
 4 Sobriety. Use no description of intoxicating drinks.
 5 Let hope predominate, but be not too visionary.
 6 Do not scatter your powers.
 7 Engage proper employees.
 8 Advertise your business. Do not hide your light under a bushel.
 9 Avoid extravagance; and always live considerably within your income, if you can do so without absolute starvation!
10 Do not depend on others.

Figure 1 P. T. Barnum's rules for success in business, 1853. *Source*: E. T. Freedley, *A Practical Treatise on Business; or How to Get Money*, London, Thomas Bosworth, 1853

Like Barnum, the early management writers were closely involved in business and they wrote as managers rather than as social scientists. Their ideas on management were derived largely from their practical experience, just as Barnum's were, and they were chiefly interested in codifying these ideas into a body of precepts that would be of practical value to other managers. They wrote at a time when there was little general interest in the notion that management could be systemized as a body of knowledge and before the social sciences had shown much interest in it, so their work needs to be seen in this light. They were in essence pioneers venturing into largely unexplored territory.

The classical management thinkers drew part of their inspiration from the example of the American engineer, F. W. Taylor (1856–1917). Taylor became famous, indeed infamous, for developing an approach to the organization and management of work which placed heavy stress on the need to specialize labour, to observe and measure work tasks 'scientifically' in order to identify the 'one best way' of executing them, to carefully select and train workmen, and to pay workers strictly according to output.

Although Taylor was an energetic advocate of his system of 'scientific management', and even though his ideas have been profoundly influential, their relevance to the concerns of the classicists was limited. Taylor's system was intended as a guide to the organization of all forms of work, but in practice it was most readily applied to job design at the shopfloor level where manual work tasks could be readily observed and measured. The classical management thinkers, however, were concerned more broadly with the tasks of general management and with the design of the total set of arrangements which make up an organization. So although Taylor used the language of principles in his writings and was explicitly acknowledged by some classical writers (Fayol called him 'the great American engineer'), the debate on management principles has tended to focus on these broader issues.

In 1887, Woodrow Wilson, the 28th President of the United States, made a bold call to the nation's scientists for the study of administration. This was urgently needed, he suggested, in order to 'rescue executive methods from the confusion and costliness of empirical experiment', by which he meant trial and error, 'and set them upon foundations laid deep in stable principle' (Wilson, 1887). Little could he have guessed that in far-away France, Henri Fayol, the son of a construction foreman (Breeze, 1985), was about to embark on just such a study and one that was to lead to the formulation of an enduring if much criticized set of management principles.

Most of the classical writers built on Fayol's initial contribution presented in his book, *General and Industrial Management* (1916, 1949). There he wrote that 'the soundness and good working order of the body corporate depend on a certain number of conditions termed indiscriminately principles, laws, rules'. It seemed, he suggested, 'especially useful to endow management with a dozen or so well-established principles, on which it is appropriate to concentrate general discussion'. These took the form of fourteen 'general principles of management' (Figure 2).

Fayol was careful to point out the limitations of these principles. They were not to be interpreted rigidly and would have to be adapted to changing circumstances. They were not exhaustive; there was no limit to the number of principles that might be discovered. And they could not be applied in a mechanical way for it was 'a matter of knowing how to make use of them, which is a difficult art requiring intelligence, experience, decision and proportion'. He also acknowledged that the principles he had described had been derived largely from his personal experience and that they were not definitive but provisional. They were but one contribution to a theory of management which, he hoped, might be developed from general discussion and the pooling of the experiences of others. Even so, he was adamant on the need for principles. 'Be it a case of commerce, industry, politics, religion, war, or philosophy', he wrote, 'in every concern there is a management function to be performed, and for its performance there must be principles, that is to say acknowledged truths regarded as proven on which to rely.' For Fayol, then, principles were the key elements of a body of knowledge which could be taught to managers and which should be made the basis of management practice.

When Fayol's work is mentioned today, it is usually to acknowledge it as the first major analysis of the management function and the first modern statement of management principles. But it is seldom noticed that his main thesis was that management was a skill that could be taught. The first part of his book was titled 'Necessity

1 *Division of work*: tasks should be divided up and employees should specialize in a limited set of tasks so that expertise is developed and productivity increased.
2 *Authority and responsibility*: authority is the right to give orders and entails the responsibility for enforcing them with rewards and penalties; authority should be matched with corresponding responsibility.
3 *Discipline*: is essential for the smooth running of business and is dependent on good leadership, clear and fair agreements, and the judicious application of penalties.
4 *Unity of command*: for any action whatsoever, an employee should receive orders from one superior only; otherwise authority, discipline, order and stability are threatened.
5 *Unity of direction*: a group of activities concerned with a single objective should be co-ordinated by a single plan under one head.
6 *Subordination of individual interest to general interest*: individual or group goals must not be allowed to override those of the business.
7 *Remuneration of personnel*: may be achieved by various methods and the choice is important; it should be fair, encourage effort, and not lead to over-payment.
8 *Centralization*: the extent to which orders should be issued only from the top of the organization is a problem which should take into account its characteristics, such as size and the capabilities of the personnel.
9 *Scalar chain (line of authority)*: communications should normally flow up and down the line of authority running from the top to the bottom of the organization, but sideways communication between those of equivalent rank in different departments can be desirable so long as superiors are kept informed.
10 *Order*: both materials and personnel must always be in their proper place; people must be suited to their posts so there must be careful organization of work and selection of personnel.
11 *Equity*: personnel must be treated with kindliness and justice.
12 *Stability of tenure of personnel*: rapid turnover of personnel should be avoided because of the time required for the development of expertise.
13 *Initiative*: all employees should be encouraged to exercise initiative within the limits imposed by the requirements of authority and discipline.
14 *Esprit de corps*: efforts must be made to promote harmony within the organization and prevent dissension and divisiveness.

Figure 2 Fayol's general principles of management, 1916. *Source*: Adapted from H. Fayol, *General and Industrial Management*, trans. Constance Storrs, London, Pitman, 1949

and possibility of teaching management', and although he introduced his famous definition of management there, this and the general principles were not discussed in detail until later.

In this opening section Fayol argued that even though management was a distinct and important function little or no provision was being made for management education. Why was this? In practice, said Fayol, there was a recognition that management was a distinct activity requiring specifically managerial ability, for when it came to selecting people for management posts the choice was seldom made on technical grounds alone. Being a good engineer, for example, was not enough. But there was also a belief that managerial ability could only be acquired through practical experience; the idea that someone could be taught to manage was considered absurd. In Fayol's view this reason for denying the possibility of management education 'carries no weight' for 'managerial ability can and should be acquired in the same way as technical ability, first at school, later in the workshop'. 'The real reason for the absence of management teaching', he went on, 'is absence of theory; without theory no teaching is possible.'

His statement of management principles was therefore more than an attempt to provide managers with useful guidance on how to manage. It was part of a broader concern to establish a body of knowledge, to 'codify the data furnished by experience' which could form the basis for systematic education in management.

In the inter-war period several more works outlining management principles appeared. In the 1920s Oliver Sheldon, a colleague of the famous Quaker employer Seebohm Rowntree, published *The Philosophy of Management* (1923), and in the 1930s two General Motors executives, James Mooney and Alan Reiley produced *The Principles of Organization* (1939). But the next major event in the development and propagation of management principles was the publication of Lyndall Urwick's *The Elements of Administration* in 1943.

Before the publication of this book Urwick had written extensively on management matters and his thinking had been strongly influenced by both his wartime experiences and the ideas of both Fayol and Taylor. In a much cited paper (Urwick, 1933), he wrote:

> It is the general thesis of this paper that there are principles which can be arrived at inductively from the study of human experience of organization, which should govern arrangements for human association of any kind. These principles can be studied as a technical question, irrespective of the purpose of the enterprise, the personnel composing it, or any constitutional, political or social theory underlying its creation. They are concerned with the method of subdividing and allocating to individuals all the various activities, duties and responsibilities essential to the purpose contemplated, the correlation of these activities and the continuous control of the work of individuals so as to secure the most economical and the most effective realization of the purpose.

In the *Elements*, Urwick drew together the ideas of a number of classical writers including Fayol, Taylor, and Mooney and Reiley. Twenty-nine main 'principles of administration' were presented. These were discussed within Fayol's framework of managerial functions and Urwick elaborated on both Fayol's ideas and those of later classical writers. One of the, more contentious inclusions, as it turned out, was the span of control principle. This asserted that 'No superior can supervise directly the work of more than five, or at the most, six subordinates whose work interlocks.' The principle was based on the idea that the human 'span of attention' was limited; there were definite limits to the number of activities that any individual could keep under control. It was therefore necessary to take this into account when organizing.

Urwick felt that there was a 'remarkable consensus of agreement' on the part of those who had studied administration about the elements which made up its technique. But he warned against dogmatism in a field where there were 'so many unknown factors, so much territory unexplored'. In a section titled 'The danger of the easy remedy', he warned of the dangers of relying on 'potted knowledge', and he added that 'there are no hints and tips and short cuts'. While books could help towards providing a first understanding of some principles, there was still a need for 'hard study and harder thinking, mastery of intellectual principles reinforced by genuine reflection on actual problems, for which the individual has real responsibility'. But like Fayol, Urwick was clear that administration needed to be improved and that this required theory, ideas and clearer thinking about the nature of administration, its methods and its principles. He was strongly committed to the belief that management skills could be taught, even though, like medical skills, they could only be refined and developed in practice. And he noted, as Fayol had done, that many 'practical men' would be impatient with such ideas. They would prefer to rely on habit and custom despite the fact that these were often 'highly irrational'.

The elaboration of management principles reached its high point with the publication of Ralph Davis's *The Fundamentals of Top Management* (1951); Davis presented more than a hundred principles! Although this growth in numbers could be seen as a sign of progress, the tendency for the principles to multiply, while extending their scope, also tended to weaken their impact and undermine their status as fundamentals. More concise lists therefore continue to appear.

In 1954, the American National Industrial Conference Board published a set of twelve Organization Principles (Figure 3). These continued to be reproduced in various management texts in the 1960s and 1970s. In one (Richards and Nielander, 1969), the principles were introduced by saying:

---

1 There must be clear lines of authority running from the top to the bottom of the organization.
2 No one in the organization should report to more than one line supervisor. Everyone in the organization should know to whom he reports, and who reports to him.
3 The responsibility and authority of each supervisor should be clearly defined in writing.
4 Responsibility should always be coupled with corresponding authority.
5 The responsibility of higher authority for the acts of its subordinates is absolute.
6 Authority should be delegated as far down the line as possible.
7 The number of levels of authority should be kept to a minimum.
8 The work of every person in the organization should be confined as far as possible to the performance of a single leading function.
9 Whenever possible, line functions should be separated from staff functions, and adequate emphasis should be placed on important staff activities.
10 There is a limit to the number of positions that can be co-ordinated by a single executive.
11 The organization should be flexible, so that it can be adjusted to changing conditions.
12 The organization should be kept as simple as possible.

Figure 3 Organization principles, 1954. *Source*: National Industrial Conference Board, *Company Organization Charts*, New York, NICB, 1954

Like the engineer who builds his bridge to meet special needs, the organization planner, in designing a company structure, applies principles. For through years of experience it has been learned that if certain principles are followed, regardless of the size of the enterprise, the result will be good organization. Some of these basic laws follow.   (Raube, 1954).

The same list was included in books by Copeman (1962) and Hunt (1979) and is still drawn on by some of today's popular management writers.

The classical writers did not form a close-knit, consensual 'school' but they did tend to share certain assumptions about the nature of management and management knowledge. Firstly, they held a firm belief in the existence of general principles or rules which could and should be applied to the management of organizations. Their orientation was deliberately 'managerial' in that they wrote chiefly for, and usually as, practising managers and aimed to provide them with useful guidance.

Secondly, the various principles put forward by different writers pointed fairly consistently to a definite model of good organization. Nowadays this model is often referred to as the 'mechanistic' or 'military' model, invoking images of machines and armies. Terms such as 'discipline', 'command', 'orders', 'subordinates', 'personnel', 'esprit de corps' and even 'initiative' have unmistakable military associations. The principles can be seen as prescriptions for the tight control of behaviour by means of discipline, clearly defined tasks, carefully circumscribed spheres of authority, limited spans of control, and so on. They seek to reproduce the regularity, smooth functioning and orderliness of the machine in the human context much as Frederick the Great of Prussia had tried to do by organizing his armies on 'mechanical' lines (Morgan, 1986).

Thirdly, there was a tendency to assume not just that there could be principles of management but that valid principles had already been arrived at through reflection on managerial experience. While some classicists were vague about the status of the principles they proposed others tended to treat them as established truths rather than as provisional generalizations. As Massie (1965) noted, the classical writers were not research-oriented and based their propositions largely on their personal knowledge instead of systematic research evidence. For example, despite his belief in the universal applicability of scientific method (Breeze, 1985), Fayol's conception of 'theory' seems to have been in terms of a set of principles which could be constructed by pooling the experiences of many managers and which would be evaluated by means of discussion.

Given the lack of formal research investigation into management and organization at the time, this somewhat unsophisticated approach to the development of sound principles was understandable. But could this be an adequate basis for an applied science of management?

The challenge of social science

From their first appearance, management principles proved controversial but this early criticism tended to come from the 'practical men' whose attitudes Fayol and Urwick were keen to challenge. These people tended to reject the possibility of the existence of principles of management because they believed that organizations were too dissimilar to allow useful generalizations to be made, and because they tended to see success in management as dependent upon personal leadership qualities which were difficult to define and impossible to teach. Management, on this view, was an art not a science. These 'empiricists', as Urwick called them, were therefore unimpressed by the notion of management principles.

After the Second World War a second major line of criticism emerged from a different quarter, the social sciences. In 1947, an American professor of public administration, Herbert Simon, who was later to win a Nobel Prize for Economics, made what has come to be seen as the classic critique of management principles. In his book *Administrative Behaviour* (1947), Simon mounted a sustained attack on 'the so-called "principles" of classical organization theory'.

Taking the work of Urwick and his colleague, Luther Gulick, as his main reference point, Simon examined three of the classical principles: division of work (specialization), unity of command, and span of control. He also looked at a further elaboration of the specialization principle which we can omit without doing violence to his main argument.

Specialization, said Simon, is simply a characteristic of any work based on group effort because it simply means different people doing different things. Work is always specialized but not necessarily in ways that are efficient. There are many different ways in which work can be divided up but the principle of specialization gives no guidance on which ways lead to efficiency and which do not.

Similarly, the principle of unity of command was always followed in practice, 'for it is physically impossible for a man to obey two contradictory commands'. But perhaps the principle was intended to mean that it was undesirable for a subordinate to be put in a position where he receives orders from more than one superior as Gulick had indeed stated. If so, this was at least a clear and unambiguous way of putting it. However, it then contradicted the principle of specialization without giving any indication of how the contradiction could be resolved. For example, unity of command would mean that technical specialists working for a general manager could not be given orders on the technical aspects of their work by the technical manager. But employees may need to receive orders from a diverse set of specialists to work efficiently. Yet this violates the principle of unity of command.

As for the span of control principle, which 'is confidently asserted as a third incontrovertible principle of administration', it was possible to state an equally plausible 'proverb'; that 'administrative efficiency is enhanced by keeping at a minimum the number of organizational levels through which a matter must pass before it is acted upon'. When the span of control (the average number of subordinates reporting to a superior) is narrow, the number of levels in the organization will tend to be greater than when it is wide. So any specified span of control will have implications for the number of levels in the organization. Narrow spans may promote efficiency by enabling closer control of subordinates; but this gain may be offset by the correspondingly large number of levels which will then exist in the organization. So to advocate a specific size of span as a principle leading to efficiency was misleading. In any case, the classicists disagreed among themselves on the ideal span – some said three, some five, some eleven – and gave no reasons for their choice.

Simon concluded that for each of the principles he had examined 'there was found, instead of a unequivocal principle, a set of two or more mutually incompatible principles apparently applicable to the administrative situation'. They were vague, ambiguous and mutually contradictory, and little more than 'proverbs'. They could not provide a useful basis for practice and could therefore be dispensed with.

Although Simon rejected the classical principles, it is worth noting that he accepted that a science of administration might still generate principles. But this would take the form of statements relating different kinds of administrative arrangement to their effects on efficiency. They would not be based on a priori, armchair reasoning but on experimental research using clearly defined measures. And although the results of administrative research might have implications for practice the first task was to describe and analyse administrative situations. Decisions about how to manage effectively presupposed a knowledge of the effects of management actions under different conditions. Efficient administration could only be based on this kind of knowledge, just as 'sound medical practice can only be founded on a thorough knowledge of the biology of the organism'.

Simon's rejection of the classical principles was largely based on a logical critique; the principles were contradictory and illogical rather than demonstrably false in the face of evidence of actual practice. But when the British organizational researcher, John Child, came to review the state of classical theory twenty years later (Child, 1969), he was able to draw on a growing body of research evidence. One study was particularly significant.

Perhaps the most important challenge to the classical precepts came from the results of a research project carried out by Joan Woodward, Britain's first female professor of industrial sociology. This research set out explicitly to discover whether firms which adhered to the principles of organization proposed in classical management theory were, in fact, any more efficient than those which did not.

Woodward's study focused on a sample of 100 industrial plants with over 100 employees operating in south Essex in the mid-1950s. She found that although none of the plants displayed all the attributes advocated by the classicists, about half of them had been organized along classical lines. But these firms seemed to perform no differently to those which ignored the classical prescriptions; 'conformity with the "rules" of management did not necessarily result in success or non-conformity in commercial failure' (Woodward, 1958). The classical principles, however reasonable and logical they might have seemed, were not indispensable to business success. So there could be 'no one best way of organising a business'.

If conformity with the classical principles did not have much impact on business performance, was there some other factor which did? Woodward found that when the firms were grouped according to the type of production technology they employed they tended to display common organizational patterns. For example, in mass-production firms, such as auto-assemblers, the span of control of foremen tended to be larger than in process production firms, such as chemical-makers. Differences in technology seemed to impose different requirements on organizations, and firms whose organization structures were closer to the average of the technological group to which they belonged performed better than those which deviated from it. Although there was no one best way of organizing, some ways were better than others provided that allowance was made for the technological conditions under which the firm operated.

Woodward's general conclusion, that a firm's organization has to fit the circumstances of its operations if it is to be effective, has been supported by a wide range of research studies. Later work showed, however, that technology was but one of many influences on organizational structure. Perhaps this finding is not too surprising. Indeed, it might appear to be rather obvious. But it certainly discomforted many of those who understood the classical principles as the basic laws of good organization. One college lecturer stated that 'Practical men will insist that there are principles of management, and I think that the social scientists who attack this idea are being academic and unconstructive' (quoted in Child, 1969). Nonetheless, as Rose (1988) has noted, such studies appeared to have 'put paid to traditional administrative theory'.

Research evidence seemed, then, to give strong support to Simon's scepticism, for it indicated that 'the management principles and many elements in scientific management presented an appearance of established knowledge and unchallengeable [sic] expertise which subsequent analysis and investigation has shown to be largely spurious' (Child, 1969).

Child (1969) summarized the limitations of the classical approach as follows. It had proposed a standardized organizational model (the military or machine model) as the optimum but this was misleading. The classical prescriptions for tight control and narrow specialization of tasks had overlooked their negative implications for motivation. When work was organized in this way it could prevent employees from experiencing fulfilment and so lead to an unwillingness to contribute effort which would hinder rather than promote efficiency. The tendency to assert principles of universal application had had to give way to a situational approach. By concentrating on the formal structure of the organization, the blueprint which could control behaviour, the classical theorists had ignored the processes of management such as decision-making, communication, and conflict-management. And by its failure to acknowledge the complexity of organizational life, the classical approach had oversimplified the problems of management and had given it an aura of 'ease, rationality and uniformity which it rarely possessed in reality'. Thus, he concluded, 'Social science has today discredited some of the most important assumptions of management thought.'

In defence of principles

If Simon's comments can be regarded as the classic critique of management principles, the counter-arguments put forward by another American professor, Harold Koontz, might well be seen as the classic defence. It might also be called the 'neo-classical' defence because Koontz's position broadly reflects the modern stream of classical thinking.

In his paper 'The Management Theory Jungle' (1961), Koontz argued that the classicists, who had been 'branded as "universalists" ' by their critics, could not reasonably be regarded as mere armchair theorists. Although their precepts had not been derived from rigorous empirical research they were none the less based on observations made over the course of lengthy practical experience. Their ideas had been called platitudes but 'a platitude is still a truism and a truth does not become worthless because it is familiar'. Often those who delighted 'in casting away anything which smacks of management principles' themselves offered generalizations which simply amounted to a restatement of the classical principles in a different guise.

One of the 'favourite tricks' of the critics, he said, was to use examples of the non-application of a single principle as grounds for rejecting the whole framework. Some critics seemed to have misunderstood and misapplied the principles which 'simply proved that wrong principles badly applied will lead to frustration'. In fact, Koontz proposed, management principles were far from being dispensable. They were, on the contrary, an essential part of management science and it would continue to be necessary to develop and test these fundamentals.

Koontz set out seven 'fundamental beliefs' of current classical thinking (Figure 4).

---

1. That managing is a process that can best be dissected intellectually by analysing the functions of the manager.
2. That long experience with management in a variety of enterprise situations can be grounds for distillation of certain fundamental truths or generalizations – usually referred to as principles – which have a clarifying and predictive value in the understanding and improvement of managing.
3. That these fundamental truths can become focal points for useful research both to ascertain their validity and to improve their meaning and applicability in practice.
4. That such truths can furnish elements, at least until disproved, and certainly until sharpened, of a useful theory of management.
5. That managing is an art, but one like medicine or engineering, which can be improved by reliance on the light and understanding of principles.
6. That principles in management, like principles in the biological and physical sciences, are none the less true even if a prescribed treatment or design by a practitioner in a given case situation chooses to ignore a principle and the costs involved, or attempts to do something else to offset the costs incurred (this is, of course, not new in medicine, engineering, or any other art, for art is the creative task of compromising fundamentals to attain a desired result).
7. That, while the totality of culture and of the physical and biological universe has varying effects on the manager's environment and subjects, as indeed they do in every other field of science and art, the theory of management does not need to encompass the field of all knowledge in order for it to serve as a scientific or theoretical foundation.

Figure 4 Koontz's fundamental beliefs of the 'management process school'. *Source*: H. Koontz, 'The Management Theory Jungle', *Journal of the Academy of Management*, 4 (3), 1961

It can be seen from these that Koontz shared the classicists' belief that management science should be devoted to the improvement of practice, but unlike them he emphasized the need for rigorous empirical research.

Koontz elaborated his defence of principles in a series of textbooks written with his colleague, Cyril O'Donnell. In *Essentials of Management* (1974), they wrote that 'Principles are used here in the sense of fundamental truths applicable to a given set of circumstances which have value in predicting results.' These truths were provisional rather than final. None the less, principles were 'believed to be a convenient and useful way of packaging some of the major truths that experience and research have found to have a high degree of credibility and predictability'. They were predictive and descriptive statements depicting relationships between variables which, when related in a systematic way, constituted a theory. Such a theory was not, as managers often seemed to assume, inherently impractical. On the contrary, it could be used to derive practical applications.

Management was an art but, like medicine or engineering, its practice could be improved by drawing on fundamental principles. But it was important to avoid applying them in a mechanical way as if they were exact formulae. It was also important to recognize that no set of principles could deal with every eventuality because this would require complete knowledge. And when principles had contradictory implications this simply pointed to the need for compromise; the costs and benefits of applying or ignoring principles had to be assessed in any real-world situation.

Koontz regarded it as obvious that management principles could have 'a tremendous impact on the practice of management, simplifying and improving it'. Admittedly, no two management situations were ever identical but there might be common elements in different situations which could be abstracted from them and related to a general conceptual scheme. Causal relationships might then be identified. This knowledge could be used to manage future situations of the same type without the need to conduct costly original research or to engage in the risky business of trial and error. The identification and use of principles, then, promised more efficient and more effective management.

Like the early classical writers, Koontz argued for both the possibility and the necessity of management principles. Where he and later neo-classical writers have tended to differ from the early thinkers is in a greater recognition of the need for their empirical validation and in greater sensitivity to the idea that the conditions under which particular principles apply need to be identified. Koontz's definition of a principle reflects this. Similarly, a number of the principles discussed were presented in contingent form. For example, the 'correct principle' of span of control was given as that 'there is a limit in each managerial position to the number of persons an individual can effectively manage, but the exact number in each case will vary in accordance with the effect of underlying variables and their impact on the time requirements of effective management'.

The neo-classicists have also tended to distance themselves from the newer approaches to the analysis of management and organization which have developed within the social sciences. Koontz's original defence of management principles, reiterated in 1980 (Koontz, 1980) was also a complaint that the burgeoning social science 'schools' of management were becoming unintelligible to managers and too far removed from their practical concerns. The emergence of new 'intellectual cults' had brought with it 'a kind of confused and destructive jungle warfare' that was threatening to obscure the existing achievements and potential for an applied science of management. As Lussato (1976) put it, the neo-classicists were in revolt against what they saw as a growing divorce between theory and practice 'or rather between the business manager and the organizational specialists'.

The continuing controversy

Before the Second World War, the main protagonists in the management principles controversy were the classicists and the empiricists (the 'practical men'), but after the war it was the social scientists who increasingly challenged classical ideas. Their line of attack was similar to that of the practical men in at least one respect because they too were sceptical of the possibility of formulating universal principles in the management field. Rather they proposed a different approach which became known as 'contingency theory' (Lawrence and Lorsch, 1967).

Many people find the contingency approach or contingency theory puzzling at first sight but it is no more than an unfamiliar name for a very simple idea. It can be stated quite readily as an approach to the study of management problems which assumes that the effects of any managerial or organizational practice will differ according to the circumstances in which it is implemented. What 'works' in one context will not necessarily work in another so that the effects of a particular management practice are contingent upon the prevailing circumstances. Hence there are no universal principles.

Thompson (1956) put the matter clearly when he wrote:

> Much of our literature [on administration] is lore, spelling out how a procedure or technique is carried out in current practice or proclaiming that 'this is the way' to do it. This material contains rather bold and often implicit assumptions about the relationships between the procedure or technique under consideration and other things which take place within the organization. This type of literature frequently asserts that a certain device is proper, i.e. gets desired results, on the grounds that 'General Motors has it' or that the one hundred 'best-managed' companies use it. But a particular budgeting procedure, for example, may be appropriate for General Motors and not for Company X, and it may be appropriate for General Motors in 1956 but less appropriate in 1960. Any particular item, that is, may show a high correlation with 'success' when imbedded [sic] in one context but show a low correlation in a different context.

The contingency approach suggests that any organizational alternative, such as the classical mechanistic/military model, may work in some circumstances but not in others. The task of the organizational scientist is therefore to identify relationships between different types of managerial practice and organizational arrangements and business outcomes in different situations. Woodward's (1958) study provides an illustration, in that the mechanistic/military model worked for firms using mass-production technology but not for those using process technologies. The optimum form of organization therefore seemed to be contingent upon the type of technology in use.

Contingency theory came to be seen as a distinct alternative to the classical approach (Luthans, 1977; Child, 1977) and was the centrepiece of the emerging social science of organization. As the contingency approach crystallized, classical ideas tended to be relegated in the social science literature to a place in the pre-scientific history of the field. Thus the classicists, with their determination to remain faithful to their principles, seemed doomed to suffer much the same fate as King Canute, overwhelmed by the fast-rising tide of social science.

Developments in the 1980s suggest, however, that classical ideas have not only survived but have flourished to an unprecedented degree. In 1982, two business consultants, Tom Peters and Robert Waterman, published a 400-page book that has been described as 'a prime example of the success of the new management books' (Soeters, 1986). Within five years, *In Search of Excellence* had sold over ten million copies and seems to have sparked off an explosive growth in popular business publishing. Yet despite its modern style its approach closely resembled that of the classicists of old.

In this book Peters and Waterman described the characteristics which seemed common to 'excellent' US companies (Figure 5). Their work was based on forty-three firms which had remained in the top half of their industries in terms of growth and profitability over a twenty-year period. Evidence on the characteristics of the firms which were claimed to account for their excellence seems to have been gathered mainly through interviews with some of the firms' managers and more generally from the authors' consulting experience.

---

1 *A bias for action*
   ‣ Project teams that tend to be small, fluid, ad hoc, and problem/action focused.
   ‣ Communications are of the essence, and there is an important commitment to learning and experimentation.
   ‣ Complex problems are tackled through a willingness to shift resources to where they are needed to encourage fluidity and action (chunking).

2 *Close to the customer*
   ‣ The market-driven principle of commitment to service, reliability, and quality, based on an appreciation of 'nichemanship' and the ability to custom-tailor a product or service to a client's needs.

3 *Autonomy and entrepreneurship*
   ‣ A principle which champions innovation, decentralization, the delegation of power and action to the level where they are needed, and a healthy tolerance of failure.

4 *Productivity through people*
   ‣ The principle that employees are people and a major resource, and should be trusted, respected, inspired, and made 'winners'.
   ‣ Organizational units should be small-scale to preserve and develop a people-oriented quality.

5 *Hands-on, value-driven*
   ‣ Organization guided by a clear sense of shared values, mission, and identity, relying on inspirational leadership rather than bureaucratic control.

6 *Stick to the knitting*
   ‣ The principle of building on strengths and knowledge of one's niche.

7 *Simple form, lean staff*
   ‣ Avoid bureaucracy; build main commitments to projects or product division rather than to the dual lines of responsibility found in formal matrix organizations; use small organizational units.

8 *Simultaneous loose-tight properties*
   ‣ The principle that reconciles the need for overall control with a commitment to autonomy and entrepreneurship.

Figure 5 Peters and Waterman's basic practices of excellently managed companies. *Source*: G. Morgan, Images of Organization, Beverly Hills, Sage, 1986

Perhaps because of the extensive popularity of their book, Peters and Waterman's claims have been subjected to considerable scrutiny in the years since its publication. One prominent critic (Carroll, 1983) pointed to the methodological weaknesses of the study; confusion over which firms had actually been used to draw conclusions about excellence, vagueness about the ways in which data were obtained and analysed, and the absence of comparisons with non-excellent companies which might have helped to show whether the observed practices were causally related to excellent performance. A later commentator described the research underpinning the book as a methodological disaster (Lawler, 1985). In a report of a British study Saunders and Wong (1985) are somewhat more charitable, seeing Peters and Waterman's volume as more important as a source of hypotheses concerning the possible determinants of corporate performance than as a statement of definitive findings. Even so their research gave only limited support to Peters and Waterman's conclusions.

In his commentary on *In Search of Excellence*, Child (1984) observed that its recommendations suffered from much the same limitations as had attended previous work in the classical tradition. By treating the attributes of the chosen firms as ones that would be displayed by any excellent company, no account had been taken of differences in firms' activities and situations. Since many of the firms in the study were high-technology and project management organizations, the excellent characteristics they showed might only be found in firms of that type and not, for example, in excellent firms in traditional industries such as coal and steel. Even then, high technology and project management firms operating in different countries with different cultural assumptions and values might find it detrimental to implement some of Peters and Waterman's prescriptions. The delegation of authority, for example, is much less acceptable in some countries than it is in others (Hofstede, 1980b).

There was also a fundamental weakness in the design of the research as Carroll (1983) had noted. Studying only excellent companies made it impossible to tell whether their common attributes were uniquely associated with performance. If low-performing firms have the same characteristics as excellent ones what relevance could those characteristics have to excellence? Peters and Waterman's study, Child noted, did not provide an answer to this question so that the key issue of what it is that causes excellent performance remained unresolved.

In short, Peters and Waterman, like their classical predecessors, had generalized from the experience of particular types of firms in particular contexts to all firms in all contexts. Just as the classical mechanistic/military model of organization did not amount to the 'one best way' to manage neither could the 'excellence model'. It was not so much wrong as incomplete and therefore inadequate as a valid and reliable guide to management practice. As Thompson (1956) had pointed out nearly thirty years previously, prescriptions based solely on the grounds that 'the best-managed companies do it' were little more than folklore.

Commentary

It was an accident of history that the earliest attempts to set out in a systematic fashion what was known about management took place at a time when the social sciences were little concerned with management and managers were little concerned with social science. But one consequence of this has been the creation of a sharp divide between the 'modern' management disciplines and the works of the 'classical' management theorists, with the latter often treated as if they were relics from the past and of purely historical interest. In their attempts to legitimize their own projects, managerial scientists have perhaps over-reacted against the 'unscientific' legacy of the past, much as the classical writers had attempted to establish their ideas by exaggerating the gap between the irrational, habitual outlook of 'practical men' and the new world of management principles. In any event the notion of management principles has continued to provoke considerable debate.

The classical principles have been subjected to extensive criticism over the years and, as with many controversies, the arguments have not necessarily been particularly clear nor altogether dispassionate. At this point we will try to isolate the underlying themes of the debate and offer some general comments. Our aim is not to adjudicate between the arguments of specific thinkers but to examine the major points of dispute within the controversy.

There are at least three major sources of contention in the management principles controversy. The first of these concerns definitions: how is the term 'principle' to be understood? Are we talking about universal scientific laws or perhaps general rules-of-thumb? The second is what might be called an existential issue; do or can principles of management exist irrespective of whether they actually exist now? The third is the validation issue; on what basis can a principle be claimed to be true? Clearly these issues are related and if we were to disagree about the first it is very likely that we will disagree about the second and third as well. Of course, in reality things are seldom quite as simple as this! Our discussion will therefore have to deal with several of these issues simultaneously.

As we saw at the start of this chapter the term 'principles' has a number of connotations but perhaps the most contentious one has been that of 'universality'. Critics of the classical approach claim that any assertion that principles are of universal application is unwarranted either because this leads to logical contradictions or because there is evidence of counter-instances or both.

A lot depends on how we interpret the term 'universal'. If we take this to mean literally something which applies at all times and in all places then there certainly cannot be any universal principles which can be demonstrated with evidence to be true because we can never obtain information on all past occurrences and certainly not on all future ones. Even if the notion of universality is given a more restricted meaning, for example as true for all known cases, anyone asserting such a universal principle is on inherently weak ground (Thouless, 1953). Anyone saying something like 'all x are y' or 'x always leads to y' is liable to be contradicted if it can be shown that there is even one counter-instance. If even one x is not y, then the universal claim is false. Not surprisingly, universal generalizations are difficult to sustain. If, however, the claim is softened to something like 'most x are y' or 'x usually leads to y' it becomes more robust but at the cost of losing some of the dramatic impact which tends to be associated with universal claims.

In criticizing the classical approach on the grounds that it claimed universal validity for its principles the critics therefore scored an easy point. Certainly some of the classical writers did make sweeping claims for their principles but it must be remembered that they were engaged in a polemical struggle with a management audience that was dedicated to a belief in 'empiricism' and which denied the possibility of forming any generalizations about management at all. The assertion of universality could therefore be seen as a potent weapon in their battle to be heard. As it turned out it was also one which could be turned against them by their later critics from social science.

A charitable interpretation of the key idea of the classical view is that it claimed that it was possible to create generalized knowledge of management and organizations. Moreover, subsequent research studies indicated that the mechanistic/military model of classical theory probably *is* effective under certain circumstances. Woodward's study, for example, was widely understood to have destroyed the classical case. But among her conclusions was the finding that within the large-batch and mass-production firms there *was* a relationship between conformity to the classical rules of management and business success (Woodward, 1958). Thus valid generalizations about the relationship between management and business performance could be made provided that the conditions under which they held were specified. For large-batch and mass-production firms it was the mechanistic/military model which seemed to work best.

The contingency approach is often contrasted with the classical one (Donaldson, 1985) but it shares with it much the same commitment to generalization. The contingency theorist aims to establish generalizations of the kind 'x usually leads to y under condition z'. If successful the result is not a universal principle but it is a principle, a statement about regularities between phenomena that can be observed, nevertheless. The difference between the two approaches lies not so much in their dedication to principles as in their definition of a principle, as a universally true statement or as a contingently true one, and in the basis upon which they are prepared to grant principles the status of knowledge. For the early classicists that basis emphasized generalization from experience whereas social scientists required validation by means of rigorously conducted empirical research. In that sense, the search for management principles has been continued by the modern contingency theorist.

Furthermore, the contingency approach does not eliminate the possibility that there may be some generalizations which apply irrespective of differences in context. Evidence to date suggests that this is a matter of degree. Some generalizations seem to apply only in highly specified contexts whereas others apply across such a broad range of situations that they can be considered universal at least in the weak sense of the word. That such a reconciliation of the classical and contingency approaches is possible is shown by evidence presented by Child (1974); five universal attributes of high performing organizations are stated together with five contingent ones. The contingency theorists' assertion that 'it all depends' is thus an assumption just as is the classical view that there are universal principles. Whether those assumptions are incompatible looks to be something that is best resolved by empirical evidence rather than purely by logical argument.

Another charge was that the classical principles were contradictory and that no guidance was given as to how these contradictions could be resolved. There does seem to be some truth in this but it is also apparent that contingency theory has not escaped this problem. It has been shown, for example, that large firms tend to work better when employees are more tightly controlled and that firms which are having to cope with change work better when employees are less tightly controlled. What then are the implications for a large firm which is having to cope with change, an increasingly familiar management dilemma? This sort of issue continues to be problematic for contingency theory and the problem of contradictions is therefore by no means restricted to the classical approach.

As Koontz noted, one way of claiming to have undermined the classical principles was by selecting one of them and showing that it could be contradicted. The span of control principle came in for particularly heavy criticism. Yet one review of a series of research studies on the span of control concluded that the revised version of the principle offered by neo-classicists like Koontz yielded a result remarkably close to that originally proposed by Fayol. Filley, House and Kerr (1976) found that the optimal span was somewhere between five and ten although larger spans were appropriate at higher levels of the organization. They commented that:

> Clearly, as suggested by early management theorists, there is a limit beyond which the size of a work group and the complexity of a manager's job cannot be extended without resulting in undesirable consequences for the organization, for the manager, and for the members of the work group. For managers whose subordinates' jobs interlock and require personal supervision, this limit has fairly consistently been found to be as originally stated by Henri Fayol – in the range of four to six.

Dismissals of the classical principles on empirical grounds seem unwarranted not only because of findings such as these but also because most of the principles have not, in fact, been subjected to systematic empirical test.

Despite, and perhaps because of, the 'challenge of social science', the notion of principles of management and organization has by no means been completely eradicated from management thought. Whereas the social sciences tend to offer more complexity not less, more uncertainty rather than more security, more questions instead of more answers, management principles offer rules, procedures, solutions. Relinquishing entirely a belief in principles may prove just too much to bear.

Indeed the idea of principles appears to be remarkably resilient and will probably always be so as long as people continue 'searching for certainty' (Casti, 1992). As we have seen, the messages of the most influential popular management books tend to be cast in the mould of rules and principles and bear a strong resemblance to those of the classical texts (leaving aside the fact that the former were generally concise and short whereas the latter are frequently lengthy and verbose!). Notwithstanding the understandable scepticism of professional social scientists, the idea that there may be a limited set of fundamental rules of managerial conduct which promise 'results' seems likely to continue to exert a powerful fascination over the minds of ever more beleaguered managers.

Are there then any valid principles of management? If we take principles to mean literally universal generalizations then the answer must be no. If, however, we mean broad generalizations supported by substantial evidence then there seem to be quite strong grounds for saying that there are, depending on how much evidence of what kind you are willing to accept. Some of these generalizations apply across a broad range of contexts but others are specific to more narrowly defined situations. And always these generalizations remain provisional and open to revision in the light of new evidence.

The issue of management principles remains controversial but perhaps no more so than the general question of laws in science. The law-like nature of the world is a basic article of scientific faith yet the quantum physicist and cosmologist, John Archibald Wheeler, has declared that as far as the laws of the universe go 'The only law is that there is no law' (quoted in Casti, 1992). It would seem unreasonable then to expect too much from science in the messy world of management.

In the next chapter we will be looking further into whether the social sciences can be of help to managers. For the moment our verdict on the matter of management principles is an open one. It seems that at the very least we should continue to ask, as Rose (1988) has done, whether this question has yet been settled.

contingency theory operationiized (1979)

'What is the right organization structure? Decision trees analysis provides the answer', by Robert Duncan, *Organizational Dynamics*, Winter, 1979, pp. 59–80.

The classical management theorists had offered managers simple principles concerning the one-best-way to structure all of their companies. In contrast, the recommendations of contingency writers on organization structure, were more complex. They rejected the classical idea of the one-best-way, claiming instead that different companies needed different types of organization structure. Moreover, once an appropriate structure was created, it was likely that it might have to be modified in the future, as organizational circumstances changed.

The managerial response to this new 'contingency' approach to structuring an organization was ambivalent. On the one hand, managements valued the clear simplicity of the classical writers, and found their principles easy to understand and reasonably straightforward to implement. On the other hand, common sense suggested that companies differed greatly in the nature of the product they produced; the technology that they used; and the environment in which they operated. Managers were willing to make decisions about the shape of their companies' structures, but were unclear about the options. In this context, Robert Duncan's article can be seen as an attempt to operationalize the contingency approach to organization structuring. Duncan uses decision tree analysis to spell out the process that a manager can use to select the appropriate structure to fit the demands of their company's environment, as well as suggesting ways of making that structure work in practice.

learning objectives

Once you have read and understood the prescribed material, you should be able to:

1 Define the key concepts and ideas in Chapters 11 and 15 of the core text.
2 Summarize the main elements of the contingency approach to organization structuring.
3 Understand the process of analyzing a company situation before selecting the most appropriate structure for it.

learning pre-requisites

Before proceeding, you should read Chapters 11 and 15 of the core text, and the article that follows, 'What is the right organizational structure?', by Robert Duncan.

learning activities

1 The contingency approach to organization structuring contains many different perspectives, presented by many different writers. Associating the appropriate **209**

writers with their statement or perspective is the first step in learning about it. For each of the statements that follow, match it to the correct writer(s) from the list provided below. Place the letter next to the number. There are more writers than statements.

(A) Tom Burns and G. M. Stalker	(F) Tom Peters
(B) Terrence Deal and Allen Kennedy	(G) Edgar Schein
(C) Robert Duncan	(H) James Thompson
(D) Paul Lawrence	(I) Robert Waterman
(E) Paul Lawrence and Jay Lorsch	(J) Joan Woodward

1 Success is determined by corporate culture, the stronger and more cohesive the culture, the more successful the company will be.

2 Organizational structure is determined by the predictability of the work task.

3 'Tell me what your environment is, and I shall tell you what your organization structure ought to be.'

4 As the technology in an organization becomes more complex, so its structure must change.

5 No form of organization is intrinsically efficient or inefficient, it depends on the nature of the environment.

6 Efficient performance comes from high differentiation and high integration in conditions of high uncertainty; and from low differentiation and low integration in conditions of low uncertainty.

7 We should think of structures as functional or decentralized, rather than in terms of the more abstract notions used by most theorists.

8 Organizational structure is a product of the interdependencies within the organization.

2 Answer the following ten multiple choice questions.

1 A small company manifests the following characteristics. A low level of specialization, with few different jobs; little standardization, and members concerned with achieving goals. This organization can be classed as:
   a) Mechanistic   (A)
   b) Integrated   (B)
   c) Organic   (C)
   d) Differentiated   (D)

2 In this article, Duncan takes, as the basis for organizational structuring:
   a) Product areas   (A)
   b) Geographic areas   (B)
   c) Information needs   (C)
   d) Interdependence requirements   (D)

3 Which one of the following statements is false?
   a) Integration needs increase when technology places an emphasis on co-operation between divisions.   (A)
   b) Integration needs increase when organizational environments are changing.   (B)
   c) Integration needs decrease with standardization and automation.   (C)

    d) Integration needs decrease when divisions are able to generate their
      own information. (D)

4   A company's environment is changing constantly and rapidly. Product
    demands and product technologies are changing every month. To cope with
    this situation, the management decides to improve lateral relations and com-
    munications. It can do this best by:
    a) An integrator role (A)
    b) A matrix structure (B)
    c) Liaison roles (C)
    d) Direct personal manager-unit contact (D)

5   The distinction between the classical management theory and the contingency
    approach can best be explained in terms of:
    a) Universal versus situation approach (A)
    b) Human resource versus organizational approach (B)
    c) Bureaucratic versus organic approach (C)
    d) Theoretical versus practical approach (D)

6   A small company's direct control structure has become inadequate.
    Management can no longer control the production of the different products
    manufactured, and the market has become too large to monitor. This problem
    of management control can best be solved by introducing:
    a) A functional structure (A)
    b) A matrix structure (B)
    c) Closer integration (C)
    d) Segmentation (D)

7   An organizational behaviour researcher is unable to conclude from his
    research whether the structure of a company depends on its characteristics
    (task, technology, people), or the way that these are managed. This dilemma
    can be best considered in terms of:
    a) Determinism versus strategic choice (A)
    b) Contingency versus determinism (B)
    c) Contingency versus strategic choice (C)
    d) Contingency versus classical management theory (D)

8   Prochem plc is a chemicals company which produces ammonia-related prod-
    ucts using a continuous flow process. The production of ammonia has been
    fluctuating according to external factors. Prochem is highly specialized, and its
    structure is likely to be most influenced by:
    a) Internal factors (A)
    b) Environmental factors (B)
    c) Technological factors (C)
    d) Strategic choice factors (D)

9   Declining customer demand might be the result of inappropriate organization-
    al structure. Which of the following is not a symptom of such poor structure?
    a) Substitute products entering the market (A)
    b) Product features not matching customer needs. (B)
    c) Inadequate management information preventing speedy decision-
      making. (C)
    d) Middle managers' decisions not being in line with top management's
      policies. (D)

10 A production firm relies heavily on its suppliers; is sensitive to the price of its raw materials which fluctuate daily; it is regularly affected by changes in government policies; and the demand for its product oscillates. The company manufactures one product using a large production plant. Its market is small and homogeneous. Following Duncan's decision tree analysis, this company should be structured as a_____ organization:

a) Decentralized (A)
b) Mixed decentralized (B)
c) Functional (C)
d) Mixed functional (D)

READING **15** *What is the right organization structure? Decision tree analysis provides the answer**
Robert Duncan†

Decision tree analysis spells out the process the manager can and should use in selecting the right structure to 'fit' the demands of the environment, as well as the specific steps he or she can take to make the appropriate structure work.

Organization design is a central problem for managers. What is the 'best' structure for the organization? What are the criteria for selecting the 'best' structure? What signals indicate that the organization's existing structure may not be appropriate to its task and its environment? This article discusses the purposes of organization structure and presents a decision tree analysis approach to help managers pick the right organization structure.

The objectives of organizational design

What is organization structure and what is it supposed to accomplish? Organization structure is more than boxes on a chart; it is a pattern of interactions and coordination that links the technology, task, and human components of the organization to ensure that the organization accomplishes it purpose.

An organization's structure has essentially two objectives: First, it facilitates the flow of information within the organization in order to reduce the uncertainty in decision making. The design öf the organization should facilitate the collection of the

* Reprinted by permission from *Organizational Dynamics*, Winter 1979, © 1979. AMACOM, a division of American Management Associations, New York. All rights reserved.
† Robert B. (Bob) Duncan received his Ph.D. from Yale University in 1970 and his M.A. (1966) and A.B. (1964) from Indiana University. He joined the faculty of the Graduate School of Management, Northwestern University, in 1970 and is currently professor and chairman of the organization behavior department. At Northwestern he teaches courses on the management of organizational change and organizational design. His research is concerned with implementing changes and innovation in organizations and examining processes of organizational design and strategy formulation. He has studied these processes in a variety of settings including business, police, education, and health organizations. He is the author of numerous journal articles, as well as two books, *Innovations and Organizations* with G. Zaltman and J. Holbeck (Wiley-Interscience, 1973) and *Strategies for Planned Change* with G. Zaltman (Wiley-Interscience, 1977). He serves on the editorial boards of the *Academy of Management Journal* and *Management Science*. Dr Duncan also acts frequently as a consultant on organizational change, organizational design, team building, and as a speaker in management development programs for business, public, educational, and health organizations.

information managers need for decision making. When managers experience a high degree of uncertainty—that is, when their information needs are great—the structure of the organization should not be so rigid as to inhibit managers from seeking new sources of information or developing new procedures or methods for doing their jobs. For example, in developing a new product, a manufacturing department may need to seek direct feedback from customers on how the new product is being accepted; the need to react quickly to customer response makes waiting for this information to come through normal marketing and sales channels unacceptable.

The second objective of organization design is to achieve effective coordination–integration. The structure of the organization should integrate organizational behavior across the parts of the organization so it is coordinated. This is particularly important when the units in the organization are interdependent. As James Thomspon had indicated, the level of interdependence can vary. In *pooled interdependence* the parts of the organization are independent and are linked together only in contributing something to the same overall organization. In many conglomerates, the divisions are really separate organizations linked only in that they contribute profits to the overall organization. Simple rules—procedures—can be developed to specify what the various units have to do. In *sequential interdependence*, however, there is an ordering of activities, that is, one organizational unit has to perform its function before the next unit can perform its. For example, in an automobile plant manufacturing has to produce the automobiles before quality control can inspect them. Now such organizations have to develop plans to coordinate activities; quality control needs to know when and how many cars to expect for inspection.

Reciprocal interdependence is the most complex type of organizational interdependence. Reciprocal interdependence is present when the output of Unit A become the inputs of Unit B and the outputs of B cycle back to become the inputs of Unit A. The relationship between the operations and maintenance in an airline is a good example of this type of interdependence. Operations produces 'sick' airplanes that need repair by maintenance. Maintenance repairs these planes and the repaired planes become inputs to the operations division to be reassigned to routes. When reciprocal interdependence between organization units is present, a more complex type of coordination is required. This is coordination by feedback. Airline operations and maintenance must communicate with one another so each one will know when the planes will be coming to them so they can carry out their respective functions.

Organizational design, then, is the allocation of resources and people to a specified mission or purpose and the structuring of these resources to achieve the mission. Ideally, the organization is designed to fit its environment and to provide the information and coordination needed.

It is useful to think of organization structure from an information-processing view. The key characteristic of organizational structure is that it links the elements of the organization by providing the channels of communication through which information flows. My research has indicated that when organizational structure is formalized and centralized, information flows are restricted and as a consequence, the organization is not able to gather and process the information it needs when faced with uncertainty. For example, when an organization's structure is highly centralized, decisions are made at the top and information tends to be filtered as it moves up the chain of command. When a decision involves a great deal of uncertainty, it is unlikely therefore that the few individuals at the top of the organization will have the information they require to make the best decision. So decentralization, that is, having more subordinates participate in the decision-making process, may generate the information needed to help reduce the uncertainty and thereby facilitate a better decision.

Alternative organizational designs

The key question for the manager concerned with organization design is what are the different structures available to choose from. Contingency theories of organization have shown that there is no one best structure. However, organization theorists have been less clear in elaborating the decision process managers can follow in deciding which structure to implement.

In discussing organization design, organization theorists describe structure differently from the way managers responsible for organization design do. Organizational theorists describe structure as more or less formalized, centralized, specialized, or hierarchical. However, managers tend to think of organizational structure in terms of two general types, the *functional* and the *decentralized*. Most organizations today are either functional or decentralized or some modification or combination of these two general types. Therefore, if we are to develop a heuristic for helping managers make decisions about organization structure, we need to think of structures functional or decentralized and not in terms of the more abstract dimensions of formalization, centralization, and so on, that organizational theorists tend to use.

Organizational environment and design: a critical interaction

In deciding on what kind of organization structure to use, managers need to first understand the characteristics of the environment they are in and the demands this environment makes on the organization in terms of information and coordination. Once the environment is understood, the manager can proceed with the design process.

The first step in designing an organization structure, therefore, is to identify the organization's environment. The task environment constitutes that part of the environment defined by managers as relevant or potentially relevant for organizational decision making. Figure 1 presents a list of environmental components managers might encounter. Clearly, no one organization would encounter all these components in decision making, but this is the master list from which organizational decision makers would identify the appropriate task environments. For example, a manager in a manufacturing divisions could 'define an environment consisting of certain personnel, certain staff units and suppliers, and perhaps certain technological components'. The usefulness of the list in Figure 1 is that it provides a guide for decision makers, alerting them to the elements the environment they might consider in decision making.

Once managers have defined the task environment, the next step is to understand the state of that environment. What are its key characteristics? In describing organizational environments, we emphasize two dimensions: simple–complex and static–dynamic.

The simple–complex dimension of the environment focuses on whether the factors in the environment considered for decision making are few in number and similar or many in number and different. An example of a *simple* unit would be a lower-level production unit whose decisions are affected only by the parts department and materials department, on which it is dependent for supplies, and the marketing department, on which it is dependent for output. An example of a *complex* environment would be a programming and planning department. This group must consider a wide variaty of environmental factors when making a decision. It may focus on the marketing and materials department, on customers, on suppliers, and so on. Thus this organizational unit has a much more heterogeneous group of environmental factors to deal with in decision making—its environment is more complex than that of the production unit.

Internal environment	External environment

Internal environment

Organizational personnel component
▸ Educational and technological background and skills
▸ Previous technological and managerial skill
▸ Individual member's involvement and commitment to attaining system's goals
▸ Interpersonal behavior styles
▸ Availability of manpower for utilization within the system

Organizational functional and staff units component
▸ Technological characteristics of organizational units
▸ Interdependence of organizational units in carrying out their objectives
▸ Intraunit conflict among organizational functional and staff units
▸ Intraunit conflict among organizational functional and staff units

Organizational level component
▸ Organizational objectives and goals
▸ Integrative process integrating individuals and groups into contributing maximally to attaining organizational goals
▸ Nature of the organization's product service

External environment

Customer component
▸ Distributors of product or service
▸ Actual users of product or service

Suppliers component
▸ New materials suppliers
▸ Equipment suppliers
▸ Product parts suppliers
▸ Labor supply

Competitor component
▸ Competitors for suppliers
▸ Competitors for customers

Sociopolitical component
▸ Government regulatory control over the industry
▸ Public political attitude toward industry and its particular product
▸ Relationship with trade unions with jurisdiction in the organization

Technological component
▸ Meeting new technological requirements of own industry and related industries in production of product or service
▸ Improving and developing new products by implementing new technological advances in the industry

Figure 1 Environmental components list

The static–dynamic dimension of the environment is concerned with whether the factors of the environment remain the same over time or change. A *static* environment, for example, might be a production unit that has to deal with a marketing department whose requests for output remain the same and a materials department that is able to supply a steady rate of inputs to the production unit. However, if the marketing department were continually changing its requests and the materials department were inconsistent in its ability to supply parts, the production unit would be operating in a more *dynamic* environment.

Figure 2 provides a four-way classification of organizational environments and some examples of organizations in each of these environments. Complex–dynamic (Cell 4) environments are probably the most characteristic type today. These environments involve rapid change and create high uncertainty for managers. The proper organizational structure is critical in such environments if managers are to have the information necessary for decision making. Also, as organizations move into this turbulent environment, it may be necessary for them to modify their structures. For example, AT&T has moved from a functional organization to a decentralized structure organized around different markets to enable it to cope with more competition in the telephone market and in communications. This change in structure was in response to the need for more information and for a quicker response time to competitive moves.

	Simple	*Complex*
Static	low perceived uncertainty Small number of factors and components in the environment Factors and components are somewhat similar to one another Factors and components remain basically the same and are not changing *Example:* Soft drink industry	moderately low perceived uncertainty Large number of factors and components in the environment Factors and components are not similar to one another Factors and components remain basically the same *Example:* Food products
Dynamic	moderately high perceived uncertainty Small number of factors and components in the environment Factors and components are somewhat similar to one another Factors and components of the environment are in continual process of change *Example:* Fast food industry	high perceived uncertainty Large number of factors and components in the environment Factors and components are not similar to one another Factors and components of environment are in a continual process of change *Examples:* Commercial airline industry Telephone communications (AT&T)

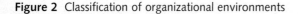

1 2

3 4

Figure 2 Classification of organizational environments

Strategies for organizational design

Once the organization's environment has been diagnosed, what type of structure the organization should have becomes the key question.

Simple design strategy

When the organization's environment is relatively simple, that is, there are not many factors to consider in decision making, and stable, that is, neither the make-up of the environment nor the demands made by environmental components are changing, the information and coordination needs for the organization are low. In such circumstances, a *functional organization structure* is most appropriate.

A key characteristic of the functional organization is specialization by functional areas. Figure 3 presents a summary of this structure's strengths and weaknesses. The key strengths of the functional organization are that it supports in-depth skill development and a simple decision-communication network. However, when disputes or uncertainty arises among managers about a decision, they get pushed up the hierarchy to be resolved. A primary weakness of the functional organization, therefore, is that when the organization's environment becomes more dynamic and uncertainty tends to increase, many decisions move to the top of the organization. Lower-level managers do not have the information required for decision making so they push decisions upward. Top-level managers become overloaded and are thus slow to respond to the environment.

Organizational design dilemma

The organizational designer faces a dilemma in such situations. Designs can be instituted that *reduce* the amount of information required for decision making.

Organizational functions	Accomplished in functional organization
Goals	Functional subgoal emphasis (projects lag)
Influence	Functional heads
Promotion	By special function
Budgeting	By function or department
Rewards	For special capability

Strengths

1 Best in *stable* environment
2 Colleagueship ('home') for technical specialists
3 Supports in-depth skill development
4 Specialists freed from administrative/coordinating work
5 Simple decision/communication network excellent in small, limited-output organizations

Weaknesses

1 Slow response time
2 Bottlenecks caused by sequential tasks
3 Decisions pile at top
4 If multiproduct, product priority conflict
5 Poor interunit coordination
6 Stability paid for in less innovation
7 Restricted view of whole

Figure 3 Characteristics of the functional organization

Decentralization is the principal strategy indicated. Or organizations can develop more lateral relations to *increase* the amount of information available for decision making.

A decentralized organization is possible whenever an organization's tasks are self-contained. Decentralized organizations are typically designed around products, projects, or markets. The decentralized healthcare organization in Figure 4 is organized around product areas (Medical and Dental) and market area (International). Each division has all the resources needed to perform its particular task. For example, Medical Products (Figure 4) has its own functional organization consisting of production, marketing, and R&D to carry out its mission. The information needed by Medical Products Division's managers is reduced because they have organized around a set of common medical products, and they don't have to worry about dental, pharmaceutical, or hospital support services or products.

In the decentralized organization, managers only have to worry about their own products or services; they have the resources to carry out these activities, and they don't have to compete for shared resources or schedule shared resources. There is also a full-time commitment to a particular product line. The decentralized structure

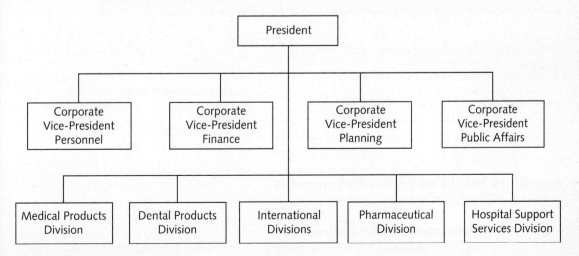

Figure 4 Decentralized organization

is particularly effective when the organization's environment is very complex, that is, there are a large number of factors to be considered in decision making, and the environment can be segmented or broken down into product or market areas around which the organization can structure itself. For example, the health products organization (Figure 4) probably started out as a functional organization. However, as its product line increased, it undoubtedly became more difficult for one manufacturing unit to have the expertise to produce such a wide range of products efficiently and to handle the diversity of information needed to do it. It would also be difficult for one marketing unit to market such a diverse group of products; different kinds of information and skills would be required to sell the different products. Segmenting this complex environment into product areas facilitates increased specialization. As a result, divisional managers need less information than if they had to deal with all the products and services of the corporation.

Figure 5 summarizes the characteristics and the strengths and weaknesses of the decentralized organization. Decentralized organizations face several problems. For example, it is sometimes difficult to decide what resources are to be pooled in a corporate staff to be used to service the entire organization. If the divisions are very different from one another in terms of products, customers, technology, and so on, however, it becomes very difficult to staff a corporate services unit with the diverse knowledge needed to be able to help the divisions. A restricted approach to innovation is another problem decentralized organizations may encounter. Because each division is organized around a particular product or geographic area, each manager's attention is focused on his or her special area. As a result, their innovations focus on their particular specialties. Managers don't have the diverse information needed to produce radical innovations.

Organizational functions	Accomplished in decentralized organization
Goals	Special product emphasis (technologies lag)
Influence	Product, project heads
Promotion	By product management
Budgeting	By product, project, program
Rewards	For integrative capability

Strengths	*Weaknesses*
1 Suited to fast change	1 Innovation/growth restricted to existing project areas
2 High product, project, or program visibility	2 Tough to allocate pooled resources (i.e., computer, lab)
3 Full-time task orientation (i.e., dollars, schedules, profits)	3 Shared functions hard to coordinate (i.e., purchasing)
4 Task responsibility, contact points clear to customers or clients	4 Deterioration of in-depth competence – hard to attract technical specialists
5 Processes multiple tasks in parallel, easy to cross functional lines	5 Possible internal task conflicts, priority conflicts
	6 May neglect high level of integration required in organization

Figure 5 Characteristics of the decentralized organization

One major liability of decentralized organizations is their relative inability to provide integration–coordination among the divisions, even when their interdependence increases. When divisions are relatively autonomous and have only pooled interdependence, there is not much need for coordination. However, when uncertainty increases and the divisions have to work together because of increased either sequential or reciprocal interdependence between the units, decentralized organizations have no formal mechanisms to coordinate and resolve the increased needs for information.

Since today's organizational environments are becoming more complex and interdependent, large decentralized corporations are finding that the need to integrate has increased for at least five reasons.

1 The increased level of regulation organizations face requires more and more coordination across divisions to be sure that all regulatory requirements are being met. For example, crackdowns by the SEC on illegal foreign payments and the increased liabilities of boards of directors have required organizations to have better control systems and information sources to enable their headquarters staff groups to know what's going on in the divisions. Affirmative action requirements have required that divisions share information on how they are doing and where possible pools of affirmative action candidates may be found.

2 Organizational environments are changing, and this can lead to a requirement of more coordination across divisions. New customer demands may require what were previously autonomous divisions to coordinate their activities. For example, if the International Group in the health products company mentioned earlier faces a demand to develop some new products for overseas, it may be necessary to provide a means by which the Medical Products and Pharmaceutical Divisions can work in a coordinated and integrated way with International to develop these new products.

3 Technological changes are placing more emphasis on increased interaction among divisions. More and more, computer systems and R&D services are being shared, thus compelling the divisions to interact more with one another.

4 The cost of making 'wrong' strategic decisions is increasing in terms of both sunk costs and losses because of failure to get market share. Since such 'wrong' decisions sometimes result from a lack of contact between divisions, it emphasizes the need to have more coordination across divisions and more sharing of information. For example, AT&T has just recently begun to market telephone and support equipment to counter the competition of other suppliers of this equipment that have entered the market. To do this AT&T has organized around market managers so they can share information, build on one another's expertise and competence, and ensure required coordination.

5 Scarce resources—for example, capital and raw materials—will require more interaction among divisions to set overall priorities. Is a university, for example, going to emphasize its undergraduate arts program or its professional schools? By setting up task forces of the deans of the schools, the university might be able to identify opportunities for new innovative programs that could benefit the entire organization. New programs in management of the arts—museums, orchestras, and so on—could draw on the expertise of the arts department and the business school and would not require a lot of new venture capital.

For a number of reasons, then, there is a need for increased coordination among divisions in decentralized organizations. Given the decentralized organization's weakness, organizational designers need to implement the second general design strategy, increasing the information flow to reduce uncertainty and facilitate coordination.

Lateral relations: increasing information available for decision making

Lateral relations is really a process that is overlaid on an existing functional or decentralized structure. Lateral relations as a process moves decision making down to where the problem is in the organization. It differs from decentralization in that no self-contained tasks are created.

Jay Galbraith has identified various types of lateral relations. *Direct contact*, for example, can be used by managers of diverse groups as a mechanism to coordinate their different activities. With direct contact, managers can meet informally to discuss their common problems. *Liaison roles* are a formal communication link between two units. Engineering liaison with the manufacturing department is an excellent example of the liaison role. The engineer serving in the liaison role may be located in the production organization as a way of coordinating engineering and production activities.

When coordinational between units becomes more complex, an *integrator role* may be established. Paul Lawrence and Jay Lorsch have indicated that the integrator role is particularly useful when organizational units that must be coordinated are differentiated from one another in terms of their structure, subgoals, time, orientation, and so on. In such situations, there is the possibility of conflict between the various units. For example, production, marketing, and R&D units in an organization may be highly differentiated from one another. Marketing, for example, is primarily concerned with having products to sell that are responsive to customer needs. R&D, on the other hand, may be concerned with developing innovative products that shape customer needs. Production, for its part, may want products to remain unchanged so that manufacturing setups don't have to be modified. Obviously there are difference among the three units in terms of their subgoals. The integrator role is instituted to coordinate and moderate such diverse orientations. The integrator could be a materials manager or a group executive whose additional function would be to coordinate and integrate the diverse units in ways that meet the organization's common objectives.

To be effective as an *integrator*, a manager needs to have certain characteristics. First, he needs wide contacts in the organization so that he possesses the relevant information about the different units he is attempting to integrate. Second, the integrator needs to understand and share, at least to a degree, the goals and orientations of the different groups. He cannot be seen as being a partisan of one particular group's perspective. Third, the integrator has to be rather broadly trained technically, so that he can talk the language of the different groups. By being able to demonstrate that he has some expertise in each area, he will be viewed as more credible by each group and will also be better able to facilitate information exchange between the units. The integrator can in effect become an interpreter of each group's position to the others. Fourth, the groups that the integrator is working with must trust him. Again, the integrator is trying to facilitate information flow and cooperation between the groups and thus the groups must believe that he is working toward a solution acceptable to all the groups. Fifth, the integrator needs to exert influence on the basis of his expertise rather than through formal power. The integrator can provide information and identify alternative courses of action for the different units as they attempt to coordinate their activities. The more he can get them to agree on solutions and courses of action rather than having to use his formal power, the more committed they will be to implementing the solution. Last, the integrator's conflict resolution skills are important. Because differentiation between the units exists, conflict and disagreement are inevitable. It is important, therefore, that confrontation is used as the conflict resolution style. By confrontation we mean that parties to the conflict identify the causes of conflict and are committed to adopting a problem-solving approach to finding a mutually acceptable solution to the conflict. The parties must also be committed, of course, to work to implement that solution.

When coordination involves working with six or seven different units, then task forces or teams can be established. Task forces involve a group of managers working together on the coordination problems of their diverse groups. For example, in a manufacturing organization, the marketing, production, R&D, finance, and engineering managers may meet twice a week (or more often when required) to discuss problems of coordination that they may be having that require their cooperation to solve. In this use a task force is a problem-solving group formed to facilitate coordination.

The matrix type of structure is the most complex form of lateral relations. The matrix is typically a formal structure in the organization: it is not a structure that is often added temporarily to an existing functional or decentralized structure. As Lawrence, Kolodny, and Davis have indicated in their article 'The Human Side of the Matrix' (*Organizational Dynamics*, Summer 1977), there are certain key characteristics of a matrix structure. The most salient is that there is dual authority, that is, both the heads of the functions and the matrix manager have authority over those working in the matrix unit.

The matrix was initially developed in the aerospace industry where the organization had to be responsive to products/markets as well as technology. Because the matrix focuses on a specific product or market, it can generate the information and concentrate the resources needed to respond to changes in that product or market rapidly. The matrix is now being used in a variety of business, public, and health organizations. Figure 6 provides a summary of the characteristics and strengths and weaknesses of the matrix form of organization.

The matrix structure is particularly useful when an organization wants to focus resources on producing a particular product or service. The use of the matrix in the aerospace industry, for example, allowed these organizations to build manufacturing units to produce particular airplanes, thus allowing in-depth attention and specialization of skills.

Matrix organizations, however, are complicated to manage. Because both project managers and traditional functional area managers are involved in matrix organizations, personnel in the matrix have two bosses, and there is an inherent potential for

Organizational functions	*Accomplished in matrix organization*
Goals	Emphasis on product/market
Influence	Matrix manager and functional heads
Promotion	By function or into matrix manager job
Budgeting	By matrix organization project
Rewards	By special functional skills and performance matrix

Strengths	*Weaknesses*
1 Full-time focus of personnel on project of matrix	1 Costly to maintain personnel pool to staff matrix
2 Matrix manager is coordinator of functions for single project	2 Participants experience dual authority of matrix manager and functional area managers
3 Reduces information requirements as focus is on single product/market	3 Little interchange with functional groups outside the matrix so there may be duplication of effort, 'reinvention of the wheel'
4 Masses specialized technical skills to the product/market	4 Participants in matrix need to have good interpersonal skills in order for it to work

Figure 6 Characteristics of the matrix organization

conflict under such circumstances. As a result, the matrix form of lateral relations should only be used in those situations where an organization faces a unique problem in a particular market area or in the technological requirements of a product. When the information and technological requirements are such that a full-time focus on the market or product is needed, a matrix organization can be helpful. Citibank, for example, has used a matrix structure in its international activity to concentrate on geographic areas. Boeing Commerical Airplane has used the matrix to focus resources on a particular product.

Lateral relations require a certain organizational design and special interpersonal skills if this process for reducing uncertainty by increasing the information available for improving coordination is going to be effective. From a design perspective, four factors are required:

1 The organization's reward structure must support and reward cooperative problem solving that leads to coordination and integration. Will a manager's performance appraisal, for example, reflect his or her participation in efforts to achieve coordination and integration? If the organization's reward system does not recognize joint problem-solving efforts, then lateral relations will not be effective.
2 In assigning managers to participate in some form of lateral relations, it is important that they have responsibility for implementation. Line managers should be involved since they understand the problems more intimately than staff personnel and, more importantly, they are concerned about implementation. Staff members can be used, but line managers should be dominant since this will lead to more commitment on their part to implementing solutions that come out of lateral relations problem-solving efforts.
3 Participants must have the authority to commit their units to action. Managers who are participating in an effort to resolve problems of coordination must be able to indicate what particular action their units might take in trying to improve coordination. For example, in the manufacturing company task force example mentioned earlier, the marketing manager should be able to commit his group to increasing the lead time for providing information to production on deadlines for delivering new products to customers.
4 Lateral processes must be integrated into the vertical information flow. In the concern for increasing information exchange *across* the units in the organization there must be no loss of concern for vertical information exchange so that the top levels in the organization are aware of coordination efforts.

Certain skills are also required on the part of participants for lateral relations to work:

1 Individuals must deal with conflict effectively, in the sense of identifying the sources of conflict and then engaging in problem solving to reach a mutually acceptable solution to the conflict situation.
2 Participants need good interpersonal skills. They must be able to communicate effectively with one another and avoid making other participants defensive. The more they can learn to communicate with others in a descriptive, nonevaluative manager, the more open the communication process will be.
3 Participants in lateral relations need to understand that influence and power should be based on expertise rather than formal power. Because of the problem-solving nature of lateral relations, an individual's power and influence will change based on the particular problem at hand and the individual's ability to provide key information to solve the problem. At various times different members will have more influence because of their particular expertise.

Lateral relations, then, is a process that is overlaid onto the existing functional or decentralized organization structure. Lateral relations requires various skills, so it is imperative that an organization never adopts this approach without training the people involved. Before implementing lateral relations, team building might be used to develop the interpersonal skills of the participating managers. These managers might spend time learning how to operate more effectively in groups, how to improve communication skills, and how to deal with conflict in a positive way so that it does not become disruptive to the organization.

The organizational design decisions tree

We have discussed the different kinds of organization structure that managers can implement. We are now prepared to identify the decision-making process the manager can use in selecting the appropriate structure to 'fit' the demands of the environment. Figure 7 presents a decision tree analysis for selecting either the functional or decentralized organization structure. This decision analysis also indicates when the existing functional or decentralized organization structure should be supplemented with some form of lateral relations in the form of a task force or team or a matrix. In general, an organization should use one of the simpler forms of lateral relations rather than the more complex and expensive matrix. In using this decision tree, there are a number of questions that the designer needs to ask.

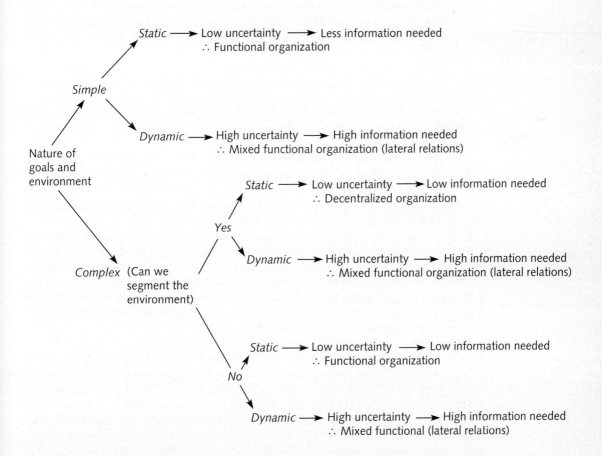

Figure 7 Organizational design decision tree heuristic

The first question is whether the organization's environment is *simple*, that is there are few factors to consider in the environment, or *complex*, that is, there are a number of different environmental factors to be considered in decision making. If the environment is defined as *simple*, the next question focuses on whether the environmental factors are *static*, that is, remain the same over time, or are *dynamic*, that is change over time. If we define the environment as static, there is likely to be little uncertainty associated with decision making. In turn, information requirements for decision making are low. In this simple–static environment, the functional organization is most efficient. It can most quickly gather and process the information required to deal with this type of environment.

At this point the question might be raised, are there any organizational environments that are in fact both simple and static or is this a misperception on the part of the managers that oversimplifies the environment? There may be environments like this, but the key is that these environments may change, that is, they may become more dynamic as the marketplace changes, as resources become scarce, or the organization's domain is challenged. For example, the motor home/recreational vehicle industry was very successful in the early 1970s. Its market was relatively homogeneous (simple) and there was a constantly high demand (static) for its products. Then the oil embargo of 1973 hit, and the environment suddenly became dynamic. The industry had a very difficult time changing because it had done no contingency planning about 'what would happen if' demand shifted, resources became scare, and so on. The important point is that an organization's environment may be simple and static today but change tomorrow. Managers should continually scan the environment and be sensitive to the fact that things can change and contingency planning may be useful.

If this simple environment is defined as dynamic, with some components in the environment changing, some uncertainty may be experienced by decision makers. Thus information needs will be greater than when the environment was static. Therefore, in this simple–dynamic environment the mixed functional organization with lateral relations is likely to be the most effective in gathering and processing the information required for decision making. Because the organization's environment is simple, the creation of self-contained units would not be efficient. It is more economical to have central functional areas responsible for all products and markets as these products and markets are relatively similar to one another. However, when uncertainty arises and there is need for more information, some form of lateral relations can be added, to the existing functional organization.

Figure 8 shows the functional organization of a manufacturing organization. The organization suddenly may face a problem with its principal product. Competitors may have developed an attractive replacement. As a result of this unique problem, the president of the firm may set up a task force chaired by the vice-president of sales to develop new products. The task force consists of members from manufacturing, sales, research, and engineering services. Its function, obviously, will be to develop and evaluate suggestions for new products.

If the organization's environment is defined by the managers as complex, that is, there are a large number of factors and components that need to be considered in decision making, the next question to ask is, can the organization *segment* its environment into geographic areas, market, or product areas? If the environment is defined as segmentable, then the next question focuses on whether the environment is static or dynamic. If the environment's defined as static, there is going to be low uncertainty and thus information needs for decision making are not going to be high. Thus, in the complex–segmentable–static environment, the decentralized organization is most appropriate, and the health products organization discussed earlier is a

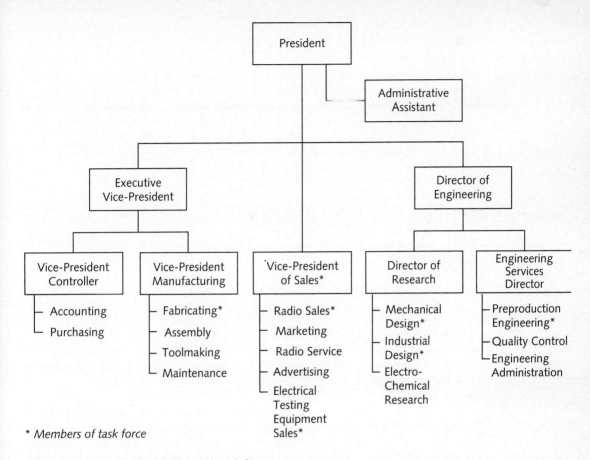

Figure 8 Functional organization with task force

good example of this. The organization can break the environment apart in the sense that it can organize around products or markets, for example, and thus information, resources, and so forth, are only required to produce and market these more homogeneous outputs of the organization.

In the complex–segmentable–dynamic environment there is a change in the components of the environment and the demands they are making on the organization, or in fact the organization has to now consider different factors in the environment that it had not previously considered in decision making. Uncertainty and coordination needs may be higher. The result is that decision makers need more information to reduce uncertainty and provide information to facilitate coordination. The mixed decentralized organization with lateral relations is the appropriate structure here.

Figure 9 presents the design of a multidivision decentralized health products organization. Some form of lateral relations may be added to this structure to help generate more information. For example, the International Division may be attempting to develop new products but may be encountering problems, with the result that the entire organization, stimulated by the president's concern, may be experiencing uncertainty about how to proceed. In such a situation, a task force of the manager of the International Group and the Dental Group and the Pharmaceutical Group might work together in developing ideas for new products in the International Division. The lateral relations mechanism of the task force facilitates information exchange *across* the organization to reduce uncertainty and increase coordination of

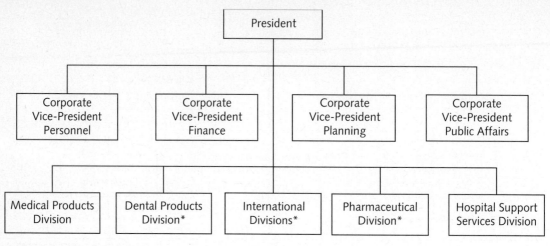

* *Members of task force*

Figure 9 Decentralized organization with lateral relations

the efforts of the divisions that should be mutually supportive. By working together, in the task force, the division managers will be exchanging information and will be gaining a better understanding of their common problems and how they need to work and coordinate with one another in order to solve these problems.

If the organization's complex environment is defined by managers as nonsegmental, the functional organization will be appropriate because it is not possible to break the environment up into geographic or product/service areas.

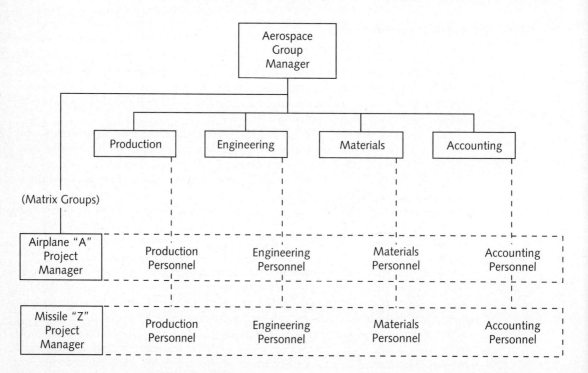

Figure 10 Functional organization with matrix

In effect, there simply might be too much interdependence among environmental components, or the technology of the organization may be so interlinked, that it is not possible to create self-contained units organized around components of the environment.

A hospital is a good example of this organization type. The environment is clearly complex. There are numerous and diverse environmental components that have to be considered in decision making (for example, patients, regulatory groups, medical societies, third-party payers, and suppliers). In the complex–nonsegmentable–static environment, environmental components are rather constant in their demands. Thus here the functional organization is most appropriate.

However, the functional organization, through its very specific rules, procedures, and channels of communication, will likely be too slow in generating the required information. Therefore, some form of lateral relations may be added to the functional organization. Figure 10 presents an example of an aerospace functional organization that uses a matrix structure for its airplane and missile products divisions. The matrix structure provides in-depth concentration of personnel and resources on these different product areas, each of which has its own very unique information and technological requirements.

Symptoms of inappropriate organizational structure

The key question at this point is 'So what?'. What are the costs to an organization if it is using the wrong structure, given its product/service and the environment in which it operates? In order to be effective, an organization needs to attain its goals and objectives, it needs to adapt to the environment, and last, it should be designed in such a way that its managers experience low role conflict and ambiguity.

Therefore, there are certain kinds of information the manager responsible for organizational design should be sensitive to in monitoring whether the appropriate structure is being used. While using the appropriate structure may have some direct impact on the organization's ability to attain its goals, its biggest impact will probably be on the adaptability of the organization and the role behavior of its managers.

Certain kinds of symptoms regarding ineffective adaptability may occur. For example:

- Organizational decision makers may not be able to anticipate problems before they occur. There may be a tendency in the organization to wait until problems occur and then react to them because the organization simply does not have enough information to develop contingency plans.
- Decision makers may err in trying to predict trends in their decision environment. Without proper coordination across divisions, the organization may lose control over the relationship between its internal functioning and its environment.
- The organization may not be able to get key information for decision making to the right place for effective decision making. For example, division managers from different product groups may have information that quality and liability standards on their respective products are unrealistically high. However, because of decentralization and lack of effective coordination through some form of lateral relations, this information may not get to the staff groups in the organization that are responsible for setting corporate policy in this area.
- The organization, having identified a problem vis-à-vis its environment, may simply not be able to take corrective action quickly enough.

Symptoms of poor fit between structure and environment may also show at the level of the individual in terms of some increase in either role conflict or role ambiguity. It is important, therefore, that the organization monitor the level of role conflict and role ambiguity among its managers and the resulting stress they experience so the system has a baseline for comparison. If there is a significant increase from this baseline in conflict and ambiguity and stress, then the organization may consider that the increase is a symptom of an organizational design problem. For example:

▶ Individuals may be experiencing increased role conflict. This may occur when the organization is implementing a functional organization in a dynamic environment. The environment may be changing and the individual may be required to make quick responses to this changing environment. Having to wait for new policy changes to come down the hierarchy may delay the organization from responding appropriately. Decision makers at the top of the organization will also suffer from role conflict when the environment is changing rapidly. In the functional organization, when new situations occur they are referred to higher levels of the organization for decision and action. The result is that top-level decision makers become overloaded and the organization's response to the environment slows down. In a dynamic environment, the functional organization constrains the decision-making adaptation process.

▶ Individuals in the organization also may experience increased role ambiguity—they may be unclear as to what is expected of them in their roles. For example, role ambiguity is likely to occur when the decentralized organization is implemented without some effective use of lateral relations. Individuals may feel they don't have the information needed for decision making. Divisional managers may not know what the corporate staff's policy is on various issues, and corporate staff may have lost touch with the divisions.

These are the kinds of information managers should be aware of as indicators of dysfunctional organization design. These data can be collected in organizational diagnosis surveys that we have developed so that a more systemic monitoring of structure exists just as we monitor organizational climate. As fine tuning the organization's design to its environment becomes more critical organizations will begin to monitor their organizational design more systematically.

Summary

What are the advantages to managers in using the design decision tree? There appear to be several:

1 It provides a *broad framework* for identifying the key factors a manager should think about in considering an organizational design. For example: What is our environment? What different structural options do we have?
2 It forces the manager to *diagnose* the decision environment. What is our environment like? How stable is it? How complex is it? Is it possible to reduce complexity by segmenting the environment into product or geographical subgroups?
3 It causes managers to think about *how much interdependence* there is among segments of the organization. How dependent on one another are different parts of the organization in terms of technology, services, support, help in getting their tasks completed? The decision points in the heuristic forces managers to question themselves about what other parts of the organization they need to coordinate their activities with, and then to think about how to do it.
4 Once the organization is in either a functional or decentralized structure, the decision tree points out what can be done to meet *the increased needs for information* through the use of lateral relations. Lateral relations provide a mechanism

for supplementing the existing structure to facilitate dealing with the organization's increased needs for information and coordination.

Managers in a variety of organizations have commented that the decision tree gives them '. . . a handle for thinking about organizational design so we can tinker with it, fine tune it and make it work better. We don't have to be coerced by structure. We now have a better feel for when certain structures should be used and for the specific steps we can take to make a given structure work.'

Selected bibliography

For a general background on organization theory as its applies to design, see James Thompson's *Organization in Action* (McGraw-Hill, 1967) and Paul Lawrence and Jay Lorsch's *Organizations and Environment* (Irwin, 1967). For a specific treatment of organizational design see Jay Galbraith's *Organizational Design* (Addison-Wesley, 1977) and (with Dan Nathanson) *Strategy Implementation: The Role of Structure and Process* (Sest Publishing, 1978). The Autumn 1977 *Organizational Dynamics* issue was devoted principally to design. Two articles are particularly helpful—Jay Lorsch's 'Organizational Design: A Situational Perspective' pp. 2–14 and Jeffrey Pfeffer and Gerald Salancik's 'Organizational Design: The Case for a Coalitional Model of Organizations' pp. 15–29. For a focus on the learning process regarding design see Robert Duncan and Andrew Weiss's 'Organizational Learning: Implications for Organizational Design' in Barry Staw's (ed.), *Research in Organizational Behavior* (JAI Press, 1978). For an excellent discussion of matrix organizations see Paul Lawrence, Harvey Kolodny, and Stan Davis' 'The Human Side of the Matrix' (*Organizational Dynamics*, Summer 1977) pp. 43–61.

Business Week and *Fortune* magazines provide numerous excellent discussions of organizations facing design problems. For example, see 'Behind the Profit Plunge at Heublein' (*Business Week*, July 4, 1977) pp. 64–65 and 'Selling Is No Longer Mickey Mouse at AT&T' (*Fortune*, July 1978) pp. 84–104.

For an excellent discussion of organizational diagnosis see Marvin Weisbord's *Organizational Diagnosis* (Addison-Wesley, 1978).

part 4 # organizational change and development

critical success factors in change (1992)

'Successful change programs begin with results', by R. H. Schaffer and H. A. Thomson, *Harvard Business Review*, January–February 1992, pp. 80–9.

Reading 17, by Warren Bennis, identifies a number of common features of organization change programmes. One of these is the elapsed time that seems to be required: from two to five years. Many organizations face problems that appear to need a much quicker response than this. Schaffer and Thomson criticize the 'flawed logic' of concentrating change efforts on 'activities' such as participation and training and management development and culture change. They argue instead for change programmes that target results, in the form of measurable improvements that can be achieved quickly. This is one argument behind business process re-engineering which also targets rapid and ambitious and quantifiable outcomes rather than 'soft' changes to organization culture.

learning objectives

Once you have read and understood this article, you should be able to:

1 Distinguish between activity-driven and results-driven approaches to organizational change.
2 Contrast the arguments for a 'quick fix' approach to performance improvement on the one hand, and the 'sustained commitment' through time to organization development on the other.
3 Present a balanced assessment of the strengths and limitations of organization development.

learning pre-requisites

You will find it useful to have read Chapter 16 on organizational change, and Chapter 17 on organization development in the core text, to put the argument of this article into context. This article is highly critical of organization development, and is cited and summarized briefly in the assessment section of Chapter 17 in the core text. The argument of this article is also relevant to the material in Chapter 18, on organization culture.

learning activities

1 You will need to have read this article and Chapters 16 and 17 to complete this learning activity. This is worth taking time over, because the output could be useful for completing coursework in this area, and for answering an examination question. The task is to produce a summary of the arguments, on the one hand for the results-driven 'quick fix' approach, and on the other hand for the 'sustained commitment' required by organization development. Use the following matrix to construct your summary.

2 Using your own judgement, and remembering the contrasting value-bases of these two broad categories, produce your own balanced assessment of the strengths and limitations of organization development. Be prepared to present and defend this judgement.

Approaches to organizational change and development: the debate

Arguments in favour of **sustained commitment** to organization development	Arguments in favour of a **quick fix approach** to performance improvement

READING

16 *Successful change programs begin with results**
Robert H. Schaffer and Harvey A. Thomson†

> Most corporate change programs mistake means for ends, process for outcome.
> The solution: focus on results, not activities.

The performance improvement efforts of many companies have as much impact on
operational and financial results as a ceremonial rain dance has on the weather.
While some companies constantly improve measurable performance, in many others, managers continue to dance round and round the campfire – exuding faith and
dissipating energy.

This 'rain dance' is the ardent pursuit of activities that sound good, look good, and
allow managers to feel good – but in fact contribute little or nothing to bottom-line
performance. These activities, many of which parade under the banner of 'total quality' or 'continuous improvement,' typically advance a managerial philosophy or style
such as interfunctional collaboration, middle management empowerment, or employee involvement. Some focus on measurement of performance such as competitive
benchmarking, assessment of customer satisfaction, or statistical process controls. Still
other activities aim at training employees in problem solving or other techniques.

Companies introduce these programs under the false assumption that if they carry
out enough of the 'right' improvement activities, actual performance improvements
will inevitably materialize. At the heart of these programs, which we call 'activity
centered,' is a fundamentally flawed logic that confuses ends with means, processes
with outcomes. This logic is based on the belief that once managers benchmark their
company's performance against competition, assess their customers' expectations,
and train their employees in seven-step problem solving, sales will increase, inventory will shrink, and quality will improve. Staff experts and consultants tell management that it need not – in fact should not – focus directly on improving results
because eventually results will take care of themselves.

The momentum for activity-centered programs continues to accelerate even
though there is virtually no evidence to justify the flood of investment. Just the opposite: there is plenty of evidence that the rewards from these activities are illusory.

In 1988, for example, one of the largest U.S. financial institutions committed itself
to a 'total quality' program to improve operational performance and win customer
loyalty. The company trained hundreds of people and communicated the program's
intent to thousands more. At the end of two years of costly effort, the program's consultants summarized progress: 'Forty-eight teams up and running. Two completed
Quality Improvement Stories. Morale of employees regarding the process is very
positive to date.' They did not report any bottom-line performance improvements –
because there were none.

The executive vice president of a large mineral-extracting corporation described
the results of his company's three-year-old total quality program by stating, 'We have
accomplished about 50% of our training goals and about 50% of our employee

* Reprinted by permission of *Harvard Business Review*. From 'Successful change programs begin with results'
by R. H. Schaffer and H. A. Thomson, January–February, 1992, pp. 80–9. Copyright © 1992 by the
President and Fellows of Harvard College; all rights reserved.
† *Robert H. Schaffer and Harvey A. Thomson are principals of the management consulting firm, Robert H.
Schaffer & Associates in Stamford, Connecticut and Toronto, Ontario, respectively. This is Mr. Schaffer's
fifth HBR article. In 1988, Harper Business published his book.* The Breakthrough Strategy: Using Short-
Term Successes to Build the High-Performance Organization. *Mr. Thomson was previously associate
professor of management at McGill University in Montreal.*

participation goals but only about 5% of our results goals.' And he considered those results meritorious.

These are not isolated examples. In a 1991 survey of more than 300 electronics companies, sponsored by the American Electronics Association, 73% of the companies reported having a total quality program under way; but of these, 63% had failed to improve quality defects by even as much as 10%. We believe this survey understates the magnitude of the failure of activity-centered programs not only in the quality-conscious electronics industry but across all businesses.

These signs suggest a tragedy in the making: pursuing the present course, companies will not achieve significant progress in their overall competitiveness. They will continue to spend vast resources on a variety of activities, only to watch cynicism grow in the ranks. And eventually, management will discard many potentially useful improvement processes because it expected the impossible of them and came up empty-handed.

If activity-centered programs have yielded such paltry returns on the investment, why are so many companies continuing to pour money and energy into them? For the same reason that previous generations of management invested in zero-based budgeting, Theory Z, and quality circles. Years of frustrating attempts to keep pace with fast-moving competitors make managers prey to almost any plausible approach. And the fact that hundreds of membership associations, professional societies, and consulting firms all promote activity-centered processes lends them an

Figure 1 Most improvement efforts have as much impact on company performance as a rain dance has on the weather

Table 1 Comparing improvement efforts

While activity-centered programs and results-driven programs share some common methodologies for initiating change, they differ in very dramatic ways.

Activity-centered programs	Results-driven programs
1 The improvement effort is defined mainly in long-term global terms. ('We are going to be viewed as number one in quality in our industry.')	1 There are measurable short-term performance improvement goals, even though the effort is a long-term, sustaining one. ('Within 60 days, we will be paying 95% of claims within 10 days.')
2 Management takes action steps because they are 'correct' and fit the program's philosophy. ('I want every manager in the division involved in an action.')	2 Management takes action steps because they appear to lead directly toward some improved results. ('Let's put together a small group to work with you to solve this machine downtime problem.')
3 The program's champion(s) counsels patience and fortitude. ('Don't be looking for results this year or next year. This is a long-term process, not a quick fix.')	3 The mood is one of impatience. Management wants to see results now, even though the change process is a long-term commitment. ('If we can't eliminate at least half of the cost disadvantage within the next three months, we should consider closing the plant.')
4 Staff experts and consultants indoctrinate everyone into the mystique and vocabulary of the program. ('It will be a Tower of Babel if we try to work on these problems before everyone, managers and employees alike, has been through the quality training and has a common vocabulary and a common tool kit.')	4 Staff experts and consultants help managers achieve results. ('We could probably work up a way to measure customer attitudes on delivery service within a week or two so that you can start improving it.')
5 Staff experts and consultants urge managers and employees to have faith in the approach and to support it. ('True employee involvement will take a lot of time and a lot of effort and though it may be a real struggle for managers, they need to understand that it is essential to become a total quality company.')	5 Managers and employees are encouraged to make certain for themselves that the approach actually yields results. ('Why don't you send a few of your people to the quality course to test out whether it really helps them achieve their improvement goals in the next month or two.')
6 The process requires management to make big investments up front – before results have been demonstrated. ('During the first year, we expect to concentrate on awareness building and skill training. Then, while managers begin to diagnose problems and opportunities in their areas, a consultant will be surveying all of our customers to get their views on the 14 critical dimensions of service. And then. . .')	6 Relatively little investment is needed to get the process started; conviction builds as results materialize. ('Let's see if this approach can help us increase sales of high-end products in a couple of branches. If it does, we can take the method to the other branches.')

aura of popularity and legitimacy. As a consequence, many senior managers have become convinced that all of these preparatory activities really will pay off some day and that there isn't a viable alternative.

They are wrong on both counts. Any payoffs from the infusion of activities will be meager at best. And there is in fact an alternative: results-driven improvement processes that focus on achieving specific, measurable operational improvements within a few months. This means increased yields, reduced delivery time, increased inventory turns, improved customer satisfaction, reduced product development time. With results-driven improvements, a company introduces only those innovations in management methods and business processes that can help achieve specific goals. (See Table 1, 'Comparing Improvement Efforts.')

An automotive-parts plant, whose customers were turning away from it because of poor quality and late deliveries, illustrates the difference between the two approaches. To solve the company's problems, management launched weekly employee-involvement team meetings focused on improving quality. By the end of six months, the teams had generated hundreds of suggestions and abundant goodwill in the plant but virtually no improvement in quality or delivery.

In a switch to a results-driven approach, management concentrated on one production line. The plant superintendent asked the manager of that line to work with his employees and with plant engineering to reduce by 30% the frequency of their most prevalent defect within two months. This sharply focused goal was reached on time. The manager and his team next agreed to cut the occurrence of that same defect by an additional 50%. They also broadened the effort to encompass other kinds of defects on the line. Plant management later extended the process to other production lines, and within about four months the plant's scrap rate was within budgeted limits.

Both activity-centered and results-driven strategies aim to strengthen fundamental corporate competitiveness. But as the automotive-parts plant illustrates, the approaches differ dramatically. The activities path is littered with the remains of endless preparatory investments that failed to yield desired outcomes. The results-driven path stakes out specific targets and matches resources, tools, and action plans to the requirements of reaching those targets. As a consequence, managers know what they are trying to achieve, how and when it should be done, and how it can be evaluated.

The activity-centered fallacy

There are six reasons why the cards are stacked against activity-centered improvement programs:

1 *Not Keyed to Specific Results.* In activity-centered programs, managers reform the way they work with each other and with employees; they train people; they develop new measurement schemes; they increase employee awareness of customer attitudes, quality, and more. The expectation is that these steps will lead to better business performance. But managers rarely make explicit how the activity is supposed to lead to the result.

Seeking to improve quality, senior management at a large telecommunications equipment corporation sent a number of unit managers to quality training workshops. When they returned, the unit heads ordered orientation sessions for middle management. They also selected and trained facilitators who, in turn, trained hundreds of supervisors and operators in statistical process control. But senior management never specified which performance parameters it wanted to improve – costs, reject rates, delivery timeliness. During the following year, some units improved performance along some dimensions, other units improved along others, and still other units saw no improvement at all. There was no way for management to assess whether there was any connection between the investment in training and specific, tangible results.

2 *Too Large Scale and Diffused.* The difficulty of connecting activities to the bottom line is complicated by the fact that most companies choose to launch a vast array of activities simultaneously across the entire organization. This is like researching a cure for a disease by giving a group of patients ten different new drugs at the same time.

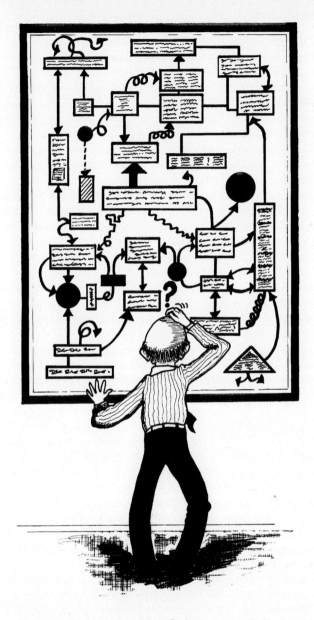

Figure 2 One company identified so many activities in so many places, it required a complex chart just to describe them

In one case, a large international manufacturer identified almost 50 different activities that it wanted built into its total quality effort. The company's list involved so many programs introduced in so many places that just to describe them all required a complex chart. Once top managers had made the investment and the public commitment, however, they 'proved' their wisdom by crediting the programs for virtually any competitive gain the company made. But in fact, no one knew for sure which, if any, of the 50 activities were actually working.

3 *Results Is a Four-Letter Word.* When activity-centered programs fail to produce improvement in financial and operational performance, managers seldom complain lest they be accused of preoccupation with the short term at the expense of the long

term – the very sin that has supposedly caused companies to defer investment in capital and human resources and thus to lose their competitive edge. It is a brave manager who will insist on seeing a demonstrable link between the proposed investment and tangible payoffs in the short term.

When one company had little to show for the millions of dollars it invested in improvement activities, the chief operations officer rationalized, 'You can't expect to overturn 50 years of culture in just a couple of years.' And he urged his management team to persevere in its pursuit of the activities.

He is not alone in his faith that, given enough time, activity-centered efforts will pay off. The company cited above, with almost 50 improvement activities going at once, published with pride its program's timetable calling for three years of preparations and reformations, with major results expected only in the fourth year. And at a large electronics company, the manual explaining its management-empowerment process warned that implementation could be 'painful' and that management should not expect to see results for a 'long time'.

4 *Delusional Measurements.* Having conveyed the false message that activities will inevitably produce results, the activities promoters compound the crime by equating measures of activities with actual improvements in performance. Companies proclaim their quality programs with the same pride with which they would proclaim real performance improvements – ignoring or perhaps even unaware of the significance of the difference.

In a leading U.S. corporation, we found that a group of quality facilitators could not enumerate the critical business goals of their units. Surprised, we asked how they could possibly assess whether or not they were successful. Their answer: success consisted of getting 100% of each unit's managers and employees to attend the prescribed quality training – a centerpiece of the corporation's total quality program.

The Malcolm Baldrige National Quality Award encourages such practices by devoting only 180 points out of a possible 1,000 points to quality results. The award gives high marks to companies that demonstrate outstanding quality processes without always demanding that the current products and services be equally outstanding.

5 *Staff- and Consultant-Driven.* The focus on activities as ends in themselves is exacerbated by the fact that improvement programs are usually designed by staff specialists, external consultants, or other experts, rather than by operating managers. In many cases, managers seek this outside help because they have exhausted their own ideas about improvement. So when staff experts and improvement gurus show up with their evangelistic enthusiasm and bright promises of total quality and continuous improvement, asking only for faith and funds, managers greet them with open arms.

But the capability of most of these improvement experts is limited to installing discrete, often generic packages of activities that are rarely aimed directly at specific results. They design training courses; they launch self-directed teams; they create new quality-measurement systems; they organize campaigns to win the Baldrige Award. Senior managers plunge wholeheartedly into these activities, relieving themselves, momentarily at least, of the burden of actually having to improve performance.

The automotive-parts plant described earlier illustrates the pattern. Senior managers had become very frustrated after a number of technical solutions failed to cure the plant's ills. When a staff group then asserted that employee involvement could produce results, management quickly accepted the staff group's suggestion to initiate employee-involvement team meetings – meetings that failed to deliver results.

The futility of expecting staff-driven programs to yield performance improvement was highlighted in a study conducted by a Harvard Business School team headed by

Michael Beer. It analyzed a number of large-scale corporate change programs, some of which had succeeded, others of which had failed. The study found that company-wide change programs installed by staff groups did not lead to successful transformation. As the authors colorfully put it, 'Wave after wave of programs rolled across the landscape with little positive impact.'[1]

6 *Bias to Orthodoxy, Not Empiricism.* Because of the absence of clear-cut beginnings and ends and an inability to link cause and effect, there is virtually no opportunity in activity-centered improvement programs to learn useful lessons and apply them to future programs. Instead, as in any approach based on faith rather than evidence, the advocates – convinced they already know all the answers – merely urge more dedication to the 'right' steps.

One manufacturing company, for example, launched almost 100 quality improvement teams as a way to 'get people involved.' These teams produced scores of recommendations for process changes. The result was stacks of work orders piling up in maintenance, production engineering, and systems departments – more than any of these groups were capable of responding to. Senior managers, however, believed the outpouring of suggestions reinforced their original conviction that participation would succeed. Ignoring mounting evidence that the process was actually counter-productive, they determined to get even more teams established.

Results-driven transformation

In stark contrast to activity-centered programs, results-driven improvements bypass lengthy preparation rituals and aim at accomplishing measurable gains rapidly. Consider the case of the Morgan Bank. When told that his units would have to compete on an equal footing with outside vendors, the senior vice president of the bank's administrative services (responsible for 20 service functions including printing, food services, and purchasing) realized that the keys to survival were better service and lower costs. To launch a response, he asked the head of each of the service functions to select one or two service-improvement goals that were important to internal 'customers' and could be achieved quickly. Unit heads participated in several workshops and worked with consultants but always maintained a clear focus on launching the improvement processes that would enable them to achieve their goals.

In the bank's microfilm department, for example, the first goal was to meet consistently a 24-hour turnaround deadline for the work of a stock-transfer department. The microfilm department had frequently missed this deadline, sometimes by several days. The three shift supervisors and their manager laid out a five-week plan to accomplish the goal. They introduced a number of work-process innovations, each selected on the basis of its capacity to help achieve the 24-hour turnaround goal, and tracked performance improvements daily.

This project, together with similar results-driven projects simultaneously carried out in the other 19 units, yielded significant service improvements and several million dollars of cost savings within the first year of the initiative – just about the time it usually takes to design the training programs and get all employees trained in a typical activity-centered effort. The experience of the Morgan Bank illustrates four key benefits of a results-driven approach that activity-centered programs generally miss:

1 *Companies introduce managerial and process innovations only as they are needed.* Results-driven projects require managers to prioritize carefully the innovations they want to employ to achieve targeted goals. Managers introduce modifications in

1. See Michael Beer, Russell A. Eisenstat, and Bert Spector, 'Why Change Programs Don't Produce Change,' HBR November–December 1990, p. 158.

management style, work methods, goal setting, information systems, and customer relationships in a just-in-time mode when the change appears capable of speeding progress toward measurable goals. Contrast this with activity-centered programs, where all employees may be ritualistically sent off for training because it is the 'right' thing to do.

In the Morgan Bank's microfilm department project, the three shift supervisors worked together as a unified team – not to enhance teamwork but to figure out how to reduce customer delivery time. For the first time ever, they jointly created a detailed improvement work plan and week-by-week subgoals. They posted this work plan next to a chart showing daily performance. Employees on all three shifts actively participated in the project, offering suggestions for process changes, receiving essential training that was immediately applied, and taking responsibility for implementation.

Thus instead of making massive investments to infuse the organization with a hodgepodge of improvement activities, the microfilm department and each of the other administrative services introduced innovations incrementally, in support of specific performance goals.

2 *Empirical testing reveals what works.* Because management introduces each managerial and process innovation sequentially and links them to short-term goals, it can discover fairly quickly the extent to which each approach yields results. In the Morgan Bank's microfilm department, for example, the creation of a detailed improvement work plan and week-by-week subgoals – which were introduced during the first two weeks of the program – enabled management to assess accurately and quickly the impact of its actions in meeting the 24-hour turnaround goal.

New procedures for communicating between shifts allowed management to anticipate workload peaks and to reassign personnel from one shift to another. That innovation contributed to meeting deadlines. A new numbering system to identify the containers of work from different departments did not contribute, and management quickly abandoned the innovation. By constantly assessing how each improvement step contributed to meeting deadlines, management made performance improvement less an act of faith and more an act of rational decision making based on evidence.

3 *Frequent reinforcement energizes the improvement process.* There is no motivator more powerful than frequent successes. By replacing large-scale, amorphous improvement objectives with short-term, incremental projects that quickly yield tangible results, managers and employees can enjoy the psychological fruits of success. Demonstrating to themselves their capacity to succeed not only provides necessary reinforcement but also builds management's confidence and skill for continued incremental improvements.

The manager of the bank's microfilm department, for example, had never had the experience of leading a significant upgrading of performance. It was not easy for her to launch the process in the face of employee skepticism. Within a few weeks, however, when the chart on the wall showed the number of missed deadlines going down, everyone took pleasure in seeing it, and work went forward with renewed vigor. The manager's confidence grew and so did employee support for the subsequent changes she implemented.

In another example, a division of Motorola wanted to accelerate new product development. To get started, a management team selected two much-delayed mobile two-way radios and focused on bringing these products to the market within 90 days. For each product, the team created a unified, multifunction work plan; appointed a single manager to oversee the entire development process as the product moved from department to department; and designated an interfunctional team to monitor progress. With these and other innovations, both radios were launched on time. This success encouraged management to extend the innovations to other new product projects and eventually to the entire product development process.

4 *Management creates a continuous learning process by building on the lessons of previous phases in designing the next phase of the program.* Both activity-centered and results-driven programs are ultimately aimed at producing fundamental shifts in the performance of the organization. But unlike activity-centered programs that focus on sweeping cultural changes, large-scale training programs, and massive process innovation, results-driven programs begin by identifying the most urgently needed performance improvements and carving off incremental goals to achieve quickly.

By using each incremental project as a testing ground for new ways of managing, measuring, and organizing for results, management gradually creates a foundation of experience on which to build an organization-wide performance improvement. Once the manager of Morgan's microfilm department succeeded in meeting the 24-hour turnaround goal for one internal customer department, she extended the process to other customer departments.

In each of the other 19 service units, the same expansion was taking place. Unit managers shared their experiences in formal review conferences so that everyone could benefit from the best practices. Within six months, every manager and supervisor in administrative services was actively leading one or more improvement projects. From a base of real results, managers were able to encourage a continuous improvement process to spread, and they introduced dozens of managerial innovations in the course of achieving sizable performance gains.

Putting the ideas into practice

Taking advantage of the power of results-driven improvements calls for a subtle but profound shift in mind-set: management begins by identifying the performance improvements that are most urgently needed and then, instead of studying and preparing and gearing up and delaying, sets about at once to achieve some measurable progress in a short time.

The Eddystone Generating Station of Philadelphia Electric, once the world's most efficient fossil-fuel plant, illustrates the successful shift from activity-centered to results-driven improvement. As Eddystone approached its thirtieth anniversary, its thermal efficiency – the amount of electricity produced from each ton of coal burned – had declined significantly. The problem was serious enough that top management was beginning to question the plant's continued operation.

The station's engineers had initiated many corrective actions, including installing a state-of-the-art computerized system to monitor furnace efficiency, upgrading plant equipment and materials, and developing written procedures for helping operating staff run the plant more efficiently. But because the innovations were not built into the day-to-day operating routine of the plant, thermal efficiency tended to deteriorate when the engineers turned their attention elsewhere.

In September 1990, the superintendent of operations decided to take a results-driven approach to improve thermal efficiency. He and his management team committed to achieve a specific incremental improvement of thermal efficiency worth about $500,000 annually – without any additional plant investment. To get started, they identified a few improvements that they could accomplish within three months and established teams to tackle each one.

A five-person team of operators and maintenance employees and one supervisor took responsibility for reducing steam loss from hundreds of steam valves throughout

Figure 3 At a power station, two tons of coal dumped in the manager's parking space dramatized poor thermal efficiency

the plant. The team members started by eliminating all the leaks in one area of the plant. Then they moved on to other areas. In the process, they invented improvements in valve-packing practices and devised new methods for reporting leaks.

Another employee team was assigned the task of reducing heat that escaped through openings in the huge furnaces. For its first subproject, the group ensured that all 96 inspection doors on the furnace walls were operable and were closed when not in use. Still another team, this one committed to reducing the amount of unburned carbon that passed through the furnace, began by improving the operating effectiveness of the station's coal-pulverizer mills in order to improve the carbon burn rate.

Management charged each of these cross-functional teams not merely with studying and recommending but also with producing measurable results in a methodical, step-by-step fashion. A steering committee of station managers met every two weeks to review progress and help overcome obstacles. A variety of communication mechanisms built awareness of the project and its progress. For example, to launch the process, the steering committee piled two tons of coal in the station manager's parking space to dramatize the hourly cost of poor thermal efficiency. In a series of 'town meetings' with all employees, managers explained the reason for the effort and how it would work. Newsletters reviewed progress on the projects – including the savings realized – and credited employees who had contributed to the effort.

As each team reached its goal, the steering committee, in consultation with supervisors and employees, identified the next series of performance improvement goals, such as the reduction of the plant's own energy consumption, and commissioned a number of teams and individuals to implement a new round of projects. By the end of the first year, efficiency improvements were saving the company over $1 million a year, double the original goal.

Beyond the monetary gains – gains achieved with negligible investment –

Eddystone's organizational structure began to change in profound ways. What had been a hierarchical, tradition-bound organization became more flexible and open to change. Setting and achieving ambitious short-term goals became part of the plant's regular routine as managers pushed decisions further and further down into the organization. Eventually, the station manager disbanded the steering committee, and now everyone who manages improvement projects reports directly to the senior management team.

Eddystone managers and workers at all levels continue to experiment and have invented a number of highly creative efficiency-improving processes. A change so profound could never have happened by sending all employees to team training classes and then telling them, 'Now you are empowered; go to it.'

In the course of accomplishing its results, Eddystone management introduced many of the techniques that promoters of activity-centered programs insist must be drilled into the organization for months or years before gains can be expected: employees received training in various analytical techniques; team-building exercises helped teams achieve their goals more quickly; teams introduced new performance measurements as they were needed; and managers analyzed and redesigned work processes. But unlike activity-centered programs, the results-driven work teams introduced innovations only if they could contribute to the realization of short-term goals. They did not inject innovations wholesale in the hope that they would somehow generate better results. There was never any doubt that responsibility for results was in the hands of accountable managers.

Philadelphia Electric – and many other companies as well – launched its results-driven improvement process with a few modest pilot projects. Companies that want to launch large-scale change, however, can employ a results-driven approach across a broad front. In 1988, chairman John F. Welch, Jr. launched General Electric's 'Work-Out' process across the entire corporation. The purpose was to overcome bureaucracy and eliminate business procedures that interfered with customer responsiveness. The response of GE's $3 billion Lighting Business illustrates how such a large-scale improvement process can follow a results-driven pathway.

Working sessions attended by a large cross-section of Lighting employees, a key feature of Work-Out, identified a number of 'quick wins' in target areas. These were initiatives that employees could take right away to generate measurable improvement in a short time. To speed new product development, for example, Work-Out participants recommended that five separate functional review sessions be combined into one, a suggestion that was eagerly adopted. To get products to customers more quickly, a team tested the idea of working with customers and a trucking company to schedule, in advance, regular delivery days for certain customers. The results of the initial pilot were so successful that GE Lighting has extended the scheduling system to hundreds of customers.

Another team worked to reduce the breakage of fragile products during shipment – costly both in direct dollars and in customer dissatisfaction. Subteams, created to investigate package design and shipping-pallet construction, followed sample shipments from beginning to end and asked customers for their ideas. Within weeks, the team members had enough information to shift to remedial action. They tried many innovations in the packaging design; they modified work processes in high-risk areas; they reduced the number of times each product is handled, they collaborated with their shippers, suppliers, and customers. The payoff was a significant reduction in breakage within a few months.

The Lighting Business has launched dozens of such results-oriented projects quickly – and as each project achieves results, management has launched additional projects and has even extended the process to its European operations.

Opportunities for change

There is no reason for senior-level managers to acquiesce when their people plead that they are already accomplishing just about all that can be accomplished or that factors beyond their control – company policy, missing technology, or lack of resources – are blocking accelerated performance improvement. Such self-limiting ideas are universal. Instead, management needs to recognize that there is an abundance of both underexploited capability and dissipated resources in the organization.

This orientation frees managers to set about translating potential into results and to avoid the cul-de-sac of fixing up and reforming the organization in preparation for future progress. Here is how management can get started in results-driven programs:

1 *Ask each unit to set and achieve a few ambitious short-term performance goals.* There is no organization where management could not start to improve performance quickly with the resources at hand – even in the face of attitudinal and skill deficiencies, personnel and other resource limitations, unstable market conditions, and every other conceivable obstacle. To begin with, managers can ask unit heads to commit to achieve in a short time some improvement targets, such as faster turnaround time in responding to customers, lower costs, increased sales, or improved cash flow. They should also be asked to test some managerial, process, or technical innovations that can help them reach their goals.

2 *Periodically review progress, capture the essential learning, and reformulate strategy.* Results-driven improvement is an empirical process in which managers use the experience of each phase as data for shaping the next phase. In scheduled work sessions, senior management should review and evaluate progress on the current array of results-focused projects and learn what is and what isn't working.

Fresh insights flood in from these early experiments: how rapidly project teams can make gains; what kind of support they need; what changes in work methods they can implement quickly; what kinds of obstacles need to be addressed at higher levels in the organization. Managers and employees develop confidence in their capacity to get things done and to challenge and overturn obsolete practices.

Armed with this learning, senior management can refine strategies and timetables and, in consultation with their people, can carve out the next round of business goals. The cycle repeats and expands as confidence and momentum grow.

3 *Institutionalize the changes that work – and discard the rest.* As management gains experience, it can take steps to institutionalize the practices and technologies that contribute most to performance improvement and build those into the infrastructure of the company. In Motorola's Mobile Division, for example, in its new product development project, a single manager was assigned responsibility for moving each new product from engineering to production and to delivery, as opposed to having this responsibility handed off from function to function. This worked so well it became standard practice.

Such change can also take place at the policy level. A petroleum company, for example, experimented with incentive compensation in two sales districts. When the trials produced higher sales growth, senior management decided to install throughout the marketing function a performance-based compensation plan that reflected what it had learned in the experiments. In this way, a company can gradually build successful innovations into its operations and discard unsuccessful ones before they do much harm.

4 *Create the context and identify the crucial business challenges.* Senior management must establish the broader framework to guide continuing performance improvement in the form of strategic directions for the business and a 'vision' of how it will operate in the future. A creative vision can be a source of inspiration and

motivation for managers and employees who are being asked to help bring about change. But no matter how imaginative the vision might be, for it to contribute to accelerated progress, managers must translate it into sharp and compelling expectations for short-term performance achievements. At Philadelphia Electric, for example, the Eddystone improvement work responded to top management's insistent call for performance improvement and cost reduction.

A results-driven improvement process does not relieve senior management of the responsibility to make the difficult strategic decisions necessary for the company's survival and prosperity. General Electric's Work-Out process augmented but could never substitute for Jack Welch's dramatic restructuring and downsizing moves. By marrying long-term strategic objectives with short-term improvement projects, however, management can translate strategic direction into reality and resist the temptation to inculcate the rain dance of activity-centered programs.

early applications of organization development techniques (1965)

'Theory and method in applying behavioral science to planned organizational change', by Warren G. Bennis, *Applied Behavioral Science*, vol. 1, no. 4, 1965, pp. 337–60.

This article was written over thirty years ago by one of the key founding figures in the organization development movement. Much of the content, however, still applies today, particularly the concerns with a broad-based, strategic, or systems approach to change, with participative approaches to organization development, with measures of effectiveness of interventions, and with the values underpinning the approach. Practitioners still expect planned change in organizations to benefit from social science knowledge. Theories of social and organizational change, however, appear to be of more value to observers than to practitioners, as Bennis complains. Implementation remains problematic.

learning objectives

Once you have read and understood this article, you should be able to:

1 Summarize Bennis' arguments about the features of valid knowledge, adequate theories of change, the flaws in most change programmes, and the factors behind effective change.
2 Understand the organization development strategies proposed by Robert Blake and by Chris Argyris, and their common features.

learning pre-requisites

You will find it useful to read Chapters 16 and 17 in the core text, on organizational change and development respectively. The argument of this article is also relevant to the discussion about the practical contributions of the social sciences, from Chapter 2 in the core text, and in Reading 2 in this volume.

learning activities

Make your own brief summary notes from this article on the following key points:

(a) Bennis notes *four* reasons for 'the emphasis on application'. What are they?
(b) Bennis argues that a theory of change should have *seven* elements. Summarize them.
(c) Bennis identifies *seven* criteria for valid knowledge. Summarize these.
(d) Bennis identifies *four* flaws in most change programmes. Restate these in positive, 'must have' terms rather than the article's 'don't have' terms.
(e) Bennis describes two organization development strategies, from Robert Blake and from Chris Argyris. He claims that these approaches have *six* features in common. What are these?

(f) Bennis identifies *four* necessary elements for effective organizational change implementation. Summarize these.

 READING **17** *Theory and method in applying behavioral science to planned organizational change**
Warren G. Bennis†

Three assumptions underlie this paper:[1] (1) that the proportion of contemporary change that is planned or that issues from deliberate innovation is much higher than in former times; (2) that man's wisdom and mundane behavior are somewhat short of perfection insofar as they regulate the fate and selective adaptation of complex human organizations; (3) that behavioral scientists in increasing numbers are called upon to influence organizational functioning and effectiveness. The paper is concerned with the strategic, methodological, and conceptual issues brought about by the emergence of the action role of the behavioral scientist.

What we have witnessed in the past two or three decades has been called the 'Rise of the Rational Spirit'—the belief that science can help to better the human condition (Merton & Lerner, 1951). The focus of this paper is on one indication of this trend: the emerging role for the behavioral scientist and, more specifically, the attempts by behavioral scientists to apply knowledge (primarily sociological and psychological) toward the improvement of human organizations.

The emergence of the action role

Many signs and activities point toward an emerging action role for the behavioral scientist. The *manipulative standpoint*, as Lasswell calls it, is becoming distinguishable from the *contemplative standpoint* and is increasingly ascendant insofar as knowledge utilization is concerned.[2] Evidence can be found in the growing literature on planned change through the uses of the behavioral sciences (Bennis, Benne & Chin, 1961; Freeman, 1963; Zetterberg, 1962; Gibb & Lippitt, 1959; Leeds & Smith, 1963; Likert & Hayes, 1957; Glock, Lippitt, Flanagan, Wilson, Shartle, Wilson, Croker, & Page, 1960) and in such additions to the vocabulary of the behavioral scientist as action research, client system, change agent, clinical sociology, knowledge centers, social catalysts. The shift is also reflected in increased emphasis on application in annual meeting time of the professional associations or in the formation of a Center for Research on the Utilization of Scientific Knowledge within The University of Michigan's Institute for Social Research.

It is probably true that in the United States there is a more practical attitude toward knowledge than anywhere else. When Harrison Salisbury (1960) traveled over Europe he was impressed with the seeming disdain of European intellectuals for practical matters. Even in Russia he found little interest in the 'merely useful.'

* Reprinted by permission from *Applied Behavioral Science*, Vol. 1, No. 4 (1965), 337–60.
† President, University of Cincinnati.
[1] Drawn from keynote address presented at International Conference on Operational Research and the Social Sciences, Cambridge, England, September 1964.
[2] For an excellent discussion of the 'value' issues in this development, see A. Kaplan, *The conduct of inquiry*. San Francisco: Chandler, 1964, chap. 10; and K. D. Benne and G. Swanson, (eds.), Values and social issues. *Journal of Social Issues*, Vol. 6 (1960).

Salisbury saw only one great agricultural experiment station on the American model. In that case professors were working in the fields. They told him, 'People call us Americans.'

Not many American professors may be found working in the fields, but they can be found almost everywhere else: in factories, in the government, in underdeveloped countries, in mental hospitals, in educational systems. They are advising, counseling, researching, recruiting, developing, consulting, training. Americans may not have lost their deep ambivalence toward the intellectual, but it is clear that the academic intellectual has become *engagé* with spheres of action in greater numbers, with more diligence, and with higher aspirations than at any other time in history.

It may be useful to speculate about the reasons for the shift in the intellectual climate. Most important, but trickiest to identify, are those causative factors bound up in the warp and woof of 'our times and age' that Professor Boring calls the *Zeitgeist*. The apparently growing disenchantment with the moral neutrality of the scientist may be due, in C. P. Snow's phrase, to the fact that 'scientists cannot escape their own knowledge.' In any event, though 'impurity' is still implied, action research as distinguished from pure research does not carry the opprobrium it once did.

Perhaps the crucial reason for the shift in emphasis toward application is simply that we know more.[3] Since World War II we have obtained large bodies of research and diverse reports on application. We are today in a better position to assess results and potentialities of applied social science.

Finally, there is a fourth factor having to do with the fate and viability of human organization, particularly as it has been conceptualized as 'bureaucracy.' I use the term in its sociological, Weberian sense, not as a metaphor *à la* Kafka's *The Castle* connoting 'red tape,' impotency, inefficiency, despair. In the past three decades Weber's vision has been increasingly scrutinized and censured. Managers and practitioners, on the one hand and organizational theorists and researchers on the other, are more and more dissatisfied with current practices of organizational behavior and are searching for new forms and patterns of organizing for work. A good deal of activity is being generated.

The lack of a viable theory of social change

Unfortunately, no viable theory of social change has been established. Indeed it is a curious fact about present theories that they are strangely silent on matters of *directing* and *implementing* change. What I particularly object to—and I include the 'newer' theories of neo-conflict (Coser, 1956; Dahrendorf, 1961), neo-functionalism (Boskoff, 1964), and neo-revolutionary theories—is that they tend to explain the dynamic interaction of a system without providing one clue to the identification of strategic leverages for alteration. They are suitable for *observers* of social change, not for practitioners. They are theories of *change*, and not of *changing*.

It may be helpful to suggest quickly some of the prerequisites for a theory of changing. I am indebted here to my colleague Robert Chin (1961, 1963):

(a) A theory of changing must include manipulable variables—accessible levers for influencing the direction, tempo, and quality of change and improvement.
(b) The variables must not violate the client system's values.
(c) The cost of usage cannot be prohibitive.
(d) There must be provided a reliable basis of diagnosing the strength and weakness

---

[3] For a recent inventory of scientific findings of the behavioral sciences, see B. Berelson and G. A. Steiner, *Human behavior*. New York: Harcourt, Brace & World, 1964.

of conditions facing the client system.

(e) Phases of intervention must be clear so that the change agent can develop estimates for termination of the relationship.

(f) The theory must be communicable to the client system.

(g) It must be possible to assess appropriateness of the theory for different client systems.

Such a theory does not now exist, and this probably explains why change agents appear to write like 'theoretical orphans' and, more important, why so many change programs based on theories of social change have been inadequate. This need should be kept in mind as we look at models of knowledge utilization.

The notion of planned change

Planned change can be viewed as a linkage between theory and practice, between knowledge and action. It plays this role by converting variables from the basic disciplines into strategic instrumentation and programs. Historically, the development of planned change can be seen as the result of two forces: complex problems requiring expert help and the growth and viability of the behavioral sciences. The term 'behavioral sciences' itself is of post-World War II vintage coined by the more empirically minded to 'safeguard' the social disciplines from the non-quantitative humanists and the depersonalized abstractions of the econometricists. The process of planned change involves a *change agent*, a *client system*, and the collaborative attempt to apply *valid knowledge* to the client's problems.[4]

Elsewhere I have attempted a typology of change efforts in which planned change is distinguished from other types of change in that it entails mutual goal setting, an equal power ratio (eventually), and deliberateness on both sides (Bennis et al. 1961, p. 154).

It may further help in defining planned change to compare it with another type of deliberate change effort, Operations Research. I enter this with a humility bordering on fear and a rueful sense of kinship in our mutual incapacity to explain to one another the nature of our work. There are these similarities. Both are World War II products: both are problem centered (though both have also provided inputs to the concepts and method of their parent disciplines).[5] Both emphasize improvement and to that extent are *normative* in their approach to problems. Both rely heavily on empirical science; both rely on a relationship of confidence and valid communication with clients; both emphasize a *systems* approach to problems—that is, both are aware of interdependence within the system as well as boundary maintenance with its environment; and both appear to be most effective when working with systems which are complex, rapidly changing, and probably science-based.

Perhaps the most crucial difference between OR and planned change has to do with the identification of strategic variables, that is, with those factors which appear to make a difference in the performance of the system. Planned change is concerned with such problems as (1) the identification of mission and values, (2) collaboration and conflict, (3) control and leadership, (4) resistance and adaptation to change, (5) utilization of human resources, (6) communication, (7) management development. OR practitioners tend to select economic or engineering variables which are more quantitative, measurable, and linked to profit and efficiency. Ackoff and Rivett

---

[4] For a fuller discussion, see R. Lippitt, J. Watson, and B. Westley, *The dynamics of planned change.* New York: Harcourt, Brace & World, 1961; and Bennis et al. (1961).

[5] For a brilliant exposition on the contributions of applied research to 'pure' theory, see A. Gouldner, Theoretical requirements of the applied social sciences, in Bennis et al. (1961)., pp. 83–95.

(1963), for example, classify OR problems under (1) inventory, (2) allocation, (3) queuing, (4) sequencing, (5) routing, (6) replacement, (7) competition, (8) search.

A second major difference has to do with the perceived importance of the relationship with the client. In planned change, the quality and nature of the relationship are used as indicators for the measure of progress and as valid sources of data and diagnosis. Undoubtedly, the most successful OR practitioners operate with sensitivity toward their clients; but if one looks at what they *say* about their work, they are clearly less concerned with human interactions.

A third major difference is that the OR practitioner devotes a large portion of his time to research, to problem solving. The change agent tends to spend somewhat more time on implementation through counseling, training, management development schemes, and so forth. Fourth, planned-change agents tend to take less seriously the idea of the *system* in their approaches. Finally, the idea of all interdisciplinary teams, central to OR does not seem to be a part of most planned-change programs.

One thing that emerges from this comparison is a realization of the complexity of modern organization. Look through the kaleidoscope one way, and a configuration of the economic and technological factors appears; tilt it, and what emerges is a pattern of internal human relations problems. It is on these last problems and their effects upon performance of the system that practitioners of planned organizational change tend to work.

A focus of convenience

To develop what George Kelley refers to as a 'focus of convenience' for planned organizational change, I want to make two key aspects clearer: the notions of 'collaborative relationships' and of 'valid knowledge.' I see the outcome of planned-change efforts as depending to some considerable extent on the relationship between client and agent. To optimize a collaborative relationship, there needs to be a 'spirit of inquiry,' with data publicly shared, and equal freedom to terminate the relationship and to influence the other.

As to valid knowledge, the criteria are based on the requirements for a viable applied behavioral science research—an applied behavioral science that:

(a) Takes into consideration the behavior of persons operating within their specific institutional environments;

(b) Is capable of accounting for the interrelated levels (person, group, role, organization) within the context of the social change;

(c) Includes variables that the policy maker and practitioner can understand, manipulate, and evaluate;

(d) Can allow selection of variables appropriate in terms of its own values, ethics, moralities;

(e) Accepts the premise that groups and organizations as units are amenable to empirical and analytic treatment;

(f) Takes into account external social processes of changes as well as interpersonal aspects of the collaborative process;

(g) Includes propositions susceptible to empirical test focusing on the dynamics of change.

These criteria must be construed as an arbitrary goal, not as all existing reality. To my knowledge, there is no program which fulfills these requirements fully. In this focus of convenience. I have arbitrarily selected change agents working on organizational dynamics partly because of my greater familiarity with their work but also because they seem to fulfill the criteria outlined to a greater extent than do other change agents. My choice of emphasis is also based on the belief that changes in the sphere of organizations—primarily industrial—in patterns of work and relationship, structure, technology, and administration promise some of the most significant changes in our society. Indeed it is my guess that industrial society, at least in the United States, is more radical, innovative, and adventurous in adapting new ways of organizing than the government, the universities, and labor unions, who appear rigid and stodgy in the face of rapid change. If space permitted, however, I would refer also to change agents working in a variety of fields—rural sociology, economics, anthropology—and in such settings as communities, hospitals, cultural-change programs.

Let us turn now to some of the 'traditional' models of knowledge utilization.

Eight types of change programs [6]

It is possible to identify eight types of change programs if we examine their strategic rationale: exposition and propagation, élite corps, human relations training, staff, scholarly consultations, circulation of ideas to the élite, developmental research, and action research.

I should like to look at each of these programs quickly and then refer to four biases which seem to me to weaken their impact.

Exposition and propagation, perhaps the most popular type of program, assumes that knowledge is power. It follows that the men who possess 'Truth' will lead the world.

Elite corps programs grow from the realization that ideas by themselves do not constitute action and that a strategic *role* is a necessity for ideas to be implemented (e.g., through getting scientists into government as C. P. Snow suggests).

Human relations training programs are similar to the élite corps idea in the attempt to translate behavioral science concepts in such ways that they take on personal referents for the men in power positions.

Staff programs provide a source of intelligence within the client system, as in the work of social anthropologists advising military governors after World War II. The strategy of the staff idea is to observe, analyze, and to plan rationally (Myrdal, 1958).

Scholarly consultation, as defined by Zetterberg (1962), includes exploratory inquiry, scholarly understanding, confrontation, discovery of solutions, and scientific advice to client.

Circulation of ideas to the élite builds on the simple idea of influencing change by getting to the people with power or influence.

Developmental research has to do with seeing whether an idea can be brought to an engineering stage. Unlike Zetterberg's scholarly confrontation, it is directed toward a particular problem, not necessarily a client, and is concerned with implementation and program. (I would wager that *little* developmental research is being done today in the behavioral sciences.)

Action research, the term coined by Kurt Lewin, undertakes to solve a problem for a client. It is identical to applied research generally except that in action research the roles of researcher and subject may change and reverse, the subjects becoming researchers engaging in action steps.

These eight programs, while differing in objectives, values, means of influence, and program implications, are similar in wanting to use knowledge to gain some

---

[6] For a fuller exposition of these ideas, see my paper, A new role for the behavioral sciences: Effecting organizational change. *Administrative Science Quarterly*, Vol. 8 (1963), pp. 125–65.

socially desirable end. Each seems successful or promising; each has its supporters and its detractors. Intrinsic to them all, I believe, is some bias or flaw which probably weakens their full impact. Four biases are particularly visible.

Rationalistic bias: no implementation of program

Most of the strategies rely almost totally on rationality. But knowledge *about* something does *not* lead automatically to intelligent action. Intelligent action requires commitment and programs as well as truth.

Technocratic bias: no spirit of collaboration

Change typically involves risk and fear. Any significant change in human organization involves rearrangement of patterns of power, association, status, skills, and values. Some may benefit, others may lose. Thus change typically involves risk and fear. Yet change efforts sometimes are conducted as if there were no need to discuss and 'work through' these fears and worries (e.g., F. W. Taylor's failure to consider the relationship between the engineer with the stopwatch and the worker, or Freud's early work when he considered it adequate to examine the unconscious of his patients and tell them what he learned—even to the extent on occasion of analyzing dreams by mail).

Individualist bias: no organization strategy is involved

This refers to strategies which rely on the individual while denying the organizational forces and roles surrounding him. There is, however, simply no guarantee that a wise individual who attains power will act wisely. It may be that *role corrupts*—both the role of power and the role of powerlessness. In any event, there is no guarantee that placing certain types of people in management—or training them or psychoanalyzing them or making scientists of them—leads to more effective action. Scientists act like administrators when they gain power. And graduates of human relations training programs tend to act like non-alumni shortly after their return to their organizational base.

The staff idea, proposed by Myrdal, is limited by the unresolved tensions in the staff-line dilemma noted by students of organizational behavior and by the conflicts derived from the role of the intellectual working in bureaucratic structures. The élite strategy has serious drawbacks, primarily because it focuses on the individual and not the organization.

Insight bias: no manipulability

My major quarrel here is not with the formulation: insight leads to change, though this can be challenged, but with the lack of provision of variables accessible to control. It is not obvious that insight leads directly to sophistication in rearranging social systems or making strategic organizational interventions. Insight provides the relevant variables for planned change as far as personal manipulation goes, but the question remains: How can that lead directly to the manipulation of external factors?

The elements of planned organizational change

In the October 7, 1963, edition of the *New York Times*, a classified ad announced a search for change agents. It read:

What's a change agent? A result-oriented individual able to accurately and quickly resolve complex tangible and intangible problems. Energy and ambition necessary for success . . .

The change agents I have in mind need more than 'energy and ambition.' They are *professionals* who, for the most part, hold doctorates in the behavioral sciences. They are not a very homogeneous group, but they do have some similarities.

They are alike in that they take for granted the *centrality of work* in our culture to men and women in highly organized instrumental settings; in their concern with improvement, development, and measurement of *organizational effectiveness*; in their *preoccupation with people* and the process of human interaction; in their interest in changing the relationships, perceptions and values of *existing personnel*. They may be members of the client system, arguing that inside knowledge is needed, or external agents, arguing that perspective, detachment, and energy from outside are needed. They intervene at different structural points in the organization and at different times.

Though each change agent has in mind a set of unique goals based on his own theoretical position and competencies as well as the needs of the client system, there are some general aims. In a paradigm developed by Chris Argyris (1962), bureaucratic values tend to stress the rational, task aspects of work and to ignore the basic human factors which, if ignored, tend to reduce task competence. Managers brought up under this system of values are badly cast to play the intricate human roles now required of them. Their ineptitude and anxieties lead to systems of discord and defense which interfere with the problem-solving capacity of the organization.

Generally speaking, the normative goals of change agents derive from this paradigm. They include: improving interpersonal competence of managers; effecting a change in values so that human factors and feelings come to be considered legitimate; developing increased understanding among and within working groups to reduce tensions; developing 'team management'; developing better methods of 'conflict resolution' than suppression, denial, and the use of unprincipled power; viewing the organization as an organic system of relationships marked by mutual trust, interdependence, multigroup membership, shared responsibility, and conflict resolution through training or problem solving.

Programs for implementing planned organizational change

Discussion here will focus on three broad types of change programs that seem to be most widely used, frequently in some combination: training, consultation, and research.

Training

Training is an inadequate word in this context, as its dictionary meaning denotes 'drill' and 'exercise.' I refer to what has been called laboratory training, sensitivity or group dynamics training, and most commonly, T-Group training.[7] The idea originated in Bethel, Maine, under the guidance or Leland Bradford, Kenneth Benne, and Ronald Lippitt, with initial influence from the late Kurt Lewin. The T-Group has evolved since 1947 into one of the main instruments for organizational change. Bradford has played a central role in this development as director of the National

---

[7] For a popular account of laboratory training, see C. Argyris, T-groups for organizational effectiveness. *Harvard Business Review*, Vol. 42 (1964), pp. 60–74. For a theoretical background, see L. P. Bradford, J. R. Gibb, and K. D. Benne (eds.), *T-group theory and laboratory method*. New York: Wiley, 1964; and E. H. Schein and W. G. Bennis, *Personal and organizational change via group methods*. New York: Wiley, 1965.

Training Laboratories. Growth has been facilitated through the active participation of a number of university-based behavioral scientists and practitioners. Tavistock Institute has played a similar role in England and recently a group of European scientists set up a counterpart to the National Training Laboratories.

The main objective at first was *personal change* or *self-insight*. Since the fifties the emphasis has shifted to *organizational development*, a more precise date being 1958, when the Esso Company inaugurated a series of laboratories at refineries over the country under the leadership of Blake and Shepard (Shepard, 1960).

Briefly, laboratory training unfolds in an unstructured group setting where participants examine their interpersonal relationships. By examining data generated by themselves, members attempt to understand the dynamics of group behavior, e.g., decision processes, leadership and influence, norms, roles, communication distortions, effects of authority on behavioral patterns, coping mechanisms. T-Group composition is itself a strategic issue. Thus the organization may send an executive to a 'stranger laboratory' which fills a 'seeding' function; 'cousin laboratories' may be conducted for persons of similar rank and occupational responsibilities within the company but from different functional groups; 'diagonal slices' may be composed of persons of different rank but not in the same work group or in direct relationship; and 'family laboratories' may by conducted for functional groups. The more the training groups approach a 'family,' the more the total organization is affected.

Consulting

The change agent *qua* consultant, perhaps best exemplified in the work of the Tavistock Institute, operates in a manner very like the practicing physician or psychoanalyst: that is, he starts from the chief 'presenting symptom' of the client, articulates it in such a way that causal and underlying mechanisms of the problem are understood, and then takes remedial action. Heavy emphasis is placed on the strategy of *role model* because the main instrument is the change agent himself. Sofer (1961) reveals this when he suggests that psychotherapy or some form of clinical experience is necessary preparation for the change agent. Argyris, as consultant, confronts the group with their behavior toward him as an analogue of their behavior *vis-a-vis* their own subordinates.

If the role of the consultant sounds ambiguous and vague, this probably reflects reality. Certainly in the consultant approach the processes of change and the change agent's interventions are less systematic and less programmed than in training or applied research programs. A word about the latter.

Applied research

I refer here to research in which the results are used systematically as an *intervention*. Most methods of research application collect information and report it. Generally, the relationship ends there. In the survey-feedback approach, as developed primarily by Floyd Mann (1957) and his associates at The University of Michigan's Institute for Social Research, this is only the beginning. Data are reported in 'feedback' meetings where subjects become clients and have a chance to review the findings, test them against their own experience, and even ask the researchers to test some of their hypotheses. Instead of being submitted 'in triplicate' and probably ignored, research results serve to activate involvement and participation in the planning, collection, analysis, and interpretation of more data.

Richard Beckhard, too, utilizes data as the first step in his work as change agent (in press). In his procedure the data are collected through formal, non-structured interviews which he then codes by themes about the managerial activities of the client for discussion at an off-site meeting with the subjects.

It should be stressed that most planned change inductions involve all three processes—training, consulting, researching—and that both agent and client play a variety of roles. The final shape of the change agent's role is not as yet clear, and it is hazardous to report exactly what change agents do on the basis of their reports. Many factors, of course, determine the particular intervention the change agent may choose: cost, tune, degree of collaboration required, state of target system, and so on.

Strategic models employed by change agents

More often than not, change agents fail to report their strategy or to make it explicit. It may be useful to look at two quite different models that are available: one developed by Robert Blake in his 'Managerial Grid' system, and one with which I was associated at an Esso refinery and which Chris Argyris evaluated some years later.

Blake has developed a change program based on his analytic framework of managerial styles (Blake, Mouton, Barnes & Greiner, 1964). Figure 1 shows the grid for

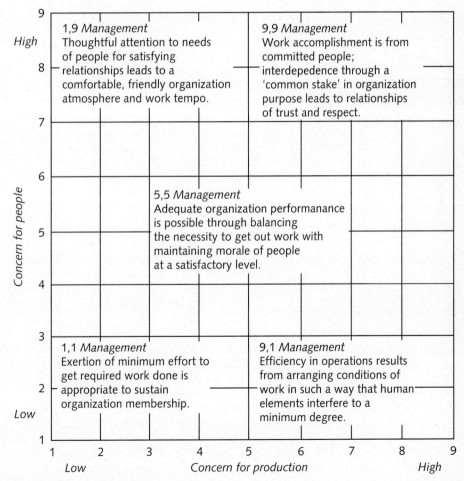

Figure 1 The managerial grid

locating types of managerial strategies. Blake and his colleagues attempt to change the organization in the direction of 'team management' (9.9 or high concern for people and high concern for production). Based on experience with 15 different factories, the Blake strategy specifies six phases: off-site laboratory for 'diagonal slice' of personnel; off-site program focused on team training for 'family' groups; training in the plant location designed to achieve better integration between functional groups; goal-setting sessions for groups of 10 to 12 managers.

Blake and his colleagues estimate that these four phases may require two years or longer. The next two, implementing plans and stabilizing changes, may require an additional two years.

Figure 2 (Argyris, 1960) presents another strategy: a change program used in a large oil company to improve the functioning of one of its smaller refineries. A new manager was named and sent to a T-Group training session to gain awareness of the human problems in the refinery. The Headquarters Organizational Development staff then conducted a diagnosis through a survey and interview of the managerial staff (70) and a sample of hourly employees (40/350). About that time the author was brought in to help the headquarters staff and the new manager.

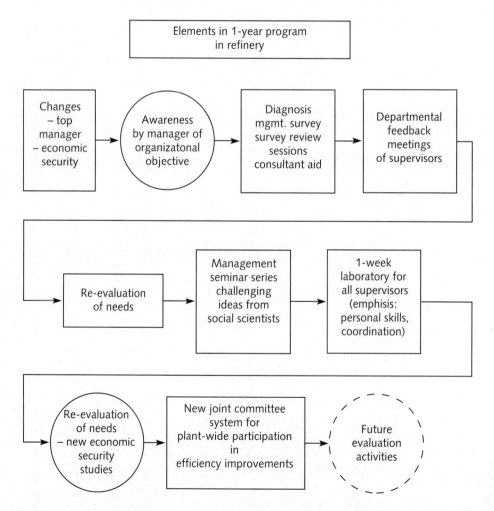

Figure 2 A change program

It was decided that a laboratory program of T-Groups might be effective but premature, with the result that weekly seminars that focused on new developments in human relations were held with top management (about 20). A one-week laboratory training program followed for all supervisors in diagonal slices, and then another re-evaluation of needs was undertaken. Some structural innovations were suggested and implemented. During the last phase of the program (not shown in the figure), the Scanlon Plan was adapted and installed (incidentally, for the first time in a 'process' industry and for the first time that a union agreed to the Plan without a bonus automatically guaranteed).

Though it cannot be said with any assurance that these two strategies are typical, it may be helpful to identify certain features: *(a) length of time* (Blake estimates five years: the refinery program took two years up to the Scanlon Plan); *(b) variety of programs* utilized (research, consulting, training, teaching, planning); *(c) necessity of cooperation* with top management and the parent organization; *(d)* approaching the organization as a *system* rather than as a collection of individuals; *(e) phasing program* from individual to group to intergroup to overall organization; *(f)* intellectual *and* emotional content.

Power and the role of the change agent

How and why do people and organizations change, and what is the nature and source of the power exerted by the change agent? We have to make inferences because change agents themselves tend to be silent on this. It is not *coercive power*, for the change agent generally does not have the ability to reward or punish. Moreover, he would prefer, at least intellectually, not to wield power at variance with his normative goals. Further, there is some evidence that coercive power is less durable than are other kinds of power, except under conditions of vigilant surveillance.

Traditional power? Almost certainly not. The change agent is, in fact, continually working without legitimization. *Expert power?* Possibly some, but it is doubtful whether his knowledge is considered 'expert' enough—in the sense that an engineer or doctor or lawyer is seen as expert. *Referent* or *identification power?* Apparently so. Sofer, for example, attributes some influence to the client system's ability and desire to emulate the change agent. Still, this will vary from a considerable degree to not at all.

This leaves us with *value power* as the likeliest candidate of the possible sources of power. Most change agents do emit cues to a consistent value system. These values are based on Western civilization's notion of a scientific humanism: concern for our fellow man, experimentalism, openness and honesty, flexibility, cooperation, democracy. If what I have said about power is correct, it is significant (at least in the United States) that this set of values seems to be potent in influencing top management circles.

Characteristics of client system

For the most part, the client systems appear to be subsystems of relatively large-scale international operations who find themselves in increasingly competitive situations, in rapidly changing environments, subjected to what have been called 'galloping variables.' Often the enterprise was founded through an innovation or monopolistic advantage which is thought to be in jeopardy.

Then there is some tension—some discrepancy between the ideal and the actual—which seems to activate the change program.

Finally, there is some faith in the idea that an intermediate proportion of organizational effectiveness is determined by social and psychological factors and that improvement here, however vague or immeasurable, may improve organizational effectiveness.

The measurement of effects

Until very recently, change agents, if they did any evaluation research at all, concentrated almost exclusively on attitudinal and subjective factors. Even so-called 'hard' behavioral variables, like absentee rates, sickness and accident rates, personnel turnover, and so forth, were rarely investigated. Relating change programs to harder criteria, like productivity and economic and cost factors, was rarely attempted and never, to my knowledge, successful.

And again, the research that was conducted—even on the attitudinal measures—was far from conclusive. Roger Harrison attempted an evaluation study of Argyris' work and found that while there was a significant improvement in the individual executive's interpersonal ability compared with a control group, there was no significant 'transfer' of this acuity to the real-life organizational setting. In short, there was a fairly rapid 'fade-out' of effects obtained in T-Group training upon return to the organization (Harrison, 1962). This study also shows that new tensions were generated between those individuals who attended the training program and those who did not—an example of the lack of a *systems* approach. Shepard's evaluation on the Esso organization shows that the impact of laboratory training was greatest on personal and interpersonal learnings, but 'slightly more helpful than useless' in changing the organization.

More recently, though, some studies have been undertaken which measure more meaningful, less subjective variables of organizational effectiveness. Blake, Mouton, Barnes, and Greiner (1964), for example, conducted an evaluation study of their work in a very large (4,000 employees) petrochemical plant. Not only did they find significant changes in the values, morale, and interpersonal behavior of the employees, but significant improvements in productivity, profits, and cost reduction. David (in press), a change agent working on a program that attempts to facilitate a large and complicated merger, attributed the following effects to the programs: increased productivity, reduced turnover and absenteeism, in addition to a significant improvement in the area of attitudes and subjective feelings.

While these new research approaches show genuine promise, much more has to be done. The research effort has somehow to equal all the energy that goes into developing the planned-change programs themselves.

Some criticisms and qualifications

The work of the change agents reported here is new and occurs without the benefit of methodological and strategic precedents. The role of the change agent is also new, its final shape not fully emerged. Thus it has both the advantage of freedom from the constraints facing most men of knowledge, and suffers from lack of guidelines and structure. Let us touch quickly on problems and criticisms facing the change agents.

Planned change and organizational effectiveness

I can identify six dimensions of organizational effectiveness: legal, political, economic, technological, social, and personal. There is a good deal of fuzziness as to which of these change agents hope to affect, and the data are inconclusive. Argyris, who is the most explicit about the relationship between performance and interpersonal competence, is still hoping to develop good measures to establish a positive relationship.

The connection has to be made, or the field will have to change its normative goal of constructing not only a *better* world but a more *effective* one.

A question of values

The values espoused indicate a way of *behaving and feeling*; for example, they emphasize openness rather than secrecy, collaboration rather than dependence or rebellion, cooperation rather than competition, consensus rather than individual rules, rewards based on self-control rather than externally induced rewards, team leadership rather than a one-to-one relationship with the boss, authentic relationships rather than those based on political maneuvering.

Are they natural? Desirable? Functional? What then happens to status or power drives? What about those individuals who have a low need for participation and/or high need for structure and dependence? And what about those personal needs which seem to be incompatible with these images of man, such as a high need for aggression and a low need for affiliation? In short, what about those needs which can be best realized through bureaucratic systems? Or benevolent autocracies? Are these individuals to be changed or to yield and comply?

The problem of values deserves discussion. One of the obstacles is the emotional and value overtones which interfere with rational dialogue. More often than not, one is plunged into a polarized debate which converts ideas into ideology and inquiry into dogma. So we hear of 'Theory X versus Theory Y,' personality versus organization, democratic versus autocratic, task versus maintenance, human relations versus scientific management, and on and on.

Surely life is more complicated than these dualities suggest, and surely they must imply a continuum—not simply extremes.

Lack of systems approach

Up to this point, I have used the term 'organizational change' rather loosely. In Argyris' case, for example, organizational change refers to a change in values of 11 top executives, a change which was not necessarily of an enduring kind and apparently brought about some conflict with other interfaces. In most other cases of planned organizational change, the change induction was limited to a small, élite group. Only the work of Blake and some others can we confidently talk about organizational change—in a systems way; his program includes the training of the entire management organization, and at several locations he has carried this step to include wage earners.

Sometimes the changes brought about simple 'fade out' because there are no carefully worked out procedures to ensure coordination with other interacting parts of the system. In other cases, the changes have 'backfired' and have had to be terminated because of their conflict with interface units. In any case, a good deal more has to be learned about the interlocking and stabilizing changes so that the total system is affected.

Some generalizations

It may be useful, as peroration, to state in the most tentative manner some generalizations. They are derived, for the most part, from the foregoing discussion and anchored in experience and, wherever possible, in research and theory.

First, a forecast: I suspect that we will see an increase in the number of planned-change programs along the lines discussed here—toward *less* bureaucratic and *more* participative, 'open system' and adaptive structures. Given the present pronounced rate of change, the growing reliance on science for the success of the industrial enterprise, the growing number of professionals joining these enterprises, and the 'turbulent contextual environment' facing the firm, we can expect increasing demand for social inventions to revise traditional notions of organized effort.

As far as adopting and acceptance go, we already know a good deal.[8] *Adoption* requires that the *type* of change should be proven quality, easily demonstrable in its effects, and with information easily available. Its cost and accessibility to control by the client system as well as its value accord have to be carefully considered.

Acceptance also depends on the relationship between the change agent and the client system: the more profound and anxiety-producing the change, the more collaborative and closer relationship required. In addition, we can predict that an anticipated change will be resisted to the degree that the client system possesses little or incorrect knowledge about the change, has relatively little trust in the source of the change, and has comparatively low influence in controlling the nature and direction of the change.

What we know least about is *implementation*—a process which includes the creation of understanding and commitment toward a particular change and devices whereby it can become integral to the client systems' operations. I will try to summarize the necessary elements in implementation:

(a) The *client system* should have as much understanding of the change and its consequences, as much influence in developing and controlling the fate of the change, and as much trust in the initiator of the change as is possible.

(b) The *change effort* should be perceived as being as self-motivated and voluntary as possible. This can be effected through the legitimization and reinforcement of the change by the top management group and by the significant reference groups adjacent to the client system. It is also made possible by providing the utmost in true volition.

(c) The *change program* must include emotional and value as well as cognitive (informational) elements for successful implementation. It is doubtful that relying solely on rational persuasion (expert power) is sufficient. Most organizations possess the knowledge to cure their ills; the rub is utilization.

(d) The *change agent* can be crucial in reducing the resistance to change. As long as the change agent acts congruently with the principles of the program and as long as the client has a chance to test competence and motives (his own and the change agent's), the agent should be able to provide the psychological support so necessary during the risky phases of change. As I have stressed again and again, the quality of the client-agent relationship is pivotal to the success of the change program.

References

Ackoff, R. L. and Rivett, P. *A manager's guide to operations research.* New York: Wiley, 1963, p. 34.

Argyris, C. *Organization development: An inquiry into the Esso approach.* New Haven, Conn.: Yale University, 1960.

[8] See in particular, E. Rogers, *The diffusion of innovations.* New York: Free Press, 1962; and M. Miles (ed.), *Innovation in education.* New York: Bureau of Publications, Teachers College, Columbia University, 1964.

Argyris, C. *Interpersonal competence and organizational effectiveness.* Homewood, Ill.: Dorsey, 1962, p. 43.

Beckhard, R. An organization improvement program in a decentralized organization. In D. Zand (ed.), *Organization development: Theory and practice*, in press.

Bennis, W. G., Benne, K. D., and Chin, R. (eds.) *The planning of change.* New York: Holt, Rinehart & Winston, 1961.

Blake, R. R., Mouton, Jane S., Barnes, L. B., and Greiner, L. E. Breakthrough in organization development. *Harvard Business Review*, 1964.

Boskoff, A. Functional analysis as a source of a theoretical repertory and research tasks in the study of social change. In C. R. Zollschan and W. Hirsch, *Explorations in social change.* Boston: Houghton Mifflin, 1964.

Chin, R. The utility of system models and developmental models for practitioners. In W. G. Bennis, K. D. Benne, and R. Chin (eds.), *The planning of change.* New York: Holt, Rinehart & Winston, 1961, pp. 201–14.

Chin, R. Models and ideas about changing. Paper read at Symposium on Acceptance of New Ideas, University of Nebraska, November, 1963.

Coser, L. *The functions of social conflict.* New York: Free Press, 1956.

Dahrendorf, R. Toward a theory of social conflict. In W. G. Bennis, K. D. Benne, and R. Chin (eds.), *The planning of change.* New York: Holt, Rinehart & Winston, 1961, pp. 445–51.

David, G. The Weldon study: An organization change program based upon change in management philosophy. In D. Zand (ed.), *Organization development: Theory and practice*, in press.

Freeman, H. E. The strategy of social policy research. *The social welfare forum*, 1963, pp. 143–60.

Gibb, J. R. and Lippitt, R. (eds.) Consulting with groups and organizations. *Journal of Social Issues*, 1959, 15.

Glock, C. Y., Lippitt, R., Flanagan, J. C., Wilson, E. C., Shartle, C. L., Wilson, M. L., Croker, G. W., and Page, H. E. *Case studies in bringing behavioral science into use.* Stanford, Calif.: Inst. Commun. Res., 1960.

Harrison, R. In C. Argyris, *Interpersonal competence and organizational effectiveness.* Homewood, Ill.: Dorsey, 1952, Chap. 11.

Leeds, R. and Smith. T. (eds.) *Using social science knowledge in business and industry.* Homewood, Ill.: Irwin, 1963.

Likert, R. and Hayes, S. P., Jr. (eds.) *Some applications of behavioral research.* Paris: UNESCO, 1957.

Mann, F. Studying and creating change: A means to understanding social organization. *Research in industrial relations.* Ann Arbor, Mich.: Industrial Relations Research Association, 1957, Publication No. 17.

Merton, R. K. and Lerner, D. Social scientists and research policy. In D. Lerner and H. D. Lasswell (eds.), *The policy sciences: Recent developments in scope and method.* Stanford, Calif.: Stanford University Press, 1951.

Myrdal, G. *Value in society theory.* New York: Harper, 1958, p. 29.

Parsons, R. T. Evolutionary universals in society. *American Sociological Review*, 1964, 29, pp. 339–57.

Salisbury, H. E. *To Moscow and beyond.* New York: Harper, 1960, p. 136.

Shepard, H. Three management programs and the theory behind them. In *An action research program for organization improvement.* Ann Arbor, Mich.: Foundation for Research on Human Behavior, 1960.

Sofer, C. *The organization from within.* London: Tavistock, 1961.

Zetterberg, H. L. *Social theory and social practice.* Totowa, N.J.: Bedminster, 1962.

modifying square-peg recruits to fit into round organizational holes (1978)

'People processing: strategies of organizational socialization', by John Van Maanen, *Organizational Dynamics*, Summer 1978, pp.19–36.

All of us are aware of socialization, either at first or second hand. During our lives, all of us have been socialized into the organizations that we have joined – primary school, secondary school, scouts, guides, church, sports club, university, supermarket, and many others. Such socialization may have been formal, when for example, we were put on a company induction programme or sent on a training course. It may have been informal, as when a senior member of the organization ticked us off for the way we spoke, or complemented us on the way that we behaved. Socialization was performed not only by company managers, but also by our fellow work mates. In addition, we also know about socialization as it is depicted in books (*Tom Brown's Schooldays, Liar's Poker*), in films (*Full Metal Jacket, Wall Street*), or on TV.

What we were probably not aware of, was that what we were undergoing or observing, was in fact a process of socialization. We just accepted it as normal practice. Organizational socialization is the way that individuals learn how to behave in a firm or company. In this article, Van Maanen, describes the different types of socialization that occur, and you may be able to identify those that you have experienced, read about, or seen. The activity that follows it, gives you the opportunity to identify and label these different *people processing strategies* as he calls them.

learning objectives

Once you have read and understood the prescribed material, you should be able to:

1 Distinguish the different types of organizational socialization techniques (people processing strategies).
2 Reflect on your own experience, and identify and correctly label the socialization techniques that were used on you, or that you have read about or seen.

learning pre-requisites

Before proceeding, you should read Chapters 5 and 18 in the core text and the article, 'People processing: strategies of organizational socialization', by John Van Maanen.

learning activities

1 Reflect on your own experience of organizational socialization, as well as any relevant book that you have read, or films or TV that you have watched. Listed below are Van Maanen's seven 'people processing' strategies. Identify an example of each strategy, and describe it briefly.

Names and definitions of Van Maanen (1978) socialization strategies

Strategy name	Definition	Your example
1 Collective	Puts newcomer through a common set of experiences as part of a group.	
2 Individual	Processes recruits singly and in isolation from each other.	
3 Formal	Segregates newcomers from regular organizational members.	
4 Informal	Treats newcomers as not differentiated from other members.	
5 Sequential steps	Requires entrant to move through a series of discrete and identifiable steps to achieve a defined role.	
6 Non-sequential steps	Accomplishes achievement of a defined role in one transitional stage.	
7 Tournament	Separates clusters of recruits into different programmes on the basis of presumed differences.	
8 Contest	Avoids sharp distinctions between clusters of recruits.	
9 Fixed	Gives the recruit complete knowledge of time required to complete passage.	
10 Variable	Offers a timetable which does not fix the length of socialization.	
11 Serial	Newcomers are provided with experienced members as role models to be followed.	
12 Disjunctive	Has no role models available since newcomers do not follow in the footsteps of predecessors.	
13 Investiture	Ratifies and documents the usefulness of personal characteristics of new recruits.	
14 Divestiture	Seeks to deny and strip away recruit's personal characteristics.	

Source: Judith R. Gordon and Jean M. Bartunek, 'Teaching organizational socialization strategies', *EXCHANGE: The Organizational Behavior Teaching Journal*, vol. 5, no. 3, 1980, pp. 37–40.

READING
18   *People processing: strategies of organizational socialization*
John Van Maanen

Van Maanen identifies seven dimensions or strategies of socialization, together with their often fateful consequences for the individual and for the organization. And he makes clear that socialization is too important to be left to chance or inertia.

Socialization shapes the person – a defensible hyperbole. Organizational socialization or 'people processing' refers to the manner in which the experiences of people learning the ropes of a new organizational position, status, or role are structured for them by others within the organization. In short, I will argue here that people acquire the social knowledge and skills necessary to assume a particular job in an organization differently not only because people are different, but, more critically, because the techniques or strategies of people processing differ. And, like the variations of a sculptor's mold, certain forms of organizational socialization produce remarkably different results.

Socialization strategies are perhaps most obvious when a person first joins an organization or when an individual is promoted or demoted. They are probably least obvious when an experienced member of the organization undergoes a simple change of assignment, shift, or job location. Nevertheless, certain people-processing devices can be shown to characterize every transition an individual makes across organizational boundaries. Moreover, management may choose such devices explicitly or consciously. For example, management might require all recruits or newcomers to a particular position to attend a training or orientation program of some kind. Or management may select people-processing devices implicitly or unconsciously. These strategies may simply represent taken-for-granted precedents established in the dim past of an organization's history. The precedent could perhaps be the proverbial trial-and-error method of socialization by which a person learns how to perform a new task on his own, without direct guidance.

Regardless of the method of choice, however, any given socialization device represents an identifiable set of events that will make certain behavioral and attitudinal consequences more likely than others. It is possible, therefore, to identify the various people-processing methods and evaluate them in terms of their social consequences.

* Reprinted by permission from *Organizational Dynamics*, vol 7 (1), Summer 1978. © 1978, AMACOM, a division of American Management Associations, New York. All rights reserved.

† John Van Maanen *has taught at Yale university; the University of Southern California and presently he is an associate professor of organization studies at the Sloan School of Management, M.I.T. He received his Ph.D. in organizational behavior from the Graduate School of Administration at the University of California, Irvine in 1972 and has published widely on the topics of work socialization, the role of the police in modern society, and the sociology of organizations. Recently, he published a book entitled* Organizational Careers: Some New Perspectives (*New York: Wiley, 1977) and co-edited a book with Peter K. Manning entitled* Policing: A View from the Streets (*Santa Monica, California: Goodyear Press, 1978). He is currently an advisory editor for the journal* Urban Life and Culture *and is engaged in a study of the fishing industry in New England. He is also completing a book on social science research methods aimed in part to promote the use of anthropological or ethnographic techniques as a means of improving our knowledge of organizational life. Dr. Van Maanen lives with his wife Colleen McCallion and their five-year-old son Casey in Nahant, Massachusetts.*

Background

Three primary assumptions underlie this analysis. First, and perhaps of most importance, is the notion that people in a state of transition are more or less in an anxiety-producing situation. They are motivated to reduce this anxiety by learning the functional and social requirements of their new role as quickly as possible.

Second, the learning that takes place does not occur in a social vacuum strictly on the basis of the official and available versions of the job requirements. Any person crossing organizational boundaries is looking for clues on how to proceed. Thus colleagues, superiors, subordinates, clients, and other work associates can and most often do support, guide, hinder, confuse, or push the individual who is learning a new role. Indeed, they can help him interpret (or misinterpret) the events he experiences so that he can take appropriate (or inappropriate) action in his altered situation. Ultimately, they will provide him with a sense of accomplishment and competence or failure and incompetence.

Third, the stability and productivity of any organization depend in large measure on the way newcomers to various organizational positions come to carry out their tasks. When positions pass from generation to generation of incumbents smoothly, the continuity of the organization's mission is maintained, the predictability of the organization's performance is left intact, and, in the short run at least, the survival of the organization is assured.

A concern for the ways in which individuals adjust to novel circumstances directs attention not only to the cognitive learning that accompanies any transition but also to the manner in which the person copes emotionally with the new situation. As sociologist Erving Goffman rightly suggests, new situations require individuals to reassess and perhaps alter both their instrumental goals (the goals they wish to achieve through their involvement in the organization) and their expressive style (the symbolic appearances they maintain before others in the organization).

In some cases, a shift into a new work situation may result in a dramatically altered organizational identity for the person. This often happens, for example, when a factory worker becomes a foreman or a staff analyst becomes a line manager. Other times, the shift may cause only minor and insignificant changes in a person's organizational identity; for instance, when an administrator is shifted to a new location or a craftsman is rotated to a new department. Yet any of these shifts is likely to result in what might be called a 'reality shock' for the person being shifted. When people undergo a transition, regardless of the information they already possess about their new role, their *a priori* understandings of that role are bound to change in either a subtle or a dramatic fashion. Becoming a member of an organization will upset the everyday order of even the most well-informed newcomer. Matters concerning such aspects of life as friendships, time, purpose, demeanor, competence, and the expectations the person holds of the immediate and distant future are suddenly made problematic. The newcomer's most pressing task is to build a set of guidelines and interpretations to explain and make meaningful the myriad of activities observed as going on in the organization.

To come to know an organizational situation and act within it implies that a person has developed some beliefs, principles, and understandings, or, in shorthand notation, a *perspective* for interpreting the experiences he or she has had as a participant in a given sphere of the work world. This perspective provides the rules by which to manage the unique and recurring strains of organizational life. It provides the person with an ordered view of the organization that runs ahead and directs experience, orders and shapes personal relationships in the work setting, and provides the ground rules to manage the ordinary day-to-day affairs.

Strategies of people processing

Certain situational variables associated with any organization transition can be made visible and shown to be tied directly to the perspective constructed by individuals in transit. The focus here is not on perspectives *per se*, however, but rather on the properties peculiar to any given people-processing situation. These properties are essentially process variables akin to, but more specific than, such generic processes as education, training, apprenticeship, and indoctrination. Further more, these properties can be viewed as organizational strategies that distinctly pattern the learning experiences of a newcomer to a particular organizational role.

The people-processing strategies examined below are associated to some degree with all situations that involve a person moving from one organizational position to another. Although much of the evidence comes from studies concerned with the way someone first becomes a member of an organization, the techniques used to manage this passage are at least potentially available for use during any transition a person undergoes during the course of a career. Thus the term 'strategy' is used to describe each examined aspect of a transition process because the degree to which a particular people-processing technique is used by an organization is not in any sense a natural condition or prerequisite for socialization. Indeed, by definition, some socialization will always take place when a person moves into and remains with a new organizational role. However, the form that it takes is a matter of organizational choice. And, whether this choice of strategies is made by design or by accident, it is at least theoretically subject to rapid and complete change at the direction of the management.

This is an important point. It suggests that we can be far more self-conscious about employing certain people-processing techniques than we have been. In fact, a major purpose of this article is to heighten and cultivate a broader awareness of what it is we do to people under the guise of 'breaking them in.' Presumably, if we have a greater appreciation for the sometimes unintended consequences of a particular strategy, we can alter the strategy to benefit both the individual and the organization.

Seven dimensions on which the major strategies of people processing can be located will be discussed. Each strategy will be presented alongside its counterpart or opposing strategy. In other words, each strategy as applied can be thought of as existing somewhere between the two poles of a single dimension. Critically, across dimensions, the strategies are not mutually exclusive. In practice, they are typically combined in sundry and often inventive ways. Thus, although each tactic is discussed in relative isolation, the reader should be aware that the effects of the various socialization strategies upon individuals are cumulative – but not necessarily compatible (in terms of outcome) with one another.

I do not claim that these strategies are exhaustive or that they are presented in any order of relevance to a particular organization or occupation. These are essentially empirical questions that can only be answered by further research. I do claim and attempt to show that these strategies are recognizable, powerful, in widespread use, and of enormous consequence to the people throughout an organization. And, since organizations can accomplish little more than what the people within them accomplish, these people-processing strategies are of undeniable importance when it comes to examining such matters as organizational performance, structure, and, ultimately, survival.

Formal (informal) socialization strategies

The formality of a socialization process refers to the degree to which the setting in which it takes place is segregated from the ongoing work context and to the degree to which an individual's newcomer role is emphasized and made explicit. The more formal the process, the more the recruit's role is both segregated and specified. The recruit is differentiated strictly from other organizational members. In an informal atmosphere, there is no sharp differentiation and much of the recruit's learning necessarily takes place within the social and task-related networks that surround his or her position. Thus informal socialization procedures are analytically similar to the familiar trial-and-error techniques by which one learns, it is said, through experience.

Generally, the more formal the process, the more stress there is influencing the newcomer's attitudes and values. The more concerned the organization is with the recruit's absorption of the appropriate demeanor and stance, the more the recruit is likely to begin to think and feel like a U.S. Marine, an IBM executive, or a Catholic priest. In other words, formal processes work on preparing a person to occupy a particular *status* in the organization. Informal processes, on the other hand, prepare a person to perform a specific *role* in an organization. And, in general, the more the recruit is separated from the day-to-day reality of the organization, the less he or she will be able to carry over, generalize, and apply any abilities or skills learned in one socialization setting to the new position.

From this standpoint, formal socialization processes are often only the 'first round' of socialization. The informal second round occurs when the newcomer is placed in his designated organizational slot and must learn informally the actual practices in his department. Whereas the first wave stresses general skills and attitudes, the second wave emphasizes specified actions, situational applications of the rules, and the idiosyncratic nuances necessary to perform the role in the work setting. However, when the gap separating the two kinds of learning is large, disillusionment with the first wave may set in, causing the individual to disregard virtually everything he has learned in the formal round of socialization.

Even when formal socialization is deliberately set up to provide what are thought to be practical and particular skills, it may be still experienced as problematic by those who pass through the process. In effect, the choice of a formal strategy forces all newcomers to endure, absorb, and perhaps become proficient with *all* the skills and materials presented to them, since they cannot know what is or is not relevant to the job for which they are being prepared. For example, in police training academies, recruits are taught fingerprinting, ballistics, and crime-scene investigation, skills that are, at best, of peripheral interest and of no use to a street patrolman. One result is that when recruits graduate and move to the mean streets of the city, a general disenchantment with the relevance of all their training typically sets in.

Even in the prestigious professional schools of medicine and law the relevance of much training comes to be doubted by practitioners and students alike. Such disenchantment is apparently so pervasive that some observers have suggested that the formal processes that typify professional schools produce graduates who have already internalized standards for their everyday work performances that are 'self-validating' and are apparently lodged well beyond the influence of others both within and outside the professional and intellectual community that surrounds the occupation.

Formal strategies appear also to produce stress for people in the form of a period of personal stigmatization. This stigmatization can be brought about by identifying garb (such as the peculiar uniform worn by police recruits); a special and usually somewhat demeaning title (such as 'rookie,' 'trainee,' or ' junior'); or an insular position (such as an assignment to a classroom instead of an office or job). A person undergoing formal socialization is likely to feel isolated, cut off, and prohibited from assuming everyday social relationships with his more experienced 'betters.'

Informal socialization processes, wherein a recruit must negotiate for himself within a far less structured situation, can also induce personal anxiety. Indeed, the person may have trouble discovering clues as to the exact dimensions of his or her assigned organizational role. Under most circumstances, laissez-faire socialization increases the influence of the immediate work group on the new employee. There is no guarantee, though, that the direction provided by the informal approach will push the recruit in the right direction so far as those in authority are concerned. Classical examples are the so-called goldbricking and quota-restriction tactics invented by employees in production situations to thwart managerial directives. Such practices are passed on informally but quite effectively to newcomers against the desires of management.

Left to his own devices, a recruit will select his socialization agents. The success of the socialization process is then determined largely on the basis of whatever mutual regard is developed between the agent and the newcomer, the relevant knowledge possessed by an agent, and, of course, the agent's ability to transfer such knowledge. In most Ph.D. programs, for example, students must pick their own advisors from among the faculty. The advisors then act as philosophers, friends, and guides for the students. And among professors – as among organization executives – it is felt that the student who pushes the hardest by demanding more time, asking more questions, and so forth, learns the most. Consequently, the recruit's freedom of choice in the more informal setting has a price. He or she must force others to teach him.

Individual (collective) socialization strategies

The degree to which individuals are socialized singly or collectively is perhaps the most critical of the process variables. The difference is analogous to the batch versus unit modes of production. In the batch or mass production case, recruits are bunched together at the outset and processed through an identical set of experiences, with relatively similar outcomes.

When a group goes through a socialization program together, it almost always develops an 'in-the-same-boat' collective consciousness. Individual changes in perspective are built on an understanding of the problems faced by all members of the group. Apparently as the group shares problems, various members experiment with possible solutions and report back. In the course of discussions that follow, the members arrive at a collective and more or less consensual definition of their situation.

At the same time, the consensual character of the solutions worked out by the group allows the members to deviate more from the standards set by the agents than the individual mode of socialization does. Therefore, collective processes provide a potential base for recruit resistance. In such cases, the congruence between managerial objectives and those adopted by the group is always problematic – the recruit group is more likely than the individual to redefine or ignore agent demands.

Classic illustrations of the dilemma raised by the use of the collective strategy can be found in both educational and work environments. In educational settings, the faculty may beseech a student to study hard while the student's peers exhort him to relax and have a good time. In many work settings, supervisors attempt to ensure that each employee works up to his level of competence while the worker's peers try to impress on him that he must not do too much. To the degree that the newcomer is backed into the corner and cannot satisfy both demands at the same time, he will follow the dicta of those with whom he spends most of his time and who are most important to him.

The strength of group understandings depends, of course, on the degree to which all members actually share the same fate. In highly competitive settings, group members know that their own success is increased through the failure of others.

Hence, the social support networks necessary to maintain cohesion in the group may break down. Consensual understandings will develop, but they will buttress individual modes of adjustment. Junior faculty members in publication-minded universities, for instance, follow group standards, although such standards nearly always stress individual scholarship.

Critically, collective socialization processes can also promote and intensify agent demands. Army recruits socialize each other in ways the army itself could never do; nor, for that matter, would it be allowed to do. Graduate students are often said to learn more from one another than from the faculty. And, while agents may have the power to define the nature of the collective problem, recruits often have more resources available to them to define the solution – time, experience, motivation, expertise, and patience (or the lack thereof).

Individual strategies also induce personal changes. But the views adopted by people processed individually are likely to be far less homogeneous than the views of those processed collectively. Nor are the views adopted by the isolated newcomer necessarily those that are the most beneficial to him in his transitional position, since he has access only to the perspectives of his socialization agents, and they may not fully apprehend or appreciate his immediate problems.

Certainly, the newcomer may choose not to accept the advice of his agents, although to reject it explicitly may well lose him his job. Furthermore, the rich, contextual perspectives that are available when individuals interact with their peers will not develop under individual strategies. In psychoanalysis, for example, the vocabulary of motives a recruit-patient develops to interpret his situation is quite personal and specific compared with the vocabulary that develops in group therapy. Of course, individual analyses can result in deep changes but they are lonely changes and depend solely on the mutual regard and warmth that exist between agent and recruit.

Apprenticeship modes of work socialization bear some similarity to therapist-patient relationships. If the responsibility for transforming an individual to a given status within the organization is delegated to one person, an intense, value-oriented process is likely to follow. This practice is common whenever a role incumbent is viewed by others in the organization as being the only member capable of shaping the recruit. It is quite common in upper levels of both public and private organizations. Because one organizational member has the sole responsibility, he or she often becomes a role model. The recruit emulates that person's thoughts and actions.

Succession to the chief executive officer level in many firms is marked by the extensive use of the individual socialization strategy. Outcomes in these one-on-one efforts depend on the affective relationships that may or may not develop between the apprentice and his master. In cases of high affect, the process works well and the new member internalizes the values of the particular role he is eventually to play quickly and fully. However, when there are few affective bonds, the socialization process may break down and the transition may not take place.

Overall, individual socialization is expensive in terms of both time and money. Failures are not recycled or rescued easily. Nor are individual strategies particularly suitable for the demands of large organizations, which process many people every year. Hence, with growing bureaucratic structures, the use of mass socialization techniques has increased. Indeed, collective tactics, because of their ease, efficiency, and predictability, have tended to replace the traditional socialization mode of apprenticeship.

Sequential (nonsequential) socialization strategies

Sequential socialization refers to transitional processes marked by a series of discrete and identifiable stages through which an individual must pass in order to achieve a defined role and status within the organization. Many banks groom a person for a particular managerial position by first rotating him or her across the various jobs that will comprise the range of managerial responsibility. Similarly, police recruits in most departments must pass successively through such stages as academy classroom instruction, physical conditioning, firearm training, and on-the-street pupilage.

Nonsequential processes are accomplished in one transitional stage. A factory worker may become a shop supervisor without benefit of an intermediary training program. A department head in a municipal government may become a city manager without serving first as an assistant city manager. Presumably, any organizational position may be analyzed to discover whether intermediate stages of preparation may be required of people taking over that position.

When examining sequential strategies, it is crucial to note the degree to which each stage builds on the preceding stage. For example, the courses in most technical training programs are arranged in what is thought to be a progression from simple to complex material. On the other hand, some sequential processes seem to follow no internal logic. Management training is often disjointed, with the curriculum jumping from topic to topic with little or no integration across stages. In such cases, a person tends to learn the material he likes best in the sequence. If, on the other hand, the flow of topics or courses is harmonious and connected functionally in some fashion, the various minor mental alterations a person must make at each sequential stage will act cumulatively so that at the end, the person may find himself considerably different from the way he was when he started.

Relatedly, if several agents handle different portions of the socialization process, the degree to which the aims of the agents are common is very important to the eventual outcome. For example, in some officers' training schools of peacetime military organizations, the agents responsible for physical and weapons training have very different attitudes toward their jobs and toward the recruits from the agents in charge of classroom instruction. Officer trainees quickly spot such conflicts when they exist and sometimes exploit them, playing agents off against one another. Such conflicts often lead to a more relaxed atmosphere for the recruits, one in which they enjoy watching their instructors pay more attention to each other than they do to the training program. An almost identical situation can be found in many police training programs.

In the sequential arrangement, agents may not know each other, may be separated spatially, and may have thoroughly different images of their respective tasks. University-trained scientists, for example, apparently have considerable difficulty moving from an academic to an industrial setting to practice their trade. The pattern disconcerts many scientists as they discover that their scholarly training emphasized a far different set of skills and interests from those required in the corporate environment. It is often claimed that to become a 'good' industrial scientist, you must learn the painful lesson that being able to sell an idea is as important as having it in the first place.

Consider, too, the range of views about a particular job an organizational newcomer may receive from the personnel department, the training division, and colleagues on the job, all of whom have a hand (and a stake) in the recruit's transition. From this standpoint, empathy must certainly be extended to the so-called juvenile delinquent who receives 'guidance' from the police, probation officers, judges, social workers, psychiatrists, and correction officers. Such a sequence may actually teach a person to be whatever his immediate situation demands.

Besides the confusion that comes from the contradictory demands that are sometimes made on people, there is also likely to be misinformation passed along by each agent in a sequential process as to how simple the next stage will be. Thus, the recruit may be told that if he just buckles down and applies himself in stage A, stages B, C, D, and E, will be easy. Agents usually mask, wittingly or unwittingly, the true nature of the stage to follow. Their reasoning is that if a person feels his future is bright, rewarding, and assured, he will be most cooperative at the stage he is in, not wishing to jeopardize the future he thinks awaits him.

When attempts are consistently made to make each subsequent step appear simple, the individual's best source of information on the sequential process is another person who has gone through it. If the recruit can find organizational members who have been through the process he can use them to help him obtain a more reality-oriented perspective. But some organizations go out of their way to isolate recruits from veteran members. Certain profit-making trade schools go to great lengths to be sure their paying clientele do not learn of the limited job opportunities in the 'glamorous and high-paying' worlds of radio and TV broadcasting, commercial art, or heavy equipment operation. Door-to-door sales trainees are continually assured that their success is guaranteed; the handy-dandy, one-of-a-kind product they are preparing to merchandise will 'sell itself.' When recruits are officially allowed the privilege of interacting with more experienced organizational members, those controlling the process invariably select a veteran member who will present a sanitized or laundered image of the future.

The degree to which an individual is required to keep to a schedule as he goes through the entire sequence is another important aspect of the sequential socialization strategy. A recruit may feel that he is being pressured or pushed into certain positions or stages before he is ready. This position is similar to that of the business executive who does not want a promotion but feels that if he turns it down, he will be damaging his career. A professor may feel that he cannot turn down the chairmanship of his department without rupturing the respectful relationships with his faculty members that he now enjoys.

On the other hand, if the person does not slip, falter, fail, or seriously discredit himself in any fashion, sequential socialization over his full career may provide him with what has been called a 'permanent sense of the unobtained.' Thus the executive who, at thirty, aims toward being the head of his department by the time he is forty, will then be attempting to make division head by fifty, and so on. The consumer sequence that stresses accumulation of material goods has much the same character as the artistic sequence that stresses the achievement of the perfect work. Sequential socialization of this sort has a rather disquieting Sisyphus-like nature as the person seeks perpetually to reach the unreachable.

Fixed (variable) socialization strategies

Organizational socialization processes differ in terms of the information and certainty an individual has regarding his transition timetable. Fixed socialization processes provide a recruit with a precise knowledge of the time it will take him to complete a given step. The time of transition is standardized. Consider the probationary systems used on most civil service jobs. The employees know in advance just how long they will be on probation. Educational systems provide another good illustration of fixed processes. Schools begin and end at the same time for all pupils. Students move through the system roughly one step at a time. Fixed processes provide rigid conceptions of 'normal' progress; those who are not on schedule are considered 'deviant.'

Variable socialization processes do not give those being processed any advance notice of their transition timetable. What may be true for one is not true for another. The recruit has to search out clues to his future. Prisoners who serve indeterminate sentences such as the legendary and properly infamous 'one to ten,' must dope out timetable norms from the scarce materials available to them. Apprenticeship programs often specify only the minimum number of years a person must remain an apprentice and leave open the precise time a person can expect to be advanced to journeyman.

Since the rate of passage across any organizational boundary is a matter of concern to most participants, transition timetables may be developed on the basis of the most fragmentary and flimsiest information. Rumors and innuendos about who is going where and when characterize the variable strategy of socialization. However, if a recruit has direct access to others who are presently in or have been through a similar situation, a sort of 'sentimental order' will probably emerge as to when certain passages can or should be expected to take place. And whether or not these expectations are accurate, the individual will measure his progress against them.

The vertically oriented business career is a good example of both variable socialization and the 'sentimental order' that seems to characterize such processes. Take the promotional systems in most large organizations. These systems are usually designed to reward individual initiative and performance on current assignments and are therefore considered, at least by upper management, to be highly variable processes. But, for those deeply concerned with their own (and others') progress in the organization, the variable process is almost inevitably corrupted, because would-be executives push very hard to uncover the signs of a coming promotion (or demotion). These people listen closely to stories concerning the time it takes to advance in the organization, observe as closely as possible the experiences of others, and develop an age consciousness delineating the range of appropriate ages for given positions. The process is judgmental and requires a good deal of time and effort. However, in some very stable organizations, such as government agencies, the expected rate of advancement can be evaluated quite precisely and correctly. Thus, the process becomes, for all practical purposes, a fixed one.

In some cases, what is designed as a fixed socialization process more closely approximates a variable process for the individual described by the cliché, 'always a bridesmaid, never a bride.' The transition timetable is clear enough but, for various reasons, the person cannot or does not wish to complete the journey. Colleges and universities have their 'professional students' who never seem to graduate. Training programs have trainees who continually miss the boat and remain trainees indefinitely. Fixed processes differ, therefore, with regard to both the frequency and the rate of the so-called role failure – the number of recruits who for one reason or another are not able to complete the process.

Some organizations even go so far as to provide a special membership category for certain types of role failures. Some police agencies, for example, give recruits unable to meet agent demands, long-term assignments as city jailers or traffic controllers. Such assignments serve as a signal to the recruit and to others in the organization that the individual has left the normal career path.

To the extent that these organizational 'Siberias' exist and can be identified by those in the fixed setting, chronic sidetracking from which there is rarely a return is a distinct possibility. On the other hand, sidetracking is quite subtle and problematic to the recruit operating in a variable socialization track. Many people who work in the upper and lower levels of management in large organizations are unable to judge where they are going and when they might get there because a further rise in the organization depends in part on such uncertain factors as the state of the economy and the turnover rates above them. Consequently, variable processes can create anxiety and frustration for people who are unable to construct reasonably valid timetables to judge the appropriateness of their movement or lack of movement in the organization.

It is clear that to those in authority within the organization, time is an important resource that can be used to control others. Variable socialization processes give an administrator a powerful tool for influencing individual behavior. But the administration also risks creating an organizational situation marked by confusion and uncertainty among those concerned with their movement in the system. Fixed processes provide temporal reference points that allow people both to observe passages ceremonially and to hold together relationships forged during the socialization experiences. Variable processes, by contrast, tend to divide and drive apart people who might show much loyalty and cohesion if the process were fixed.

Tournament (contest) socialization strategies

The practice of separating selected clusters of recruits into different socialization programs or tracks on the basis of presumed differences in ability, ambition, or background represents the essence of tournament socialization processes. Such tracking is often done at the earliest possible date in a person's organizational career. Furthermore, the shifting of people between tracks in a tournament process occurs mainly in one direction: downward. These people are then eliminated from further consideration within the track they have left. The rule for the tournament socialization strategy, according to Yale University sociologist James Rosenbaum, is simple: 'When you win, you win only the right to go on to the next round; when you lose, you lose forever.'

Contest socialization processes, on the other hand, avoid a sharp distinction between superiors and inferiors of the same rank. The channels of movement through the various socialization programs are kept open and depend on the observed abilities and stated interests of all. In perhaps 75 percent of American public high schools, school administrators and teachers have made student tracking decisions by the ninth grade (and even before). Thus only students on a college-bound track are allowed to take certain courses. But some schools practice a contest mode. They give their students great freedom to choose their classes and allow for considerable mobility in all directions within the system.

Although little empirical research has been done along these lines, there are strong reasons to believe that some version of the tournament process exists in virtually all large organizations. Often someone who is passed over for a management job once, is forever disqualified from that position. And accounts from the women's movement strongly suggest that women in most organizations are on very different tracks from men and have been eliminated from the tournament even before they began. A similar situation can be said to exist for most minority-group members.

Even the so-called 'high-potential employee' has something to worry about in the tournament process. Often the training for the 'high potentials' is not the same as that for the other employees. The 'high potential' track will differ considerably from the track afforded the average or typical recruit. But tournament strategy dictates that even among the 'high potentials' once you are dropped from the fast track you can't get back on it.

As you move through higher and higher levels in the organization, the tournament strategy becomes even more pervasive. Perhaps this is inevitable. The point here is simply that the tournament socialization process (particularly if an extreme version is used across all levels in an organization) has widespread consequences.

One consequence is that when tournament processes are used, the accomplishments of an employee are more likely to be explained by the tracking system of that organization than by the particular characteristics of the person. Thus the person who fails in organization *X* might well have succeeded in organization *Y*. Also, those who fall out of the tournament at any stage can expect only custodial socialization in the future. They are expected to behave only in ways appropriate to their plateaued position, are treated coolly, and are discouraged from making further efforts. The organization, in other words, has completed its work on them. As can be seen, tournament socialization, more than the contest mode, can shape and guide ambition in a powerful way.

Consider, too, that in tournament processes, where a single failure has permanent consequences, those passing through tend to adopt the safest strategies of passage. Low risk taking, short cycles of effort, and ever-changing spheres of interest based primarily on what those above them deem most desirable at any given time are the norm. It follows that those who remain in the tournament for any length of time are socialized to be insecure, obsequious to authority, and differentiated, both socially and psychologically, from one another. On the other hand, those who do not remain in the tournament tend to move in the other direction, becoming fatalistic, homogeneous, and, to varying degrees, alienated from the organization.

The attractiveness and prevalence of tournament socialization strategies in work organizations appear to rest on two major arguments. One is that such processes promote the most efficient allocation of resources. Organizational resources, its proponents say, should be allocated only to those most likely to profit from them. The other, closely related argument, is based primarily on the faith that an accurate and reliable judgment of an individual's potential can be made early in one's career. They believe that the principles of selection and personnel psychology (which are uncertain at best) can be used to separate the deserving from the undeserving members of the organization. Various tricks are then legitimized by testing and classifying people so that each test and the resulting classification represent another level in the tournament process. The American Telephone & Telegraph Co. is perhaps the foremost proponent and user of this socialization process. Each transition from one hierarchical level to another is accompanied by the rigorous evaluation of the ever-declining cadre still in the tournament.

Contest socialization, on the other hand, implies that preset norms for transition do not exist in any other form than that of demonstrated performance. Regardless of age, sex, race, or other background factors, each person starts out equal to all other participants. As in educational systems, this appears to be the stated policy of most American corporations. However, those who have looked closely at these organizations conclude that this Horatio Alger ideal is rarely even approximated in practice.

There is some evidence (primarily from studies conducted in public schools) that contest socialization processes, where they do exist, encourage the development of such characteristics as enterprise, perseverance, initiative, and a craftlike dedication to a job well done. We also have the occasionally impressive results of the workplace experiments that are designed to create autonomous work groups, open and competitive bidding for organizational jobs, and the phasing out of the predictive types of psychological tests used to locate people in the 'proper' career track (sometimes in secrecy). Instead of tests, a few organizations have moved toward simply providing people with more reliable career information and voluntary career counseling so that people can make more knowledgeable choices about where to go in the organization.

In summary, tournament socialization seems far more likely than contest socialization to drive a wedge between the people being processed. In tournament situations, each person is out for himself and rarely will a group come together to act in unison either for or against the organization. Contest strategies, as the label implies, appear to produce a more cooperative and participative spirit among people in an organization. Perhaps because one setback does not entail a permanent loss, people can afford to help one another over various hurdles and a more fraternal atmosphere can be maintained.

Serial (disjunctive) socialization strategies

The serial socialization process, whereby experienced members groom newcomers about to assume similar roles in the organization, is perhaps the best guarantee that an organization will not change over long periods of time. In the police world, the serial feature of recruit socialization is virtually a taken-for-granted device and accounts in large measure for the remarkable stability of patrolman behavior patterns from generation to generation of patrolmen. Innovation in serial modes is unlikely, but continuity and a sense of history will be maintained – even in the face of a turbulent and changing environment.

If a newcomer does not have predecessors available in whose footsteps he can follow, the socialization pattern may be labeled disjunctive. Whereas the serial process risks stagnation and contamination, the disjunctive process risks complication and confusion. The recruit who is left to his own devices may rely on definitions for his task that are gleaned from inappropriate others.

But the disjunctive pattern also gives a recruit the chance to be inventive and original. Without an old guard about to hamper the development of a fresh perspective, the conformity and lockstep pressures created by the serial mode are absent. Most entrepreneurs and those people who fill newly created positions in an organization automatically fall into a disjunctive process of socialization. In both cases, few, if any, people with similar experiences are around to coach the newcomer on the basis of the lessons they have learned.

Similarly, what may be a serial process to most people may be disjunctive to others. Consider a black lawyer entering a previously all-white firm or the navy's recent attempts to train women to become jet pilots. These 'deviant' newcomers do not have access to people who have shared their set of unique problems. Such situations make passage considerably more difficult, especially if the person is going it alone, as is most often the case.

Sometimes what appears to be serial is actually disjunctive. Newcomers may be prepared inadequately for spots in one department by agents from another department. This is often true when the personnel department handles all aspects of training. Only later, after the newcomers have access to others who have been through the same process, do they discover the worthlessness and banality of their training. Agent familiarity with the target position is a very crucial factor in the serial strategy.

Occasionally, what could be called 'gapping' presents a serious problem in serial strategies. Gapping refers to the historical or social distance between recruit and agent. For example, a newcomer to an organization has the greatest opportunity to learn about his future from those with whom he works. But the experiences passed on to him – no doubt with the best of intentions – by those with whom he works may be quite removed from his own circumstance.

Typically, recruits in the first class will set the tone for the classes to follow. This is not to say that those following will be carbon copies, but simply that it is easier to learn from people who have been through similar experiences than it is to devise solutions from scratch. So long as there are people available in the socialization setting the recruits consider to be 'like them,' these people will be pressed into service as guides, passing on the consensual solutions to the typical problems faced by the newcomer. Mental patients, for example, often report that they were only able to survive and gain their release because other, more experienced, patients 'set them wise' as to what the psychiatric staff deemed appropriate behavior indicating improvement.

From this perspective, serial modes of socialization provide newcomers with built-in guidelines to organize and make sense of their organizational situation. Just as children in stable societies are able to gain a sure sense of the future by seeing in their parents and grandparents an image of themselves grown older, employees in organizations can gain a sense of the future by seeing in their more experienced elders an image of themselves further along. The danger exists, of course, that the recruit won't like that image, and will leave the organization rather than face what seems to be an agonizing future. In industrial settings, where worker morale is low and turnover is high, the serial pattern of initiating newcomers into the organization maintains and perhaps amplifies an already poor situation.

The analytic distinction between serial and disjunctive socialization processes is sometimes brought into sharp focus when an organization cleans house, sweeping old members out and bringing new members to replace them. In extreme cases, an entire organization can be thrown into a disjunctive mode of socialization, causing the organization to lose all resemblance to its former self. For example, in colleges with a large turnover of faculty, long-term students exert a lot of control. Organizations such as prisons and mental hospitals, where inmates stay longer than the staff, are often literally run by the inmates.

Investiture (divestiture) socialization strategies

The last major strategy to be discussed concerns the degree to which a socialization process is set up either to confirm or to dismantle the incoming identity of a newcomer. Investiture processes ratify and establish the viability and usefulness of the characteristics the person already possesses. Presumably, recruits to most high-level managerial jobs are selected on the basis of what they bring to the job. The organization does not wish to change these recruits. Rather, it wants to take advantage of their abilities.

Divestiture processes, on the other hand, deny and strip away certain entering characteristics of a recruit. Many occupational and organizational communities almost require a recruit to sever old friendships, undergo extensive harassment from experienced members, and engage for long periods of time in what can only be called 'dirty work' (that is, low-status, low-pay, low-skill, and low-interest tasks). During such periods, the recruit gradually acquires the formal and informal credentials of full and accepted membership.

Ordained ministers, professional athletes, master craftsmen, college professors, and career military personnel must often suffer considerable mortification and humiliation to pay the dues necessary before they are considered equal and respected participants in their particular professions. As a result, closeness develops among the people in that occupation and a distinct sense of solidarity and mutual concern can be found. Pervasive and somewhat closed social worlds are formed by such diverse groups as policemen, airline employees, railroad workers, nurses, symphony musicians, and funeral directors.

Investiture processes say to a newcomer, 'We like you as you are; don't change.' Entrance is made as smooth and troublefree as possible. Members of the organization go to great lengths to ensure that the recruit's needs are met. Demands on the person are balanced to avoid being unreasonable. There is almost an explicit 'honeymoon' period. At times, even positions on the bottom rung of the organizational ladder are filled with a flurry of concern for employee desires. Orientation programs, career counseling, relocation assistance, even a visit to the president's office with the perfunctory handshake and good wishes, systematically suggest to newcomers that they are as valuable as they are.

Ordinarily, the degree to which a setting represents an ordeal to a recruit indicates the degree to which divestiture processes are operative. Rehabilitation institutions, such as mental hospitals and prisons, are commonly thought to be prototypical in this regard. But even in these institutions, initiation processes will have different meanings to different newcomers. Some 'rehabilitation' settings, for example, offer a new inmate a readymade home away from home that more or less complements his entering self-image. Thus, for some people, becoming a member of, say, the thief subculture in a prison acts more as an investiture than a divestiture socialization process. In such cases, one's preinstitutional identity is sustained with apparent ease. Prison is simply an annoying interval in the person's otherwise orderly career. The analyst must examine socialization settings closely before assuming powerful divestiture processes to be acting homogeneously on all who enter.

Yet the fact remains that many organizations consciously promote initiation ordeals designed primarily to make the recruit whatever the organization deems appropriate. In the more extreme cases, recruits are isolated from former associates, must abstain from certain types of behavior, must publicly degrade themselves and others through various kinds of mutual criticism, and must follow a rigid set of sanctionable rules and regulations.

This process, when voluntarily undergone, serves, of course, to commit and bind people to the organization. In such cases, the sacrifice and surrender on the part of the newcomers is usually premised upon a sort of institutional awe the recruits bring with them into the organization. Such awe serves to sustain their motivation throughout the divestiture process. Within this society, there are many familiar illustrations: the Marine Corps, fraternal groups, religious cults, elite law schools, self-realization groups, drug rehabilitation programs, professional athletic teams, and so on. All these organizations require a recruit to pass through a series of robust tests in order to gain privileged access to the organization.

In general, the endurance of the divestiture process itself promotes a strong fellowship among those who have followed the same path to membership. For example, college teaching, professional crime, dentistry, and the priesthood all require a person to travel a somewhat painful and lengthy road. The trip provides the newcomer with a set of colleagues who have been down the same path and symbolizes to others on the scene that the newcomer is committed fully to the organization. For those who complete the ordeal, the gap separating recruits from members narrows appreciably while the gap separating members from nonmembers grows.

Clearly, divestiture rather than investiture strategies are more likely to produce similar results among recruits. And, it should be kept in mind, the ordeal aspects of a divestiture process represent an identity-bestowing, as well as an identity-destroying, process. Coercion is not necessarily an assault on the person. It can also be a device for stimulating personal changes that are evaluated positively by the individual. What has always been problematic with coercion is the possibility for perversion in its use.

Summary and conclusions

I have attempted to provide a partial framework for analyzing some of the more pervasive strategies used by organizations to control and direct the behavior of their members. For instance, the tightness or looseness of day-to-day supervision could also be depicted as a socialization strategy. So, too, could the degree of demographic and attitudinal homogeneity or heterogeneity displayed by the incoming recruits, since it could affect the probability that a single perspective will come to dominate the group of newcomers. What I have tried to do here, however, is describe those processes that are most often both ignored by organizational researchers and taken for granted by organizational decision makers.

It is true that someone undergoing a transition is not *tabula rasa*, waiting patiently for the organization to do its work. Many people play very active roles in their own socialization. Each strategy discussed here contains only the possibility, and not the actuality, of effect. For example, those undergoing collective socialization may withdraw from the situation, abstaining from the group life that surrounds other recruits. Or a person may undergo a brutal divestiture process with a calculated indifference and stoic nonchalance. A few exceptions are probably the rule in even the most tyrannical of settings.

However, the preponderance of evidence suggests that the seven strategies discussed here play a very powerful role in influencing any individual's conception of his work role. By teasing out the situational processes variables that, by and large, define an organization passage, it becomes apparent that for most people a given set of experiences in an organization will lead to fairly predictable ends.

If we are interested in strategies that promote a relatively high degree of similarity in the thoughts and actions of recruits and their agents, a combination of the formal, serial, and divestiture strategies would probably be most effective. If dissimilarity is desired, informal, disjunctive, and investiture strategies would be preferable. To produce a relatively passive group of hard-working but undifferentiated recruits, the combination of formal, collective, sequential, tournament, and divestiture strategies should be used. Other combinations could be used to manufacture other sorts of recruits with, I suspect, few exceptions.

At any rate, the single point I wish to emphasize is that much of the control over individual behavior in organizations is a direct result of the manner in which people are processed. By directing focused and detailed attention to the breakpoints or transitions in a person's work career, much can be gained in terms of understanding how organizations shape the performances and ambitions of their members. And, most critically, the strategies by which these transitions are managed are clearly subject to both empirical study and practical change.

Increased awareness and interest in the strategies of people processing may be a matter of some urgency. The trend in modern organizations is apparently to decrease control through such traditional means as direct supervision and the immediate application of rewards and punishments and increase control by such indirect means as recruitment, selection, professionalization, increased training, and career path manipulation. To these more or less remote control mechanisms, we might well add the seven strategies described in this paper.

Certain features of organizations promote behavioral styles among subordinates, peers, and superiors. Since many of the strategies for breaking in employees are taken for granted (particularly for employees beyond the raw recruit level), they are rarely discussed or considered to be matters of choice in the circles in which managerial decisions are reached. Furthermore, those strategies that are discussed are often kept as they are simply because their effects are not widely understood.

People-processing strategies are also frequently justified by the traditional illogic of 'that's the way I had to do it, so that's the way my successors will have to do it.' Yet, as I have attempted to show, socialization processes are not products of some fixed, evolutionary pattern. They are products of both decisions and nondecisions – and they can be changed. Unfortunately, many of the strategies discussed here seem to be institutionalized out of inertia rather than thoughtful action. This is hardly the most rational practice to be followed by managers with a professed concern for the effective utilization of resources – both material and human.

Selected bibliography

For a much fuller consideration of just how these socialization strategies are linked to one another and how they can be used to help predict the behavioral responses of people in organizational settings, see John Van Maanen and Edgar H. Schein's 'Toward a Theory of Organizational Socialization,' in Barry Staw's (ed.) *Research in Organizational Behavior* (JAI Press, 1978). Some of the ideas developed in this paper are also to be found in John Van Maanen's 'Breaking-In: Socialization to Work,' a chapter in Robert Dubin's *Handbook of Work, Organization, and Society* (Rand-McNally, 1976). An examination of the contrast between the content variables of organizational socialization and the process variables treated here can be found in several of the selections in the recent book edited by Van Maanen, *Organizational Careers: Some New Perspectives* (John Wiley, 1977).

The view of the individual presented in this paper places greater emphasis on the social situations and institutions in which a person resides than it does upon the inner personality. This view suggests that man is social to the core not just to the skin and it is presented best by Erving Goffman in his classic works, *The Presentation of Self in Everyday Life* (Doubleday, 1959) and *Asylums* (Anchor, 1961). Goffman has recently published a difficult but ultimately rewarding book, *Frame Analysis* (Harvard University Press, 1974), that summarizes and ties together much of his sometimes obscure earlier writings.

Some of the better treatments of the sociology of human behavior in organizational settings of direct relevance to managers include Everett C. Hughes's *Men and Their Work* (Free Press, 1958), Melville Dalton's *Men Who Manage* (John Wiley, 1959) and, most recently Rosabeth Kanter's *Men and Women of the Corporation* (Basic Books, 1977). A somewhat broader but nonetheless still pertinent examination of the issue addressed in this paper can be found in Orville Brim and Stanton Wheeler's *Socialization After Childhood* (John Wiley, 1964) and Blanch Greer's (ed.) *Learning to Work* (Sage, 1972). And for a most practical effort at weaving many of these sociological ideas into the psychological fabric that presently informs much of our thinking about behavior in organizations, see Edgar H. Schein's suggestive treatment of *Career Dynamics* (Addison-Wesley, 1978).

change as a political process (1993)

'The organisational politics of technological change', by David A. Buchanan, in David Medyckyj-Scott and Hilary M. Hearnshaw (eds), *Human Factors in Geographical Information Systems*, Belhaven Press, London, 1993, pp. 211–22.

The process of planned change in an organizational setting is often described in a tidy, linear, rational way that starts with a definition of the problem, moves through the evaluation of possible solutions, and ends with the implementation and assessment of the chosen approach. The reality of organizational change, however, is usually different. This article deals with the politics of change. Although the focus lies with geographic information systems, the argument applies to a wide range of technological changes across different settings.

learning objectives

Once you have read and understood this article, you should be able to:

1 Identify aspects of technological and organizational change that increase the problems facing the change agent.
2 Explain and illustrate the political expertise required by the effective change agent.
3 Criticize theories and models of organizational change which ignore the significant role that organizational politics can play.

learning pre-requisites

You will find it useful to read Chapter 16, on organizational change, and Chapter 19, on technology as a trigger of change, in the core text. Chapter 17 deals with the related topic of organization development. The leading commentators in that field argue that the change agent should not be a 'political activist'. That is not the position advanced in Buchanan's article. This debate is also relevant to the material in Chapter 22 of the core text, on organizational power and politics.

learning activities

1 Let us first explore what can be called the 'hassle factor'. Buchanan identifies a number of issues that make new technology projects difficult and risky, and a number of problems that can threaten the position – even the career – of the change agent. So there are two kinds of hassle factors: *risk factors* and *vulnerability factors*. As you read the article, use the matrix on the following page to summarize these factors.
2 As you read through the second half of the article, make a note of as many *power skills* as you can find. These are covert or 'backstage' techniques for mobilizing

support, blocking interference, and focusing attention and enthusiasm on the change process.

3 Consider your own position here. How would you respond if asked to explain and justify the use of such covert or backstage actions in an organizational setting? Do you find these approaches ethical and defensible, or do you find them distasteful and objectionable?

Technological change in the organization: the hassle factor

Risk factors:	*Vulnerability factors:*
threats to the change project	threats to the change agent

Intervention in the political system: a collection of skills

READING 19   *The organisational politics of technological change**
David A. Buchanan

'Although technical issues do play a significant role in the success of a GIS implementation project, financial, organisational, and personnel factors are just as critical and may have longer term impact on the project and system's ultimate success.'

David D. Selden, American Management Systems, Inc.

Is there a problem?

Organisational applications of information technology should present few managerial or technical difficulties in the 1990s, given the significant accumulated experience of such systems. Despite continuing use of the label 'new technology', computing in general and Geographical Information Systems (GIS) in particular have a history spanning at least three decades. The technology is relatively well understood, if still evolving rapidly. There is a wealth of documented experience of applications across a wide variety of settings. The effects on jobs, skills, organisation structures, management styles and business strategies have been extensively explored. The commercial benefits of information technology applications are widely appreciated and exploited. The processes involved in managing technological change are also well documented. The 'new' technology introduced by most organisations in the 1990s will rather represent 'more of the same', in the form of extended and upgraded applications of existing and familiar systems. The novelty value has worn off.

Yet, in spite of the accumulated wisdom and experience, there is still a high problem rate in information technology applications. The available advice on implementation seems either to be inappropriate or ignored.

Evidence for the claim that the main difficulties lie with organisational and managerial rather than with technical factors is overwhelming. Miles (1990) discusses survey evidence suggesting that 30 per cent of large information technology projects in Britain run over budget and over time, mainly because of organisational problems. From an extensive review of the North American literature, Long (1987) concludes that failures in office automation applications are due 10 per cent to technical problems and 90 per cent to organisational and managerial issues. A survey of 400 British and Irish companies carried out in mid-1990 revealed that only 11 per cent had been successful in their information technology applications on criteria concerning benefits achieved, timely completion, and return on investment (Kearney 1990). The Kearney report urged management to recognise that organisation and people issues, not technical areas, are barriers to success and are also the key contributors to success.

The champion of technological change – the project leader or change agent – would on this evidence be advised to focus on managerial and organisational expertise rather than on technical competence. Some commentators have argued that information technology specialists may have a 'trained incapacity' to deal effectively with the organisational dimensions of change and that 'computer illiterate' project managers may be appropriate in many settings (Hamilton 1988; Kearney 1990; Classe 1991). The British Computer Society has been advocating since the late 1980s the development of 'hybrid managers' in this field, combining information technology expertise with business awareness and management skills (Earl and Skyrme 1990; Palmer and Ottley 1990).

---

* Reprinted by permission

What managerial and organisational expertise is required to champion change effectively? Does change involving computing technology have any special characteristics? What issues and problems can the manager seeking to introduce a GIS expect to face? How should the manager most effectively proceed in the face of such problems? In addressing these questions, the emphasis of this chapter is on the manager as change agent, and on the practical expertise required in this role. The main argument of the chapter is that effective implementation is often established in the domain of organisational politics.

Risky projects

Research into technical and organisational change in the 1980s revealed that information technology projects have special characteristics that make them particularly awkward to manage (Buchanan 1986, 1988; Boddy and Buchanan 1986). Often they are expensive and difficult to cost justify in conventional accounting terms. Implementation lead times can be protracted. The long-term commitment of finance and other resources can mean that they are therefore seen as major financial risks. Applications can often be in sectors and areas in which neither the supplier or user have much prior experience. Organisational changes cut across traditional boundaries, threatening entrenched positions and vested interests. Project team members often come from different backgrounds and functions and may not talk the same language as other team members. They are also likely to have different levels of knowledge of the technology – a factor which can inhibit discussion and decision-making because the less well-informed contributors feel unqualified to challenge other, firmly held and forcefully expressed opinions. There is often ambiguity with respect to 'final ownership'. It may not be clear where eventual responsibility for a system lies, with several departments or individuals competing for control.

These aspects of technology implementation make special demands on the manager as champion of change, particularly as the role puts the change agent in a personally vulnerable position. In this respect, information technology projects can be risky for those responsible for their implementation.

To what extent do these features, derived from studies of information technology in general, apply to applications of GIS? With respect to difficulties in cost justification, *The Economist* (1992) argues that the cost of a spatial database for a public utility can be enormous, estimating that a $500,000 investment in hardware may require a further investment ten times that size to generate the required customised database (government offices and utilities represent about three quarter's of the industry's customers). Cornelius and Medyckyj-Scott (1991) point to the difficulties in establishing tangible and measurable benefits of GIS, but also claim that users look primarily for improvements in individual and organisational effectiveness, rather than direct cost savings. Guest (1989), drawing on the experience of Lancashire County Council, argues that cost justification 'is likely to be the most awkward area of all'. The main benefits lie with improved availability of information, improved management facilities, and decision-making aids. Savings in such areas cannot easily be quantified, unless staff reductions – an obviously sensitive issue – are involved. Guest also points out that software costs alone for all but the most basic of systems can run into six figures.

With respect to protracted lead times, Todd (1989) points out that 'the overall time scale for implementation of integrated GIS will take a number of years'. The cost-benefit calculation used by Hampshire County Council (Lyon 1989) initially implied a six to eight year pay-back period. In this case, the cost of implementation was higher than initially forecast, and was inflated partly by additional unforeseen software costs. Cornelius and Medyckyj-Scott (1991) estimate that it can take three to five years to achieve benefits. The traditional commercial pay-back period used in investment appraisal is two to three years. The perceived risk in the investment is clearly increased where the time lag between investment and return is so great, and where costs and benefits are difficult to quantify.

With respect to novelty, Ventura (1989, p. 829) explores the problems of 'sorting through overstated and conflicting claims of hardware, and particularly software vendors'. Goody (1989) warns of 'suppliers eager to tell you what will be available in the future' and of the ready availability of what he calls 'vapourware' in the GIS industry. Lyon (1989) discusses the frustrations and difficulties of 'being a very early player in the game', without 'the cushion of other people's experience to fall back on' from his experience at Hampshire County Council. Lyon adds that, 'although there are a growing number of organisations embarking on a GIS course there are still very few with practical experience of implementing and running a system … consequently there is little experience of solving the sort of problems that can arise'. Guest (1989) points out that the relative infancy of contemporary applications makes it difficult to establish benefits clearly in advance, and also renders awkward the process of comparing applications in other organisations. Another consequence of infancy that Guest notes is that, 'the purchaser will almost unavoidably be breaking some new ground'. Guest also notes the absence of suitable 'off the shelf' systems and the subsequent need to invest in customising specific system requirements, retrieval sequences, output formats and other characteristics. Novelty of application can thus increase both costs and uncertainty.

With respect to the perceived threat of organisational changes, Todd (1989) argues that 'GIS applications by their very nature are likely to affect several different departments within one organisation', and that 'GIS users will challenge the need to keep and maintain all data within distinct departmental boundaries'. Cartwright (1990) argues that the need to exchange information and the technology to achieve this are constrained by traditional organisation structures that reinforce boundaries, which in turn inhibit desirable information flows. Yet the principal advantage of GIS, Cartwright argues, derives from 'the ability to pull the disparate operational parts together by means of a common access method to a common information model of the organisation's business and the environment in which it operates' (Cartwright 1990, p. 39). Cornelius and Medyckyj-Scott (1991, p. 44) also argue that the technology is, 'by its nature a force which necessitates significant change within the organisation'. However, their survey revealed that only a small proportion of users – 18 per cent – had formally discussed the organisational implications of their applications, and only 15 per cent had considered the impact on jobs and work roles. This contrasts sharply with the other finding from the survey that 90 per cent of user organisations experienced organisational difficulties. Typical changes included departmental restructuring, wider information exchange, and the formation of new specialist occupational groupings.

The evidence suggests that applications of GIS create management problems similar to those experienced in other information technology domains. The implications for the change agent, project leader or technology champion are likely also to be similar.

Readers are therefore invited to consider themselves in the highly vulnerable position of the change agent implementing a GIS in an organisation. The colleagues with whom you are working represent different levels of support for, and understanding of, the proposed system. You cannot clearly identify either the costs or the benefits of the application for which you are responsible. It is going to take about five years to finish the project and to begin to see some real returns and other managers are therefore critical about the financial uncertainty and risk involved. Neither the user organisation nor the hardware and software suppliers have any prior experience in implementing a system like the one proposed. There is a lot of anxiety in your organisation about the implications for jobs and responsibilities.

How does the manager as change agent deal with these combined pressures? Fortunately, the vulnerability of the position is offset by the rewards, in terms of both personal challenge and satisfaction and longer term career enhancement. In addition, the expertise required to deal with such issues is readily identifiable. It is important to recognise the significance of organisational factors and not overemphasise technical issues (Foley 1988), and it is important also to deploy consciously and in a planned and creative manners the organisational and political expertise identified below.

Strategy, participation and project management

There is a wealth of practical advice available concerning the implementation of technological and organisational change. That advice has three main dimensions.

First, most commentators argue the need for a long-term strategic view of technology investment, for two reasons. One is that technological innovation can open up new commercial opportunities, in terms of products and services, and should therefore not be regarded merely as a route to streamlining current operations and cost cutting. The second is that, as we have seen, implementation lead times can be extended and the strategic benefits likewise can take time to develop. Kearney (1990) claims that successful users of information technology are more likely to have adopted a long-term strategic view of their investment, and that less successful users adopted a short-term, pragmatic approach to their investment. Boddy and Buchanan (1986) similarly distinguish between an 'opportunistic' and a 'strategic' approach to new technology investment, advocating the latter. Earl (1989), amongst others, makes a compelling case for linking technology strategy with corporate strategy. This advice implies board level representation of technological expertise and planning, or at least that the project champion has the ear of influential senior executives.

Second, it is commonplace in management writing to find advocated a participative approach to the implementation of change (e.g. Eason 1988; Preece 1989; Carnall 1990). The rationale for this is straightforward and difficult to challenge. Those who will be affected, directly or indirectly, by change are in a good position to identify the benefits and problems if they are involved in the planning and decision-making process. Those who contribute to the planning and decision-making are more likely to feel 'ownership' of events and outcomes, and are therefore more likely to be committed to making the changes successful than if they are simply told at a late stage what they have to do (see Chapter 16).

Third, a project management approach to change implementation is widely advocated and adopted (Darnell and Dale 1985; Ahituv and Neumann 1986; Hinton 1988). This involves the establishment of a planned process in which the change is seen to unfold in a logical, phased manner that proceeds from an analysis of the problem, through evaluation of different solutions, to implementation and review. Given the characteristics of the risky, vulnerable task confronting the change agent, to what extent are these structured, phased approaches relevant? Gunton (1990) argues that these simple models are irrelevant and that other methods are required to manage the attitudes and perceptions of organisational members – to generate enthusiasm, to win commitment, to overcome resistance to change. Such considerations move the action of the change agent into the domain of organisational politics.

Power skills and the change agent

It is not the intention here to challenge directly any of the above advice. However, it is necessary to demonstrate that this advice is partial, in that it oversimplifies the reality of the change agent's position. The change agent often cannot action the advice offered due to constraints on personal time, expertise and other resources. That advice also implies that organisational priorities remain stable, which is rarely the case, and also ignores the reality of resistance to change due to personal motives related to job, status, influence and career opportunities. In this section, techniques for dealing with such issues are explored.

Pettigrew (1985, 1987, 1988) has been a major British contributor to thinking in this area. He sees change in organisations not as a logical process but as an untidy cocktail of quests for power, competing views, rational assessment and manipulation, combined with the 'subtle processes of additively building up a momentum of support for change and then vigorously implementing change' (Pettigrew 1985, p. xviii). He notes the growing distrust of 'formalised strategic planning procedures' and 'an increased sensitivity to more informal processes of leadership, vision building, and to team and commitment building as sufficient conditions to manage processes of creating strategic change' (Pettigrew 1988, p. 2). He depicts strategic change as 'in essence a long-term conditioning, educating, and influence process designed to establish the dominating legitimacy of a different pattern of relations between strategic context and content' (Pettigrew 1985, p. 455). For Pettigrew,

> the real problem of strategic change is anchoring new concepts of reality, new issues for attention, new ideas for debate and resolution, and mobilising concern, energy and enthusiasm often in an additive and evolutionary fashion to ensure these early illegitimate thoughts gain powerful support and eventually result in contextually appropriate action. (Pettigrew 1985, p. 438)

By defining 'the real problem of change' in these terms, Pettigrew places on the change agent's agenda a set of items quite different from those typically found in project management texts. The concerns with involvement and ownership expressed in the participative management literature acquire different connotations in the attempt to stimulate debate and mobilise concern. The emphases on goals, deadlines, controls and involvement are here displaced by a concern with legitimacy.

How can the change agent address these issues? How does the project manager intervene in organisational politics to progress technological changes more effectively?

Dutton (1988), in exploring how attention becomes allocated to strategic issues, identifies specific tactics for manipulating the meaning – or 'orchestrating the impressions' – attached to management proposals. These concern 'issue salience', 'issue sponsorship', and 'agenda structure'. There are, for example, four sets of tactics that can be used to alter issue salience. The magnitude of an issue can be manipulated, perhaps by describing it as critical to survival, competitiveness, profitability or to other key organisational goals. The abstractness of the issue can be changed by grounding or by clouding it, by generalising the issue to broaden support in some cases, or by making the issues more specific and focused in others. The simplicity of the issue can be manipulated, either by 'going to the heart of the matter', or by relating it in more complex ways to other concerns. The immediacy of the issue can be manipulated, making it a pressing concern to stimulate action, or by playing it down. These manipulations are achieved through the forms of language and presentation in which proposals and issues are couched and communicated.

Dutton also identifies similar tactics for modifying issue sponsorship. The location of an issue can be manipulated by attaching a powerful individual to it in some way, or by recruiting influential friends to its support. In the same way, attachment can be altered, through allowing more people to participate, and to get involved to increase commitment. Finally, Dutton identifies tactics for modifying agenda structure, through changing the size or length of the current agenda (depending on what is realistic and manageable), and by changing the agenda variety, which can help to determine support for or resistance to new items. The direction of manipulation in each case will depend on the issue and on the context in which it is being introduced and pursued, and this is a matter of management judgement for the change agent.

Pettigrew (1985) indicates the management actions which contribute to effective change implementation. One of the underlying concerns of this approach is with how changes acquire legitimacy on the one hand, and with how proposals find disfavour on the other. A second underlying concern is with the timing of change – with the sequencing of events, the building of awareness and the establishment of consensus. The process of change thus involves the development of concern about the status quo; acknowledgement and understanding of the problem; planning and acting; and finally stabilisation.

In the 'problem sensing' stage, in which concern is aroused and developed in the organisation, the role played by visionary leaders and 'early adopters' is critical. This stage is time consuming, and is often politically sensitive. The task of the change agent is to establish activities that 'educate the organisation', and which broaden the support group. In the 'acknowledgement' phase, the key management tasks are to keep talking and to sustain momentum. This also is time consuming, but the talking is often necessary to make sure that the support for and recognition of the problem are not deflected by other issues and priorities. Pettigrew's advice with respect to planning and acting includes:

▶ setting up management development initiatives which challenge existing thinking;
▶ altering administrative mechanisms and career paths and reward systems;
▶ forming task forces around issues and problems;
▶ fragmenting a global vision into manageable bits;
▶ the exercise of patience, repetition and perseverance (which may involve waiting for individuals to leave or retire);
▶ backing off and waiting until the time is right for other reasons;
▶ replacing those who leave – 'creative retirals' – with known supporters of the change proposals;
▶ changing the organisation structure and procedures;
▶ promoting key individuals or 'role models' and changing their responsibilities at the same time.

These activities express Pettigrew's view of intervention in the organisation's political system, and of the symbolic activity involved in managing change. These constitute deliberate actions to support and to perpetuate the required 'ideological reorientation'. At the stabilisation stage, the key management task is 'making things which happen stick', and this may again involve combinations of substantive and symbolic action such as adjusting rewards and information flows, and adjusting the distribution of power and authority in the organisation. Tangible changes in communications, responsibilities and rewards are also symbolic in that they send signals to other members of the organisation concerning management priorities and future intentions.

A number of commentators have argued that project managers, even in technically sophisticated domains, are at an advantage if they possess strong interpersonal, communication and social skills. Ring (1989, p. 28), for example, reporting on a survey of 191 management information system professionals carried out by the

Andersen Consulting firm, claims that 'The most important element was to have a good project manager with good interpersonal skill.' The selection of a good 'technician' was often regarded as a problem. Ring concludes that the effective project manager has to be an 'all-rounder', with competence in team-building, staff motivation, empowering others, giving others responsibility, credit and independence, giving feedback, listening, picking up problems quickly, taking criticism, and accepting responsibility. Ring (1989) quotes one manager as commenting that:

> I doubt whether the average IT person has a wide enough breadth of vision to do this. If you're looking for project leaders, I think it's easier to teach a little bit of IT to a businessman than it is to teach business to IT people. (p. 29).

Kanter (1983) identifies what she calls 'change architect skills' for the change agent, which include effective articulation or definition of proposals for change. The standard project management advice is: define your project, your problem and your goal clearly. That is easier to say than it is to achieve in practice. There are some clear definitions that are better and more effective than others, particularly when it comes to winning ready support, and anticipating resistance. Kanter suggests that there are at least seven attributes of a 'good' project definition. These are attributes that increase the acceptability of what is being proposed. She suggests that, where possible, a proposal should be presented in terms that make it sound:

▶ *Trial-able*   It should appear capable of being subjected to a pilot before going the whole way down the track with the scheme and with all its effort and expense.

▶ *Reversible*   Convince your audience that what you are proposing can be changed back to today's status quo if it falls to pieces.

▶ *Divisible*   Where your project has a number of separate dimensions, present these as potentially independent aspects of a broader change programme so when single issues cause problems the whole package doesn't have to fold.

▶ *Concrete*   Make the changes and their outcomes tangible and avoid expressing what will happen in abstract and general terms which do not convey an accurate feel for the proposals.

▶ *Familiar*   Make proposals in terms that other people in the organisation can recognise and feel familiar with, because if what you propose is so far over the horizon that people don't recognise it, they'll feel out of their comfort zones and start resisting.

▶ *Congruent*   Proposals for change should where possible be seen to 'fit' within the rest of the organisation and be consistent with existing policy and practice – or at least consistent with other parallel changes.

▶ *Sexy*   Choose projects that have publicity value – whether in terms of external or media relations, or in terms of the internal politics of the organisation.

We are here not dealing directly with deceit, but with the careful construction of the language of change proposals, in a covert attempt to win acceptability and to deflect counter-argument and resistance.

Keen (1981) offers interesting advice on the organisational politics of counter-implementation and counter-counter-implementation strategies respectively. His prescription is aimed at change agents dealing with applications of management information systems, but it is a simple matter to translate this advice into other settings. Keen suggests the following counter-implementation strategies.

▶ *Divert resources*   Split the budget across other projects, have key staff given other priorities and allocate them to other assignments; arrange for equipment to be moved or shared.

▶ *Exploit inertia*   Suggest that everyone wait until a key player has taken action, or read the report, or made an appropriate response; suggest that the results from some other project should be monitored and assessed first.

▶ *Keep goals vague and complex*   It is harder to initiate appropriate action in pursuit of aims that are multi-dimensional and that are specified in generalised, grandiose or abstract terms.

▶ *Encourage and exploit lack of organisational awareness*   Insist that 'we can deal with the people issues later', knowing that these will delay or kill the project.

▶ *'Great idea – let's do it properly'*   And let's bring in representatives from this function and that section, until we have so many different views and conflicting interests that it will take forever to sort them out.

▶ *Dissipate energies*   Have people conduct surveys, collect data, prepare analyses, write reports, make overseas trips, hold special meetings …

▶ *Reduce the champion's influence and credibility*   Spread damaging rumours, particularly amongst the champion's friends and supporters.

▶ *Keep a low profile*   It is not effective openly to declare resistance to change because that gives those driving change a clear target to aim for.

This advice is helpful to the change agent in two respects. First, in attempts to block changes promoted by others in the organisation. Second, in recognising counter-implementation strategies being used to block the change in hand. Counter-implementation is not always easily recognised, and in this respect, the last point on Keen's list of strategies is the most significant. It is not necessary in attempting to block change publicly to declare resistance. On the contrary, some counter-implementation behaviour is covert, and it may be just as effective, or more effective, openly to support change by using, for example, the 'let's do it properly' approach.

What does the change agent do when confronted by the use of counter-implementation strategies of this kind? Keen suggests some counter-counter-implementation strategies:

▶ *Establish clear direction and objectives*   Goal clarity enables action to proceed more effectively than ambiguity and complexity which can slow down action.

▶ *Establish simple, phased programming*   For the same reasons as having clear goals.

▶ *Adopt a fixer-facilitator-negotiator role*   Resistance to change can rarely be overcome by reason alone and the exercise of these interpersonal skills is required.

▶ *Seek and respond to resistance*   It can be more effective to take a proactive approach to resistance in order to overcome, mitigate or block it.

▶ *Rely on face to face*   Personal influence and persuasion are usually more effective in winning and sustaining support than the impersonal memo or report (see Keen's earlier point about the fixer role).

▶ *Create a prior 'felt need'*   If people want change because they have had the reasons explained to them, then resistance is likely to be minimal.

▶ *Build personal credibility*   By sustaining a professional image and integrity, by displaying expertise and credibility.

▶ *Co-opt support early*   Kanter (1983) speaks of coalition building, and of recruiting backers, as of prior importance in comparison with team building.

▶ *Exploit a crisis*   Which may be part of creating the felt need – people will often respond more positively to a crisis which they understand and face collectively than to personal attempts to change their behaviour.

▶ *The meaningful steering committee*   Should include in its membership key players in the organisation who carry 'weight', and authority and respect.

Here again, we are dealing with covert action, rather than with public behaviour, designed to side-step as well as to overcome resistance and to stimulate support through means other than reasoning and argument. The change agent is thus advised to follow the conventional advice about strategic planning, participation and project management. But the change agent is advised also to complement this approach with appropriate 'backstage activity', which involves manipulating language, organisation structures and personal relationships in ways which contribute substantively and symbolically to the winning of support and the blocking of resistance.

The management of change as the management of meaning

The key point is that the practical implications of a political perspective on organisational change are different from those derived from the project management emphasis on goals, roles, deadlines and budgets, and with the participative management advice about sympathetic involvement to ease acceptance and increase commitment. This suggests both a tension and a separation between the *public* performance of the change agent in justifying action in a manner acceptable to and credible in the organisation, and the covert or backstage activity in drawing attention to, establishing discussion around, and marshalling support for change.

The change agent is concerned partly with how proposals address an organisational problem. The change agent is also partly concerned with the involvement and ownership of those affected by the change. In the perspective explored here, the change agent is advised also to be concerned with how the change is perceived by other actors in the organisation, with how it is understood. Those perceptions and that understanding can be managed; they can be manipulated through the methods and approaches outlined in the previous section. In this perspective, therefore, the key to the management of change is the management of meaning (Pettigrew 1985).

The available research and documented experience with respect to applications of GIS are inadequate to confirm whether these management issues – derived from studies of other technological and organisational changes – are relevant. The evidence to hand suggests however that GIS can be expected to generate managerial, organisational and political issues similar to those discussed in this chapter.

References

Ahituv, N. and Neumann, S., 1986, *Principles of information systems for management*, W. C. Brown Publishers, Dubuque, Iowa.

Boddy, D. and Buchanan, D. A., 1986, *Managing new technology*, Blackwell, Oxford.

Buchanan, D. A., 1986, The management essentials of IT projects, *Technology Strategies*, July: 7–8.

Buchanan, D. A., 1988, New technology requires skilled management, *Employment Bulletin*, 4 (5): 1–2.

Carnall, C., 1990, *Managing change in organisations*, Prentice Hall, Hemel Hempstead.

Cartwright, J., 1990, Thinking corporately, in Foster, M. and Shand, P. (eds), *The AGI Yearbook 1990*, Taylor and Francis, London, 35–40.

Classe, A., 1991, Top dogs, *Computing*, 31 January: 18–19.

Cornelius, S. and Medyckyj-Scott, D., 1991, If only someone had said: human and organisational barriers to GIS success, *Mapping Awareness*, 5 (7): 42–5.

Darnell, H. and Dale, M. W., 1985, *Total project management: an integrated approach to the management of capital investment projects in industry*, British Institute of Management, London.

Dutton, J. E., 1988, Understanding strategic agenda building and its implications for managing change, in Pondy, L. R., Boland Jr., R. J. and Thomas, H. (eds), *Managing ambiguity and change,* John Wiley, Chichester, 127–55.

Earl, M., 1989, *Management strategies for information management,* Prentice Hall, Hemel Hempstead.

Earl, M. and Skyrme, D., 1990, *Hybrid managers: what do we know about them?,* Oxford Institute of Information Management, Research and Discussion Papers, Oxford.

Eason, K., 1988, *Information technology and organisational change,* Taylor and Francis, London.

The Economist, 1992, The delight of digital maps, 21 March: 91–2.

Foley, M. E., 1988, Beyond the bits, bytes, and black boxes: institutional issues in successful LIS/GIS management, in *Proceedings, GIS/ LIS '88 Conference,* vol. 2, 30 November–2 December, San Antonio, Texas, American Society for Photogrammetry and Remote Sensing, Falls Church, VA., 608–17.

Goody, C. A., 1989, GIS: thoughts for a first time buyer, paper presented at the *Managing Geographical Information Systems and Databases Conference,* September 20–22, North West Regional Research Laboratory, Lancaster University, Lancaster, UK.

Guest, R., 1989, Implementing a geographical information system – benefits and problems, paper presented at the *Managing Geographical Information Systems and Databases Conference,* September 20–22, North West Regional Research Laboratory, Lancaster University, Lancaster, UK.

Gunton, T., 1990, *Inside information technology: a practical guide to management issues,* Prentice Hall, Hemel Hempstead.

Hamilton, S., 1988, The complex art of saying no, *Computing,* 13 October: 30–1.

Hinton, R., 1988, *Information technology and how to use it: a handbook of effective practice,* ICSA Publishing, Cambridge.

Kanter, R. M., 1983, *The change masters: corporate entrepreneurs at work,* Unwin, London.

Kearney, A. T., 1990, *Barriers to the successful application of information technology – A management perspectiue,* Department of Trade and Industry and Chartered Institute of Management Accountants, HMSO, London.

Keen, P., 1981, Information systems and organisational change, in Rhodes, E. and Weild, D. (eds), *Implementing new technologies: choice, decision and change in manufacturing,* Basil Blackwell/The Open University Press, Oxford, 361–73.

Long, R., 1987, *New office information technology: human and managerial implications,* Croom Helm, London.

Lyon, F., 1989, Implementing a GIS: the Hampshire experience, *Mapping Awareness,* 3 (6): 19–21.

Miles, R., 1990, A stitch in time, *Computing,* 11 October: 22–3.

Palmer, C. and Ottley, S., 1990, *From potential to reality: 'Hybrids' – a critical force in the application of information technology in the 1990s,* British Computer Society, London.

Pettigrew, A. M., 1985, *The awakening giant: continuity and change in ICI,* Basil Blackwell, Oxford.

Pettigrew, A. M., 1987, Context and action in the transformation of the firm, *Journal of Management Studies,* 24 (6): 649–70.

Pettigrew, A. M. (ed.), 1988, *The management of strategic change,* Basil Blackwell, Oxford.

Preece, D. A., 1989, *Managing the adoption of new technology,* Routledge, London.

Ring, T., 1989, When it's not enough to be technically brilliant, *Computing,* 14 September: 28–9.

Selden, D., 1987, Success criteria for GIS, in Aangeenbrug, R. T. and Schiffman, Y. M. (eds), *International Geographic Information Systems (IGIS) Symposium,* vol. 3, Arlingron, VA., NASA, Washington DC, 239–43.

Todd, P., 1989, GIS solutions can't be bought, they must be built, paper presented at the *Managing Geographical Information Systems and Databases Conference,* September 20–22, North West Regional Research Laboratory, Lancaster University, Lancaster, UK.

Ventura, S. J., 1989, Framework for evaluating GIS implementation, in *Proceedings, GIS/LIS '89 Conference,* vol. 2, 26–30 November, Orlando, Florida, American Society for Photogrammetry and Remote Sensing, Falls Church, VA., 825–36.

part 5 # management in the organization

where have we been, and where are we going? (1984)

'Leadership and supervision', by Phil Yetton, in M. Gruneberg and T. Wall (eds), *Social Psychology and Organizational Behaviour*, John Wiley, London, 1984, pp. 9–35.

Phil Yetton presents this excellent summary of leadership research as an attempt to find 'alternatives to heredity as the basis of leadership, and to authoritarianism as the dominant form of management control' – a neat description of a research tradition spanning over half a century. He takes us through early trait approaches, behavioural models, and a range of contemporary contingency theories of leadership, including the influential 'Vroom–Yetton' normative model. His presentation explores the merits, weaknesses and practical implications of these theories. He then identifies what is missing from current approaches. The article ends with a statement of 'where we are going' in this field.

learning objectives

Once you have read and understood this article, you should be able to:

1 Explain and illustrate trends in the study of leadership.
2 Assess the strengths, limitations and practical implications of a range of leadership theories and models.
3 Appreciate the extent to which leadership theories which are apparently contradictory can be viewed as complementary.

learning pre-requisites

You will find it helpful first to read Chapter 20 in the core text, on leadership and management style, where some of the issues covered by Yetton are introduced. We hope you will find that Yetton builds significantly on that chapter.

learning activities

1 Produce your own summary of Yetton's article, by noting the approaches to leadership that he covers, and their respective merits, weaknesses and practical implications. You can do this by drawing up a matrix with the following column headings: Approach; Merits; Weaknesses; and Practical implications. You may find it useful to refer both to Chapter 20 in the core text and to your own experience to complete this assessment.
2 In his concluding remarks, Yetton describes 'where we are going' with leadership research and theory. Make sure that you can explain his argument here, primarily in your own words. But let's go beyond this statement. Take the range of factors covered in this review (traits, followers, trust, context, nature of problem, personalities, goals, and so on) and experiment with drawing up your own model of

leadership. Get creative here. Build on the simple models shown in the article. Or perhaps create a model similar to, or a bit more complex than, the model of personality and job performance from Ivan Robertson in Reading 6. Be innovative. These are just some suggestions.

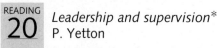

READING
20 Leadership and supervision*
P. Yetton

The First World War and Crimean War were led by officers who were '*born to rule*'; and fought by soldiers whose role has been classically described as follows—'Theirs not to reason why. Theirs but to do and die'.

This chapter is about the alternatives to heredity as the basis of leadership, and to authoritarianism as the dominant form of managerial control. Its structure follows the historical pattern of research, which itself reflects the sequence of questions that Western society has asked since the First World War about the appropriate distribution of power in institutions.

Central to that general debate has been the specific question of participative versus autocratic management. It is this recurrent issue of the social structure of decision making which is the focus of this chapter. The discussion is limited in this way to provide coherence to a topic which has filled many books as authors have tried to explain why one president, executive, manager, or administrator is more successful than another.

More specifically the aim of this chapter is to provide understanding of: (i) early approaches to leadership, namely trait theory and behavioural models; and (ii) current contingency approaches as represented by Fiedler's LPC model, Path–Goal theory, the Vroom–Yetton model, and Graen's dyad model. Throughout comment will be made on each of these approaches, on their respective merits, weaknesses and implications for practice. The chapter begins, however, with some illustrations of managerial decision-making which serve as a reference point throughout the remainder of the text.

Some introductory illustrations

All of us have observed leader behaviour varying from autocratic to democratic to laissez-faire. An autocratic decision style is one in which the manager retains the decision-making rights to him or herself, is task orientated, gives orders to his or her subordinates, and for which communication is typically one-way and downwards. The manager is the initiator of all salient actions. In contrast, in a laissez-faire decision style, the manager imposes few, if any, controls on subordinates. Decisions are left to subordinates and it is they who are the principal initiators of actions. A continuum between these two extremes is presented in Figure 1.

Let us begin by listing four cases in which different styles identified in Figure 1 are illustrated. By returning to and re-examining these cases throughout the chapter, they will provide a relatively concrete application and integration of the theories discussed.

* Reproduced by permission from *Social Psychology and Organizational Behaviour*, Edited by M. Gruneberg and T. Wall © 1984 John Wiley & Sons Ltd.

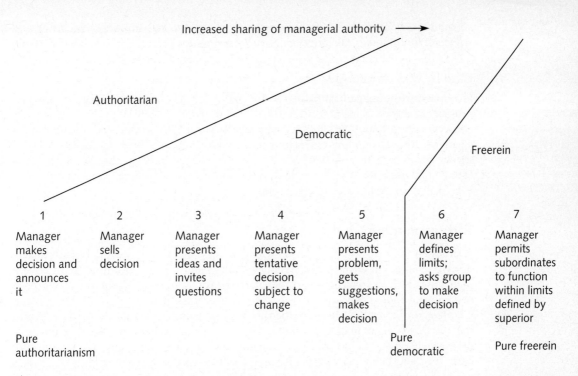

Figure 1 A continuum of leader behaviour and leadership styles. *Source*: Adapted from R. Tannenbaum and W. H. Schmidt (1958), 'How to choose a leadership pattern', *Harvard Business Review*, March–April, 96

Case A: Market research consultant

Kent Department Stores asks a market research agency for a cost estimate for a quote on a corporate image survey in Coventry where they opened a new store twelve months ago. Field work and computer cost estimates have already been obtained from the field force co-ordinator and computer bureau, respectively. It would fit easily into the current project schedule. *The consultant reviews all the information and submits a quote: autocratic.*

Case B: Buying controller Davids Ltd

Davids Ltd is a small department store chain. It is the responsibility of the fashion buying controller to finalize the fashion direction and budgets for next spring. The dress, suits, coats, separates, and sportswear buyers are in general agreement. All that is required is to make slight adjustments to achieve over-all balance within the total fashion budget. *The buying controller negotiates agreement with each buyer: individual consultation.*

Case C: Product manager Crutch Jeans

Crutch Jeans U.K. is an off-shoot from the U.S. parent which was formed to exploit the fashion end of the punk jean market. It is time to finalize the product line for next season. Five new styles have been field tested against the existing six style product line, and detailed costings are available on all options. The problem is whether to expand the product to seven rather than six styles and which to select. *The product manager calls a meeting of sales manager, designer, production manager, and accountant, he shares the problem with them, and listens to their arguments and advice before making the decision: group consultation.*

Case D: Fashion manager

Five product managers responsible for men's shirts, women's shirts, swimwear, sportswear, and jean tops report to the merchandise manager. While they have company cars, they do not park in the company car park. This is reserved for senior management. Recent building extensions have made available three additional covered spaces which have been assigned to the product managers. How should they be allocated? *The manager calls a meeting in which his product managers work out a satisfactory assignment: democratic group.*

Early approaches

A simple trait or personality model of leadership may explain the differences in style described above in terms of the manager's personality. The consultant might have a higher need for dominance than the merchandise manager. Alternatively, within a behavioural model the link between personality and behaviour would be relaxed. The fashion buyer may be described as high on initiating structure behaviour and the merchandise manager as high on consideration behaviour. To explain both descriptively (what happened) and normatively (what should have happened), the early trait and behavioural models assume differences between managers.

Trait theory

Between the First and Second World Wars, researchers attempted to answer the question of how leaders differed from followers. If heredity could not be relied on as a selection mechanism, could personality and/or other individual trait tests provide alternatives? Such strategies implicitly or explicitly assumed differences in individual performance to result from pre-existing trait differences (Figure 2).

Stogdill (1976) reviews an impressive range of trait studies. However, it is the number of such studies and not the consistency of their findings which is impressive. Factors which discriminated between leaders and followers in one study typically failed to replicate in subsequent research. Jenkins (1947) and Gibb (1969) present major reviews of the literature and find no universal trait or set of traits common among leaders and their subordinates. On the other hand, Stogdill (1976) reports evidence that leaders and followers differ with respect to their intelligence, need for power, dependability, sense of responsibility, social participativeness, and the socio-economic status of their parents.

Figure 2 Trait models of leadership

In a recent major replication, Ghiselli (1971) reports that compared with ineffective managers, effective managers score higher on intelligence, self-assurance, supervisory ability, need for occupational achievement, decisiveness, and need for self-actualization, and lower on need for security. He also reports effectiveness to be independent of need for power, socio-economic background, need for money, maturity, and relative masculinity/femininity orientation.

There appears to be agreement that effective managers have above average scores on intelligence, self-confidence, need for job success, and initiative. The literature says nothing about the additivity or substitutability of the various characteristics. The implication is that it is better to be high on all. Of course, if we try to select someone in the top 10% on five independent dimensions such as those above, we have restricted the domain of potential candidates to one in 100,000 from the total population. In addition, the choice may be further restricted by other requirements. For example, he or she should be an accountant between 30 and 40 years old!

Of course, these dimensions may not be independent. It is likely that self-confidence and initiative are as much outcomes of past successes as they are independent predictors of future success. In addition, the high need for power among managers may reflect assumptions made by those appointing managers to senior positions rather than any causal relation between it and performance. Evans (1979), using a crude classification system, summarizes Stogdill's (1976) review as follows:

Appointed leaders:
    Twelve of 23 studies found intelligence higher for leaders.
    Five of 23 studies found social skills higher for leaders.
Emergent leaders:
    20 of 40 studies found intelligence higher for leaders.
    22 of 40 studies found social skills higher for leaders.

This pattern is consistent with the author's recent experience in examining three years of performance appraisals for 45 senior managers in one company. In no case was a manager graded as currently promotable if he or she did not score well above average in technical knowledge, but over 50% of the currently promotable managers were scored adequate or below on interpersonal skills!

After a massive research effort, we seem to be confident of little more than intelligence being positively related to managerial success. In a technologically-based industrial society this must come as little surprise to most. However, our major gain is probably the lack of any findings. To be able to conclude that personality does not dominate managerial performance is of great importance. Researchers are thereby freed to look elsewhere for the determinants of effective managerial behaviour.

Behavioural models

After the First World War, the search for a theory of leadership sought personality and other individual difference correlates of managerial performance. After the Second World War, the research focus shifted to behavioural differences and the human relations school of management emerged. This asserted that increased participation leads to increased morale which then generates high performance. After all, had not the forces of democracy been shown to triumph over the autocratic forces of fascism?

We are all familiar with stories of leadership portrayed in the cinema, whether it is John Wayne winning the war single-handed or Luke Skywalker defeating the Empire. The leader of the good guys is usually inexperienced, his/her troops are outgunned and outnumbered, and they begin by losing. Finally, as survival is threatened, the leader takes advice from his experienced NCO or other mentor, and begins to treat his troops as individuals. The unit develops tremendous morale, and defeats the enemy who lose because they act rigidly and stupidly. Given the social acceptability of this form of leadership it was rational to prove scientifically that effective leaders participated with and were considerate of their subordinates/followers.

The basic behavioural model is presented in Figure 3. Research consistently reports positive correlations between participative styles of decision taking and subordinates' satisfaction (see for example review by House and Baetz, 1979). While the relationship between satisfaction and participation is consistently strong, the relationship with performance is both variable and weak. It would therefore be a poor guide to managerial behaviour and/or training.

Figure 3 Behavioural models

There are two other major research themes in the behavioural literature. One was developed at Ohio State University and the other at Michigan University in the U.S.A. At Ohio, Halpin and Winer (1957) factor analysed over 1,500 items descriptive of managerial behaviour and identified four principal factors. Two of these, *consideration* and *initiating structure*, accounted for the majority of the explained variance.

Consideration is the empathy a manager shows for subordinates' emotional needs, and the warmth, support, and respect he or she shows for them. The shift from low to high consideration in the John Wayne war film is always very obvious, and is immediately followed be a rise in morale. In contrast, initiating structure reflects the level of organization and structuring of subordinates' actions by the manager. The shift in the typical film from low to high initiating structure is less obvious and the research findings less consistent than for the parallel consideration shift (Stogdill, 1976).

Again there is an extensive body of research findings. For example, Halpin (1957) reports a positive correlation between initiating structure and performance. Korman (1966) presents a positive relationship between consideration and subordinates' satisfaction and a negative one between turnover and consideration.

The above and other similar findings were summarized by Blake and Mouton (1964) in their Managerial Grid, according to which effective managers are high in both consideration and initiating structure. The leader benefits from the advantages associated with a high score on each dimension. The high consideration characteristic would offset any tendency for the high initiating structure behaviour to generate high grievance rates. Fleishman and Harris (1962) report that managers high on initiating structure tend to generate both high performance and high grievance rates among their subordinates. However, those who are also high on consideration avoid the high grievance rates.

Whereas the Ohio group began by attempting to identify the major dimensions of leader behaviour, the Michigan team classified managers as effective or ineffective and then attempted to isolate leader behaviour which differentiated between them. Their findings are summarized in Table 1.

In an early study Katz, Maccoby and Morse (1950) report that high performance managers tend to be person-centred as opposed to production-centred. They provide general rather than close supervision, and differentiate their own from their subordinates' roles. The first two findings were subsequently replicated by Katz, Maccoby, Gurin, and Floor (1951). They found no evidence for the effectiveness of role

Table 1 Michigan model

	Effective managers	Ineffective managers
I	Concerned about subordinates	Task focused
II	General supervision	Close supervision

differentiation. The findings for consideration versus task and general versus close supervision have been replicated frequently (Stogdill, 1976).

Does Table 1 present the basis for an adequate theory? Unfortunately, the general conclusion is no. The early research at Ohio was preoccupied with developing instruments to measure consideration and initiating structure. Their existence encouraged replication and facilitated cross validation. The chance of finding any inconsistencies which existed was therefore high. In contrast, the Michigan research classification was derived from in-depth interviews. Errors in variables across studies are likely and few studies could be and were replicated. As such the consistency of their results is more apparent than real.

The three sets of research findings can be integrated at a very general level. Participation is likely to map into general supervision and high initiating structure.* A participative style would also be likely to emphasize people and consideration towards subordinates. At this level of generalization, the three models are equivalent and all appear plausible.

Two major reservations limit this integration. First, the level of participation in the cases above may be a property of the four jobs rather than of the leadership strategy. If similar problems occur within, rather than between jobs, then the within manager's style variance would dominate the between job variance. That is, an individual manager could act autocratically on Monday morning and participatively in the afternoon. This shift may be large relative to any average difference in participation comparing his or her behaviour with that of a colleague. This is the pattern reported by Vroom and Yetton (1973). Similar arguments could be made with respect to the other variables, in which case, while the theory would be valid, it would explain little of importance.

The second major reservation is the lack of longitudinal studies establishing causality. The few such studies reported tend to suggest that low performance leads to both low morale and close supervision (Lawler and Porter, 1972). It may be that style, as measured above, is as much an outcome as it is a cause of performance and satisfaction. Of course, causality was not a problem for the personality theorists who simply assumed that personality caused behaviour rather than itself being formed by the leadership experience. We will return to this issue later as it is also of major concern in the review of current theories.

Comment on the early approaches

The answers we get nearly always depend on the questions we ask. Even with similar questions, a different frame of reference can substantially alter the answers or, at least, their interpretation. This is the case here. Let us re-examine the four illustrative cases described earlier.

For a reader who assumed a personality or individual differences frame of reference for leadership, it is natural to expect that four different managers were

---

* An examination of the items in a typical initiating structure questionnaire suggest that while high scores would tend to weight onto general supervision, a few items (telling subordinates what to do) would weight onto close supervision.

described. After all, there are four different jobs and four very different leadership styles. In fact, all refer to a single manager and were taken from her employment history when interviewed for the position of managing director for a major fashion company. She is not atypical. Table 2 presents the style choices made by 35 managers when asked how they would act in each of the four situations. On three of the cases, they report a high degree of consistency both with each other and the actual manager involved. The exception is the parking lot problem (Case D, p. 11).

Table 2 Leadership style choices of 35 managers

	Autocratic	Individual consultation	Group consultation	Democratic group
Research consultant	33*	2	0	0
Buying controller	5	23*	6	1
Product manager	3	6	26*	0
Fashion manager	13	5	3	14*

Source: *Mary Derbyshire's choice

It is easy to see, from an examination of the four illustrative cases, that participation and performance can only be weakly linked within a personality or behavioural main effect model. Our successful applicant for the managing director's job, Mary Derbyshire, varies her behaviour from highly autocratic to highly participative. This is consistent with the patterns for the other managers. Only in the parking lot problem do we observe a wide variation in autocratic and participative managerial behaviours. A general relationship between participation and performance takes no account of the variation in style variance across situations.

How do we explain Mary's apparently inconsistent participative behaviour? Just as the behavioural models questioned the link between personality and behaviour, the recent theories challenge the assumption that an individual has a single dominant leadership style. Instead, he or she is fitted (Fiedler, 1967) or fits his or her style (Path–Goal: House and Mitchell, 1974) to the situation. Vroom and Yetton (1973) also fit the manager's style to the situation, but distinguish situations in terms of different problems within the manager's role. They define situations in terms of the characteristics of problems which the manager confronts. Graen also disaggregates, in his case, across different subordinates rather than across problems (Dansereau, Graen, and Haga, 1975). By relaxing different assumptions, each of these theories attempts to resolve inconsistent findings apparent in the simple personality and behavioural main effect models.

Current approaches

The human relations school of management was finally buried by the management community with Richard Nixon and the Vietnam War. The general belief in the obvious rightness of being considerate to subordinates and others engendered by the Second World War had been dissipated. The shift in both the management and academic community was towards contingent models in which the situational context both does and should influence both behaviour and its outcomes.

This next generation of models is significantly more complex than the earlier ones. In addition, unlike the trait and behavioural models discussed above, the contingency models discussed here have very different internal structures. There is no single, all embracing contingency model. Different assumptions are relaxed in each of Fiedler's, Path–Goal, Vroom–Yetton's and Graen's models. Indeed, these models are often presented not only as competing but as mutually exclusive. If one is validated, the others are wrong. Because most researchers defend one model at the expense of the others, the relative importance of the phenomena they address is inadequately discussed in the literature. In fact, they attempt to explain different phenomena. As far as this author knows, there is no single empirical comparative study of these theories.

Fiedler's (1967) theory is the earliest and the most extensively researched. Three situational factors, *leader–member relations*, *task structure*, and *leader position power* determine the favourability of the situation for managers high or low on the Least Preferred Coworker (LPC) trait. It holds that low LPC managers perform best in situations of either high or low favourableness, whereas high LPC managers fit situations of medium favourableness. This is a trait-contingency model with an initial emphasis on the selection of managers to match the situation followed by some situation engineering and manager training to correct mismatches. It fits within the person–situation interaction paradigm.

Path–Goal makes the influence of leader behaviour, initiating structure and consideration, dependent on the degree of structure present in the situation (House and Mitchell, 1974). This is a behaviour–contingency model. Both this and Fiedler's theory average across leader behaviours in a particular role. The different styles a manager uses on different problems and in his/her interactions with different subordinates are ignored.

Both Vroom–Yetton and Graen disaggregate manager behaviour. Vroom and Yetton (1973) show that variation in style for an individual manager is greater than the difference between managers. They identify seven situational dimensions which both should and do influence the level of subordinate participation in decision-making. Graen differentiates between subordinates instead of problems (Dansereau, Graen, and Haga, 1975). Managers act differently towards different subordinates. Members of the in group are consulted like colleagues, whereas members of the out group are treated as hired workers and told what to do.

Each of the four models is considered in greater detail next.

Fiedler's LPC model

Fiedler's LPC model was the first sustained attempt to develop a contingent model of leadership (Fiedler, 1967). Others such as Tannenbaum and Schmidt (1958) had advocated situation based models but Fiedler's was the first such systematic empirical investigation. His model has three situational factors which define the degree of situational favourableness for the leader.

Leaders are differentiated by their LPC score. The meaning of LPC and its behavioural correlates are still a matter of conjecture and some controversy. A manager's score is his or her average score on the 16 item scale in Figure 4. A manager with a low score sees his least preferred coworker in a generally poor light. In contrast, a manager with a high score differentiates between performance and individual differences among his work colleagues.

In their initial studies, Fiedler and his associates found correlations between LPC scores and managerial performance ranging from +0.8 to −0.8 (Fiedler, 1967). This is typical of the trait research findings discussed above. Instead of rejecting LPC as a leadership trait, Fiedler examined why successful board chairmen were high LPC, whereas the best open heart supervisors were low LPC. Situational favourableness was found to moderate the LPC/performance relationship. Fiedler argues that under

	8	7	6	5	4	3	2	1		
Pleasant									Unpleasant	____
Friendly	8	7	6	5	4	3	2	1	Unfriendly	____
Rejecting	1	2	3	4	5	6	7	8	Accepting	____
Tense	1	2	3	4	5	6	7	8	Relaxed	____
Distant	1	2	3	4	5	6	7	8	Close	____
Cold	1	2	3	4	5	6	7	8	Warm	____
Supportive	8	7	6	5	4	3	2	1	Hostile	____
Boring	1	2	3	4	5	6	7	8	Interesting	____
Quarrelsome	1	2	3	4	5	6	7	8	Harmonious	____
Gloomy	1	2	3	4	5	6	7	8	Cheerful	____
Open	8	7	6	5	4	3	2	1	Guarded	____
Backbiting	1	2	3	4	5	6	7	8	Loyal	____
Untrustworthy	1	2	3	4	5	6	7	8	Trustworthy	____
Considerate	8	7	6	5	4	3	2	1	Inconsiderate	____
Nasty	1	2	3	4	5	6	7	8	Nice	____
Agreeable	8	7	6	5	4	3	2	1	Disagreeable	____
Insincere	1	2	3	4	5	6	7	8	Sincere	____
Kind	8	7	6	5	4	3	2	1	Unkind	____
									Total score	====

Figure 4 Least preferred coworkers (LPC) scale

high situational favourableness subordinates accept being directed. A low LPC or task-orientated manager fits such a situation. In the converse situation, with everything stacked against the leader, he or she must intervene decisively and direct subordinates' actions. Here again a low LPC task focussed manager is needed. On the other hand, when the situation is moderately favourable, a high LPC or person-centred management style is required to work through the issues involved. These results are presented in Figure 5 which reports the correlation between performance and LPC under different conditions of situational favourableness. (Note that correlations vary from strongly positive to strongly negative.)

This theory is inductive in that it was developed to account for the variance in correlations observed between LPC and manager performance. Naturally, it explains much of the variance in this relationship reported in the initial research. The validation studies report contradictory results. For example, Graen, Orris, and Alvares (1971) in a laboratory experiment failed to replicate the earlier findings. This study was undertaken after Graen, Alvares, Orris, and Martella (1970) re-analysed Fiedler's initial results and questioned his interpretation. The controversy has raged ever since. Chemers and Rice (1974) review the literature and conclude the theory is valid, whereas, Ashour (1973) argues it is false. Recently, Schrieheim and Kerr (1977) and Fiedler (1977) reviewed the evidence. The former came down against the theory, the latter, not surprisingly, in favour.

The problem in all the reviews is how to aggregate across different studies. Recently developments in meta analysis have resolved some of these issues. In meta analysis the studies to be reviewed are treated as a sample of the possible studies which could be done. Variations in results are compared to the variance expected given sampling error, measurement reliability, range restriction and other sample characteristics. Using this technique, Strube and Garcia (1982) find strong evidence in support of the theory. The exceptions are Octants II and III (the second and third from the left in Figure 5). They also note that the majority of studies are of Octants I, III, and V. In Octant I with very high situational favourableness a task focussed manager is needed is run an efficient operation with few problems. In Octant V with

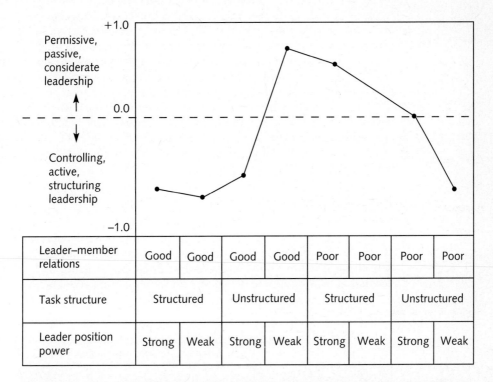

Figure 5 Fiedler's LPC model. Correlation between performance and LPC under different conditions of situational favourableness. Reproduced with permission from F. E. Fiedler (1972). *Source*: F. E. Fiedler (1972), 'The effects of leadership training and experience: a contingency model interpretation', *Administrative Science Quarterly*, December 1972, 455

poor leader member relations but otherwise a favourable situation, a person-centred manager is needed. As already noted, the results for Octant III are inconclusive.

Assuming that the theory is valid, how could it be used? Selection and placement are obvious options, however, there are two major difficulties. One is that managers may take their LPC scan. The other is that leader–member relations need to be predicted before the manager is appointed. For internal promotion under relatively stable conditions this might be possible. However, if the situation is Octant V with poor leader–member relations due to the previous manager's behaviour, the new high LPC (person-centred) manager might improve the situation and create an Octant I situation in which he or she is a mismatch. If the future situational favourableness is a function of present leader behaviour, there is a major validity threat to the theory.

If an error in selection is made and a mismatch is appointed, what action should be taken? Initially Fiedler favoured engineering the situation to fit the person. However, in practice this option may be limited. For example, an increase in position power may be unacceptable to his or her colleagues, or more generally within the over-all power structure of the organization. Conversely, where a decrease is called for, the manager may not find it acceptable. Similarly, any change in the level of task structure may require major alterations in responsibilities and the associated information and other decision-making and implementing technologies. These could result in mismatches elsewhere.

More recently, Fiedler has advocated training to resolve mismatches. Typically, this is in reference to a mismatch due to the presence of low task structure. This is resolved by training the manager in the skills necessary to get on top of the problems and structure the work situation. This moves us in a direction in which the contingency conditions are themselves a function of managerial behaviour.

While meta analysis has established general support for the theory, the discussion above raises some important reservations about its application. The interactions between both engineering and training solutions to mismatches and matters of system design and efficiency warrant careful examination. Most importantly, the behavioural correlates of LPC under different conditions of favourableness need to be established. Fiedler provides no direct evidence that high LPC managers are person-centred or low LPC managers task-centred. Yet much of the arguments supporting the theory rest on this assumption.

Path–Goal theory

Fiedler's theory is a trait-contingency model. The situation determines the effectiveness of the trait. The Path–Goal model is a behavioural–contingency model. The inconsistencies in the behavioural model discussed above are assumed to be a function of the situation. Both high and low initiating structure and consideration are deemed to be appropriate depending on the situation (see Figure 6).

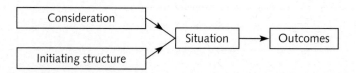

Figure 6 Path–Goal model

The underlying theory is an expectancy model. The manager satisfies his or her subordinates to the extent that they find their work experience intrinsically or extrinsically rewarding. The manager's behaviour is motivating in the degree to which he or she makes those rewards contingent on task performance. Effective leadership involves the joint event of anticipated satisfactions by subordinates perceived by them as contingent on organization performance.

This is the basic structure of any expectancy model. While the above statement appears simple, its operationalization has led to many very complex models. Both subordinates' utility functions (value of a reward) and their risk preferences and other determinants of subjective probabilities are complex issues. For example Schuler (1976) shows that only when the task is well structured and non-ego involving, do subordinate personalities moderate the style–satisfaction–performance relationship.

This relationship is likely to be sensitive not only to personality and other individual differences among subordinates, but also to management team dynamics and organization structural characteristics. For example, Miles and Petty (1977) report that organization size moderates the basic model. In small government agencies, the correlation between initiating structure and subordinates' satisfaction is positive, and negative for large agencies. In contrast, the correlation between consideration and satisfaction is higher for large rather than small agencies.

A leadership theory in which the moderators for secondary hypotheses span personality and organization theory suffers from a lack of specification The problem with the Path–Goal model is that it is simply too general. Rather than being a theory about leadership, it is the application of the general expectancy model to the area of leadership. All the problems experienced with expectancy models elsewhere are then encountered in the context of leadership. Even House (House, Filley, and Kerr, 1976) reviews the evidence and concludes that the theory is not sufficiently developed and well-specified to be used as a prescriptive theory.

Vroom–Yetton model

Like Fiedler's theory, the Vroom–Yetton model is essentially a diagnostic one. Unlike Fiedler, Vroom and Yetton assume that managers can vary their style from situation to situation (see Figure 7). The model is concerned with deriving and implementing a solution to a recognized problem. Thus the model is different from Fiedler's in two major ways. First, the situational characteristics are properties of specific decisions confronting the manager, rather than being general characteristics of the manager's position or role. (The Path–Goal model, like Fiedler's, generates behaviour at the role level.) Second, the leader is assumed to have a flexible style. He or she may use all the styles employed in the four illustrative cases, as did Mary Derbyshire. It could be appropriate for a manager to be autocratic Monday morning and participative in the afternoon because the problems are different.

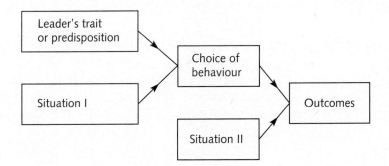

Figure 7 Vroom–Yetton model of leadership

Vroom and Yetton identify five different leadership styles which span a continuum from autocratic to participative (see Figure 8). These are similar to those proposed earlier by Tannenbaum and Schmidt (1958) (see Figure 1) and Heller (1971). Seven problem characteristics define the situation (see Figure 9). A problem's situational characteristics define a feasible set of styles which is used to generate a solution which meets the necessary acceptance and quality constraints. The feasible set may contain up to five styles. The normative model is presented in Figure 9. To apply it, the manager begins at the left-hand side and asks himself or herself the first question: 'Is there a quality requirement such that one solution is likely to be more rational than

AI You solve the problem or make the decision yourself, using information available to you at the time.

AII You obtain the necessary information from your subordinates, then decide the solution to the problem yourself. You may or may not tell your subordinates what the problem is in getting the information from them. The role played by your subordinates in making the decision is clearly one of providing the necessary information to you, rather than generating or evaluating alternative solutions.

CI You share the problem with the relevant *subordinates individually*, getting their ideas and suggestions without bringing them together as a group. Then *you* make the decision, which may or may not reflect your subordinates' influence.

CII You share the problem with your subordinates *as a group*, obtaining their collective ideas and suggestions. Then you make the decision, which may or may not reflect your subordinates' influence.

GII You share the problem with your subordinates as a group. Together you generate and evaluate alternatives and attempt to reach agreement (consensus) on a solution. Your role is much like that of chairman. You do not try to influence the group to adopt 'your' solution, and you are willing to accept and implement any solution which has the support of the entire group.

Figure 8 Leadership styles

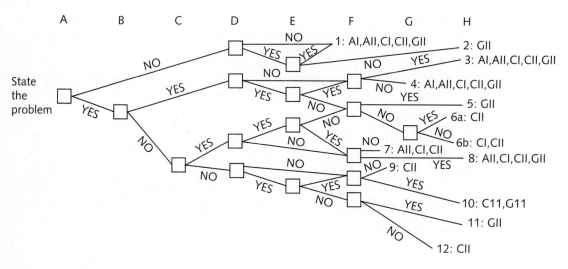

Figure 9 Vroom–Yetton normative model
Decision-process flow chart for group problems (feasible set):

A Is there a quality requirement such that one solution is likely to be more rational that another?
B Do I have sufficient information to make a high-quality decision?
C Is the problem structured?
D Is acceptance of decision by subordinates critical to effective implementation?
E If I were to make the decision by myself, is it reasonably certain that it would be accepted by my subordinates?
F Do subordinates share the organizational goals to be attained in solving this problem?
G Is conflict among subordinates likely in preferred solutions? (This question is irrevelent to individual problems.)
H Do subordinates have sufficient information to make a high-quality decision?

another?' If the answer is no, the manager follows the upper route, if the answer is yes, he or she follows the lower route. Whenever a box is encountered the corresponding question above is asked. This is repeated until a terminal node is reached. Each node is labelled with the styles which satisfy that type of problem.

The structure of the decision tree in Figure 9 incorporates seven rules. Three protect the quality of the decision and four protect its acceptance by subordinates. Any particular rule states that under given circumstances, a subset of the five styles should be eliminated from the set of styles considered feasible. These are avoided because they involve a potential risk to quality and/or acceptance. The rules are presented in Figure 10.

Rules protecting quality requirements

The leader information rule
If the quality of the decision is important and the leader does not possess enough information or expertise to solve the problem by himself, then AI is eliminated from the feasible set.

The goal congruence rule
If the quality of the decision is important and subordinates are not likely to pursue the organizational goals in their efforts to solve this problem, then GII is eliminated from the feasible set.

The unstructured problem rule
In decisions in which the quality of the decision is important, if the leader lacks the necessary information or expertise to solve the problem by himself, and if the problem is unstructured, the method of solving the problem should provide for interaction among subordinates likely to possess relevant information. Accordingly, AI, AII, and CI are eliminated from the feasible set.

The acceptance rule
If the acceptance of the decision by subordinates is critical to effective implementation and if it is not certain that an autocratic decision will be accepted, AI and AII are eliminated from the feasible set.

The conflict rule
If the acceptance of the decision is critical, an autocratic decision is not certain to be accepted and disagreement among subordinates in methods of attaining the organizational goal is likely, the methods used in solving the problem should enable those in disagreement to resolve their differences with full knowledge of the problem. Accordingly, under these conditions, AI, AII, and CI, which permit no interaction among subordinates and therefore provide no opportunity for those in conflict to resolve their differences, are eliminated from the feasible set. Their use runs the risk of leaving some of the subordinates with less than the needed commitment to the final decision.

The fairness rule
If the quality of the decision is unimportant, but acceptance of the decision is critical, and not certain to result from an autocratic decision, it is important that the decision process used generate the needed acceptance. The decision process used should permit the subordinates to interact with one another and AI, AII, CI, and CII are eliminated from the feasible set.

The acceptance priority rule
If acceptance is critical, not certain to result from an autocratic decision and if subordinate(s) is(are) motivated to pursue the organizational goals represented in the problem, then methods which provide equal partnership in the decision-making process can provide greater acceptance without risking decision quality. Accordingly, AI, AII, CI, and CII are eliminated from the feasible set.

Figure 10 Vroom–Yetton model rules

The decision tree format makes two features very obvious. First, there is not necessarily a single best style for a problem. In some instances any of the five styles would do, while in others the model recommends a single best decision method. Where more than one style is feasible, additional criteria for restricting the choice are suggested. These include, for example, minimizing the managerial resources involved in the decision, or developing the subordinates' understanding of the problem.

Second, it is also immediately apparent from the tree that if a manager makes incorrect judgements about the answers to any of the seven situational questions, then the style recommended by the model may be inappropriate. For example, an incorrect judgement as to the likelihood that subordinates would accept and be committed to a given decision could lead to the model prescribing an autocratic process (AI) rather than a participative style (GII). Examining managers' codings of standard cases and both managers' and their subordinates' codings of on-line problems, Yetton (1980) concludes that perceptual errors in judgements are not a major problem for the implementation of the theory.

Vroom and Jago (1978) report a test of the normative theory using managers' reports of recalled problems. Each manager was asked to recall and describe two problems, one of which was successfully managed, the other unsuccessfully. After identifying their problems, the managers were trained in the use of the model. They were asked to compare the style they actually used with that prescribed by the decision tree. When the styles used agreed with the model, the outcomes were more frequently successful (68%) than unsuccessful (32%). When the styles were in violation of the model, the outcomes were most frequently unsuccessful (78%) than successful (22%).

While this evidence appears to be strong, there is a major weakness. Self reports tend to be biased (Bass, 1957). This is supported by differences in managers' self-report style and similar judgements by their subordinates (Jago and Vroom, 1975). However, the latter data refer to expected behaviour on hypothetical questions and not to recalled behaviour from actual situations.

House, Filley, and Kerr (1976) question the parsimony of the model and the capacity of the average manager to use such a complex strategy. Following this line, Field (1979) presents a simplified version of the model. However, to do this he increases the average level of participation for a range of problems which would substantially raise the cost of the strategy. The trade-off of simplicity for higher costs may be inappropriate. Certainly, with over 5,000 managers in the U.S.A., Europe and Australia trained in the original model, few have complained that it is too complex. Indeed, in personalizing the model many increase its complexity.

As well as proposing a normative model describing how managers should act, Vroom and Yetton investigated how they do in fact behave. They found that managers were more participative on problems with a quality requirement, or where they lack some of the relevant information or expertise, or which are unstructured, than on problems without one or more of those characteristics. Managers are also more participative if acceptance of the decision by subordinates is important and when acceptance is unlikely to exist for an autocratic decision taken by themselves. If acceptance is important, and the subordinates share the manager's goals, and there is no conflict among subordinates, managers are again more participative than if any or all of these conditions are not satisfied.

A comparison of these descriptive findings reveals that, with one exception, the normative and descriptive patterns of behaviour have the same sign but the variance in behaviour within the descriptive model is less than within the normative. That is, when the normative model says a manager should be very participative, he does tend to act participatively as indicated by the model but not to the degree prescribed. Similarly, when the model advocates autocratic behaviour, managers are typically autocratic but are slightly less so than is suggested by the normative model.

The exception to this general pattern is the typical manager's avoidance of highly participative styles when conflict among his subordinates is strong. In contrast, the Vroom and Yetton normative model advocates participative styles when, in addition to the presence of conflict, it is also necessary to develop the subordinates' commitment to the resultant decision in order to safeguard its effective implementation. While investigating possible differences among managers' responses to situational variables, Jago (1978) found some evidence for a manager-situation interaction with respect to conflict. While the typical manager is averse to conflict, there are perhaps a quarter of managers who are not. These appear to be comfortable in using participative decision modes even when a high level of conflict is present. Vroom and Yetton (1973) speculate that such interactions may be just as important as determinants of behaviour as the direct situational effects. Jago's recent research seems to confirm this (Jago, 1978). No major changes in theoretical framework are required to take account of any such individual situation interactions.

Whereas application is problematic with both Fiedler's and the Path–Goal theory this is not so for the Vroom–Yetton model. The five styles are already in most managers' repertoires and upgrading their skills in this area simply requires the application of existing training technologies. In addition, managers can make judgements about problem characteristics. So, improving a manager's choice of style is only a matter of learning to apply the rules combined with training in group dynamics and problem solving, with an emphasis on coping with conflict.

Graen's dyad model

Whereas Vroom and Yetton disaggregate across problem situations, Graen's dyad theory disaggregates across subordinates (Dansereau, Graen, and Haga, 1975). Instead of an emphasis on subordinates as potential team members, Graen's theory explicitly assumes managers do not act in the same undifferentiated way towards all subordinates. In particular, subordinates are divided into in and outgroup members. The in group members are allowed access to more information, given more discretion, and have more influence, than members of the out group.

Graen and his associates describe the relationships between managers and subordinates in terms of task interactions to the exclusion of social processes. The supervisor gives members of his or her in group information on a 'want to know' basis, influence through participative decision making, and task support. The manager's relationship with these favoured subordinates depends little on the formal authority portrayed in an organization chart. Rather than subordinates, they are 'trusted assistants' or colleagues. These subordinates reciprocate with greater expenditure of time and effort than formally required. Conversely, other subordinates are treated as 'ordinary workers'. For them, communication is formal, access to information is restricted to a 'need to know' basis, and they carry out their manager's instructions. They experience a formal contractual relationship with their manager.

Crouch and Yetton (1982) elaborate the basic dyad model to include social relationships. Following Homans (1950), they argue that work group members who have more frequent task contact, form social relationships. Over time, stable cliques develop. The pattern is presented in Figure 11.

These results challenge two basic assumptions central to current leadership theories. These are social/task independence and subordinate homogeneity. Instead, the

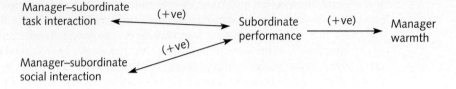

Figure 11 Manager–subordinate dyad

levels of manager–subordinate task and social contact, manager warmth, and subordinate performance are found to be highly interdependent. These results have substantial implications for the Fiedler, Path–Goal and Vroom–Yetton theories.

Comments on the contingency models

In the introduction to this section, it was noted that the contingency models described above are typically treated as if they are competing, even mutually exclusive, rather than complementary. In contrast, it is assumed here that the four models explain different phenomena.

Let us begin by exploring the overlap between Graen's dyad and the Vroom–Yetton models. To integrate this with the Vroom–Yetton model, Crouch and Yetton (1982) show that it is sufficient to assume that the in and out groups experience a different mix of problems. The in group is both allocated responsibility for a high proportion of the complex problems experienced by the work group and encouraged to redefine and expand problems at their own discretion. In contrast, out group members' responsibilities are well structured and they are given little discretion in problem redefinition. Given these two different problem mixes, the Vroom–Yetton model would descriptively predict and normatively advocate a participative highly involved task and social structure for the in group; and an autocratic relationship between the manager and the out group.

This identifies two important qualifications which should be made to the Vroom–Yetton model. One is that problem characteristics are not dictated by an autonomous environment but are frequently under the control of the manager. The other is that problem characteristics are frequently a function of subordinates' abilities and predispositions towards participative decision taking, properties which differ across subordinates. For example, those with weak performance records should and would have tasks structured for them. With them, the manager would act in an authoritative manner.

Crouch and Yetton (1982) extend this analysis to the Path–Goal model. Members of the in group participate with their manager and experience his or her behaviour as supportive. They would code their manager as high in consideration. Conversely, the out group would score their manager as low. It follows that variance in subordinates' coding of their manager's level of consideration should not be treated as error.

Furthermore, assume high performing groups have a high proportion of in group members and vice versa for poor groups Then, there would be a positive relationship between consideration and performance across groups. For example, Lowin and Craig (1968) found that high subordinate performance leads to increased considerate manager behaviour. This is a complete reversal of the Path–Goal model. Considerate manager behaviour is a joint outcome with, rather than a determinant of, high performance.

The research findings for the relationship between initiating structure and performance within the Path–Goal model are less consistent than those in relation to consideration. This may be so because when subordinates experience the same level of *initiating structure*, its form may be very different. For the in group, the manager helps members to structure up complex and ill-defined problems. The group codes the manager high on initiating structure. Out group members may also rate their manager high on initiating structure but this is the result of close supervision rather than in joint problem solving.

Finally, Fiedler's theory assumes *situational favourableness* as defined by *task structure*, *leader–subordinate relations*, and *leader position power* to be independent of the manager's style. The above speculation suggests that these three characteristics are as much outcomes as determinants of leader effectiveness. Furthermore, the in groups tend to be characterized by low structure and good leader–member relations, while the out group are the converse. As such, leader–member match and mismatch occurs within the same work team. Only for the limited case of relatively undifferentiated groups is Fiedler's theory unconfounded. An examination of group differentiation may account for the inconsistent findings in that literature.

The above discussion implicitly argues that there is a general theory for which the four contingency models described above are special cases. Each explain some of the observed leader behaviour and group performance. The inconsistencies reported in the literature should then be interpreted not as evidence against one of the theories, but of its incompleteness. The formulation of such a theory requires two shifts in leadership research. One is to treat the theories as potentially complementary rather than competitive. The other is to conduct research simultaneously on at least two and, preferably, all four theories. In the interim, the practising manager or academic consultant should simply apply each model and review carefully any dissimilar recommendations, in the light of his or her own experience.

A more general perspective: what is missing from current approaches?

The contingency theories resolve some of the problems associated with the earlier trait and behavioural models. However, as Kuhn (1962) comments, a paradigm shift retains most but not all of the explanatory power of the rejected paradigm. Nearly always something is lost. This is the case with leadership theory. Below four areas of loss are considered.

Individual differences

Trait theories were concerned not only with personality but all individual differences. As noted earlier, intelligence is positively correlated with managerial performance. Certainly, Mary Derbyshire is of above average intelligence, performing at the top of both her undergraduate and MBA classes. Even with no account for industry, staff/line, and other differentials, research reports positive correlations between MBA grade point average and managerial performance.

Of course, most people would accept that subordinate ability is a major determinant of work group performance. Yet of the contingency theories, only Graen addresses the issue of subordinate ability. For Vroom and Yetton, it is the style rather than the members selected for that style which is central to their theory. Similarly, Path–Goal and Fiedler make little reference to ability differentials. This probably reflects the emphasis on group process rather than member ability in the small group literature since the Second World War.

Prior to that war, the greater emphasis was on ability rather than group dynamics. Recently, there is a developing literature which reemphasizes the importance of member ability (Einhorn, Hogarth, and Klempner, 1977; Laughlin, Kerr, Davis, Halff, and Marcinak, 1975). In particular, Yetton and Bottger (1982) show that group composition effects are likely to dominate process gains and losses.

It may be that individual differences among managers and, perhaps more importantly among their subordinates, are an important determinant of work group performance. For example, it is likely that a high need for power by senior managers combined with a low need for power by their subordinates leads to a high risk of 'group think'. This is described by Janis and Mann (1977) as a process in which subordinates censor their own criticisms. This results in a spurious consensus around their perception of their leader's preference. Little real problem solving takes place and a poor decision may be accepted.

On a very different tack, it appears that females are better than males at interpreting non-verbal cues. It may be that there are a number of individual differences which are more important than the recent literature acknowledges. Subordinates' characteristics, or those interacting with their manager's profile, may have important consequences for performance. Certainly, this is believed by a wide cross section of managers.

One individual difference has been purposely excluded from the discussion so far. This is charisma. There is no doubt that some leaders including Jesus Christ, Gandhi, Mao Tse Tung, Patton, Stalin and de Gaulle, held a very strong magnetic attraction for their followers. While the existence of charismatic leadership is not in doubt, its nature is not understood and does not fit within any of the patterns described here.

Interpersonal trust

Just as the rejection of the trait paradigm in favour of behavioural models of leadership may have led to an inappropriate de-emphasis of individual differences, so did the subsequent shift to contingent models tend to lose sight of the importance of interpersonal trust. While the behavioural models measured and researched initiating structure and consideration, the underlying philosophy of the human relations movement emphasized trust and openness (Golembiewski and McConkie, 1975).

Again returning to Mary Derbyshire, we find that on more than one occasion when she moved jobs, one of her subordinates followed her to the new organization. A major factor in this was the subordinate's trust that Mary would be open, honest with, and not exploitative. In contrast, low trust generates defensiveness and team disintegration which effectively blocks both learning and problem solving (Gibb, 1969). Gibb argues that trust facilitates increased feedback and more effective communication which jointly generate increased performance.

The contingency models do not reject the importance of trust. Rather, the development and maintenance of high interpersonal trust simply ceases to be a central focus. In Fiedler's theory, leader member relations are a contextual factor rather than an important outcome of the manager's behaviour. The other three contingent models are essentially diagnostic. In general, they lack an effective implementation strategy. The development of interpersonal trust between manager and subordinates is central to any such strategy.

Goal setting

Leadership theories are concerned with getting things done, as are theories of work motivation. Both involve the identification of, and commitment to, goals. Goal theory (not to be confused with the Path–Goal model, though there is overlap) rests on a simple assumption. The greater the magnitude and specificity of a goal, the greater its impact on behaviour. Of course, goals can be impossible. The objectives, while difficult, should be achievable. Research on the goal setting techniques shows impressive results with employees ranging from waiters and truck drivers to research scientists and managers (Locke, Shaw, Saari, and Latham, 1981).

The basic steps are as follows. Required performance behaviours are specified in detail, levels of performance are agreed (or imposed), feedback on performance is given regularly and goal attainment is rewarded. It should be noted in the context of participative leadership theories that in goal setting, participation leads to greater performance than imposed standards only in so far as participation leads to the setting of more difficult goals. The basic model introduces structure and direction into work activity, monitors progress, and rewards it. Here, there is a link with the early Michigan studies of close versus general supervision. The intention and effect of setting performance behaviours is to prevent the manager from constantly reciting them to subordinates. Rather, the discussion and thinking generated by the process of identifying required performance behaviours, especially under co-operative conditions, is to socialize the subordinate into acceptance of role requirements. When such norms are internalized, the manager's supervisory style would tend to be general rather than close. Within the framework agreed, the subordinates assume responsibility for task completion.

Concluding remarks

This 'review' of the leadership literature attempts to show how and why the questions asked by both managers and researchers have changed over time. Through new questions we learn more about leadership but forget some of the things we knew. In conclusion, it might be interesting to sketch this author's view of 'where we are' and 'where we are going'.

Where we are is learning to discriminate among the needs of different situations: across roles for Fiedler and Path–Goal; across problems for Vroom–Yetton; and across subordinates for Graen. While doing this, we need to remember the importance of ability (selection and training) and interpersonal trust contained in the early trait and human relations theories, respectively. Given our strong socialization towards democracy and egalitarianism, this capacity to discriminate among colleagues and subordinates will not come easily. Where we are going, is to examine the current theories as complementary rather than competing. This will facilitate an interpretation across existing theories. It will require the development of a theory of followership to integrate subordinates' and managers' behaviour in a single leadership model. The initial directions for this are indicated in the elaborations by Crouch and Yetton (1982) on Graen's dyad model. Within this perspective, the inconsistent findings, particularly with respect to Fiedler and Path–Goal, would be treated not as evidence against those theories but as evidence of their incompleteness. Factors treated as fixed in one theory, for example leader–member relations in Fiedler's theory, would be treated as the outcomes from Path–Goal or Vroom–Yetton. The resultant integration is likely to be at least an order of magnitude more complex than the current contingency models.

However, the greatest challenge to theory is not the above. Rather, it is the need to extend the range of leader behaviour which is the subject of research and theory development. The literature has been dominated by a concern with, for example, participation and consideration, which are a limited subset of leader behaviour. The domain of leadership is much wider. This can be seen if we simply observe managers' actions.

References

Ashour, A. S. (1973) Further discussions of Fiedler's contingency model of leadership effectiveness, *Organizational Behavior and Human Performance*, 9, pp. 369–376.

Bass, B. M. (1957) Leadership opinions and rotated characteristics of salesmen and sales managers, in Stogdill, R. M., and Coons, A. E. (eds.), *Leader Behaviour: Its Description and Measurement*, Ohio State University, Bureau of Business Studies, Columbus, Ohio.

Blake, R. R., and Mouton, J. S. (1964) *The Managerial Grid*, Gulf Publishing Co., Houston, Texas.

Chemers, M. J., and Rice, R. W. (1974) A theoretical and empirical examination of Fiedler's contingency model of leadership effectiveness, in Hunt, J. G., and Larson, L. L. (eds.), *Contingency Approaches to Leadership*, Southern Illinois University Press, Carbondale, Illinois.

Crouch, A. C., and Yetton, P. W. (1982) Manager-subordinate relationships in vertical dyad linkages, *AGSM Working Paper No. 82–001*, February 1982.

Dansereau, F., Graen, G., and Haga, W. S. (1975) A vertical dyad linkage approach to leadership within formal organizations: a longitudinal investigation of the role making process, *Organization Behaviour and Human Performance*, 13, pp. 46–78.

Einhorn, H. J., Hogarth, R. M., and Klempner, E. (1977) Quality of group judgment, *Psychological Bulletin*, 84, pp. 158–172.

Evans, M. G. (1979) Leadership, in Kerr, S. (ed.), *Organizational Behavior*, Grid Publishing, Columbus, Ohio, pp. 207–240.

Fiedler, F. E. (1967) *A Theory of Leadership Effectiveness*, McGraw-Hill, New York.

Fiedler, F. E. (1976) The leadership game: matching the man to the situation, *Organizational Dynamics*, Winter, 1976, 6–16.

Fielder, F. E. (1977) Validation and extension of the contingency model of leadership effectiveness: a review of empirical findings, *Psychological Bulletin*, 26, pp. 128–148.

Field, R. H. G. (1979) A critique of the Vroom–Yetton contingency model of leadership behavior, *Academy of Management Review*, 4 (2), pp. 249–258.

Fleishman, E. A., and Harris, E. E. (1962) Patterns of leadership behaviour related to employ grievances and turnover, *Personnel Psychology*, **15**, pp. 43–56.

Ghiselli, E. E. (1971) *Exploration in Managerial Talent*, Goodyear, Santa Monica.

Gibb, C. A. (1969) Leadership, in Lindzery, G., and Aronson, E. (eds.), *The Handbook of Social Psychology* (2nd Edn.), Addison–Wesley, Reading, pp. 205–282.

Golembiewski, R. T., and McConkie, M. (1975) The centrality of interpersonal trust in group processes, in Cooper, C. L. (eds.), *Theories of Group Processes*, John Wiley, London, 1975.

Graen, G., Alvares, K., Orris, J. B., and Martella, J. A. (1970) Contingency model of leadership effectiveness: antecedent and evidential results, *Psychological Bulletin*, 74, pp. 285–296.

Graen, G., Orris, J. B., and Alvares, K. (1971) Contingency model of leadership effectiveness: some experimental results, *Journal of Applied Psychology*, 55, pp. 196–201.

Halpin, A. W. (1957) The leader behaviour and effectiveness of aircraft commanders, in Stogdill, R. M., and Coons, A. E. (eds.), *Leader Behaviour: Its Description and Measurement*, Ohio State University, Bureau of Business Research, Columbus, Ohio.

Halpin, A. W., and Winer, B. J. (1957) A factorial study of leader behavior descriptions, in Stogdill, R. M., and Coons, A. E. (eds.), *Leader Behavior: Its Description and Measurement*, Ohio State University, Bureau of Business Research, Columbus, Ohio.

Heller, F. A. (1971) *Managerial Decision-Making*, Tavistock, London.

Homans, G. (1950) *The Human Group*, Harcourt, Brace, and Jovanovich, New York.

House, R. J. (1971) A path goal of leader effectiveness, *Administrative Science Quarterly*, 16, pp. 321–338.

House, R. J. (1971) A path goal of leader effectiveness, in Fleishman, E. A., and Hunt, J. G. (eds.), *Current Developments in the Study of Leadership*, Southern Illinois University Press, Carbondale, Illinois..

House, R. J. (1977) A theory of leader effectiveness, in Hunt, J. G., and Larson, L. L. (eds.), *Leadership: The Cutting Edge*, Southern Illinois University Press, Carbondale, Illinois, pp. 189–207.

House, R. J., and Baetz, M. L. (1979) Leadership: some empirical generalizations and new research directions, in Staw, B. M. (ed.), *Research in Organizational Behavior*, JAL Press, Greenwich, Connecticut, pp. 341–423.

House, R. J., and Mitchell, T. R. (1974) Path goal theory of leadership, *Journal of Contemporary Business*, **5**, 81–97.

Jago, A. G. (1978) Configured cue utilization in implicit models of leader behavior, *Organizational Behaviour and Human Performance*, **22**, 474–496.

Jago, A. G., and Vroom, V. H. (1975) Perceptions of leadership style: superior and subordinate descriptions of decision making behavior, in Hunt, J. G., and Larson, L. L. (eds.), *Leadership Behavior*, Kent State University Press, Kent, Ohio, pp. 103–120.

Janis, I., and Mann, L. (1977) *Decision Making: A Psychological Analysis of Conflict Choice and Commitment*, Free Press, New York.

Jenkins, W. O. (1974) A review of leadership studies with particular reference to military problems, *Psychological Bulletin*, **44**, 54–79.

Katz, D., Maccoby, N., Gurin, G., and Floor, L. (1951) *Productivity, Supervision, and Morale Among Railroad Workers*, University of Michigan, Institute of Social Research, Ann Arbor.

Katz, D., Maccoby, N., and Morse, N. (1950) *Productivity, Supervision, and Morale in an Office Situation*, University of Michigan, Institute for Social Research, Ann Arbor.

Korman, A. K. (1966) Consideration, initiating structure, and organizational criteria: a review, *Personnel*, **19**, 349–361.

Kuhn, T. S. (1962) *The Structure of Scientific Revolution*, University of Chicago Press, Chicago.

Laughlin, P. L., Kerr, N. L., Davis, J. H., Halff, H. M., and Marcinak, K. A. (1975) Group size, member ability and social schemes on an interactive task, *Journal of Personality and Social Psychology*, **31**, 522–535.

Lawler, E. E., III, and Porter, L. W. (1972) The Effect of Performance on Satisfaction, in Bass, B. M., and Deep, S. D. (eds.), *Studies in Organizational Psychology*, Allyn and Bacon, Boston.

Locke, E. A., Shaw, K. N., Saari, L. M., and Latham, G. (1981) Goal setting and task performance: 1969–1980, *Psychological Bulletin*, **90**, 125–152.

Lowin, A., and Craig, J. R. (1968) The influence of level of performance on managerial style: an experimental object lesson in the ambiguity of correlation data, *Organization Behavior and Human Performance*, **3**, 440–458.

Miles, D. H., and Petty, M. M. (1977) Leader effectiveness in small bureaucracies, *Academy of Management Journal*, **20**(2), 238–250.

Schrieheim, C. A., and Kerr, S. (1977) RIP LPC: a response to Fiedler, in Hunt, J. G., and Larson, L. L. (eds.), *Leadership: The Cutting Edge*, Southern Illinois University Press, Carbondale, Illionis, pp. 51–56.

Schuler, R. S. (1976) *Handbook of Leadership*, Free Press, Glencoe, Illinois.

Strube, M. J., and Garcia, J. E. (1982) A meta-analytic investigation of Fiedler's contingency model of leadership effectiveness, *Psychological Bulletin*, **90**(2), 307–321.

Tannenbaum, R., and Schmidt, W. (1958) How to choose a leadership pattern, *Harvard Business Review*, **36**(2), 95–102.

Vroom, V. H., and Jago, A. G. (1978) On the validity of the Vroom–Yetton Model, *Journal of Applied Psychology*, **63**, 151–162.

Vroom, V. H., and Yetton, P. W. (1973) *Leadership and Decision Making*, University of Pittsburgh Press, Pittsburgh.

Yetton, P. W. (1980) Managers' subjective perception of their work situation with regard to the application of Vroom–Yetton leadership model, *Technical Report No. 1*, Australian Graduate School of Management, University of New South Wales.

Yetton, P. W., and Bottger, P. C. (1982) Individual versus group problem solving: an empirical test of a best member strategy, *Organization Behavior and Human Performance*, **29**, 307–321.

'Toward multi-dimensional values in teaching: the example of conflict behaviours', by Kenneth W. Thomas, *Academy of Management Review*, July 1977, pp. 484–90.

The topic of conflict resolution revolves around three major issues. The first concerns the range of approaches that are used. Most people use the same one or two, with varying degrees of success. Knowledge of, and the ability to apply, a greater number would enhance their level of success. The second issue relates to knowing when to use which conflict resolution approach – that is, using it appropriately in a given situation. Third is the issue of which approaches are to be preferred and avoided. Historically, some have been considered to be more correct than others.

This article and its associated activity address these issues. The five different conflict resolution approaches are listed by the author, and the different contexts in which each is most applicable, are defined. The article considers the values that guide the adoption of different approaches, and the consequences of such choices.

learning objectives

Once you have read and understood the prescribed material, you should be able to:

1 Assess your knowledge of Thomas's five conflict resolution approaches described in Chapter 21 of the core text.
2 Appreciate that conflict resolution is not value-free, but has to take account of different issues.
3 Understand the importance of taking a relative rather than an absolute view towards conflict resolution.
4 Identify examples of situations in which a particular conflict resolution style would appear to be most appropriate.

learning pre-requisites

Before proceeding, you should read Chapter 21 of the core text, and the article, 'Towards multi-dimensional values in teaching: the example of conflict behaviours', by Kenneth Thomas.

learning activities

1 Below are listed Thomas's 27 situations, classified under their respective conflict resolution approaches. Reflect on your own experience, and identify those situations in which you last used that approach. Insert brief details of each of them.
2 It is unlikely that you will be able to supply an illustration for all 27 situations. Where you have gaps, consult a relation, friend or work colleague. Explain the

conflict resolution approach to them, and describe the situation(s) that you are missing. Ask if they can supply you with an example from their experience.

3 Once you have acquired examples of all 27 situations, your conflict resolution situation 'bingo card' will be complete. Moreover, you will be more aware of the differences between the five approaches, and the circumstances in which you and others use each of them.

Conflict resolution approach	Situation	Available example
Competition	1. When quick decisive actions vital (e.g. in emergencies).	
	2. On important issues where unpopular actions need implementing (e.g. in cost cutting, enforcing unpopular rules, discipline).	
	3. On issues vital to an organization's welfare, when you know you're right.	
	4. Against people who take advantage of non-competitive behaviour.	
Collaboration	5. To find an integrative solution when both sets of concerns are too important to be compromised.	
	6. When your objective is to learn.	
	7. To merge insights from people with different perspectives.	
	8. To gain commitment by incorporating concerns into consensus.	
	9. To work through feelings which have interfered with a relationship.	
Avoidance	10. When an issue is trivial or more important issues are pressing.	
	11. When you perceive no chance of satisfying your concerns.	
	12. When potential disruption outweighs the benefits of resolution.	
	13. To let people cool down and regain perspective.	
	14. When gathering information supersedes immediate decision.	
	15. When others can resolve the conflict more effectively.	
	16. When issues seem tangential or symptomatic of other issues.	
Accommodation	17. When you find you are wrong – to allow a better position to be heard, to learn, and to show your reasonableness.	
	18. When issues are more important to others than yourself – to satisfy these and maintain co-operation.	
	19. To build social credits for later issues.	
	20. To minimize loss when you are outmatched and losing.	
	21. When harmony and stability are particularly important.	
	22. To allow subordinates to develop by learning from mistakes.	
Compromise	23. When goals are important, but not worth the effort or potential disruption of more assertive modes.	
	24. When opponents with equal power are committed to mutually exclusive goals.	
	25. To achieve temporary settlements to complex issues.	
	26. To arrive at expedient solutions under time pressure.	
	27. As a backup when collaboration or competition is unsuccessful.	

Toward multi-dimensional values in teaching: the example of conflict behaviors*
Kenneth W. Thomas†

It no longer seems possible to retain the image of management education as an objective, value-free transmission of knowledge. The political and ethical consciousness-raising of the past decade has heightened awareness that management education transmits values, whether explicitly or implicitly. This note examines the role of values in the management classroom and proposes a general philosophy of education with respect to value positions. The subject area of conflict management is used as a focal example.

Values and 'facts'

An instructor cannot convey facts without involving values. The term 'value' is used here in its most generic sense to indicate any judgment of good-bad, desirable-undesirable, important-unimportant. Laszlo (11) argues that the individual is not 'an abstract observer perceiving facts in pristine purity'. Rather, individuals pursue, attend to, and remember facts which relate to their goals. As Maslow (15) noted, 'Facts don't just lie there, like oatmeal in a bowl...' As they become more certain, they take on a normative quality for directing behavior.

In selecting the 'facts' which constitute course content, any instructor makes and conveys value judgments about what is important and useful for guiding managerial behavior. On a given day, the instructor exercises and conveys value judgments in emphasizing certain points, drawing implications, selecting anecdotes from experience, and so on.

Instructors would be conveying value judgments even if they restricted their role to recounting a random sample of research findings. Research itself is guided by values. Baritz (2) has emphasized that research topics are selected as important by the values of the researcher and of funding agencies. Hypotheses often reflect value judgments (or expectations) that a given behavior, condition, or intervention is related to good (functional, satisfying, productive, etc.) outcomes. These expectations can be self-confirming to the degree that researchers select situations, measures, etc. which are likely to yield the expected results. Finally, there is empirical evidence that scientists tend to selectively interpret results in favor of their hypotheses – to rationalize away contradictory evidence (16) and to be relatively critical of the methodologies of studies which support competing hypotheses (14). After his study of NASA scientists, Mitroff (16) concluded that the objectivity of science is more likely to occur in the checks and balances between adversary schools of thought than in the objectivity of individual researchers.

* This note is based on a paper presented at the Western Academy of Management, Las Vegas, 1975. Appreciation is extended to Brian Kleiner and Uma Sekaran for their help with literature reviews, to Warren Schmidt for his collaboration in designing the conflict laboratory from which some of the data came, and to Rob Martin of the President's Association of the American Management Association, for sponsoring these laboratories. The author is also indebted to Will McWhinney, Michael McCaskey, and Kenneth Moore for comments on earlier drafts. Portions of this work were supported by the Institute of Industrial Relations, UCLA. Reprinted by permission from *Academy of Management Review*, July 1977.
† Kenneth W. Thomas (Ph.D. – Purdue University) is Associate Professor of Industrial Relations and Organization Behavior in the School of Business Administration, Temple University.

Value trends

Developmental research (8) indicates that individuals' value systems, as they mature, tend to metamorphose from universal, absolute notions of good and bad toward what Lombard (13) calls 'relativism' – 'the philosophy of guiding one's action in the light of multiple values and goals'. Lombard observes that widespread, analogous changes have been occurring in the value systems which underlie the sciences.

Within management literature of the past few years, important changes appear to represent the beginnings of a quantum step toward relativism. Established, absolutistic normative stances have been questioned, issues have been placed in more complex perspective, and contingency theories have become more popular. But these developments are only beginnings. A number of sacred cows remain ensconced in the pantheon of management values. In the field of Organizational Behavior (OB), for example, consider the high regard for collaboration, self-actualization, two-way communication, authenticity and spontaneity, achievement motivation, etc. An instructor must still choose how to deal with these and other value positions.

A central consideration in selecting an approach to value issues in the classroom is its effect upon the diversity of students who comprise the class. The thrust of this note is that a relativistic or multi-valued approach to value issues (to be described in detail) will prove more beneficial to students than single-valued or absolutistic stances. The field of conflict management illustrates absolutist vs. multi-dimensional value positions.

Value issues in conflict management: the 'collaborative ethic'

In conflict management, predominant emphasis in OB literature has been upon collaboration – variously called 'confrontation', 'problem-solving', 'integrating', or 'integrative bargaining'. This behavioral mode seeks joint optimization of the concerns of two or more parties, with an emphasis upon openness and trust.

Advocates for this mode have often lapsed into absolutism. Blake and Mouton (4, p. 95) once referred to competitive intergroup relations as 'pathological' and contrasted them with 'intergroup health, as revealed through cooperative problem solving that leads to concord'. Likewise, Bennis wrote:

> The value system presented here, an amalgam of democracy, collaboration, and science, represents the most civilized and advanced system available (3, p. 206).

Although this stance has been qualified in other writings, collaboration has remained an explicitly stated ideal in a number of influential works, and has received primary emphasis in OB education.

The research base

Empirical studies which support the usefulness of collaboration have been almost entirely correlational, tending to rely upon questionnaire measures. In a study of such questionnaires, Thomas and Kilmann (22) found that collaborating was rated by individuals as highly socially desirable and that ratings of collaborating tended to vary with ratings of other 'good' constructs, so that evidence for collaboration may largely be due to halo effects in ratings. Alternative causal interpretations can be made from existing correlational results – for example, that it is simply easier to be collaborative when things are going well.

The point is not that collaboration is unrelated to good outcomes, but that empirical evidence which supports the benefits of collaboration is weaker than it first appears. The issue of the functionality of different conflict-handling modes seems more complex than the simple superiority of collaboration in all situations.

Alternative value systems

When behavior is construed in terms of the single dimension of collaborative-uncollaborative, it is difficult to appreciate the value of being 'uncollaborative' – a negative concept without clear behavioral referents. To assess more fully the trade-offs involved, the behaviors which are alternatives to collaboration should be specified, and the merits of each examined. The classification used here is Thomas' (19, 20) reinterpretation of the Blake and Mouton (5) framework. That classification identifies four alternatives to collaboration. Each can be interpreted as the manifestation of an alternative value system which is highly regarded in our culture.

Competing – Consider the veneration of successful, courageous, and resourceful leaders in competitive endeavors – the heroes of wars, sports, and (perhaps to a lesser extent now) industry. The challenging and energizing aspects of competition are reflected in the popularity of competitive games and the prevalence of adversary plots in movies and television.

Compromising – It appears to be a cornerstone of American pragmatism, which emphasizes practicality, realism, workability, expediency, and the search for satisfactory solutions rather than optimal ones.

Avoiding – It is associated with the goals of tranquility, peace, and harmony, and with diplomacy, tact, discretion, and caution. Many Eastern philosophies gaining popularity in our society emphasize the maintenance of inner harmony, supported by a partial withdrawal from worldly, day-to-day concerns.

Accommodating – Much of the Christian ethic is based upon the values of unselfish (or even self-sacrificing) attention to the needs of others. Related values include: humility, pacifism, brotherly love, kindness, and generosity.

All five value systems represent subsystems of the American character (and probably the character of all cultures). Moreover, all five appear to be represented to varying degrees within the personal value systems of individuals in our culture. Myrdal (17) indicated that individual value systems contain apparently contradictory subsystems which can be evoked by different situations. Each subsystem emphasizes different behaviors as valuable skills and can be evoked as a 'frame of mind' when one's appreciation of a situation suggests that those particular skills are relevant. Lawrence and Lorsch's (12) collection of proverbs indicates that on different occasions one's common sense can say apparently contradictory things like: 'Come, let us reason together,' 'Put your foot down where you mean to stand,' 'Half a loaf is better than none,' 'Don't stir up a hornet's nest,' and 'Turn the other cheek.'

The five conflict modes as managerial skills

To indicate situational contingencies which managers consider in conflict situations, 28 chief executives in two laboratories on conflict management were asked to furnish lists of managerial situations in which each of the five modes would be useful. They had been given definitions of the five conflict modes before the exercise, and were self-selected into small groups to explore the uses of a given mode. A compilation and condensation of responses from two laboratories is shown in Table 1. Each entry represents a potential diagnosis of a situation which would strongly suggest the value of a particular mode.

This list is not offered as a definitive statement on the functionality of each conflict mode, but as evidence that, when asked to think in specifics instead of abstractions, experienced managers (a) see the usefulness of conflict modes as depending upon a

Table 1 Situations in which to use the five conflict-handling modes, as reported by 28 chief executives of organizations

Conflict mode	*Situation*
Competing	1 When quick, decisive action is vital – e.g., emergencies.
	2 On important issues where unpopular actions need implementing – e.g., cost cutting, enforcing unpopular rules, discipline.
	3 On issues vital to company welfare when you know you're right.
	4 Against people who take advantage of non-competitive behavior.
Collaborating	1 To find an integrative solution when both sets of concerns are too important to be compromised.
	2 When your objective is to learn.
	3 To merge insights from people with different perspectives.
	4 To gain commitment by incorporating concerns into a consensus.
	5 To work through feelings which have interfered with a relationship.
Compromising	1 When goals are important, but not worth the effort or potential disruption of more assertive modes.
	2 When opponents with equal power are committed to mutually exclusive goals.
	3 To achieve temporary settlements to complex issues.
	4 To arrive at expedient solutions under time pressure.
	5 As a backup when collaboration or competition is unsuccessful.
Avoiding	1 When an issue is trivial, or more important issues are pressing.
	2 When you perceive no chance of satisfying your concerns.
	3 When potential disruption outweighs the benefits of resolution.
	4 To let people cool down and regain perspective.
	5 When gathering information supersedes immediate decision.
	6 When others can resolve the conflict more effectively.
	7 When issues seem tangential or symptomatic of other issues.
Accommodating	1 When you find you are wrong – to allow a better position to be heard, to learn, and to show your reasonableness.
	2 When issues are more important to others than yourself – to satisfy others and maintain cooperation.
	3 To build social credits for later issues.
	4 To minimize loss when you are outmatched and losing.
	5 When harmony and stability are especially important.
	6 To allow subordinates to develop by learning from mistakes.

complex set of situational circumstances, and (b) see all five modes as useful skills in appropriate situations.

Dysfunctions of the single-valued approach in teaching

Discussion of value systems and the specific example of conflict suggest several dysfunctional consequences of a single-valued approach to teaching. These principles apply to any content area discussed in terms of a single, valued construct – for example, discussing motivation in terms of need achievement, leadership in terms of participative management or decision styles in terms of risk preference.

Rejecting the Input – Single-valued emphasis may not fit the complex considerations which weigh in students' own decision making. Alternatively, the prescribed value system may be incompatible with their own most salient value subsystems and the experiences which gave rise to them. Accordingly, students may reject the inputs as simplistic, incorrect, or simply irrelevant – especially when they have only brief exposure to the new material.

Threat to Self-Esteem – The single-valued approach reduces a content area to a single construct (e.g., collaborative-uncollaborative) which becomes a good-bad dimension. Individuals who place low on that dimension encounter threat to self-esteem, which may produce defensiveness, close the student, and make things difficult for the instructor/trainer. For example, Archer's (1) recent study indicates that a considerable proportion of individuals in human relations groups undergo a reduction in self-esteem, and suggests that it may occur among individuals whose behavior receives least reinforcement. Kilmann and Taylor (9) found that hostile ratings of a human relations course tended to come from students whose decision-making styles were least compatible with the emphasis upon intuition and feelings.

Abandoning Strengths – If the single-valued approach is effective in producing more of the prescribed behavior, it will in some cases mean that individuals abandon non-sanctioned strengths for prescribed behaviors at which they are clumsier and less effective. The range of effective adaptability for an individual, although sizeable, is limited.

Reducing Flexibility – Laszlo (11) cites the need for behavioral flexibility to cope with wide ranges of environmental circumstances. Reliance upon a single behavior reduces one's repertoire, and accordingly restricts one's range of competence.

Driving Issues Underground – Each value system generates its own variety of 'sins'. For example, a single-valued collaborative ethic may construe other modes as varieties of sins: competing may appear antisocial and defensive, reflecting basic insecurities; compromising may be superficial and myopic, missing basic issues; etc. A value system which denies the legitimacy of non-collaborative behaviors can cause individuals to hide various motives and needs – competitive motives, hostility, needs for privacy, etc. – depriving individuals of the motive force of those needs, and making it more difficult to deal with them effectively. On the group level, collaborative norms can drive non-collaborative issues underground, to appear as hidden agendas which interfere with other issues (7).

A multi-valued approach to teaching

The multi-valued approach described here is an attempt to crystallize tentative guidelines for overcoming these dysfunctions. Like all approaches to education, it is manifestly not value-free. Value underpinnings include a strong concern for the welfare and self-esteem of the student or trainee and a desire for students to act in accordance with their own skills, perceptions, and values. These values are supplemented by a mistrust of universal principles. The approach has three main elements.

A Complex Perspective on functionality Issues – In considering a given topic (leadership, conflict, etc.), the question of Functionality is introduced as a complex and important issue which has not been fully settled. Glasser (6) has observed that such important and open-ended issues require thinking and generate student interest. By not becoming a personal advocate for a position, the instructor fosters student involvement and does not force students into the choice of either passively accepting that value position or treating the instructor as an antagonist. The instructor is also freed from the responsibility of having ultimate answers.

The instructor still teaches facts in the form of research findings, anecdotes, etc., and still presents prevalent theories as inputs to the discussion. But they are presented as considerations rather than solutions, and students are encouraged to feed in their own experiences as well. The objective is to combine these different facts and experiences into a larger and more complex perspective. By building upon the insights of individual students, the resulting perspective is more likely to be seen as relevant to their world and as a contribution to their own efforts to understand it.

Emphasizing Individual Strengths – The multi-valued approach legitimates different behaviors as skills which are useful in different situations. The individual's behavioral predispositions can be interpreted as a repertoire of specialized skills. The emphasis on strengths provides a supportive climate in which individuals can more easily and objectively assess their own behaviors. This assessment can be aided by role-playing simulations, reflective exercises, and pencil-and-paper measures – especially those already tied to multi-valued theories. The responses of the chief executives in Table 1, for example, have been incorporated into feedback materials for a multi-valued measure of conflict behavior (10, 21).

One implication of the multi-valued approach is that no behavioral profile is perfect; each set of specialized strengths implies the existence of flat sides which are less developed. But these become a condition of human existence rather than personal failings, making it easier to view them in perspective. This perspective may also make it easier for the instructor to treat his or her *own* foibles with a sense of humor and help to 'humanize' the classroom atmosphere.

Preparing for Opportunities and Problems – An individual's effectiveness is seen as depending largely upon the fit between personal strengths and the requirements of a situation. The multi-valued approach can help students manage this degree of fit by anticipating potentially advantageous and difficult situations for their strength profiles. Another approach is to acquaint students with danger signals to help them recognize their overuse of particular behaviors (21).

Acceptance of one's strengths and weaknesses does not imply resignation to stasis. Rogers (18) emphasized awareness and acceptance of one's current self as a necessary precursor to change. If students perceive significant problem areas in particular settings, the multi-valued approach can suggest options. Having recognized problem areas, they may try to develop minimal competencies in the required behaviors. Recognizing that they are building upon strengths may make the clumsiness of this learning period less threatening. They can also learn to use the skills of other people who are strong in complementary areas – viewing individual differences as resources rather than annoyances and threats. Finally, if mismatches between skills and situations are great enough, they may choose to seek new situations which are more favorable.

Conclusions

The issue of the functionality of any behavior is extremely complex. It varies not only with managerial situations, but also with the skills and flat sides of the individuals who must implement the behavior. Although we pay lip service to the fact that we are dealing with *individuals* in the classroom, we have often espoused normative positions which ignore individual differences. The fact remains that individuals are good at different things, and that almost any behavior can constitute a skill in an appropriate situation. There is a need to adopt teaching strategies which reflect these realities – strategies which fit the realities of different individuals and which allow them to value and to capitalize upon their own strengths.

References

1. Archer, Dane. 'Power in Groups: Self-Concept Changes of Powerful and Powerless Group Members,' *Journal of Applied Behavioral Science*, Vol. 10 (1974), 208–220.
2. Baritz, Loren. *The Servants of Power* (Middletown, Conn.: Wesleyan University Press, 1960).
3. Bennis, Warren G. *Changing Organizations* (New York: McGraw-Hill, 1966).
4. Blake, Robert R., and Jane S. Mouton. 'The Intergroup Dynamics of Win-Lose Conflict and Problem-Solving Collaboration in Union-Management Relations,' in Muzafer Sherif (Ed.), *Intergroup Relations and Leadership* (New York: Wiley, 1962).
5. Blake, Robert R., and Jane S. Mouton. *The Managerial Grid* (Houston: Gulf Publishing, 1964).
6. Glasser, William. *Schools Without Failure* (New York: Harper and Row, 1969).
7. Harrison, Roger. 'Role Negotiation: A Tough-Minded Approach to Team Development,' in Warren G. Bennis, David E. Berlew, Edgar H. Schein, and Fred I. Steele, *Interpersonal Dynamics*, 3rd ed. (Homewood Ill.: Dorsey, 1973).
8. Harvey, O. J., David E. Hunt and Harold M. Schroder. *Conceptual Systems and Personality Organization* (New York: Wiley, 1961).
9. Kilmann, Ralph H., and Vern Taylor. 'A Contingency Approach to Laboratory Learning: Psychological Types Versus Experiential Norms,' *Human Relations*, Vol. 27 (1974), 891–909.
10. Kilmann, Ralph H., and Kenneth W. Thomas. 'Developing a Forced-Choice Measure of Conflict-Handling Behavior: The MODE Instrument,' *Educational and Psychological Measurement*, Vol. 37 (1977), in press.
11. Laszlo, Erwin. 'A Systems Philosophy of Human Value,' *Behavioral Science*, Vol. 18 (1973), 250–259.
12. Lawrence, Paul R., and Jay W. Lorsch. *Organization and Environment* (Boston: Graduate School of Business Administration, Harvard University, 1967).
13. Lombard, George F. F. 'Relativism in Organizations,' *Harvard Business Review*, Vol. 49 (1971), 55–65.
14. Mahoney, Michael J. 'The Truth Seekers,' *Psychology Today*, Vol. 12, No. 11 (1976), 64–65.
15. Maslow, Abraham H. 'Fusion of Facts and Values,' *The American Journal of Psychoanalysis*, Vol. 23 (1963), 117–131.
16. Mitroff, Ian I. *The Subjective Side of Science* (Amsterdam: Elsevier, 1974).
17. Myrdal, Gunnar. *An American Dilemma: The Negro Problem and Modern Democracy* (New York: Harper and Row, 1962).
18. Rogers, Carl R. 'A Process Conception of Psychotherapy,' *The American Psychologist*, Vol. 13 (1958), 142–149.
19. Ruble, Thomas L., and Kenneth W. Thomas. 'Support for a Two-Dimensional Model of Conflict Behavior,' *Organizational Behavior and Human Performance*, Vol. 16 (1976), 143–155.
20. Thomas, Kenneth W. 'Conflict and Conflict Management,' in Marvin D. Dunnette (Ed.), *The Handbook of Industrial and Organizational Psychology* (Chicago: Rand McNally, 1976), 889–935.
21. Thomas, Kenneth W., and Ralph H. Kilmann. *The Thomas-Kilmann Conflict Mode Survey* (Tuxedo, N.Y.: Xicom, 1975).
22. Thomas, Kenneth W., and Ralph H. Kilmann. 'The Social Desirability Variable in Organizational Research: An Alternative Explanation for Reported Findings,' *Academy of Management Journal*, Vol. 18 (1975), 741–752.

come back Machiavelli, all is forgiven (1973)

'Power and the ambitious executive', by Robert N. McMurry, *Harvard Business Review*, vol. 51, no. 6, 1973, pp. 140–5.

This article has a potentially unfashionable message. McMurry argues that, to be successful, executives have to be 'politically astute' in their acquisition and use of power in the organization. And he offers specific and detailed guidance on just what this means in practice, apparently from personal experience. Most commentators in the field of organizational behaviour this century have advised management to be open, communicative, trusting, honest, participative, sharing and involving. McMurry advises almost the opposite in this article.

learning objectives

Once you have read and understood this article, you should be able to:

1 Explain the potential significance of 'Machiavellian' tactics to the survival of senior executives in an organization.
2 Describe and illustrate these tactics.

learning pre-requisites

The argument of this article is relevant to three topics in the core text. First, Chapter 16, on organizational change, explores the *power skills* of the change agent – these are similar to the 'Machiavellian' tactics discussed by McMurry. Second, Chapter 20, on leadership and management style, discussed the many *power bases* of the manager. Third, Chapter 22, on organizational power and politics, puts these issues in a wider context. McMurry is, of course, offering advice to the individual manager or executive, not specifically to the change agent.

learning activities

1 Like many American articles, this one is deceptively easy to summarize into a set of main, or 'bullet', points. The author has built this into the structure of the article for you. However, in this case, the broad structure of the article conceals much of the guidance on offer. If you just pick out the main headings, you will miss some of the nuances, subtleties and detail in McMurry's argument and advice. So, make your own detailed list of 'bullet points' summarizing the advice that McMurry wants to give to the executive struggling to survive in the senior executive power game.
2 Some of your 'bullet points' will come from the section on 'personal style' towards the end of this article. This advice seems to cut across the message of the 'humanist' writers in organizational behaviour. What is your personal position on McMurry's argument? Is what he suggests realistic and defensible, or odious and reprehensible? Share your opinion with colleagues and instructors on your course.

READING
22   *Power and the ambitious executive**
Robert N. McMurry

The methods of holding top-management power in a company strike many people as devious and Machiavellian. They involve calculated alliances, compromises, and 'deals' – and often they fly in the face of practices advocated by experts on organizational behavior. From the standpoint of the beleaguered and harassed executive, however, there may be no substitute for them – if he wants to survive at the top.

Mr. McMurry has been writing for HBR since 1952, when an article he wrote on 'The Executive Neurosis' caused a minor sensation in the management community. Executive recruiting, labor relations, management communications, value conflicts, and other matters have been the subjects of his articles since then. The article in this issue is inspired by material in a book manuscript he has recently completed. It will be published by Amacom (the publishing subsidiary of the American Management Association) in 1974 under the title, *The Maverick Executive*. The author heads up The McMurry Company, a firm of management psychologists and personnel consultants in Chicago.

The most important and unyielding necessity of organizational life is not better communications, human relations, or employee participation, but power. I define *power* as the capacity to modify the conduct of other employees in a desired manner, together with the capacity to avoid having one's own behavior modified in undesired ways by other employees. Executives must have power because, unfortunately, many employees resent discipline; to these employees, work is something to be avoided. In their value systems 'happiness' is the ultimate goal. For the organization to be made productive, such persons must be subjected to discipline.

Without power there can be no authority; without authority, there can be no discipline; without discipline, there can be difficulty in maintaining order, system, and productivity. An executive without power is, therefore, all too often a figurehead – or worse, headless. The higher an executive is in his management hierarchy, the greater his need for power. This is because power tends to weaken as it is disseminated downward.

Gaining and keeping power

If the executive owns the business, that fact may ensure his power. If he does not, and sometimes even when he does, his power must be acquired and held by means which are essentially political. Of critical importance, since most of his power is derived or delegated, his power must be dependable. Nothing is more devastating to an executive than to lose support and backing in moments of crisis. It is for this reason that the development of continuing power is the most immediate and nagging concern of many professional managers.

How can chief executives and other managers who possess little or no equity in a business consolidate enough power to protect their jobs and enforce their dictates when necessary? The eight recommendations which follow are the fruit of 30 years of observation of a great number of executives managing a variety of enterprises.

A number of these conclusions conflict with the findings of other writers. The most that can be said in defense of my recommendations is that they did not spring from an ivory tower. They are based on strategies and tactics employed by demonstrably successful executives who lacked financial control of their enterprises. The executives were working pragmatists. Their prime criteron of a desirable course of action was: Will it work? While the strategies presented here are not infallible, they have proven their worth more often than not in the hard and competitive world of business.

1 *The executive should take all the steps he can to ensure that he is personally compatible with superiors.*
In the case of the chief executive, this means compatibility with the owners and/or their representatives, such as bankers, lawyers, and family members; in the case of other managers, senior executives and owners are the key groups. The point is that though a manager may have all the skills, experience, and personal attributess his position requires, if his values and goals are not reasonably consonant with those of the persons who hold power and he is not acceptable to them personally, his tenure will probably be brief.

To protect against subsequent disillusionment and conflict, the prospective manager should, before he joins the comapny, endeavor to become acquainted with his prospective superior of superiors informally. This could be done at dinner with them, on the golf course, or on a trip. At such a meeting he can learn his superior's values, standards, prejudices, and expectations. If any significant evidence of incompatibility emerges, he should call off negotiations–incompatibility tends to worsen rather than improve with continued contact.

If at all possible, the manager's wife should meet the superior, also under informal conditions, since compatibility with her can play an important part in the new man's acceptance. Likewise, it can be arranged for the manager's wife to meet the chief's wife, early in the course of negotiations, that should be done. Compatibility between these two can be very advantageous; incompatibility can be fatal.

2 *Whether he comes to the company from outside or is being promoted from within, the executive should obtain an employment contract.*
While many owners and senior executives protest that they never make such agreements and that it is against their policy to do so, the prospective manager must insist that every policy is subject to change and that he will not accept the position without one. A failure to win out at this most critical juncture can be fatal to him. The reason is not so much that failure strips him of any vestige of job security and power but that it indicateds to those in command that he is somewhat docile and submissive and probably can be pushed about at their whim.

This is particularly true where the executive's primary assignment is to salvage and rehabilitate a sick or failing operation or to initiate and pioneer a new and radically different field of activity that no one in the business knows much about. The compensation may be alluring, the status attractively elevated, and the challenge exciting. But the risks have to be great. If worse comes to worst and the executive is removed, he will have a tidy sum to carry him over the six months or longer that he needs to find a new job.

3 *On taking a major assignment, the executive should obtain from his superiors a clear, concise, and unambiguous statement in writing of his duties, responsibilities, reporting relationships, and scope of authority.*
Such a document is absolutely essential if the manager is not later to make the humiliating and frustrating discovery that the parameters of his job have been changed, often with no notice to him. He may have been led to believe at the outset that he

had certain responsibilities and commensurate authority to carry them out. Later he may learn that he has no such authority and that some of the people who were to report to him in effect do not do so. He may discover that figuratively he has been castrated; all of his authority has been taken from him, leaving him powerless. If, when he protests, he cannot substantiate his charges with a written commitment, he is likely to be told, 'You have misunderstood our original agreement.'

4 *The executive should take exceptional care to find subordinates who combine technical competence with reliability, dependability, and loyalty.*
As many a top executive has learned to his sorrow, he is constantly vulnerable to sabotage by his underlings. This is especially the case where he comes in from outside and 'does not know where the bodies are buried.' It is for this reason that he should be so careful in the choice of his immediate subordinates.

In theory, each superior, regardless of his level in the management hierarchy, should have a strong, competent number-two man who is ready and willing to step into his place should he be promoted, retire, leave the company, or for any reason be unable to continue to function. Some executives do just this. But in practice the policy can be hazardous, at least in terms of the senior man's job security.

An aggressive, ambitious, upwardly mobile number-two man is dangerous to any chief, weak or strong. For one thing, the number-two man is often very difficult to control. He has his own personal array of goals and objectives which may or may not be consistent with those of his superior and/or the company. Since he is usually inner directed and a man of strong convictions, it is often difficult to divert him from the course which he has set for himself and which he sincerely believes to be best for him (and secondarily for the company). The risk is considerably lessened if the chief has only one strong subordinate, for then it is easier to watch and constrain him.

Moreover, since the strong subordinate tends to be an individualist, he is more apt to find himself in conflict with his peers. He has a compulsive need to achieve *his* goals regardless of the needs or expectations of the others or of the welfare of the enterprise as a whole. Not only may his influence be seriously divisive, but he tends to fragment the enterprise, to induce a centrifugal effect in it. This is why such businesses as advertising and consulting are so notoriously prone to fragmentation; they attract too many entrepreneurs.

Strong, decisive, qualified men are rarely willing to remain for more than a brief time in a secondary role. Their impatience is accentuated if, for any reason, they do not respect their superior or feel frustrated in their careers. Sometimes they conclude that their greatest opportunity lies not in seeking advancement by moving to another company but by undermining and eventually supplanting their present superior.

In consequence, the politically astute top executive seeks subordinates who not only have the requisite technical skills but who are also to some degree passive, dependent, and submissive. Their 'loyalty' is often a euphemism for docility. They tend to be security-conscious and prone to form a dependent relationship with their chief. If the chief has held his position for many years, this building of a submissive group has usually taken place slowly by a process of trial and error. But when he comes in from outside or takes over as the result of a merger, he is often prone (and is usually well advised) to bring his own associates with him or to give preferment to men whom he knows and has worked with previously.

5 *A useful defensive tactic for the executive is to select a compliant board of directors.*
Of course, the chief executive is the one most immediately concerned with this ploy, but second- and third-level managers, too, may have a vital interest in this matter. In recent years, changes in directors' responsibilities have made it somewhat more

difficult to stack the board in the old-fashioned sense. But its membership and operation can still be influenced in a significant way.

Inside directors tend usually to be more malleable than outside directors. Few will be courageous enough to cross swords with the chief executive. While board members by law are the stockholders' representatives and thus are the holders of ultimate power in the business, in practice this is often little more than a polite fiction. In many instances they have largely abdicated their management or even corporate supervisory responsibilities.

Sometimes the directors are too busy to interfere in operations. Not infrequently they have little equity in the business and, hence, are disinterested in it. Sometimes they have been chosen principally because they are 'big names' who add status and respectability to the company but can devote little time to its affairs. Much as some observers and authorities dislike such tendencies, they are the realities. The top-management group that knows how to use and exploit power will make sure that it, too, enjoys the blessings of a compliant board.

6 *In business, as in diplomacy, the most important stratagem of power is for the executive to establish alliances.*
The more alliances the executive can build, the better. He can establish several kinds of relationships:

▶ *With his superiors* – He can make personal contact with and sell himself to the owner of the business or, where the ownership is widely diversified, to the more influential stockholders. One chief executive I know has luncheon once each month with the widow of the founder of his company. As long as she is convinced that he is a 'wonderful man,' he has both power and tenure.

Where banks, insurance companies, or mutual funds have a controlling voice in the company, the executive can seek to ingratiate himself with their key executives. If certain of his directors are unusually dominant, he does everything he can to win their favor and support. This does not necessarily mean that he is obsequious and sycophantic in his relationships with them. On the contrary, he may regularly stand up to them and confront them directly.

The key to success in a relationship of this nature is the ascertainment of the other person's expectations. If the man or woman whose support he hopes to win likes tigers, he is a tiger; it the person prefers a mouse, he restrains his more aggressive impulses. Above all, he studies each person's prejudices and values and is careful never to offend them.

▶ *With his peers* – The adroit manager also builds allegiances with others at his own level. While these people may not be direct sources of power to him, they can often be valuable as supplementary means of support and intelligence. Included among his contacts should be prominent industry figures. Since government intervention in business is increasing daily, acquaintance with senators, congressmen, and major department heads in government can also be helpful. (The owners of a company doing business with the Defense Department will think twice before sacking an executive who is on intimate terms will the Secretary or his deputy.)

One good means of ensuring support from peers is to identify common goals and objectives towards which all can strive. An even more powerful step is to find a common enemy – an antibusiness government official, let us say, or a hostile labor leader. Often influential rivals for power or even disgruntled subordinates can be neutralized by being taken into groups having common goals or enemies.

▶ *With subordinates* – I have already mentioned the importance of selecting dependent subordinates in whose selfish interest it is to support their chief. Such persons
may also be useful as sources of internal intelligence. The information they provide is not always completely accurate or reliable, but it can be cross-checked
against data from a variety of other sources.

7 *The executive should recognize the power of the purse.*
He knows that the best control he can exercise over his subordinates is fiscal. Hence
he seeks as quickly as possible to position himself where he approves all budgets.
Nothing is as effective in coping with a recalcitrant staff as the power to cut off financial support for their projects. On the other hand, nothing so often promotes grati-
tude and cooperation as fiscal support of subordinates' favorite projects.

8 *The executive should understand the critical importance of clear and credible
channels of communication upward from all levels of his personnel and downward
from him to them.*
Without such channels the executive is an isolate who does not know what is tran-
spiring in his enterprise. His commands will be heard only partially by his subordinates; they will be infrequently understood and rarely acted on. He should recognize
that many of his staff have strong motives to keep the truth from him and to block or
distort his downward communications.[1]

To overcome deficiencies of communication, the executive must learn not to
depend too much on his hierarchy of assistants (many of whom are not communication centers at all, but barriers to it). Where possible, he will address his people directly, conducting periodic 'State of the Company' reports to them and encouraging
direct feedback from them by soliciting anonymous questions and expressions of dissatisfaction. He must supplement his formal channels of upward and downward
communication by all available means, such as work councils, opinion polls, interviews with natural leaders, and community surveys.

Personal style

The place of a chief or other top executive in a business in which he has little or
no equity is somewhat analogous to that of a diplomat working in an unfriendly, if
not openly hostile, country. He may have much overt status and prestige, but he
has little real power. He needs to accomplish certain goals, but he has little true
leverage to apply to those people whom he seeks to influence. In view of this, he
sometimes finds it necessary to use indirect, oblique, Machiavellian stratagems to
gain his ends.

Observation of many politically astute executives in action indicates that most of
them utilize supplementary ploys in coping with and influencing owners, associates,
employees, and other groups. They know that an executive-politician must:

▶ Use caution in taking counsel – He may take the views of others into account, but
he knows the decisions must be his. Advice is useful, but unless its limits are recognized, it can easily become pressure.
▶ Avoid too close superior-subordinate relationships – While he must be friendly
with his subordinates, he is never intimate with them. His personal feelings must
never be a basis for action concerning them. His door may be 'open' – but not too
far.

1. For a fuller explanation of this point, see my article 'Clear Communications for Chief Executives,' HBR
March–April, 1965, p. 131.

- Maintain maneuverability – He never commits himself completely and irrevocably. If conditions change, he can gracefully adapt himself to the altered circumstances and change course without loss of face.
- Use passive resistance when necessary – When under pressure to take action which he regards as inadvisable, he can stall. To resist such demands openly is likely to precipitate a crisis. Therefore he initiates action, but in such a manner that the undesired program suffers from endless delays and ultimately dies on the vine.
- Not hesitate to be ruthless when expedient – No one really expects the boss to be a 'nice guy' at all times. If he is, he will be considered to be a softy or a patsy and no longer deserving of respect. (A surprisingly large segment of the population has a strong need to be submissive. Hence these people are more comfortable under a ruthless superior. This can be clearly seen in the rank and file of many labor organizations.)
- Limit what is to be communicated – Many things should not be revealed. For instance, bad news may create costly anxieties or uncertainties among the troops; again, premature announcements of staff changes may give rise to schisms in the organization.
- Recognize that there are seldom any secrets in an organization – He must be aware that anything revealed 'in confidence' will probably be the property of everyone in the establishment the next morning.
- Learn never to place too much dependence on a subordinate unless it is clearly to the latter's personal advantage to be loyal – Although some people are compulsively conscientious, most are not. Most give lip service to the company or the boss, but when the crunch comes, their loyalty is exclusively to themselves and their interests.
- Be willing to compromise on small matters – He does this in order to obtain power for further movement. Nothing is more often fatal to executive power than stubbornness in small matters.
- Be skilled in self-dramatization and be a persuasive personal salesman – He is essentially an actor, capable of influencing his audiences emotionally as well as rationally. He first ascertains his audience's wants and values. He then proceeds to confirm them, thus absolutely ensuring his hearer's acceptance of his message.
- Radiate self-confidence – He must give the impression that he knows what he is doing and is completely in command of the situation, even though he may not be sure at all.
- Give outward evidence of status, power, and material success – Most people measure a leader by the degree of pomp and circumstance with which he surrounds himself. (This is why the king lives in a palace and the Pope in the Vatican.) Too much modesty and democracy in his way of life may easily be mistaken for a lack of power and influence. For example, most subordinates take vicarious pride in being able to say, 'That's my boss who lives in the mansion on the hill and drives a Rolls Royce.'
- Avoid bureaucratic rigidity in interpreting company rules – To win and hold the allegiance of his subordinates, an executive must be willing to 'bend the rules' from time to time and make exceptions, even when they are not wholly justified.
- Remember to give praise as well as censure – Frequently, because he is under pressure from his superiors, he takes out his frustrations on his subordinates by criticizing them, sometimes unreasonably. He must remember that, if their loyalty is to be won and held, they merit equal amounts of praise and reassurance.
- Be open-minded and receptive to opinions which differ from his – If he makes

people feel that anyone who disagrees with him is, ipso facto, wrong, his power will suffer. Listening to dissent is the principal means by which he can experience corrective contact with reality and receive warning that the course he is following will lead to trouble. Also, openness to disagreement helps him to use his power fairly – or, more accurately, use it in a manner that will be perceived as fair by subordinates.

Conclusion

The position of a top executive who has little or no equity in the business is often a perilous one, with little inherent security. If things go well, his tenure is usually ensured; if they go badly, all too often he is made the scapegoat. Since many of the factors that affect his performance are beyond his control, he is constantly subject to the threat of disaster. His only hope for survival under these conditions is to gain and retain power by tactics that are in a large measure political and means that are, in part at least, Machiavellian.

Such strategies are not always noble and high-minded. But neither are they naive. From the selfish standpoint of the beleaguered and harassed executive, they have one primary merit: they enhance his chances of survival.

revolution – what revolution? (1985)

'From control to commitment in the workplace', by Richard E. Walton, *Harvard Business Review*, March–April 1985, pp. 77–84.

Walton argues that a revolution is under way. This revolution concerns strategies for managing an organization's workforce. Walton describes the choice between a strategy of control, and a strategy of commitment. The strategy of control, he argues, is no longer appropriate for several reasons. The survival and development of contemporary organizations, he claims, require the adoption of a strategy of commitment. However, he does point out that there are problems with the strategy of commitment, which may explain why this approach is not particularly widespread. Walton's argument from the mid-1980s is probably just as relevant to the twenty-first century and the late 1990s. Walton's argument is wide ranging. He combines in this clearly written article elements of theory and research in organizational behaviour which are treated in the core text, of necessity, as separate topics.

learning objectives

Once you have read and understood this article, you should be able to:

1 Explain Walton's argument in support of a strategy of commitment, as an approach to organizational management, and in criticism of a strategy of control.
2 Identify the five unresolved problems with the commitment strategy.
3 Summarize the pressures behind the development of commitment strategies, and also the pressures to retain control strategies.

learning pre-requisites

See *Learning activities*. You are not getting any help with this one.

learning activities

1 Walton's argument is particularly wide ranging. He provides his own summary 'exhibit', and you will find a further summary of this point in Chapter 23 of the core text. In this short article, he brings together a number of strands of thinking in organizational behaviour, to support a central argument. Identify for yourself the chapters in the core text which contain material relevant to Walton's argument.
2 Walton argues that there are factors encouraging the introduction and development of the commitment strategy. However, he also argues that there are problems, which suggest that the control strategy will also continue to find support. Summarize the driving and resisting factors in a force field analysis, similar to the learning activity for Reading 16. Use the template and guidance notes on the following page.

> **The transition from a strategy of control to a strategy of commitment: a force field analysis**
>
> Target situation: widespread adoption of the commitment strategy
>
> | driving forces $\longrightarrow$ | $\longleftarrow$ restraining forces |
> |---|---|
> | | |

1 Driving and restraining forces can be arguments, evidence, economic or environmental pressures, social movements, ideas, people, pressure groups, and so on.
2 Using the article by Walton as your main source, but drawing on other sources and your own experience, list the driving and restraining forces at work in this field.
3 Give each of these forces a weight from 1 (weak) to 10 (strong).
4 In your judgement, how would you assess the balance of forces here – are either driving or restraining forces dominant, or is the field close to equilibrium?
5 Action planning: what recommendations can you make about weakening or eliminating resisting forces, and about strengthening the driving forces and introducing new ones?

READING
23

From control to commitment in the workplace*
Richard E. Walton

The symptoms are familiar: a good strategy is not executed well; costs rise out of all proportion to gains in productivity; high rates of absenteeism persist; and a disaffected work force, taking little pride or pleasure in what it does, retards innovation and quality improvements. To those at the top of the corporate ladder, it seems as if they are the captains of a ship in which the wheel is not connected to the rudder. Whatever decisions get made, little happens down below. Only lately have managers themselves begun to take responsibility for these symptoms and for the approach to work-force management out of which they grow. Only lately have they begun to see that workers respond best – and most creatively – not when they are tightly controlled by management, placed in narrowly defined jobs, and treated like an unwelcome necessity, but, instead, when they are given broader responsibilities, encouraged to contribute, and helped to take satisfaction in their work. It should come as no surprise that eliciting worker commitment – and providing the environment in which it can flourish – pays tangible dividends for the individuals and for the company. The author describes these opposing approaches to a company's human capital and points out the key challenges in moving from one to the other.

Mr. Walton, Jesse Isidore Straus Professor of Business Administration at the Harvard Business School, is a recognized authority on issues related to work-force management. His prior articles in HBR include 'Improving the Quality of Work Life' (May–June 1974) and 'Work Innovations in the United States' (July–August 1979). For some time now, his research interests have addressed the evolution of the 'commitment model' discussed in this article.

The larger shape of institutional change is always difficult to recognize when one stands right in the middle of it. Today, throughout American industry, a significant change is under way in long-established approaches to the organization and management of work. Although this shift in attitude and practice takes a wide variety of company-specific forms, its larger shape – its overall pattern – is already visible if one knows where and how to look.

Consider, for example, the marked differences between two plants in the chemical products division of a major U.S. corporation. Both make similar products and employ similar technologies, but that is virtually all they have in common.

The first, organized by businesses with an identifiable product or product line, divides its employees into self-supervising 10- to 15-person work teams that are collectively responsible for a set of related tasks. Each team member has the training to perform many or all of the tasks for which the team is accountable, and pay reflects the level of mastery of required skills. These teams have received assurances that management will go to extra lengths to provide continued employment in any economic downturn. The teams have also been thoroughly briefed on such issues as market share, product costs, and their implications for the business.

Not surprisingly, this plant is a top performer economically and rates well on all measures of employee satisfaction, absenteeism, turnover, and safety. With its employees actively engaged in identifying and solving problems, it operates with fewer levels of management and fewer specialized departments than do its sister plants. It is also one of the principal suppliers of management talent for these other plants and for the division manufacturing staff.

In the second plant, each employee is responsible for a fixed job and is required to perform up to the minimum standard defined for that job. Peer pressure keeps new employees from exceeding the minimum standards and from taking other initiatives that go beyond basic job requirements. Supervisors, who manage daily assignments and monitor performance, have long since given up hope for anything more than compliance with standards, finding sufficient difficulty in getting their people to perform adequately most of the time. In fact, they and their workers try to prevent the industrial engineering department, which is under pressure from top plant management to improve operations, from using changes in methods to 'jack up' standards.

A recent management campaign to document an 'airtight case' against employees who have excessive absenteeism or sub-par performance mirrors employees' low morale and high distrust of management. A constant stream of formal grievances, violations of plant rules, harassment of supervisors, wildcat walkouts, and even sabotage has prevented the plant from reaching its productivity and quality goals and has absorbed a disproportionate amount of division staff time. Dealings with the union are characterized by contract negotiations on economic matters and skirmishes over issues of management control.

No responsible manager, of course, would ever wish to encourage the kind of situation at this second plant, yet the determination to understand its deeper causes and to attack them at their root does not come easily. Established modes of doing things have an inertia all their own. Such an effort is, however, in process all across the industrial landscape. And with that effort comes the possibility of a revolution in industrial relations every bit as great as that occasioned by the rise of mass production the better part of a century ago. The challenge is clear to those managers willing to see it – and the potential benefits, enormous.

Approaches to work-force management

What explains the extraordinary differences between the plants just described? Is it that the first is new (built in 1976) and the other old? Yes and no. Not all new plants enjoy so fruitful an approach to work organization; not all older plants have such intractable problems. Is it that one plant is unionized and the other not? Again, yes and no. The presence of a union may institutionalize conflict and lackluster performance, but it seldom causes them.

At issue here is not so much age or unionization but two radically different strategies for managing a company's or a factory's work force, two incompatible views of what managers can reasonably expect of workers and of the kind of partnership they can share with them. For simplicity, I will speak of these profound differences as reflecting the choice between a strategy based on imposing *control* and a strategy based on eliciting *commitment*.

The 'control' strategy

The traditional – or control-oriented – approach to work-force management took shape during the early part of this century in response to the division of work into small, fixed jobs for which individuals could be held accountable. The actual definition of jobs, as of acceptable standards of performance, rested on 'lowest common denominator' assumptions about workers' skill and motivation. To monitor and control effort of this assumed caliber, management organized its own responsibilities into a hierarchy of specialized roles buttressed by a top-down allocation of authority and by status symbols attached to positions in the hierarchy.

For workers, compensation followed the rubric of 'a fair day's pay for a fair day's work' because precise evaluations were possible when individual job requirements were so carefully prescribed. Most managers had little doubt that labor was best thought of as a variable cost, although some exceptional companies guaranteed job security to head off unionization attempts.

In the traditional approach, there was generally little policy definition with regard to employee voice unless the work force was unionized, in which case damage control strategies predominated. With no union, management relied on an open-door policy, attitude surveys, and similar devices to learn about employees' concerns. If the work force was unionized, then management bargained terms of employment and established an appeal mechanism. These activities fell to labor relations specialists, who operated independently from line management and whose very existence assumed the inevitability and even the appropriateness of an adversarial relationship between workers and managers. Indeed, to those who saw management's exclusive obligation to be to a company's shareowners and the ownership of property to be the ultimate source of both obligation and prerogative, the claims of employees were constraints, nothing more.

At the heart of this traditional model is the wish to establish order, exercise control, and achieve efficiency in the application of the work force Although it has distant antecedents in the bureaucracies of both church and military, the model's real founder is Frederick W. Taylor, the turn-of-the-century 'father of scientific management,' whose views about the proper organization of work have long influenced management practice as well as the reactive policies of the U.S. labor movement.

Recently, however, changing expectations among workers have prompted a growing disillusionment with the apparatus of control. At the same time, of course, an intensified challenge from abroad has made the competitive obsolescence of this strategy clear. A model that assumes low employee commitment and that is designed to produce reliable if not outstanding performance simply cannot match the standards of excellence set by world-class competitors. Especially in a high-wage country like the United States, market success depends on a superior level of performance, a level that, in turn, requires the deep commitment, not merely the obedience – if you could obtain it – of workers. And as painful experience shows, this commitment cannot flourish in a workplace dominated by the familiar model of control.

The 'commitment' strategy

Since the early 1970s, companies have experimented at the plant level with a radically different work-force strategy. The more visible pioneers – among them, General Foods at Topeka, Kansas; General Motors at Brookhaven, Mississippi; Cummins Engine at Jamestown, New York; and Procter & Gamble at Lima, Ohio – have begun to show how great and productive the contribution of a truly committed work force can be. For a time, all new plants of this sort were nonunion, but by 1980 the success of efforts undertaken jointly with unions – GM's cooperation with the UAW at the Cadillac plant in Livonia, Michigan, for example – was impressive enough to encourage managers of both new and existing facilities to rethink their approach to the work force.

Stimulated in part by the dramatic turnaround at GM's Tarrytown assembly plant in the mid-1970s, local managers and union officials are increasingly talking about common interests, working to develop mutual trust, and agreeing to sponsor quality-of-work-life (QWL) or employee involvement (EI) activities. Although most of these ventures have been initiated at the local level, major exceptions include the joint effort between the Communication Workers of America and AT&T to promote QWL throughout the Bell System and the UAW-Ford EI program centrally directed by Donald Ephlin of the UAW and Peter Pestillo of Ford. In the nonunion sphere, the spirit of these new initiatives is evident in the decision by workers of Delta Airlines to show their commitment to the company by collecting money to buy a new plane.

More recently, a growing number of manufacturing companies has begun to remove levels of plant hierarchy, increase managers' spans of control, integrate quality and production activities at lower organizational levels, combine production and maintenance operations, and open up new career possibilities for workers. Some corporations have even begun to chart organizational renewal for the entire company. Cummins Engine, for example, has ambitiously committed itself to inform employees about the business, to encourage participation by everyone, and to create jobs that involve greater responsibility and more flexibility.

In this new commitment-based approach to the work force, jobs are designed to be broader than before, to combine planning and implementation, and to include efforts to upgrade operations, not just maintain them. Individual responsibilities are expected to change as conditions change, and teams, not individuals, often are the organizational units accountable for performance. With management hierarchies relatively flat and differences in status minimized, control and lateral coordination depend on shared goals, and expertise rather than formal position determines influence.

People Express, to cite one example, started up with its management hierarchy limited to three levels, organized its work force into three- or four-person groups, and created positions with exceptionally broad scope. Every full-time employee is a 'manager': flight managers are pilots who also perform dispatching and safety checks; maintenance managers are technicians with other staff responsibilities; customer service managers take care of ticketing, security clearance, passenger boarding, and in-flight service. Everyone, including the officers, is expected to rotate among functions to boost all workers' understanding of the business and to promote personal development.

Under the commitment strategy, performance expectations are high and serve not to define minimum standards but to provide 'stretch objectives,' emphasize continuous improvement, and reflect the requirements of the marketplace. Accordingly compensation policies reflect less the old formulas of job evaluation than the heightened importance of group achievement, the expanded scope of individual contribution, and the growing concern for such questions of 'equity' as gain sharing, stock ownership, and profit sharing. This principle of economic sharing is not new. It has long played a role in Dana Corporation, which has many unionized plants, and is a fundamental part of the strategy of People Express, which has no union. Today, Ford sees it as an important part of the company's transition to a commitment strategy.

Equally important to the commitment strategy is the challenge of giving employees some assurance of security, perhaps by offering them priority in training and retraining as old jobs are eliminated and new ones created. Guaranteeing employees access to due process and providing them the means to be heard on such issues as production methods, problem solving, and human resource policies and practices are also a challenge. In unionized settings, the additional tasks include making relations less adversarial, broadening the agenda for joint problem solving and planning, and facilitating employee consultation.

Underlying all these policies is a management philosophy, often embodied in a published statement, that acknowledges the legitimate claims of a company's multiple stakeholders – owners, employees, customers, and the public. At the center of this philosophy is a belief that eliciting employee commitment will lead to enhanced performance. The evidence shows this belief to be well-grounded. In the absence of genuine commitment, however, new management policies designed for a committed work force may well leave a company distinctly more vulnerable than would older policies based on the control approach. The advantages – and risks – are considerable.

The costs of commitment

Because the potential leverage of a commitment-oriented strategy on performance is so great, the natural temptation is to assume the universal applicability of that strategy. Some environments, however, especially those requiring intricate teamwork, problem solving, organizational learning, and self-monitoring, are better suited than others to the commitment model. Indeed, the pioneers of the deep commitment strategy – a fertilizer plant in Norway, a refinery in the United Kingdom, a paper mill in Pennsylvania, a pet-food processing plant in Kansas – were all based on continuous process technologies and were all capital and raw material intensive. All provided high economic leverage to improvements in workers' skills and attitudes, and all could offer considerable job challenge.

Is the converse true? Is the control strategy appropriate whenever – as with convicts breaking rocks with sledgehammers in a prison yard – work can be completely prescribed, remains static, and calls for individual, not group, effort? In practice, managers have long answered yes. Mass production, epitomized by the assembly line, has for years been thought suitable for old-fashioned control.

But not any longer. Many mass producers, not least the automakers, have recently been trying to reconceive the structure of work and to give employees a significant role in solving problems and improving methods. Why? For many reasons, including to boost in-plant quality, lower warranty costs, cut waste, raise machine utilization and total capacity with the same plant and equipment, reduce operating and support personnel, reduce turnover and absenteeism, and speed up implementation of change. In addition, some managers place direct value on the fact that the commitment policies promote the development of human skills and individual self-esteem.

The benefits, economic and human, of worker commitment extend not only to continuous-process industries but to traditional manufacturing industries as well. What, though, are the costs? To achieve these gains, managers have had to invest extra effort, develop new skills and relationships, cope with higher levels of ambiguity and uncertainty, and experience the pain and discomfort associated with changing habits and attitudes. Some of their skills have become obsolete, and some of their careers have been casualties of change. Union officials, too, have had to face the dislocation and discomfort that inevitably follow any upheaval in attitudes and skills. For their part, workers have inherited more responsibility and, along with it, greater uncertainty and a more open-ended possibility of failure.

Part of the difficulty in assessing these costs is the fact that so many of the following problems inherent to the commitment strategy remain to be solved.

Employment assurances

As managers in heavy industry confront economic realities that make such assurances less feasible and as their counterparts in fiercely competitive high-technology areas are forced to rethink early guarantees of employment security, pointed questions await.

Will managers give lifetime assurances to the few, those who reach, say, 15 years' seniority, or will they adopt a general no-layoff policy? Will they demonstrate by policies and practices that employment security, though by no means absolute, is a higher priority item than it was under the control approach? Will they accept greater responsibility for outplacement?

Compensation

In one sense, the more productive employees under the commitment approach deserve to receive better pay for their better efforts, but can managers balance this claim on resources with the harsh reality that domestic pay rates have risen to levels that render many of our industries uncompetitive internationally? Already, in such industries as trucking and airlines, new domestic competitors have placed companies that maintain prevailing wage rates at a significant disadvantage. Experience shows, however, that wage freezes and concession bargaining create obstacles to commitment, and new approaches to compensation are difficult to develop at a time when management cannot raise the overall level of pay.

Table 1 Work-force strategies

	Control	Transitional	Commitment
Job design principles	Individual attention limited to performing individual job. Job design deskills and fragments work and separates doing and thinking. Accountability focused on individual. Fixed job definition.	Scope of individual responsibility extended to upgrading system performance, via participative problem-solving groups in QWL, EI, and quality circle programs. No change in traditional job design or accountability.	Individual responsibility extended to upgrading system performance. Job design enhances content of work, emphasizes whole task, and combines doing and thinking. Frequent use of teams as basic accountable unit. Flexible definition of duties, contingent on changing conditions.
Performance expectations	Measured standards define minimum performance. Stability seen as desirable.		Emphasis placed on higher, 'stretch objectives,' which tend to be dynamic and oriented to the marketplace.
Management organization: structure, systems, and style	Structure tends to be layered, with top-down controls. Coordination and control rely on rules and procedures. More emphasis on prerogatives and positional authority.	No basic changes in approaches to structure, control, or authority.	Flat organization structure with mutual influence systems. Coordination and control based more on shared goals, values, and traditions. Management emphasis on problem solving and relevant information and expertise.

	Status symbols distributed to reinforce hierarchy.	A few visible symbols change.	Minimum status differentials to de-emphasize inherent hierarchy.
Compensation policies	Variable pay where feasible to provide individual incentive. Individual pay geared to job evaluation. In downturn, cuts concentration on hourly payroll.	Typically no basic changes in compensation concepts. Equality of sacrifice among employee groups.	Variable rewards to create equity and to reinforce group achievements: gain sharing, profit sharing. Individual pay linked to skill and mastery. Equality of sacrifice.
Employment assurances	Employees regarded as variable costs.	Assurances that participation will not result in loss of job. Extra effort to avoid layoffs.	Assurances that participation will not result in loss of job. High commitment to avoid or assist in reemployment. Priority for training and retaining existing work force.
Employee voice policies	Employee input allowed on relatively narrow agenda. Attendant risks emphasized. Methods include open-door policy, attitude surveys, grievance procedures, and collective bargaining in some organizations. Business information distributed on strictly defined 'need to know' basis.	Addition of limited, ad hoc consultation mechanisms. No change in corporate governance. Additional sharing of information.	Employee participation encouraged on wide range of issues. Attendant benefits emphasized. New concepts of corporate governance. Business data shared widely.
Labor-management relations	Adversarial labor relations; emphasis on interest conflict.	Thawing of adversarial attitudes; joint sponsorship of QWL or EI; emphasis on common fate.	Mutuality in labor relations; joint planning and problem solving on expanded agenda. Unions, management, and workers redefine their respective roles.

Which approach is really suitable to the commitment model is unclear. Traditional job classifications place limits on the discretion of supervisors and encourage workers' sense of job ownership. Can pay systems based on employees' skill levels, which have long been used in engineering and skilled crafts, prove widely effective? Can these systems make up in greater mastery, positive motivation, and work-force flexibility what they give away in higher average wages?

In capital-intensive businesses, where total payroll accounts for a small percentage of costs, economics favor the move toward pay progression based on deeper and broader mastery. Still, conceptual problems remain with measuring skills, achieving consistency in pay decisions, allocating opportunities for learning new skills, trading off breadth and flexibility against depth, and handling the effects of 'topping out' in a system that rewards and encourages personal growth.

There are also practical difficulties. Existing plants cannot, for example, convert to a skill-based structure overnight because of the vested interests of employees in the higher classifications. Similarly, formal profit- or gain-sharing plans like the Scanlon Plan (which shares gains in productivity as measured by improvements in the ratio of payroll to the sales value of production) cannot always operate. At the plant level, formulas that are responsive to what employees can influence, that are not unduly influenced by factors beyond their control, and that are readily understood, are not easy to devise. Small stand-alone businesses with a mature technology and stable markets tend to find the task least troublesome, but they are not the only ones trying to implement the commitment approach.

Yet another problem, very much at issue in the Hyatt-Clark bearing plant, which employees purchased from General Motors in 1981, is the relationship between compensation decisions affecting salaried managers and professionals, on the one hand, and hourly workers, on the other. When they formed the company, workers took a 25% pay cut to make their bearings competitive but the managers maintained and, in certain instances increased, their own salaries in order to help the company attract and retain critical talent. A manager's ability to elicit and preserve commitment, however, is sensitive to issues of equity, as became evident once again when GM and Ford announced huge executive bonuses in the spring of 1984 while keeping hourly wages capped.

Technology

Computer-based technology can reinforce the control model or facilitate movement to the commitment model. Applications can narrow the scope of jobs or broaden them, emphasize the individual nature of tasks or promote the work of groups, centralize or decentralize the making of decisions, and create performance measures that emphasize learning or hierarchical control.

To date, the effects of this technology on control and commitment have been largely unintentional and unexpected. Even in organizations otherwise pursuing a commitment strategy, managers have rarely appreciated that the side effects of technology are not somehow 'given' in the nature of things or that they can be actively managed. In fact, computer-based technology may be the least deterministic, most flexible technology to enter the workplace since the industrial revolution. As it becomes less hardware-dependent and more software-intensive and as the cost of computer power declines, the variety of ways to meet business requirements expands, each with a different set of human implications. Management has yet to identify the potential role of technology policy in the commitment strategy, and it has yet to invent concepts and methods to realize that potential.

Supervisors

The commitment model requires first-line supervisors to facilitate rather than direct the work force, to impart rather than merely practice their technical and administrative expertise, and to help workers develop the ability to manage themselves. In practice, supervisors are to delegate away most of their traditional functions – often without having received adequate training and support for their new team-building tasks or having their own needs for voice, dignity, and fulfillment recognized.

These dilemmas are even visible in the new titles many supervisors carry – 'team advisers' or 'team consultants,' for example – most of which imply that supervisors are not in the chain of command, although they are expected to be directive if necessary and assume functions delegated to the work force if they are not being performed. Part of the confusion here is the failure to distinguish the behavioral style required of supervisors from the basic responsibilities assigned them. Their ideal style may be advisory, but their responsibilities are to achieve certain human and economic outcomes. With experience, however, as first-line managers become more comfortable with the notion of delegating what subordinates are ready and able to perform, the problem will diminish.

Other difficulties are less tractable. The new breed of supervisors must have a level of interpersonal skill and conceptual ability often lacking in the present supervisory work force. Some companies have tried to address this lack by using the position as an entry point to management for college graduates. This approach may succeed where the work force has already acquired the necessary technical expertise, but it blocks a route of advancement for workers and sharpens the dividing line between management and other employees. Moreover, unless the company intends to open up higher level positions for these college-educated supervisors, they may well grow impatient with the shift work of first-line supervision.

Even when new supervisory roles are filled – and filled successfully – from the ranks, dilemmas remain. With teams developed and functions delegated, to what new challenges do they turn to utilize fully their own capabilities? Do those capabilities match the demands of the other managerial work they might take on? If fewer and fewer supervisors are required as their individual span of control extends to a second and a third work team, what promotional opportunities exist for the rest? Where do they go?

Union-management relations

Some companies, as they move from control to commitment, seek to decertify their unions and, at the same time, strengthen their employees' bond to the company. Others – like GM, Ford, Jones & Laughlin, and AT&T – pursue cooperation with their unions, believing that they need their active support. Management's interest in cooperation intensified in the late 1970s, as improved work-force effectiveness could not by itself close the competitive gap in many industries and wage concessions became necessary. Based on their own analysis of competitive conditions, unions sometimes agreed to these concessions but expanded their influence over matters previously subject to management control.

These developments open up new questions. Where companies are trying to preserve the non-union status of some plants and yet promote collaborative union relations in others, will unions increasingly force the company to choose? After General Motors saw the potential of its joint QWL program with the UAW, it signed a neutrality clause (in 1976) and then an understanding about automatic recognition in new plants (in 1979). If forced to choose, what will other managements do? Further, where union and management have collaborated in promoting QWL, how can the union prevent management from using the program to appeal directly to the workers about issues, such as wage concessions, that are subject to collective bargaining?

And if, in the spirit of mutuality, both sides agree to expand their joint agenda, what new risks will they face? Do union officials have the expertise to deal effectively with new agenda items like investment, pricing, and technology? To support QWL activities, they already have had to expand their skills and commit substantial resources at a time when shrinking employment has reduced their membership and thus their finances.

The transitional stage

Although some organizations have adopted a comprehensive version of the commitment approach, most initially take on a more limited set of changes, which I refer to as a 'transitional' stage or approach. The challenge here is to modify expectations, to make credible the leaders' stated intentions for further movement, and to support the initial changes in behavior. These transitional efforts can achieve a temporary equilibrium, provided they are viewed as part of a movement toward a comprehensive commitment strategy.

The cornerstone of the transitional stage is the voluntary participation of employees in problem-solving groups like quality circles. In unionized organizations, union-management dialogue leading to a jointly sponsored program is a condition for this type of employee involvement, which must then be supported by additional training and communication and by a shift in management style. Managers must also seek ways to consult employees about changes that affect them and to assure them that management will make every effort to avoid, defer, or minimize layoffs from higher productivity. When volume-related layoffs or concessions on pay are unavoidable, the principle of 'equality of sacrifice' must apply to all employee groups, not just the hourly work force.

As a rule, during the early stages of transformation, few immediate changes can occur in the basic design of jobs, the compensation system, or the management system itself. It is easy, of course, to attempt to change too much too soon. A more common error, especially in established organizations, is to make only 'token' changes that never reach a critical mass. All too often managers try a succession of technique-oriented changes one by one: job enrichment, sensitivity training, management by objectives, group brainstorming, quality circles, and so on. Whatever the benefits of these techniques, their value to the organization will rapidly decay if the management philosophy – and practice – does not shift accordingly.

A different type of error – 'overreaching' – may occur in newly established organizations based on commitment principles. In one new plant, managers allowed too much peer influence in pay decisions; in another, they underplayed the role of first-line supervisors as a link in the chain of command; in a third, they overemphasized learning of new skills and flexibility at the expense of mastery in critical operations. These design errors by themselves are not fatal, but the organization must be able to make mid-course corrections.

Rate of transformation

How rapidly is the transformation in work-force strategy, summarized in the *Exhibit*, occurring? Hard data are difficult to come by, but certain trends are clear. In 1970, only a few plants in the United States were systematically revising their approach to the work force. By 1975, hundreds of plants were involved. Today, I estimate that at least a thousand plants are in the process of making a comprehensive change and that many times that number are somewhere in the transitional stage.

In the early 1970s, plant managers tended to sponsor what efforts there were. Today, company presidents are formulating the plans. Not long ago, the initiatives were experimental; now they are policy. Early change focused on the blue-collar work force and on those clerical operations that most closely resemble the factory. Although clerical change has lagged somewhat – because the control model has not produced such overt employee disaffection, and because management has been slow to recognize the importance of quality and productivity improvement – there are signs of a quickened pace of change in clerical operations.

Only a small fraction of U.S. workplaces today can boast of a comprehensive commitment strategy, but the rate of transformation continues to accelerate, and the move toward commitment via some explicit transitional stage extends to a still larger number of plants and offices. This transformation may be fueled by economic necessity, but other factors are shaping and pacing it – individual leadership in management and labor, philosophical choices, organizational competence in managing change, and cumulative learning from change itself.

Suggested readings

Irving Bluestone, 'Labor's Stake in Improving the Quality of Working Life,' *The Quality of Working Life and the 1980s*, ed. Harvey Kolodny and Hans van Beinum (New York: Praeger, 1983).

Robert H. Guest, 'Quality of Work Life – Learning from Tarrytown,' HBR, July–August, 1979, p. 76.

Janice A. Klein, 'Why Supervisors Resist Employee Involvement,' HBR, September–October, 1984, p. 87.

John F. Runcie, '"By Days I Make the Cars",' HBR, May–June, 1980, p. 106.

W. Earl Sasser and Frank S. Leonard, 'Let First-Level Supervisors Do Their Job,' HBR, March–April, 1980, p. 113.

Leonard A. Schlesinger and Janice A. Klein, 'The First-Line Supervisor: Past, Present and Future,' *Handbook of Organizational Behavior*, ed. Jay W. Lorsch (Englewood Cliffs, N.J.: Prentice-Hall, 1983).

Richard E. Walton, 'Work Innovations in the United States,' HBR, July–August, 1979, p. 88; 'Improving the Quality of Work Life,' HBR, May–June, 1974, p. 12; 'How to Counter Alienation in the Plant,' HBR, November–December, 1972, p. 70.

Richard E. Walton and Wendy Vittori, 'New Information Technology: Organizational Problem or Opportunity?' *Office: Technology and People*, No. 1, 1983, p. 249.

Richard E. Walton and Leonard A. Schlesinger, 'Do Supervisors Thrive in Participative Work Systems?' *Organizational Dynamics*, Winter 1979, p. 25.